AUTOMOTIVE
ELECTRICAL
AND
ELECTRONIC
SYSTEMS

FRANK C. DERATO

GREGG DIVISION

McGRAW-HILL BOOK COMPANY

New York ■ Atlanta ■ Dallas ■ St. Louis ■ San Francisco ■ Auckland
Guatemala ■ Hamburg ■ Lisbon ■ London ■ Madrid
Mexico ■ Montreal ■ New Delhi ■ Panama ■ Paris ■ San Juan ■ São Paulo
Singapore ■ Sydney ■ Tokyo ■ Toronto

12052912

7-90

Sponsoring Editor: D. Eugene Gilmore
Editing Supervisor: Larry Goldberg
Design and Art Supervisor: Frances Conte Saracco
Production Supervisor: Priscilla Taguer

Text Designer: Pencil Point Studio/Gene Garone
Cover Designer: Sulpizio Associates Graphic Design

Series Consultant: Donald L. Anglin

Library of Congress Cataloging in Publication Data

Derato, Frank C.
  Automotive electrical and electronic systems.

  Includes index.
  1. Automobiles—Electric equipment.   2. Automobiles
—Electric equipment—Maintenance and repair.
3. Automobiles—Electronic equipment.   4. Automobiles
—Electronic equipment—Maintenance and repair.
I. Title.
TL272.D44   1986   629.2'54   85-11302
ISBN 0-07-067041-2 {TEXT}
ISBN 0-07-067043-9 {SHOP MANUAL}
ISBN 0-07-079803-6 {SET}

AUTOMOTIVE ELECTRICAL AND ELECTRONIC SYSTEMS

234567890 SEMSEM 8921098

ISBN 0-07-067041-2 {TEXT}
ISBN 0-07-067043-9 {SHOP MANUAL}
ISBN 0-07-079803-6 {SET}

CONTENTS

FOREWORD

Automotive Electrical and Electronic Systems by Frank Derato is the first two-volume text in the McGraw-Hill Basic Automotive Series. The series offers a fresh start in automotive service training. Each book is totally new and not a revision of any previous book or manual.

Each text was prepared by an outstanding teacher in the subject-matter area and then reviewed by other experts in automotive service training. The result is a two-book set— a textbook and a shop manual—that provides the needed basics both for the classroom and for the shop.

The textbooks in the Basic Automotive Series will cover each area of the National Institute for Automotive Service Excellence (ASE) certification tests for Master Automobile Technician. The content of each was selected after careful analysis of the latest available task lists, ASE test-preparation guidelines, manufacturers' service recommendations, and, most importantly, the needs and experiences of automotive teachers.

Pedagogically, each two-book set in the McGraw-Hill Basic Automotive Series is a thoroughly researched and field-tested textbook and shop manual. Each task leads the student toward the development of skills capable of objective measurement.

For schools seeking program certification by the National Automotive Technicians Education Foundation (NATEF), every attempt has been made to include the *high-priority* items from their task list. At least ninety percent of these must be included in the curriculum to meet the minimum standards for certification.

The style of the series has been designed to attract the student, cultivate interest, and enhance learning. Review questions at the end of each chapter reinforce key points, while providing practice with ASE-type questions. Key words are defined in the text, and again in the chapter vocabulary review.

The author of each book has included the latest information and service procedures available from the automotive and test equipment manufacturers. In addition, a complete new illustration program has been prepared for each book. These illustrations provide new insights into the construction and operation of the latest and most advanced automotive components.

Donald L. Anglin
Series Consultant

PREFACE

With each new model year, the automobile becomes more complex. Some of the greatest changes take place in the electrical system. A few years ago it was a novelty to have a computer in an automobile. Now, it is commonplace. Since the development of the microprocessor, microcomputers have become an integral part of electrical system design. Most cars are now produced with an on-board microcomputer which controls such functions as ignition, fuel delivery, and emission control. More and more convenience items which use microcomputers are being developed. Voice warning systems use computer-synthesized speech to alert the driver to certain conditions in the vehicle. Keyless entry systems allow the driver to unlock the doors by punching a numerical code into a keypad mounted on the door. Travel information systems allow the driver to obtain digital readouts of miles per gallon, miles to destination, and miles to fuel tank empty. Antitheft alarm systems provide increased vehicle security. Instrument panels which use vacuum fluorescent displays and digital readouts are gradually replacing those with gauges and indicator lights.

The increasing complexity of the automobile creates the need for more sophisticated service techniques. The service methods of a few years ago are no longer adequate. This two-book set, textbook and shop manual, provides information on the latest electronic systems. These books have been designed to prepare a technician for the ASE Electrical Systems Test. The information provided is relevant to that required for the test, and the end-of-chapter questions are similar in format to questions found in the test.

The *textbook* presents a background of basic electricity, magnetism, and semiconductors. Then, the battery and the charging and starting systems are analyzed in detail. The theory of operation of the horn, windshield wiper, lighting, signal, and power accessory circuits is covered. Finally, after a brief introduction to microcomputers, advanced systems such as keyless entry, antitheft, travel information, entertainment, and speed control are covered. A detailed description of the types of instrument panel displays is included.

The shop manual covers the service aspect of the systems listed above. Chapters on the use of test equipment and basic electrical troubleshooting are also presented.

These two books provide automotive students with the means to learn electrical systems from basic concepts to the advanced electronic systems. They also provide experienced technicians the opportunity to learn the latest troubleshooting methods.

The author wishes to acknowledge some of the people who helped in the preparation of these books. James E. Raymond, Louis Jacobson, George Whitehouse, Les Goings, and Bill Steen read portions of the manuscript and offered many suggestions for improving it. Ted Armstrong, Bill Hamer, Frank Ofiero, and F. Wendell Tietsworth provided valuable technical assistance. Philip Calabrese, David T. Currin, and Tom Starkey aided in preparing some of the illustrations, with the cooperation of Kenneth W. Miller.

Frank C. Derato

CHAPTER 1

ELECTRICITY AND THE AUTOMOBILE

OBJECTIVES

After you have studied this chapter, you should be able to:

1. Understand the basic operation of the internal combustion engine.

2. Explain the purposes of the various parts of the automotive electrical system and the relation of these parts to the operation of the automobile.

3. Explain the functions of the major electrical components used in the automobile.

4. Understand the basic principles of emission control and the purposes of the various emission control devices.

The first electrical device used on an automobile was the spark plug. Jean J. Lenoir is credited with inventing the spark plug in 1860, 26 years before the first automobile. He was working on an internal combustion engine to be used as a stationary engine for industrial purposes.

In 1886, Gottlieb Daimler and Karl Benz, working independently, each built an automobile. These vehicles are considered the first successful automobiles. Both were powered by internal combustion engines, but only the engine designed by Benz used a spark plug. He used a small battery to provide electric energy to the spark plug. (*Energy* is the ability to do work.) The engine designed by Daimler used a gas flame as the method of ignition and did not require electricity in any form. In fact, the first automobiles did not use electricity for lighting. Acetylene gas lamps were used when automobiles were driven at night.

In 1912, an electric starter motor was developed by Charles F. Kettering. It was first used on the 1912 Cadillac. This was the first car to combine ignition, starting, and lighting in a complete electrical system. It represented the most advanced technology of the time

Since then, the automobile electrical system has gone through many changes and has become increasingly complex. The modern automobile uses electricity and electronics in all phases of vehicle operation. Today's automobile uses the latest in electronic technology—from the microprocessors in computerized engine control systems to the electronic displays on instrument panels. In fact, some automobiles use a voice from a computer to alert the driver to certain conditions in the automobile. In the near future, a computer voice will advise the service technician of where to look for a malfunction. This will greatly simplify the job of troubleshooting.

THE INTERNAL COMBUSTION ENGINE

Combustion is a burning process (fuel is burned in the presence of air), and *internal combustion* means that the burning process takes place inside the engine. The part of the engine where the burning takes place is called the *cylinder*. Engines are classified by the number of cylinders they have. The most common engines have either four, six, or eight cylinders. The cylinders can be arranged in a row, and this type of engine is called a *straight,* or *in-line,* engine (Fig. 1-1). Another type of engine has the cylinders arranged in a V form (Fig. 1-2). V-6 and V-8 engines are common examples of this type.

An engine produces power because the heat energy of the fuel is converted into mechanical energy during combustion. The heat energy produces high pressure inside the cylinder. The part that moves inside the cylinder is called the *piston* (Fig. 1-3). The part of the cylinder that is above the piston is called the *combustion chamber*.

Combustion takes place in the combustion chamber, and forces the piston downward. The piston is attached to one end of a *connecting rod.* The other end of the connecting rod is attached to a crank (Fig. 1-4). The downward motion of the piston and connecting rod causes the crank to rotate. Each piston and connecting rod is attached to a crank, and the cranks are all part of a shaft called the *crankshaft* (Fig. 1-5). The cranks on the crankshaft are called *crankpins.* The up-and-down (reciprocating) motion of the pistons is converted into rotary motion by the actions of the connecting rods and crankshaft (Fig. 1-6).

The rotary motion of the crankshaft is transmitted through the transmission, drive shaft, and differential to the

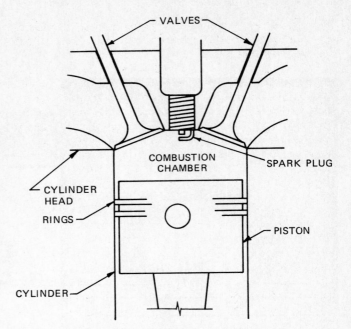

Fig. 1-3. Piston, cylinder, cylinder head, and valves.

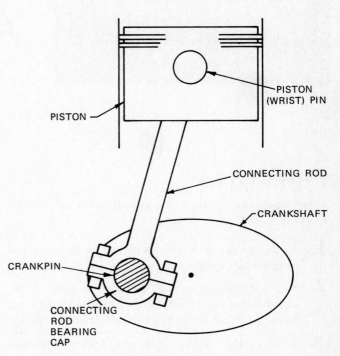

Fig. 1-4. Piston and connecting rod attached to crank.

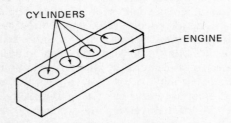

Fig. 1-1. Cylinder arrangement in an in-line, or straight, engine.

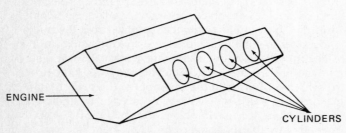

Fig. 1-2. Cylinder arrangement in a V-8 engine.

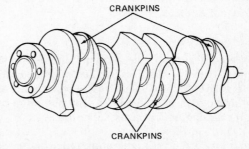

Fig. 1-5. Engine crankshaft. *(Chrysler Corporation)*

rear wheels in rear-drive vehicles. In front-drive vehicles, the rotary motion is transmittted to the front wheels through the transaxle.

Engines are also classified by the method used to ignite the air-fuel mixture to start combustion. In one type of engine, a spark at a spark plug (Fig. 1-7) ignites the air-fuel mixture. This is called a *spark-ignition engine*. Gasoline is usually the fuel for a spark-ignition engine. In another type of engine, the fuel is ignited by the *heat of compression*. This is known as a *compression-ignition,* or *diesel, engine*. The heat of compression is the increase in temperature of a gas when it is compressed into a small volume. In a diesel engine, air is compressed to a higher temperature than is needed to burn the fuel. Fuel is then sprayed into the hot cylinder at the proper time, and combustion takes place. The fuel used in a diesel engine is called *diesel fuel*. Diesel engines do not use spark plugs, but they do have *glow plugs* which are used in starting a cold engine (Fig. 1-8). A glow plug is a small electric heater that warms the combustion chamber so that the heat of compression will be high enough for ignition. Once the engine starts, the glow plugs no longer function. Glow plugs promote easier starting, especially in cold weather.

Operation of the Engine

The part of an engine that covers the openings of the cylinders is called the *cylinder head*. Each engine cylinder usually has two valves which are located in the cylinder head (Fig. 1-3). One valve, called the *intake valve*, controls the admission of the air-fuel mixture to the cylinder in a spark-ignition engine. In a diesel engine, the intake valve controls the admission of air only. The other valve, called the *exhaust valve*, controls the release of burned gases to the exhaust system. For the engine to operate, a sequence of events (called *strokes*) must take place.

A stroke is a piston movement from the uppermost position of the piston (called *top dead center,* or *TDC*) to the lowermost position (*bottom dead center,* or *BDC*). A stroke is also a motion in the upward direction, from BDC to TDC.

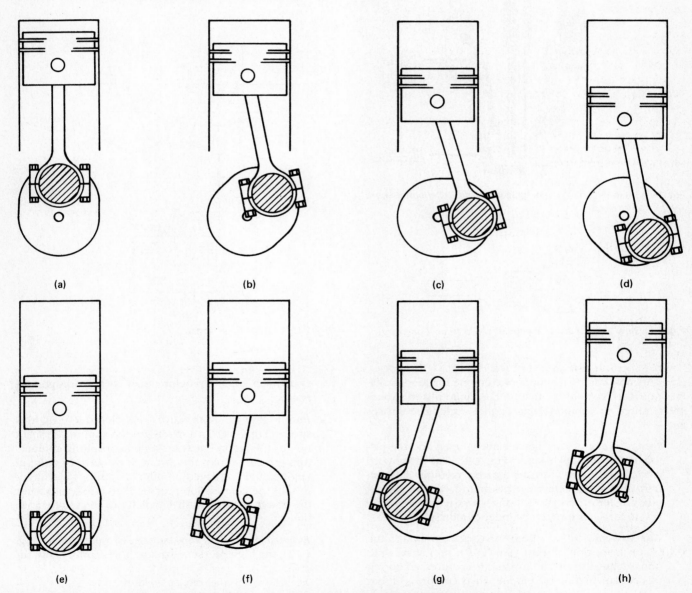

(a)	(b)	(c)	(d)
(e)	(f)	(g)	(h)

Fig. 1-6. Motion of piston and connecting rod to produce one crankshaft revolution (positions a through h).

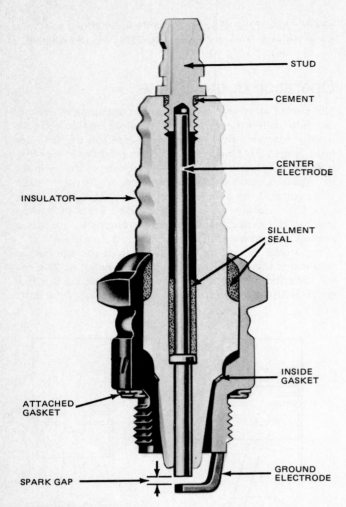

Fig. 1-7. Spark plug for a spark-ignition engine. (*Champion Spark Plug Company*)

STUD

CEMENT

CENTER ELECTRODE

INSULATOR

SILLMENT SEAL

INSIDE GASKET

ATTACHED GASKET

SPARK GAP

GROUND ELECTRODE

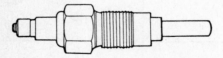

Fig. 1-8. Glow plug for a diesel engine. (*Ford Motor Company*)

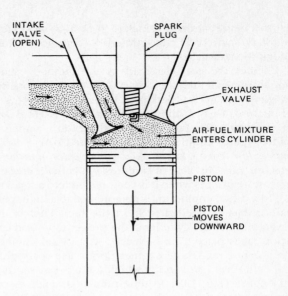

INTAKE VALVE (OPEN)

SPARK PLUG

EXHAUST VALVE

AIR-FUEL MIXTURE ENTERS CYLINDER

PISTON

PISTON MOVES DOWNWARD

Fig. 1-9. Intake stroke.

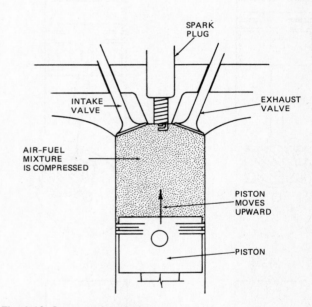

SPARK PLUG

INTAKE VALVE

EXHAUST VALVE

AIR-FUEL MIXTURE IS COMPRESSED

PISTON MOVES UPWARD

PISTON

Fig. 1-10. Compression stroke.

The most common automobile engine is a four-stroke-cycle engine. This means that four separate piston strokes are required to complete one engine cycle. The strokes are:

- *Intake stroke*   The intake valve is open and the piston is moving downward (Fig. 1-9). The downward motion of the piston creates a partial vacuum. This vacuum allows atmospheric pressure to force the air-fuel mixture into the cylinder of a spark-ignition engine and to force air into the cylinder of a diesel engine.

- *Compression stroke*   Both valves are closed and the piston is moving upward (Fig. 1-10). In a spark-ignition engine, the air-fuel mixture is compressed during this stroke. In a diesel engine, air is compressed, but

to a much higher pressure than in a spark-ignition engine.

- *Power stroke*   Both valves are closed during this stroke (Fig. 1-11). In a spark-ignition engine, the spark ignites the air-fuel mixture, and the resulting combustion pressure forces the piston downward. In a diesel engine, fuel is sprayed into the hot air in the cylinder to start the combustion process. This stroke produces the power at the crankshaft which can be used to move the car.

- *Exhaust stroke*   When the exhaust valve opens (Fig. 1-12), the high-pressure exhaust gases rapidly flow out of the cylinder as the piston moves upward. These gases flow into the exhaust system.

When the exhaust stroke is completed, the next cycle immediately begins with another intake stroke. At high engine speeds, an engine cycle takes place in a small fraction of a second. At any one moment, each piston in an engine is in a different part of the cycle than any other piston is in. When one piston is on its intake stroke, another piston is on its power stroke. This is how an individual piston is moved through the intake, compression, and exhaust strokes. The power strokes of the other pistons drive the crankshaft around. A large, heavy metal disk is bolted to the end of the crankshaft (Fig. 1-13). This disk is called a *fly-wheel*. The purpose of the flywheel is to help carry the crankshaft around between power strokes to smooth out the operation of the engine.

Valves

The valves are controlled by *cams*—one cam per valve. A cam is a rotating part with a raised portion, or lobe, that pushes open the valve each time the cam rotates. The cams are part of a shaft called the *camshaft* (Fig. 1-14).

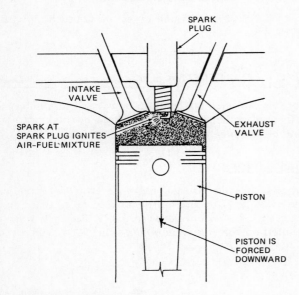

Fig. 1-11. Power stroke.

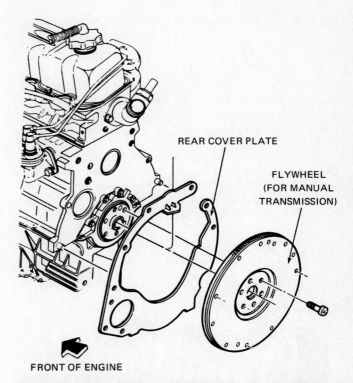

Fig. 1-13. Flywheel, which bolts to the end of the crankshaft. *(Ford Motor Company)*

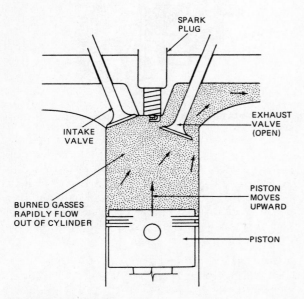

Fig. 1-12. Exhaust stroke.

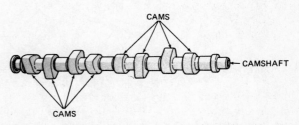

Fig. 1-14. Camshaft for a four-cylinder engine. *(Chrysler Corporation)*

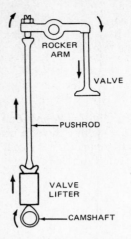

Fig. 1-15. Valve train. *(Deere and Company Technical Services)*

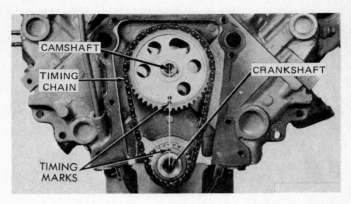

Fig. 1-17. Timing chain, which drives the camshaft. *(Chrysler Corporation)*

In some engines, a series of parts is used to transmit the cam action to the valves. These parts are called the *valve train* (Fig. 1-15). In other engines, called *overhead-camshaft engines,* the camshaft operates the valves directly (Fig. 1-16).

The camshaft is driven from the crankshaft by gears (timing gears) or by a chain called a *timing chain* (Fig. 1-17). Most overhead-camshaft engines use a toothed belt called a *timing belt* (Fig. 1-16). However, some overhead camshafts are driven by a chain.

FUEL SYSTEM

There are two methods that can be used to supply fuel to an internal combustion engine. These methods are *carburetion* and *fuel injection.*

Carburetion

Carburetion is the mixing of fuel with air so that a combustible mixture is obtained. The mixing takes place in a device called a *carburetor* (Fig. 1-18). The carburetor is mounted on the *intake manifold* (Fig. 1-19). The intake

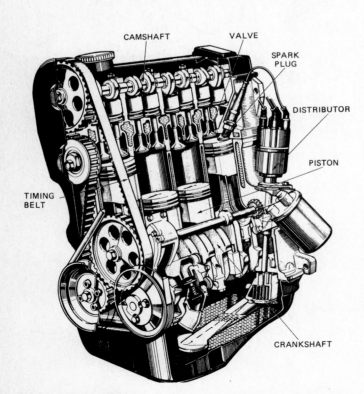

Fig. 1-16. Four-cylinder overhead-camshaft engine. *(Chrysler Corporation)*

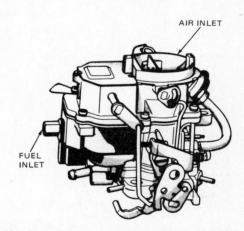

Fig. 1-18. Carburetor for a spark-ignition engine. *(Chrysler Corporation)*

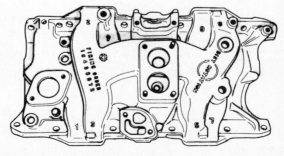

Fig. 1-19. Intake manifold for a V-8 engine. *(Chrysler Corporation)*

manifold is the part of the engine that distributes the air-fuel mixture to the intake ports. The ports are the passages to the cylinders which are opened and closed by the valves. The partial vacuum caused by the individual intake strokes of the pistons accumulates in the intake manifold and is called the *intake manifold vacuum*. The intake manifold vacuum allows atmospheric pressure to force air into the engine through the carburetor, where the proper amount of fuel is mixed with the air.

The carburetor can provide a lean mixture or a rich mixture, depending on the operating conditions and speed of the engine. *Rich* and *lean* refer to the amount of fuel in the air-fuel mixture. A rich mixture has a greater proportion of fuel than a lean mixture.

The speed of the engine is controlled by the carburetor throttle valve (Fig. 1-20). This valve is operated by the accelerator pedal and linkage, and it regulates the amount of air-fuel mixture that enters the intake manifold. When the accelerator pedal is depressed, the throttle valve opens to admit a greater amount of air-fuel mixture, increasing the engine speed. When the pedal is released, the throttle valve closes and reduces the amount of air-fuel mixture, decreasing the engine speed.

Fuel Injection

In fuel injection, the intake manifold carries air only. Fuel is carried through a system of tubes that connect directly to the cylinders or to the intake manifold at each intake valve (Fig. 1-21). The fuel is injected or sprayed into the cylinders of a diesel engine or into the intake air before it reaches the intake valves of a spark-ignition engine. Fuel injection can provide a more precise quantity of fuel to the cylinders than can a carburetor.

Fuel injection can be mechanical. The amount of fuel delivered is determined by moving parts. Fuel injection can also be electronic. In electronic fuel injection, electronic circuits accurately determine the amount of fuel that is delivered to the cylinders.

Throttle Body Fuel Injection

A *throttle body* is a device that resembles a carburetor (Fig. 1-22). It is mounted on the intake manifold in the same manner as a carburetor, and it has throttle valves that control engine speed. In throttle body fuel injection, fuel is injected into the throttle body. Therefore, the intake manifold carries both air and fuel. All throttle body fuel-injection systems are electronically controlled.

IGNITION SYSTEM

Spark-ignition internal combustion engines have an electric ignition system to ignite the air-fuel mixture in the cylinders. The ignition system distributes the electric energy to the proper spark plugs at the proper times.

The ignition system includes the battery, the ignition switch, the ignition coil, and the distributor (Fig. 1-23). The battery supplies electric energy to the ignition system, which converts that energy into the form needed to produce sparks at the spark plugs.

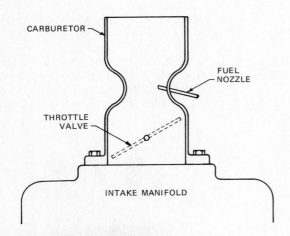

Fig. 1-20. Carburetor throttle valve.

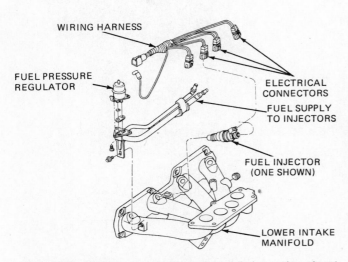

Fig. 1-21. Fuel-injection system for a four-cylinder engine. (*Ford Motor Company*

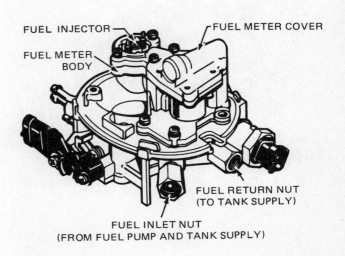

Fig. 1-22. Throttle body. (*General Motors Corporation*)

7

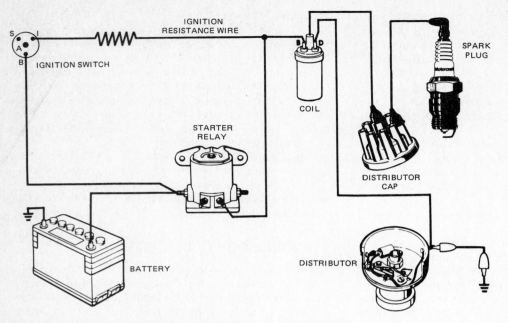

Fig. 1-23. Components of a breaker-point ignition system. *(Ford Motor Company)*

The distributor has a central shaft which is free to rotate (Fig. 1-24). A gear pinned to the bottom end of the shaft meshes with a gear on the camshaft. Therefore, as the camshaft rotates, the distributor shaft rotates.

Pulses of electric energy are generated in the ignition coil. This energy is distributed to the spark plugs by means of a rotary switch. The rotary switch consists of the distributor cap and the rotor (Fig. 1-25). The distributor cap has a number of towers around its outside edge. The towers are raised portions of the cap which hold the wires that connect to the spark plugs. The towers have conductors which extend through to the inside of the cap. These conductors are called *electrodes* (Fig. 1-26). The cap has a center tower with one outer tower for each spark plug. The output wire from the ignition coil is connected to the center tower of

the distributor cap. The rotor mounts on the top of the distributor shaft and rotates with the shaft. A spring contact on the rotor touches the center electrode of the cap. As the rotor rotates, its tip passes close to each electrode around the outside edge of the cap (Fig. 1-27). Electric energy is transferred to the electrode and flows through the wire to the spark plug. Therefore, as the distributor shaft rotates, the energy from the ignition coil is connected to each spark plug in turn.

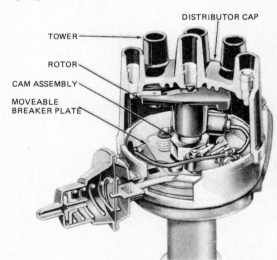

Fig. 1-25. Distributor cap and rotor. *(Ford Motor Company)*

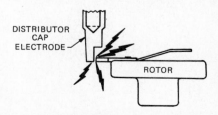

Fig. 1-26. Rotor aligned with distributor cap electrode. *(Ford Motor Company)*

Fig. 1-24. Ignition distributor. *(Delco-Remy Division of General Motors Corporation)*

8

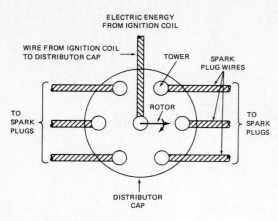

Fig. 1-27. Rotor and distributor cap.

The ignition coil must be triggered to produce a pulse of energy each time the rotor is aligned with a distributor cap electrode. There are two methods of doing this, and the method used determines the type of ignition system. The two types of ignition systems are the *breaker-point ignition system* and the *electronic ignition system*.

Breaker-Point Ignition System

In a breaker-point ignition system, there is a cam mounted on the distributor shaft (Fig. 1-28). A set of switch contacts *(breaker points)* is mounted near the cam. One contact is fixed, and the other contact is moveable. The moveable contact is mounted on an arm that pivots about one end. The arm has a small rubbing block which rests against the cam. As the distributor shaft rotates, the cam lobes push the arm and the moveable contact moves away from the fixed contact. Each time the contacts are opened, the ignition coil is triggered to produce one pulse of energy. A condenser (Chap. 3) is used in the distributor to prevent excessive arcing at the points and to ensure that the maximum electric energy reaches the spark plugs.

Electronic Ignition System

In an electronic ignition system, a magnetic-pickup coil (Fig. 1-29) and electronic circuits are used instead of breaker points. A small, toothed wheel *(reluctor)* is mounted on the distributor shaft in place of the distributor

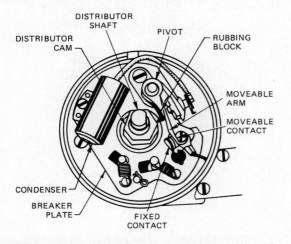

Fig. 1-28. Breaker-point distributor. *(Ford Motor Company)*

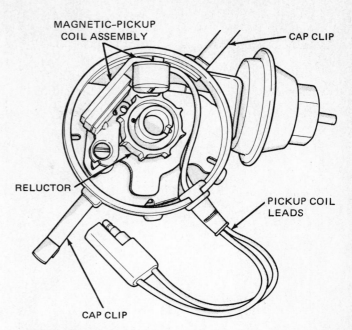

Fig. 1-29. Electronic ignition distributor. *(Chrysler Corporation)*

cam. As the distributor shaft rotates, the toothed wheel causes magnetic impulses to occur in the pickup coil. These impulses trigger the ignition coil to produce the pulses of energy that are distributed to the spark plugs. The operation of magnetic-pickup coils is covered in Chap. 3. The advantage of an electronic ignition system is that there are no moving parts which contact each other. Therefore, wear cannot take place. Electronic ignition systems have widely replaced breaker-point ignition systems, although many vehicles with breaker-point systems are still being used. A complete electronic ignition system is shown in Fig. 1-30.

Electronic ignition systems differ from one manufacturer to another. In the high-energy ignition (HEI) system made by General Motors, the ignition coil is mounted in the distributor cap (Fig. 1-31). This eliminates the wire from the coil to the distributor cap.

Ignition Timing

An important consideration in any type of ignition system is the *ignition timing*. Ignition timing is defined as the time the spark occurs in relation to the position of the piston. Timing greatly affects the performance and fuel economy of an engine.

The ignition timing is adjusted during an engine tuneup while the engine is running at idle speed. This is called the *initial timing*. Proper engine timing depends on many factors. The two most important factors are engine speed and engine load. The timing must be automatically changed from the initial timing as engine speed and load change. When the timing is changed so that the spark occurs earlier in the engine cycle, the spark is *advanced*. When the timing is changed so that the spark occurs later in the engine cycle, the spark is *retarded*.

Most distributors use a centrifugal advance mechanism and a vacuum advance diaphragm to adjust the timing automatically. Centrifugal advance, vacuum advance, and computer-controlled advance are discussed in the following paragraphs.

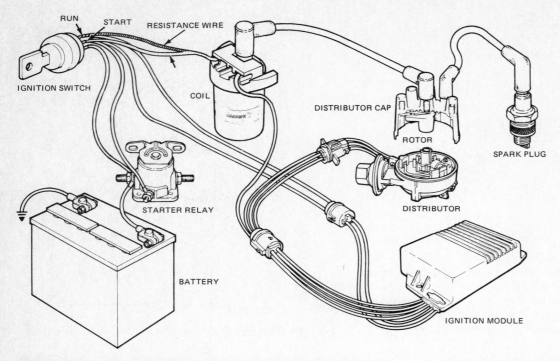

Fig. 1-30. Components of an electronic ignition system. *(Ford Motor Company)*

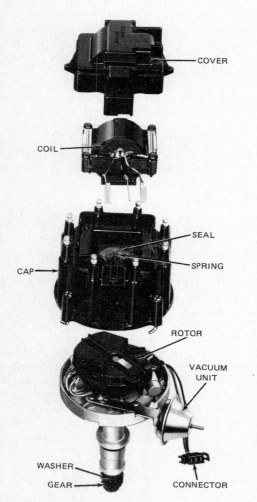

Fig. 1-31. HEI distributor. *(Delco-Remy Division of General Motors Corporation)*

Centrifugal Advance   A centrifugal (or mechanical) advance mechanism consists of two weights that swing outward as the distributor shaft rotates (Fig. 1-32). The faster the shaft rotates, the farther the weights swing outward. The outward movement causes the spark to occur earlier in the engine cycle. Therefore, the mechanical advance automatically adjusts the ignition timing based on the speed of the engine.

Vacuum Advance   A vacuum diaphragm unit is mounted on the side of the distributor (Fig. 1-33). The *diaphragm* is a thin membrane which is mounted inside a metal case. One side of the diaphragm is linked to the plate on which the points or pickup coil is mounted (depending

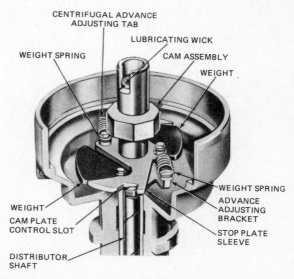

Fig. 1-32. Centrifugal weights, which control ignition timing based on engine speed. *(Ford Motor Company)*

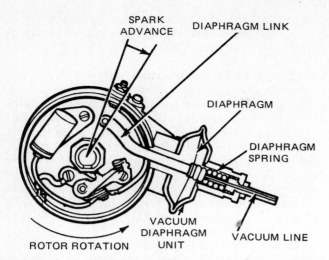

Fig. 1-33. Vacuum diaphragm, which controls ignition timing based on engine load. *(Ford Motor Company)*

on the type of ignition system). The other side of the diaphragm is exposed to either the intake manifold vacuum or the vacuum present in the carburetor. A change in vacuum changes the position of the diaphragm, which, in turn, changes the position of the distributor plate. When the distributor plate moves, the timing changes. Therefore, when there is a change in vacuum, the timing changes. Because either intake manifold or carburetor vacuum is a measure of the load on the engine, the vacuum diaphragm changes the timing based on engine load.

Computer-Controlled Advance   Some vehicles use microcomputers to control ignition timing. Microcomputer systems are capable of maintaining the timing at the correct setting under all engine operating conditions. Microcomputers are discussed later in this chapter.

EMISSION CONTROL

In recent years, a major concern has been the amount of air pollution that a vehicle produces. Pollution comes from three different sources: fuel evaporation, crankcase vapors, and exhaust emissions from the tailpipe (Fig. 1-34).

Fuel Evaporation

Fuel evaporation has been controlled by the use of sealed fuel-tank caps and charcoal canisters. A *charcoal canister* is a device which traps fuel vapors and later releases them to be burned in the cylinders (Fig. 1-35).

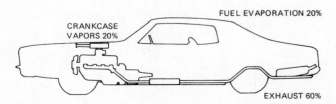

Fig. 1-34. Sources of air pollution from an automobile. *(Cadillac Motor Division of General Motors Corporation)*

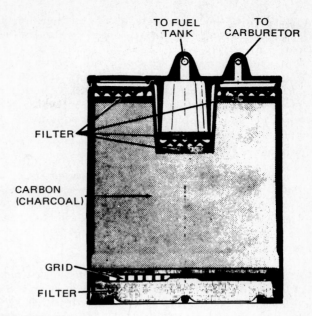

Fig. 1-35. Charcoal canister. *(Cadillac Motor Division of General Motors Corporation)*

Crankcase Vapors

The *crankcase,* or oil pan, is the pan which covers the crankshaft of an engine. Crankcase vapors have been controlled by positive crankcase ventilation (PCV) systems. The PCV system circulates crankcase vapors back into the intake manifold, where they are burned in the cylinders (Fig. 1-36).

Exhaust Emissions

Gasoline is a *hydrocarbon* (HC). It is composed of the elements hydrogen and carbon. The combustion process that takes place in the cylinders is a rapid chemical reaction between gasoline and air. Air is composed of approximately 20 percent oxygen (O) and 80 percent nitrogen (N). If combustion in the cylinders were complete, the gasoline and air would combine to form carbon dioxide (CO_2)

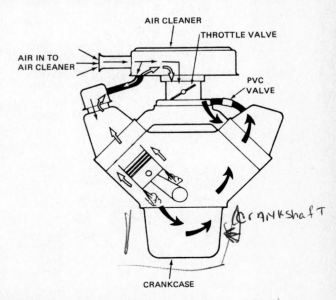

Fig. 1-36. PCV system. *(Ford Motor Company)*

and water (H_2O)—both harmless substances. The nitrogen would not react, and it would pass out of the exhaust system unchanged (Fig. 1-37).

In actual combustion, carbon dioxide and water are still formed, but in addition, carbon monoxide (CO), unburned hydrocarbons (HC), and oxides of nitrogen (NO_x) are produced (Fig. 1-38). These substances are released into the atmosphere and cause air pollution.

Emission Control Devices

The effort to reduce exhaust emissions has produced a number of different devices which are now used on automobiles. These devices, many of which are electrically operated, are designed to minimize CO, HC, and NO_x. The most common emission control devices are briefly described below.

Air Pump   An air pump is belt-driven by the crankshaft and supplies air to the exhaust system (Fig. 1-39). Additional air in the exhaust system causes the CO and HC to react further to form CO_2 and H_2O. On some vehicles, air delivery can be switched to different parts of the exhaust system or diverted to the atmosphere. Electrical controls are often used to perform these functions.

Carburetor Controls   Carburetors are controlled to minimize exhaust emissions. Some of these controls are electrical and provide precise adjustment of the air-fuel ratio. One common electrical component is the electric

choke (Fig. 1-40). This device reduces exhaust emissions during cold engine warm-up by reducing the length of time the choke valve is closed.

Exhaust-Gas Recirculation   Oxides of nitrogen are formed when combustion temperatures exceed 2500°F [1370°C]. If combustion temperatures are kept below this level, NO_x emissions will be minimized. The exhaust-gas-recirculation (EGR) system recirculates burned exhaust gases back into the intake manifold (Fig. 1-41). Exhaust gases will not burn. Therefore, they dilute and cool the burning air-fuel mixture in the cylinders. The result is lower combustion temperatures and less NO_x. Some vehicles use electrically operated solenoids to control EGR operation. Solenoids are covered in Chap. 3.

Catalytic Converters   A catalytic converter is located in the exhaust system. It provides an additional space for HC and CO to burn more completely into CO_2 and H_2O (Fig. 1-42). The word *catalytic* comes from the word *catalyst*. A catalyst is something that aids a chemical reaction but does not enter the reaction itself.

Another type of catalytic converter is the dual-bed, or three-way, catalytic converter (Fig. 1-43). These devices reduce NO_x emissions in addition to minimizing CO and HC. Three-way catalytic converters require a supply of air from the air pump and an accurately controlled air-fuel ratio. Microcomputers are used to control three-way catalytic converter systems. Microcomputers are discussed later in this chapter.

Fig. 1-37. Perfect combustion.

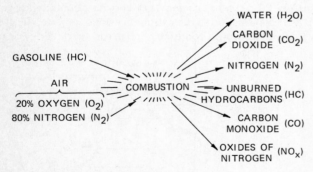

Fig. 1-38. Actual combustion.

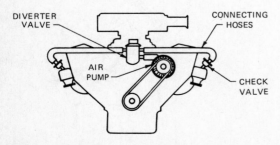

Fig. 1-39. Air pump system. *(Colorado State University)*

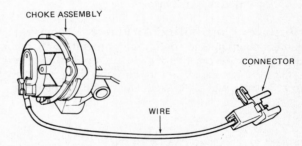

Fig. 1-40. Electric choke. *(Ford Motor Company)*

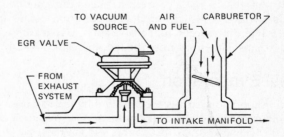

Fig. 1-41. EGR system. *(Colorado State University)*

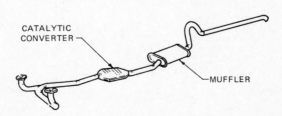

Fig. 1-42. Catalytic converter located in the exhaust system. *(Chrysler Corporation)*

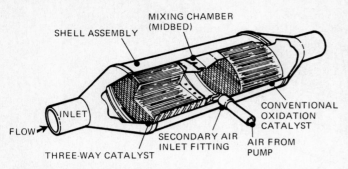

SHELL ASSEMBLY
MIXING CHAMBER (MIDBED)
INLET
FLOW
THREE-WAY CATALYST
SECONDARY AIR INLET FITTING
AIR FROM PUMP
CONVENTIONAL OXIDATION CATALYST

Fig. 1-43. Three-way catalytic converter. *(Ford Motor Company)*

STARTING SYSTEM

An engine cannot be started if the pistons are not moving. This is because the pistons must be moving on their intake strokes for the air-fuel mixture to enter the cylinders. If the pistons were standing still, no fuel would enter the cylinders and combustion could not take place.

The first cars were started by being cranked by hand. This was not too difficult on one- and two-cylinder engines (although it was inconvenient). But as engines became larger, hand cranking became more difficult.

The *starter motor* replaced the hand crank. The starter motor is an electric motor which operates when the ignition switch is turned to the START position (Fig. 1-44). The motor has a gear on the end of its shaft that engages a large gear mounted on the outside edge of the flywheel (Fig. 1-45).

The large-diameter flywheel is used as the point of engagement for the starter motor for two reasons:

- The flywheel is bolted to the crankshaft, so when the flywheel is rotated, the pistons move.

- Because of the mechanical advantage of a small gear driving a large gear, a relatively small starter motor can crank the engine.

Other components used in starting systems are relays and solenoids (Chap. 3). They are used to direct electric energy from the battery to the starter motor when the ignition switch is turned to the START position. In addition, solenoids engage the starter motor gear into the flywheel gear. Once the engine starts, the gear automatically·disengages from the flywheel. If the starter motor remained engaged after the engine started, the starter motor would be driven at an excessive speed and would be damaged.

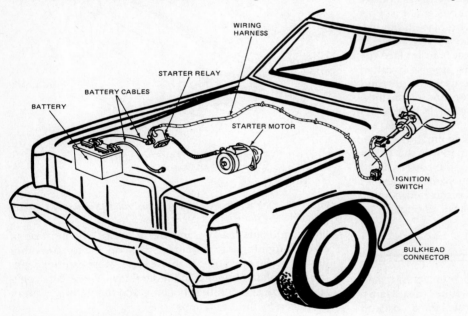

WIRING HARNESS
STARTER RELAY
BATTERY CABLES
BATTERY
STARTER MOTOR
IGNITION SWITCH
BULKHEAD CONNECTOR

Fig. 1-44. Components of a starting system. *(Ford Motor Company)*

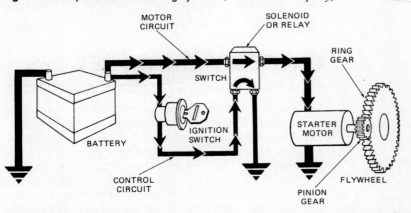

MOTOR CIRCUIT
SOLENOID OR RELAY
SWITCH
RING GEAR
BATTERY
IGNITION SWITCH
STARTER MOTOR
CONTROL CIRCUIT
PINION GEAR
FLYWHEEL

Fig. 1-45. Diagram of a starting system. *(Chevrolet Division of General Motors Corporation)*

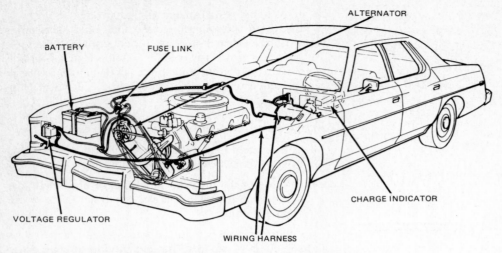

Fig. 1-46. Components of a charging sytem. *(Ford Motor Company)*

CHARGING SYSTEM

The charging system includes the battery, the alternator, and the regulator (Fig. 1-46). A *battery* is a device that converts chemical energy into electric energy. When the engine is started, the battery supplies the energy to operate the starter motor. However, the battery cannot supply energy indefinitely. If the energy is not replaced, the battery runs down and stops functioning.

The purpose of the charging system is to replace the energy removed from the battery. This process is called *charging the battery*. The alternator is used for this purpose. An *alternator* is a device that converts mechanical energy into electric energy. The alternator is belt-driven from the crankshaft.

The *regulator* is used to control how much the alternator charges the battery. The regulator adjusts the charging rate of the alternator to the needs of the battery. Until recently, regulators were electromechanical devices (Chap. 3). Now most regulators use electronic components, and some regulators are made small enough to be built into the alternator (Fig. 1-47).

LIGHTING

Automotive lighting can be separated into exterior and interior lighting. Exterior lighting includes headlamps, parking lamps, stoplamps, turn signal lamps, backup

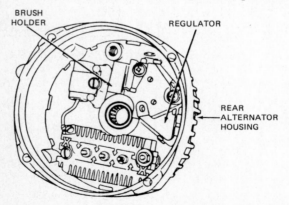

Fig. 1-47. Rear housing of an alternator, showing the location of the electronic regulator. *(Chevrolet Division of General Motors Corporation)*

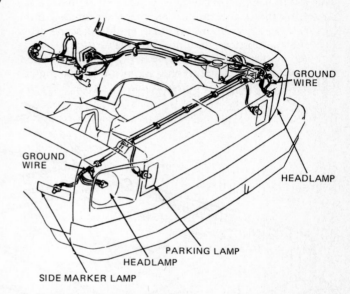

Fig. 1-48. Exterior (front) lighting. *(Chevrolet Division of General Motors Corporation)*

lamps, and side marker lamps (Fig. 1-48). The purpose of exterior lighting is to illuminate the road and to warn other drivers of the operation of the vehicle. Most exterior lighting is regulated by state and federal law. These laws regulate the size and numbers of lamps and the lighting pattern produced by the headlamps.

Interior lighting includes instrument-panel lamps, map lamps, dome lamps, and courtesy lamps. Interior lighting is used for safety and convenience. Vehicle lighting is covered in Chap. 12.

GAUGES, WARNING DEVICES, AND DISPLAYS

Gauges and warning devices provide information to the driver on the operating conditions of the vehicle (Fig. 1-49). This information includes fuel level, oil pressure, engine-coolant temperature, and the condition of the brake system. As the use of electronics increases in automobiles, more vehicle information is provided to the driver. For example, some vehicles have electronic circuits that warn the driver if the fuel drops below a certain level or if a headlamp or taillamp has burned out.

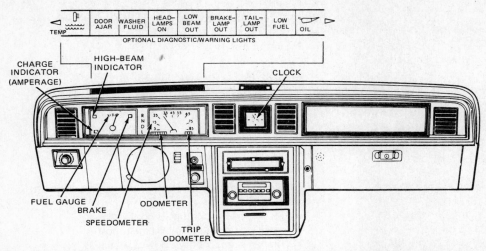

Fig. 1-49. Automobile instrument panel, showing the location of gauges and warning lamps. *(Ford Motor Company)*

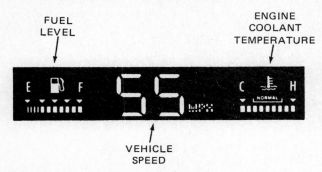

Fig. 1-50. Electronic display. *(Ford Motor Company)*

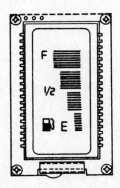

Fig. 1-51. Electronic display of fuel level, presented in graphic form. *(Ford Motor Company)*

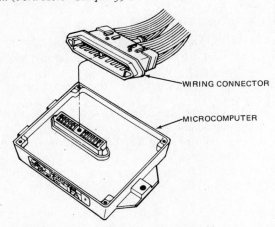

Fig. 1-52. Microcomputer. *(Ford Motor Company)*

Information is also presented to the driver in the form of electronic displays (Fig. 1-50). Displays use symbols and graphs (Fig. 1-51) to represent operating conditions in the vehicle. Gauges, warning devices, and displays are covered in Chap. 14.

MICROCOMPUTER SYSTEMS

A *microcomputer* is a miniature computer (Fig. 1-52). Microcomputers are used in an increasing number of ways on automobiles. One common application of microcomputers is in computer-controlled engine systems. These systems are used to control ignition timing, air-fuel mixture, and some emission control devices.

The microcomputer uses sensors to provide it with information on engine operation. The sensors measure such things as coolant temperature, air temperature, engine speed, and barometric pressure. On the basis of the information provided by the sensors, the microcomputer makes decisions and sends signals to control devices. In this way, the ignition timing, air-fuel mixture, and emission controls are constantly maintained at their best adjustment.

Other applications of microcomputers are in antilock brake systems, keyless-entry door locks, antitheft alarm systems, and engine diagnostic systems. Microcomputers are covered in Chap. 15.

OTHER ELECTRICAL COMPONENTS

There are many other electrical components used in the automobile as accessories that provide safety, comfort, convenience, and entertainment. These components include:

- *Safety* Windshield wipers, windshield washers, horns, and window defrosters
- *Comfort* Heaters and air conditioners
- *Convenience* Power windows, power seats, electric door locks, speed control, and antitheft alarm systems
- *Entertainment* AM and FM radios, tape players, and citizens band (CB) radios

Accessories are covered in Chaps. 15 and 16.

VOCABULARY REVIEW

Bottom dead center (BDC) The lowermost position of the piston in the cylinder.

Cam A rotating device with a raised portion (or lobe) which opens a valve each time the cam rotates.

Catalyst A substance that aids a chemical reaction but does not enter the reaction itself.

Combustion The burning of the air-fuel mixture in the combustion chamber.

Combustion chamber The space in the cylinder above the piston.

Connecting rod The part of an engine that connects the piston to the crankshaft.

Cylinder The part of an engine in which the piston moves and combustion takes place.

Cylinder head The part of an engine that covers the top openings of the cylinders.

Energy The ability to do work.

Flywheel A large rotating mass, bolted to the end of the crankshaft, which smooths out the engine vibrations.

Glow plug A small electric heater used in a diesel engine to warm the combustion chamber during cold starts.

Heat of compression The increase in temperature of a gas when it is compressed.

Hydrocarbon (HC) A substance which is composed of hydrogen and carbon.

Ignition timing The time the spark occurs at a spark plug in relation to the position of the piston.

Intake manifold The part of an engine that distributes the air-fuel mixture to the intake ports.

Intake manifold vacuum The vacuum, caused by the individual intake strokes of the pistons, which accumulates in the intake manifold.

Piston The part of an engine that fits inside the cylinders and is forced downward by combustion.

Port A passage to a cylinder which is opened and closed by a valve.

Stroke A piston movement from top dead center to bottom dead center or from bottom dead center to top dead center.

Top dead center (TDC) The uppermost position of the piston in the cylinder.

Valve Engine part that permits air and fuel to enter or exhaust gases to leave the cylinder.

Valve train The series of components that open and close valves.

REVIEW QUESTIONS

Select the *one* correct, best, or most probable answer to each question.

1. What part of the electrical system supplies energy to the battery?
   a. ignition system
   b. charging system
   c. microcomputer
   d. starter motor

2. Which of the following is part of the ignition system?
   a. distributor cap
   b. alternator
   c. starter relay
   d. regulator

3. In which part of the engine does combustion take place?
   a. intake manifold
   b. crankshaft
   c. piston
   d. cylinder

4. In a four-stroke-cycle engine, the order of the strokes is
   a. intake, power, compression, exhaust
   b. intake, compression, exhaust, power
   c. intake, compression, power, exhaust
   d. compression, power, intake, exhaust

5. Which of the following is *not* a part of a diesel electrical system?
   a. charging system
   b. ignition system
   c. starter motor
   d. alternator

6. What are the products of complete combustion?
   a. carbon monoxide and water
   b. oxides of nitrogen
   c. hydrocarbons and carbon monoxide
   d. water and carbon dioxide

7. Which of the following emission control devices lowers combustion temperatures?
   a. EGR system
   b. air pump
   c. catalytic converter
   d. PCV system

8. Combustion temperatures above 2500°F [1370°C] produce which pollutant?
   a. HC
   b. CO
   c. NO_x
   d. CO_2

9. Which of the following is part of the charging system?
   a. distributor
   b. regulator
   c. solenoid
   d. carburetor

10. All of the following statements are true *except*
    a. centrifugal advance changes the timing based on engine speed
    b. vacuum advance changes the timing based on engine load
    c. timing refers to how long the spark occurs in relation to flywheel speed
    d. timing affects engine performance and fuel economy

CHAPTER 2

BASIC ELECTRICITY

OBJECTIVES

After you have studied this chapter, you should be able to:

1. Describe the structure of matter in terms of molecules, atoms, and electrons.

2. Explain the basic principles of electricity.

3. Define *voltage, current,* and *resistance.*

4. Perform Ohm's law calculations.

DISCOVERY OF ELECTRICITY

The study of electricity can be traced back approximately 3000 years to the ancient Greeks. They observed the effects of static electricity and, through experimentation, tried to understand them. In 1600, the first book appeared that logically attempted to explain electricity. It was written in England by William Gilbert, a physician.

In the years that followed, many scientists studied electricity, each one contributing a little more to the total amount of knowledge. It has taken hundreds of years for the most brilliant scientists to develop the theories of electricity known today.

MOLECULES, ATOMS, AND ELECTRONS

Everything around us is made of *matter.* Matter is anything that has mass and occupies space. All matter is made up of *molecules.* A molecule is the smallest particle of a substance that has all the properties of that substance. For example, if a molecule of water is broken apart, it will no longer be water. It will be hydrogen and oxygen.

There are forms of matter that exist in a pure form, and these substances are called *elements.* Elements are pure substances, ones that have not combined or reacted with any other substance. Some examples of elements are hydrogen, oxygen, iron, gold, silver, copper, chlorine, and uranium. There are many others.

An *atom* is the smallest part of an element that has all the properties of that element. The atoms of the various elements combine to form molecules of all the chemical substances known. A molecule of water, for example, is composed of two hydrogen atoms and one oxygen atom (Fig. 2-1).

To investigate electricity, we must study the construction of atoms. An atom has a central core, or *nucleus,* around which a number of tiny particles revolve. The particles are called *electrons,* and they revolve around the nucleus in paths called *orbits.*

It is helpful to think of the electrons revolving around the nucleus just as planets revolve around the sun in the solar system (Fig. 2-2). This is an excellent comparison because the nucleus is roughly as many times more massive than an electron, as the sun is more massive than a planet. In addition, the distance from an electron to the nucleus, compared with the size of an electron, is similar to distances found in the solar system. This may seem surprising considering the fact that the diameter of an atom is approximately 0.0000000039 inch (in.) [0.0000001 millimeter (mm)].

The number of electrons that a particular atom has determines which element that atom is from. All the atoms of a particular element have the same number of electrons. There are no two elements whose atoms have the same number of electrons. The number of electrons in the atoms of some typical elements is shown in Fig. 2-3.

Element	Electrons	Element	Electrons
Hydrogen	1	Gold	79
Oxygen	8	Carbon	6
Iron	26	Chlorine	17
Copper	29	Uranium	92
Silver	47	Aluminum	13

Fig. 2-3. Some typical elements and the number of electrons in their atoms.

The nucleus of an atom is made up of two other types of particles: *protons* and *neutrons.* Both of these particles are very much heavier than the electron. There is a difference in electric charge among these three particles. Electrons are negatively charged. Protons are positively charged. Neutrons are neutral.

The law of electric charge, which was developed to explain the effects of static electricity (described later in this chapter), can also be used to explain what happens inside an atom. The law of electric charge states that:

- Unlike charges attract.

- Like charges repel.

It is the electrical attraction between positive and negative charges that holds the electrons in their orbit around the nucleus (Fig. 2-4). Because atoms are electrically neutral, there must be an equal number of protons and electrons. Neutrons do nothing to affect the charge; they only affect the weight of the atom.

There are a number of different orbit levels for the electrons, each at certain distances from the nucleus (Fig. 2-2). Each particular orbit level can hold a certain number of electrons. The inner levels of an atom are always filled, but the outer levels may or may not be filled, depending on the number of electrons in that particular atom.

The electrons in the outermost orbit of an atom are of interest in a discussion of electric current. In a good *conductor* of electricity (a substance which allows electric current flow), the electrons in the outermost orbit are not held too tightly to the nucleus. In copper, which is a good conductor, the electrons in the outer orbits of the atoms are held so loosely that many electrons tend to break away from their atoms. These electrons are called *free electrons.*

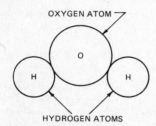

Fig. 2-1. Molecule of water.

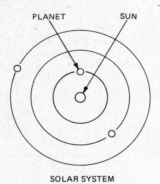

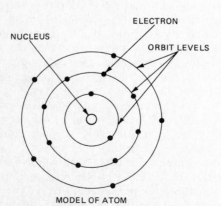

Fig. 2-2. Comparison between an atom and the solar system.

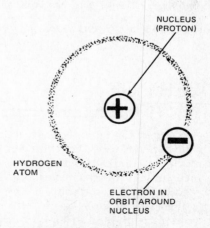

Fig. 2-4. Electrical attraction between an electron and the nucleus of an atom. *(Delco-Remy Division of General Motors Corporation)*

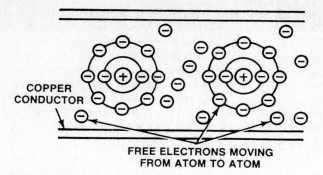

Fig. 2-5. Free electrons in a copper wire. *(Ford Motor Company)*

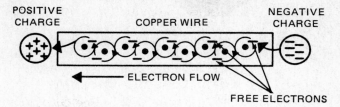

Fig. 2-6. Electron movement in a wire. *(Delco-Remy Division of General Motors Corporation)*

Free electrons move about randomly and often join other atoms that have lost electrons (Fig. 2-5). There are many free electrons in copper and other conductors such as gold, silver, and aluminum.

In some materials, the outer electrons of the atom are held very tightly to the nucleus, and there are no free electrons. These materials will not conduct electricity, and they are known as *insulators.* Examples of insulators are plastic, rubber, paper, and glass.

When an electron breaks away from an atom in a conductor, the atom is no longer neutral. Because it has lost a negative charge, and is no longer balanced electrically, it has a positive charge. A charged atom is called an *ion.* In this example, it is a positive ion. If a free electron attaches itself to a neutral atom, the result is a negative ion.

An atom can never lose a proton. Protons are so tightly bound to the nucleus that they cannot break away. Therefore, there are no free protons as there are free electrons. When a positive charge is referred to, it is a positive ion.

ELECTRIC CURRENT FLOW

When the free electrons in a conductor all move in the same direction, the movement is called *electric current.* Therefore, electric current is defined as the flow of electrons all moving in the same direction. Electric current is measured in *amperes* (A), or *amps.* The name of the unit of current was chosen to honor André Ampère (1775–1836), an early experimenter in electricity. An ampere is 6,250,000,000,000,000,000 (6.25 quintillion) electrons moving past a given point in 1 second. This number of electrons is called a *coulomb,* and an ampere is defined as the flow of a coulomb of charge per second. The ampere is a more convenient way of describing the flow of electric current.

An electron does not move from one end of a wire to the other, traveling only in a straight line. As one electron moves, it may bump into another electron and cause it to move. The first electron may stop, with the second one continuing the motion. There may be millions of such collisions in a very short length of wire. If an electron collides with an atom, it may remain with that atom, while another electron leaves the atom to continue the motion (Fig. 2-6). The electron motion is similar to a row of falling dominoes. Each domino (or electron) does not move very far, but the result is very rapid movement covering large distances. Electric current travels at the speed of light. This is 186,000 miles per second (mi/s) [299,000 kilometers per second km/s].

The random movement of free electrons in a conductor is not electric current. The electrons must all move in the same direction. For this to happen, there must be a force that moves the electrons. In electricity, this force is called *voltage.*

VOLTAGE

Voltage was named in honor of Alessandro Volta (1775–1827), who built the first battery in 1800. Voltage is the driving force that makes electric current flow; it is also called electrical pressure or *electromotive force (emf).* Voltage is measured in *volts* (V).

Figure 2-7 shows two isolated packages of electric charge—one negative and one positive. These packages are located near each other and are an example of *static electricity.* Static electricity is electric charge which has accumulated on the surface of an insulator and, therefore, cannot flow. The electrons in the negative package are attracted to the positive charge. Because there is no conducting path between them, the electrons cannot flow. However, there is a voltage, or force, between the two packages.

If the packages are connected by a conductor (Fig. 2-8), the electrons will quickly flow to the positive charge. The flow will not last very long—only a small fraction of a second. But this will be long enough to equalize the charge in both packages. The movement of electrons is electric current, and a voltage caused the current to flow. Voltage can exist without current. But for current to flow, there must be a voltage.

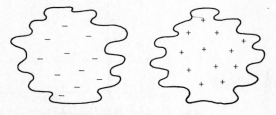

Fig. 2-7. Two isolated packages of electric charge.

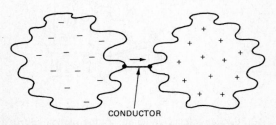

Fig. 2-8. Two packages of charge connected by a conductor.

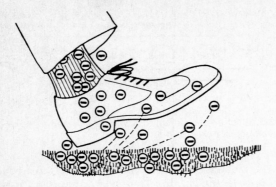

Fig. 2-9. Walking across a carpet strips electrons from the atoms in the carpet. *(Ford Motor Company)*

The idea of two packages of electric charge represents a common example of static electricity. If you walk across a carpet (Fig. 2-9) on a dry, cold day, you will get a shock if you touch a wall switch or a lamp, for example (Fig. 2-10). Both the carpet and the soles of your shoes are insulators. The friction between your shoes and the carpet causes electrons to be stripped from the outer orbits of the atoms of the carpet. These electrons build up on your body, and you become a package of negative charge. Because you are highly negative, the lamp switch represents a positive charge in comparison. When you touch it, there is a brief current flow.

The current flow described in these examples is not very useful, because it only lasts a fraction of a second. Something is needed that will continually produce a voltage. *Batteries* do this by chemical reactions. *Generators* and *alternators* do this through mechanical motion. Batteries are covered in Chap. 7, generators and alternators in Chaps. 3 and 11.

RESISTANCE

There is a third factor in an electric circuit—*resistance*. Resistance is the opposition to flow of electric current. As the electrons flow through a conductor, they meet with a certain amount of opposition. Some conductors are better than others, but even with a good conductor, there is a

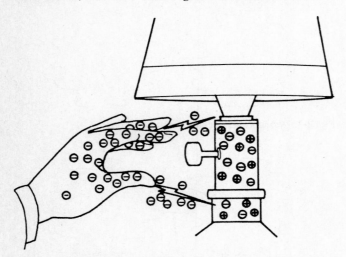

Fig. 2-10. Excess electrons jump to the lamp. *(Ford Motor Company)*

small amount of resistance. The resistance can be thought of as the collisions between electrons and other electrons or between electrons and atoms or as a type of friction.

Devices which use electricity to function, such as lights or motors, have a greater amount of resistance. Resistance is measured in *ohms*. The unit was named in honor of George Ohm (1789–1854), who discovered a formula in 1827 which is called *Ohm's law*. The symbol for the ohm is the Greek letter omega (Ω). Ohm's law is covered later in this chapter.

THREE-PART SYSTEM

There are three factors in any electric circuit: voltage, current, and resistance, or *driving force, flow,* and *opposition to flow*. Figure 2-11 shows how these factors function together in a three-part system. Current flow is represented by the arrows labeled FLOW. Opposition to flow is represented by a box, and its location shows that the flow must pass through the opposition. Driving force is represented by two dotted lines with arrows marked − and +. The driving force is shown with two arrows, one on each side of the opposition. Current must have a place to start from and a place to go. Otherwise, it will not flow.

A diagram of a simple electric cicuit is shown in Fig. 2-12. The lines in the diagram represent wires, and symbols are used to represent the battery and the resistance. A resistance is shown connected to the battery. The resistance may represent the opposition to flow caused by a light

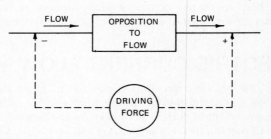

Fig. 2-11. Model of a three-part system.

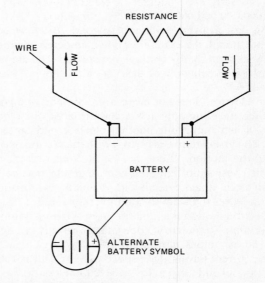

Fig. 2-12. Simple electric circuit.

bulb, for example. The driving force is provided by the battery. The flow of current is represented by the two arrows.

In this circuit, a path is provided for the electrons to flow from the negative terminal to the positive terminal of the battery. This path is called a *complete circuit*. For current to flow, the circuit must be complete. A break anywhere in the circuit will prevent the flow of current.

Sometimes, electricity can be easier to understand if you compare current flow to water flow or heat flow.

Water Flow

A simple water system is shown in Fig. 2-13. The water flows from the pump through a restricting valve and then back to the pump. The water pump provides the driving force by creating water pressure. The flow is the actual movement of water molecules, and the restricting valve is the opposition to flow.

Heat Flow

The flow of heat is another three-part system. Consider a building that is being heated in cold weather (Fig. 2-14). Heat flows through the walls to the colder temperature outside. In a three-part system, the driving force is the difference in temperature from inside to outside. The flow is the actual flow of heat, shown by the arrows. The opposition to flow is the insulation value of the walls.

EFFECT OF RESISTANCE ON CURRENT FLOW

Varying the resistance has a great effect on current flow. If a resistor is placed across a battery (Fig. 2-15), the resistance determines how much current flows. A small resistance allows a large current flow. A large resistance allows a small current flow. The word *draw* is sometimes used to describe the effect of resistance on current flow. For example, a mechanic might say that a starter motor draws a certain amount of current from a battery.

The resistance shown in Fig. 2-12 may represent any device connected to the battery. Anything that operates by using electricity has resistance. In automotive electrical systems, the resistance may be a light, a horn, a radio, or any of the many other electrical and electronic devices. Because instrument-panel lamps have a large resistance,

they draw a small amount of current. A starter motor has a very low resistance. Therefore, it draws a large amount of current.

Any device that draws current from the battery or alternator is also called a *load*. If the resistance of the device is low, so that it draws a large current, it is called a heavy load. If the resistance is high, so that it draws a small current, it is called a light load.

There are also resistances called *resistors*. Resistors are made of carbon or resistance wire. They are manufactured to have a certain resistance value. Resistors are used to limit the amount of current that flows in a circuit. An example of a resistor used in the automobile is the ignition resistor (Fig. 2-16). Generally, this is a 1-Ω resistor which is used to limit the current flow to the ignition coil.

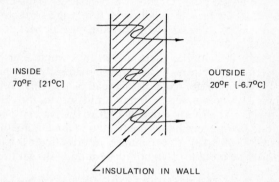

INSIDE 70°F [21°C]

OUTSIDE 20°F [-6.7°C]

INSULATION IN WALL

Fig. 2-14. Heat loss through a wall. (Arrows indicate heat flow.)

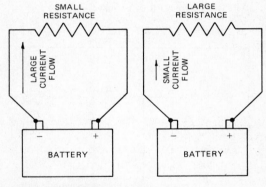

SMALL RESISTANCE

LARGE RESISTANCE

LARGE CURRENT FLOW

SMALL CURRENT FLOW

BATTERY

BATTERY

Fig. 2-15. Effect of resistance on current flow.

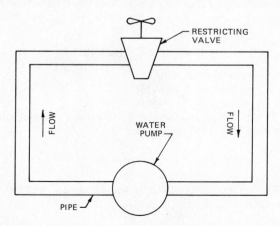

RESTRICTING VALVE

FLOW

FLOW

WATER PUMP

PIPE

Fig. 2-13. Water system.

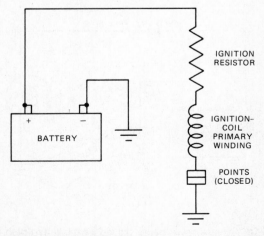

IGNITION RESISTOR

IGNITION-COIL PRIMARY WINDING

POINTS (CLOSED)

BATTERY

Fig. 2-16. Resistor used in the ignition system.

In a circuit, resistance limits only the amount of current flow. Electric current always flows at the speed of light, whether the resistance is large or small.

To help understand the effect of resistance on current flow, refer to the water system of Fig. 2-13. If the valve is turned to a small opening (large opposition to water flow), very little water flows. If the valve is opened wide (small opposition to flow), a large amount of water flows.

GROUND

For a circuit to be complete, there must be a path from one terminal of the battery through the circuit (or component) and back to the other terminal of the battery. This means there must be a *feed,* or *supply,* wire bringing current to the component and a *return* wire carrying current back to the battery (Fig. 2-17).

In an automobile, there are many components that connect to the battery: headlamps, taillamps, radio, horn, and starter motor, for example. Instead of a separate return wire for each component, the frame and body of the car are used to carry the return currents back to the battery. Therefore, one battery terminal is connected to the engine block or frame (Fig. 2-18). This common return circuit is called *ground.* The electrical symbol for ground is shown in Fig. 2-18.

The name *ground* is a carryover from the early days of telegraph circuits, when return currents actually flowed through the ground. Imported-car service manuals often use the word *earth* instead of ground.

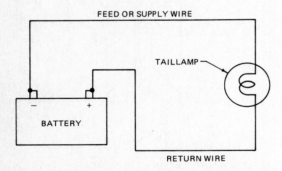

Fig. 2-17. Taillight circuit, showing feed wire and return wire.

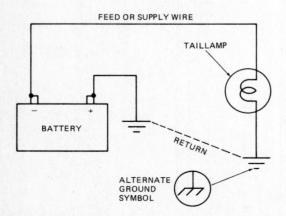

Fig. 2-18. Taillight circuit using ground as the return path to the battery.

DIRECTION OF CURRENT FLOW

Electric current is the flow of electrons in a conductor, with the direction of flow from negative to positive. It is also possible to think of *positive current* flow, which means the direction of flow is from positive to negative. You may assume current flow in either direction, as long as you are consistent. All the rules, measurements, and calculations will work either way.

Electron flow has been used so far, because that is what actually takes place in a wire. This presents a problem in the automobile, however. In the mid-1950s, the automobile manufacturers made negative ground the industry standard. Prior to that, many cars had positive ground.

With negative ground, electrons flow out of the negative terminal of the battery and through the frame and body of the car to a component (such as a radio). Then the electrons return to the positive terminal of the battery along a feed, or supply, wire. Although this is what actually happens, it is easier to visualize positive current flow: Positive current flows out of the positive battery terminal to the component and returns to the battery through ground (Fig. 2-19). In this way, the wires going to the components can still be called feed wires, and ground can still be considered the return. In this book, positive current flow is used.

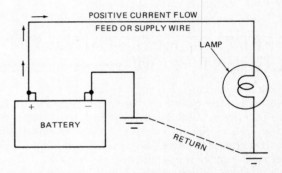

Fig. 2-19. Negative ground system, showing positive current flow.

OHM'S LAW

In 1827, George Ohm introduced a simple mathematical formula which relates voltage, current, and resistance. This formula is called Ohm's law. Ohm's law says that voltage is equal to current times resistance. A force of 1 V is required to push a current of 1 A through a resistance of 1 Ω. Ohm's law is

$$V = I \times R \qquad \text{1st form}$$

where V = voltage in volts
$\quad I$ = current in amperes
$\quad R$ = resistance in ohms

The current can be found if the voltage and resistance are known by using the formula

$$I = \frac{V}{R} \qquad \text{2d form}$$

The resistance can be found if the voltage and current are known by using the formula

$$R = \frac{V}{I} \qquad \text{3d form}$$

TYPES OF CIRCUITS

There are two basic types of electric circuits. They are called *series* and *parallel*.

Series Circuit

A series circuit is shown in Fig. 2-20. In a series circuit, there is only one current path. The same battery current flows through each component (or resistance).

The total resistance in a series circuit is the sum of the individual resistors. This is written as

$$R_{total} = R_1 + R_2 + R_3$$

In the example shown,

$$R_{total} = 5\,\Omega + 3\,\Omega + 4\,\Omega = 12\,\Omega$$

Parallel Circuit

A parallel circuit is shown in Fig. 2-21. In a parallel circuit, there is more than one current path. The current splits up, with the greater current flowing through the smallest resistance. The total resistance in a parallel circuit is found by using the formula

$$R_{total} = \frac{1}{1/R_1 + 1/R_2 + 1/R_3}$$

In the example shown,

$$R_{total} = \frac{1}{1/10 + 1/5 + 1/2} = \frac{1}{(1 + 2 + 5)/10}$$
$$= \frac{1}{8/10} = \frac{10}{8} = 1.25\,\Omega$$

The total resistance in a parallel circuit is always less than the value of the smallest resistance. In Fig. 2-21, 1.25 Ω is less than 2 Ω.

If there are only two resistors in parallel, the total resistance can be found by using the formula

$$R_{total} = \frac{R_1 \times R_2}{R_1 + R_2}$$

In this formula, the total resistance is equal to the product of the resistances divided by the sum of the resistances. This formula is called "the product over the sum" method.

EXAMPLE: Find the total resistance in the circuit shown in Fig. 2-22.

SOLUTION:

$$R_{total} = \frac{R_1 \times R_2}{R_1 + R_2} = \frac{5\,\Omega \times 3\,\Omega}{5\,\Omega + 3\,\Omega} = \frac{15}{8} = 1.9\,\Omega$$

Series-Parallel Circuit

A combination of series circuits and parallel circuits is often used. This is called a *series-parallel* circuit. An example of a series-parallel circuit is shown in Fig. 2-23.

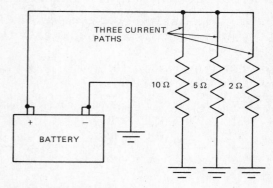

Fig. 2-21. Parallel circuit.

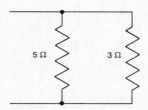

Fig. 2-22. Parallel circuit with two resistors.

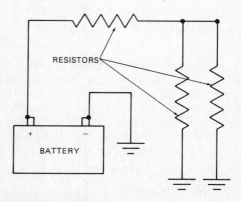

Fig. 2-23. Series-parallel circuit.

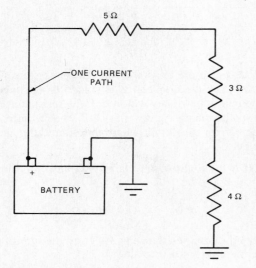

Fig. 2-20. Series circuit.

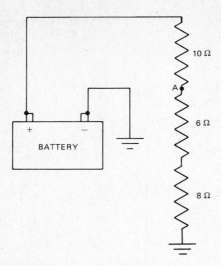

Fig. 2-24. Circuit diagram of examples 1 and 2.

EXAMPLES OF OHM'S LAW

To illustrate how Ohm's law is used, examples of the three forms of Ohm's law are given below, using the various types of electric circuits.

EXAMPLE 1: Find the current flowing in the circuit shown in Fig. 2-24.

SOLUTION: The total resistance in the circuit is found by using the series resistance formula:

$$R_{total} = R_1 + R_2 + R_3 = 10\ \Omega + 6\ \Omega + 8\ \Omega = 24\ \Omega$$

Using the second form of Ohm's law,

$$I = \frac{V}{R} = \frac{12\ V}{24\ \Omega} = 0.5\ A$$

EXAMPLE 2: In Fig. 2-24, find the voltage across each resistance. (The term *voltage across* means the voltage from one side of the resistor to the other.)

SOLUTION: The voltage across each resistor can be found by using the first form of Ohm's law:

Voltage (across the 10-Ω resistor)
$$= I \times R = 0.5\ A \times 10\ \Omega = 5\ V$$

Voltage (across the 6-Ω resistor)
$$= I \times R = 0.5\ A \times 6\ \Omega = 3\ V$$

Voltage (across the 8-Ω resistor)
$$= I \times R = 0.5\ A \times 8\ \Omega = 4\ V$$

The voltage across each resistor is called a *voltage drop,* or an *IR drop.* This expression is used because of the reductions of voltage around the circuit. The voltage at point A, for example, is 5 V less than the battery voltage. That is, the voltage has dropped 5 V across the 10-Ω resistor.

If the individual voltage drops are added together, the total will equal the battery voltage, that is,

$$5\ V + 3\ V + 4\ V = 12\ V$$

In all series circuits the sum of the voltage drops equals the applied voltage.

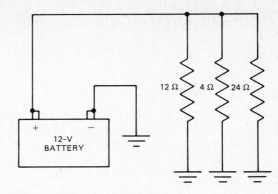

Fig. 2-25. Circuit diagram of example 3.

EXAMPLE 3: Find the current in each resistor and the total current supplied by the battery in the circuit shown in Fig. 2-25.

SOLUTION: Since 12 V appears across each resistor, the current flowing in each resistor can be found by using the second form of Ohm's law:

$$I = \frac{V}{R}$$

Current (12-Ω resistor) $= \dfrac{12\ V}{12\ \Omega} = 1\ A$

Current (4-Ω resistor) $= \dfrac{12\ V}{4\ \Omega} = 3\ A$

Current (24-Ω resistor) $= \dfrac{12\ V}{24\ \Omega} = 0.5\ A$

Note that the greatest current flows through the smallest resistance.

To find the total current supplied by the battery, add the individual currents:

$$I_{total} = 1\ A + 3\ A + 0.5\ A = 4.5\ A$$

ALTERNATE SOLUTION: Another way to find the total current supplied by the battery is to find the total resistance in the circuit and then use the second form of Ohm's law:

$$R_{total} = \frac{1}{1/R_1 + 1/R_2 + 1/R_3} = \frac{1}{1/12\ \Omega + 1/4\ \Omega + 1/24\ \Omega}$$

$$= \frac{1}{(2 + 6 + 1)/24} = \frac{1}{9/24} = \frac{24}{9} = 2.7\ \Omega$$

$$I = \frac{V}{R} = \frac{12\ V}{2.7\ \Omega} = 4.5\ A$$

EXAMPLE 4: In the breaker-point ignition system shown (Fig. 2-26), the ignition coil is designed to operate with 5 A flowing in the primary winding. If the resistance of the ignition-coil primary winding is 1.6 Ω, and if there is no resistance across the points, what value should the ignition resistor be?

SOLUTION: Using the third form of Ohm's law, the total resistance should be

$$R = \frac{V}{I} = \frac{12\ V}{5\ A} = 2.4\ \Omega$$

Since the total resistance is 2.4 Ω and the ignition coil is 1.6 Ω, the ignition resistor should be

$$2.4\ \Omega - 1.6\ \Omega = 0.8\ \Omega$$

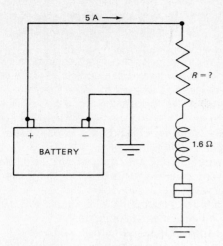

Fig. 2-26. Circuit diagram of example 4.

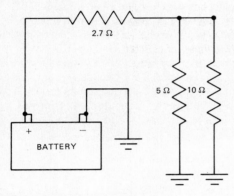

Fig. 2-27. Circuit diagram of example 5.

EXAMPLE 5: In the series-parallel circuit shown in Fig. 2-27, find the current flowing in each resistor and the voltage across each resistor.

SOLUTION: A series-parallel circuit requires a systematic, step-by-step solution. First, find the resistance of the parallel branch. Since there are two resistors, you can use the simplified version of the parallel resistance formula:

$$R = \frac{R_1 \times R_2}{R_1 + R_2} = \frac{5\,\Omega \times 10\,\Omega}{5\,\Omega + 10\,\Omega} = \frac{50}{15} = 3.3\,\Omega$$

$$R_{total} = 2.7\,\Omega + 3.3\,\Omega = 6.0\,\Omega$$

The current flowing into the circuit can be found by using the second form of Ohm's law:

$$I = \frac{V}{R} = \frac{12\,V}{6\,\Omega} = 2\,A$$

Now the voltage drop can be found across the 2.7-Ω resistor by using the first form of Ohm's law:

$$V\,(2.7\text{-}\Omega \text{ resistor}) = I \times R = 2\,A \times 2.7\,\Omega = 5.4\,V$$

The voltage across the parallel branch of the circuit is

$$12\,V - 5.4\,V = 6.6\,V$$

Therefore, the current through each resistance is

$$I\,(5\text{-}\Omega \text{ resistor}) = \frac{V}{R} = \frac{6.6\,V}{5\,\Omega} = 1.3\,A$$

$$I\,(10\text{-}\Omega \text{ resistor}) = \frac{V}{R} = \frac{6.6\,V}{10\,\Omega} = 0.66\,A$$

	Current	Voltage
2.7-Ω resistor	2 A	5.4 V
5-Ω resistor	1.3 A	6.6 V
10-Ω resistor	0.66 A	6.6 V

Fig. 2-28. Table showing the currents and voltages found in example 5.

A tabulation of the currents and voltages in the circuit is shown in Fig. 2-28.

ENERGY, WORK, AND POWER

Energy is the capacity or ability to do *work*. Work is defined as the application of a force to move an object. For work to be done, the object must move. If a force is applied and the object does not move, work is not done. Energy can take many forms. Some examples are mechanical energy, electric energy, heat energy, and chemical energy. A battery contains chemical energy. This means the battery has the capacity to move electrons (to do work).

Power is the rate, or speed, at which work is done. It is measured in *watts (W)*. One watt represents the work done by one volt moving a coulomb of charge in one second. The watt was named in honor of James Watt (1736–1819), who experimented with steam power.

The formula for power is

$$P = V \times I$$

where P = power in watts
V = voltage in volts
I = current in amperes

EXAMPLE: How much power is used in an automotive headlamp that draws 5 A?

SOLUTION:

$$P = V \times I = 12\,V \times 5\,A = 60\,W$$

The power formula can be stated another way. By substituting $(I \times R)$ in the place of V (from Ohm's law),

$$P = V \times I = (I \times R) \times I = I^2 \times R \quad \text{or} \quad I^2R$$

Power in electric circuits often takes the form of heat. The term I^2R represents the heat energy given off in a resistance when current flows through the resistance.

EXAMPLE: How much power (heat) is given off in a 0.9-Ω ignition resistor when 8 A flows through it?

SOLUTION

$$P = I^2 \times R = 8^2 \times 0.9\,\Omega = 64 \times 0.9 = 57.6\,W$$

Electric power can be related to mechanical power (horsepower, or hp) by the following:

$$1\text{ hp} = 746\,W$$

25

VOCABULARY REVIEW

Alternator A device that generates electricity by mechanical means. It converts mechanical energy into electric energy.

Ampere (A) The unit of measurement of electric current. An ampere is the flow of a coulomb of charge per second.

Atom the smallest part of an element that has all the properties of that element.

Battery A device that produces electricity by chemical means. It converts chemical energy into electric energy.

Complete circuit A conducting path from the negative terminal of a battery to the positive terminal.

Conductor A substance which allows electric current to flow.

Coulomb A quantity of electric charge equal to 6,250,000,000,000,000,000 (6.25 quintillion) electrons.

Draw To cause current to flow from a battery or an alternator.

Earth Ground.

Electric current The flow of electrons all moving in the same direction.

Electromotive force (emf) Voltage.

Electron A particle which orbits around the nucleus of an atom. Electrons are negatively charged.

Element A pure substance which has not combined or reacted with any other substance.

Energy The capacity or ability to do work.

Feed wire The circuit wiring which carries electric current from the battery or alternator to a component.

Free electron An electron which is present in a material but is not part of an atom.

Generator A device that generates electricity by mechanical means. It converts mechanical energy into electric energy.

Ground The circuit which uses the engine, frame, and body of the vehicle to carry return current back to the battery or alternator.

Insulator A substance which does not allow electric current to flow.

Ion A charged atom.

Load A device which uses electric energy in a circuit and converts that energy into another form.

Matter Anything that has mass and occupies space.

Molecule The smallest particle of a substance that has all the properties of that substance.

Neutron A neutral particle which is part of the nucleus of an atom.

Nucleus The central core of an atom.

Ohm (Ω) The unit of measurement of resistance.

Ohm's law A mathematical formula which relates voltage, current, and resistance.

Orbit The path that electrons take as they revolve around the nucleus of an atom.

Parallel circuit A circuit having more than one current path.

Positive current Electric current which is assumed to flow from positive to negative.

Power The rate, or speed, at which work is done.

Proton A positively charged particle which is part of the nucleus of an atom.

Resistance The opposition to flow of electric current.

Resistor A device which has a certain resistance value.

Return wire The circuit wiring which carries electric current from a component to the battery or alternator.

Series circuit A circuit in which the same current flows through each component.

Series-parallel circuit A circuit which is a combination of series and parallel circuits.

Static electricity Electric charge which has accumulated on the surface of an insulator.

Volt (V) The unit of measurement of voltage.

Voltage The electrical pressure, or driving force, behind electric current flow.

Voltage drop The reduction in voltage from that of the source as current passes through resistors in a series circuit. Also known as the *IR drop.*

Watt (W) The unit of measurement of power.

Work The application of a force to move an object.

REVIEW QUESTIONS

Select the *one* correct, best, or most probable answer to each question.

1. The central core of an atom is called the
   a. orbit
   b. electron
   c. neutron
   d. nucleus

2. Resistance is measured in
   a. volts
   b. ohms
   c. amperes
   d. watts

3. Electromotive force is also called
   a. electric current
   b. voltage
   c. resistance
   d. power

4. Electric current is measured in
   a. volts
   b. ohms
   c. amperes
   d. watts

5. A molecule of water is composed of
   a. two hydrogen atoms and one oxygen atom
   b. one hydrogen atom and two oxygen atoms
   c. one hydrogen atom and one oxygen atom
   d. two hydrogen atoms and two oxygen atoms

6. The smallest particle of a substance that still retains all the properties of the substance is
   a. a molecule
   b. an electron
   c. an atom
   d. a nucleus

7. The smallest particle of an element that still retains all the properties of that element is
   a. a molecule
   b. an electron
   c. an atom
   d. a nucleus

8. Atoms of a particular element can be distinguished by the number of
   a. electrons
   b. neutrons
   c. molecules
   d. orbit levels

9. What is the name given to an atom that has lost an electron?
   a. negative atom
   b. molecule
   c. nucleus
   d. ion

10. An ampere is
    a. the unit of voltage
    b. the unit of power
    c. a coulomb per second
    d. the work done by 1 V

11. The flow of electrons all moving in the same direction in a wire is called
    a. power
    b. voltage
    c. current
    d. electromotive force

12. Which of the following statements is true of a parallel circuit?
    a. there is only one current path
    b. the sum of the currents through the individual branches equals the total current supplied by the battery
    c. the total resistance is equal to the sum of the individual resistances
    d. the smallest resistance has the smallest current

13. Which of the following statements is true of a series circuit?
    a. the sum of the voltage drops should equal the applied voltage
    b. there is more than one current path
    c. the total resistance is less than the smallest resistance value
    d. the smallest resistance has the greatest current

14. Ohm's law can be written as
    a. $I = \dfrac{V}{R}$
    b. $R = \dfrac{V}{I}$
    c. $V = I \times R$
    d. all of the above

15. An electrical device that has 12 V applied to it draws 24 A. How much power does the device use?
    a. 2 W
    b. 0.5 W
    c. 288 W
    d. 36 W

16. How much power is used in a 25-Ω resistor if 2 A flows through it?
    a. 50 W
    b. 12.5 W
    c. 100 W
    d. 27 W

17. Two 10-Ω resistors are connected in parallel. What is the total resistance?
    a. 20 Ω
    b. 10 Ω
    c. 100 Ω
    d. 5 Ω

18. What resistance should a circuit have to limit the current to 8 A? The battery voltage is 12 V.
    a. 96 Ω
    b. 1.5 Ω
    c. 20 Ω
    d. 0.66 Ω

19. A 24-Ω resistor is connected to a 12-V battery. How much current flows?
    a. 0.5 A
    b. 2 A
    c. 0.2 A
    d. 288 A

20. Which of the following statements is true?
    a. the current is the driving force in an electric circuit
    b. power is equal to current times resistance
    c. a large resistance results in a large current
    d. none of the above

CHAPTER 3

MAGNETISM AND MAGNETIC DEVICES

OBJECTIVES

After you have studied this chapter, you should be able to:

1. Discuss the basic principles of magnetism.

2. Describe the operation of electromagnets, relays, and solenoids.

3. Describe the operation of a motor.

4. Explain how electric current is generated.

5. Describe the operation of a transformer.

PERMANENT MAGNETS ══════

Magnetism has been known for thousands of years. Lodestones, which are natural magnets, were used by ancient sailors to navigate. They would place a lodestone on a small wooden raft in a container of water. The raft would swing around and help them determine direction. However, this method was not very accurate, and the sailors did not understand how or why it worked. It was, in effect, a very primitive compass.

The book written by William Gilbert in 1600 included a chapter on magnetism, in which he explained the oper-

ation of the compass. He said that the earth was a large magnet (Fig. 3-1) and that the compass needle (being slightly magnetized) was attracted to the poles. This attraction always caused the compass needle to point north. Gilbert's theory was startling in its day, but it was accepted,

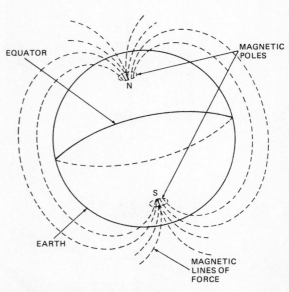

Fig. 3-1. The earth as a large magnet.

and the scientists began to study magnetism. They learned that every magnet has two *poles*. Poles are the places on a magnet where the magnetic force is the strongest. The poles were named *north* and *south* to correspond with the poles of the earth. However, the magnetic poles of the earth are not the same as the geographic poles. In fact, the position of the magnetic poles changes from year to year.

The idea of magnetic *lines of force* was also developed (Fig. 3-1). Magnetic lines of force are imaginary lines joining the north and south poles of a magnet. On earth, the compass needle aligns itself along a line of force.

Each line of force is thought of as a complete loop. The loop travels from the north pole, through the air surrounding the magnet to the south pole, and returns to the north pole through the magnet itself. There are many lines of force surrounding a magnet; the stronger the magnet, the greater the number of lines. All the lines of force taken together as a whole are called the *magnetic field*. Figure 3-2 shows the magnetic field of a bar magnet, and Fig. 3-3 shows the magnetic field of a horseshoe magnet.

From the early experimentation, the law of magnetism was developed. It states:

- Like magnetic poles repel.

- Unlike magnetic poles attract.

This means that a north pole and a south pole will be attracted to each other. However, two north poles will repel each other, as will two south poles.

Bar magnets and horseshoe magnets are called *permanent magnets*. A permanent magnet is a magnet that retains its magnetism for a long period of time. Another type of magnet is called an *electromagnet*.

ELECTROMAGNETS

In 1820, Hans Oersted made a very important discovery. While performing some electrical experiments, he passed a large electric current through a wire. He noticed that the needle of a nearby compass moved. Further experimentation showed that whenever a compass is placed over a wire with current flowing in it, the needle will always point at right angles to the wire (Fig. 3-4).

Because a compass needle will always attempt to align itself along a line of force, Oersted concluded that a magnetic field was present around the wire. Therefore, he established the fact that electricity causes magnetism. The magnetic field around a wire carrying electric current is shown in Fig. 3-5.

Further experimentation showed that the magnetic strength could be increased by winding the wire into a coil. In this way, the small circular lines of force add together as turns of wire are added (Fig. 3-6). This is called an electromagnet. The electromagnet has the same field pattern as the bar magnet shown in Fig. 3-2.

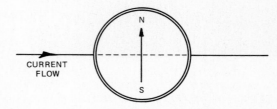

Fig. 3-4. Compass needle affected by current flow.

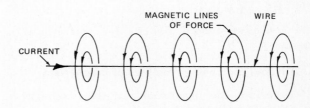

Fig. 3-5. Magnetic field around a wire carrying electric current.

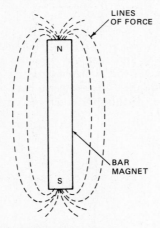

Fig. 3-2. Magnetic field of a bar magnet.

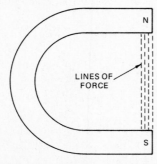

Fig. 3-3. Magnetic field of a horseshoe magnet.

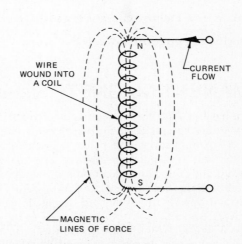

Fig. 3-6. Magnetic field of an electromagnet.

The electromagnet has two advantages over a permanent magnet:

- The magnetic field can be turned on and off at will by switching the current on and off.
- The strength of the field can be increased by increasing the current, or by adding more turns of wire.

The strength of the electromagnet can also be increased by placing an iron core inside the coil of wire. This is because iron is a better path than air for the lines of force. The iron concentrates and increases the number of lines of force.

OHM'S LAW FOR MAGNETISM

Magnetism can be related to the three-part system described in Chap. 2 and shown in Fig. 2-11. A formula similar to Ohm's law can be used. The formula is

$$F = \phi R$$

where F = magnetomotive force
ϕ = flux
R = reluctance

The *magnetomotive force* is the magnetic driving force. It is equivalent to electromotive force (voltage) in an electric circuit.

The *flux* is the flow of lines of force. It is equivalent to current in an electric circuit.

The *reluctance* is the opposition to flow of lines of force. It is equivalent to resistance in an electric circuit.

Ohm's law for magnetic circuits helps describe what happens to an electromagnet when an iron core is inserted. Iron is a much better magnetic material than air, with a much lower reluctance. A lower reluctance results in a greater flux (stronger magnetism). Therefore, when an iron core is inserted into an electromagnet, the magnetic force is greatly increased. This is equivalent to a lower resistance, resulting in a larger current flow in an electric circuit.

PERMEABILITY

Permeability describes magnetic conductivity, or the ease with which a substance concentrates and increases the number of lines of force. Permeability is the magnetic conductivity of a substance compared with the magnetic conductivity of air. The greater the permeability, the greater the magnetic conductivity and the easier a substance can be magnetized. The effect of permeability is the opposite of that of reluctance. When reluctance is high, permeability is low, and when reluctance is low, permeability is high.

MAGNETIC DEVICES

There are a number of magnetic devices used on automobiles. These devices include relays, solenoids, buzzers, motors, alternators, and magnetic-pickup coils. The operation of each of these devices is described below.

RELAYS AND SOLENOIDS

Two magnetic devices used in automotive electrical systems are *relays* and *solenoids*. The relay has switch contacts which are magnetically operated. The solenoid may have switch contacts, but when operated, it can apply a large force. A relay is used to control another circuit. A solenoid is used to control a mechanical movement.

Solenoids

A solenoid is an electromagnet with a moveable magnetic core (Fig. 3-7). Magnetic cores are usually made of iron, because of its high permeability. If a magnetic core is free to move, it will always move in a direction that will decrease the reluctance in the magnetic circuit. This is the basic principle of operation of a solenoid.

In Fig. 3-7, the solenoid is shown in the deenergized position. *Deenergized* means that no current is flowing in the coil. Notice that the core is only partially inside the coil. The lower portion of the coil has air inside it, and air has a much higher reluctance than the iron core. When current flows through the coil (solenoid energized), the resulting magnetism pulls the core into the coil (Fig. 3-8). With the core completely within the coil, the reluctance of the magnetic path inside the coil is much lower. When current flows, the core could not move in the other direction because that would increase the reluctance.

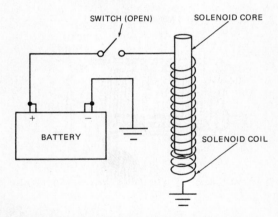

Fig. 3-7. Solenoid shown in the deenergized position.

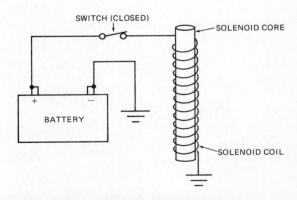

Fig. 3-8. Solenoid shown in the energized position.

Figure 3-9 shows a starter solenoid. In some starter motors, the starter solenoid is used to engage the starter motor pinion gear into a ring gear around the engine flywheel to crank the engine. In Fig. 3-10, the solenoid is shown with the coil in the deenergized position. When the coil is energized, the magnetic force pulls the core into the coil to decrease the reluctance of the magnetic path (Fig. 3-11). Because of the large force exerted on the core, the pinion gear is engaged into the flywheel ring gear.

Some solenoids also have contacts which close to send current to the starter motor at the same time the pinion gear engages the ring gear. When the contacts close, the starter motor operates to crank the engine. Other solenoids may have an additional set of contacts to apply full battery voltage directly to the ignition coil while the engine is cranking.

Solenoids are also used as automatic trunk releases (Fig. 3-12) and to control engine idle speed and the operation of valves in emission control systems and carburetors.

Relays

A common type of relay has a fixed core and a moveable arm called an *armature* (Fig. 3-13). When the relay coil is energized, the armature is attracted to the core (Fig. 3-14). In moving toward the core, the armature decreases the reluctance in the magnetic circuit. The relay shown in Fig. 3-14 has one set of switch contacts. One contact is located

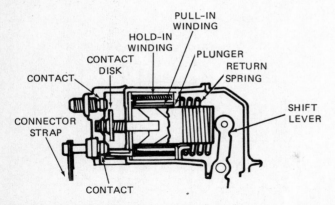

Fig. 3-9. Starter solenoid. (*Delco-Remy Division of General Motors Corporation*)

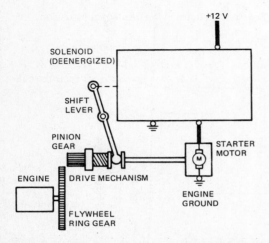

Fig. 3-10. Starter solenoid shown in the deenergized position. (*Chevrolet Division of General Motors Corporation*)

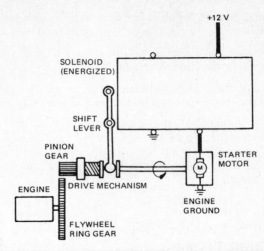

Fig. 3-11. Starter solenoid shown in the energized position, with the pinion gear engaged into the flywheel ring gear. (*Chevrolet Division of General Motors Corporation*)

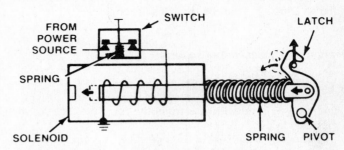

Fig. 3-12. Solenoid used as a trunk-latch release. (*Ford Motor Company*)

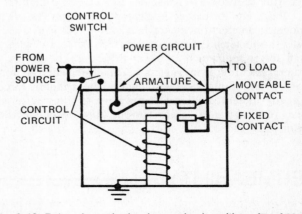

Fig. 3-13. Relay shown in the deenergized position. (*Ford Motor Company*)

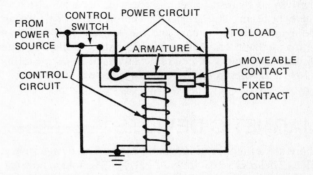

Fig. 3-14. Relay shown in the energized position. (*Ford Motor Company*)

on the armature. The other contact is located in a fixed position a small distance from the armature. The switch contacts are controlled by the movement of the armature. When the relay is deenergized, the contacts are open. When the relay is energized, the armature moves (down in Fig. 3-14) and closes the contacts.

Relays are often used in starter motor circuits, and these are called *starter relays*. In a starter relay, the contacts are designed to carry a large current to the starter motor. By using a relay, the small current to energize the relay coil can control the large starter motor current (Fig. 3-15). Therefore, the switch contacts that carry the current to control the relay can be small. The *ignition switch* controls the starter relay. Some starter relays are built as solenoids (with a moveable core). They are called relays because their purpose is only to switch current, not to apply a force.

A relay can have more than one set of contacts. The contacts can either be normally open or normally closed. The "normal" position of a relay is the deenergized position. Relays are also used to switch current to horns, alarm devices, power door locks, and power windows.

BUZZERS

A buzzer is similar in construction to a relay (Fig. 3-16). The internal wiring is different, however. The wire which connects to the coil of the buzzer is connected through a set of normally closed contacts. When voltage is applied to the buzzer, the contacts conduct current and the coil is energized. The armature is attracted toward the coil, but the movement of the armature opens the contacts. When the contacts open, the coil deenergizes and the armature is released. The contacts close, and the armature is again attracted to the coil. This action occurs rapidly (and continuously), causing a buzzing sound. Buzzers are used as warning devices in an automobile.

METER MOVEMENTS

An *ammeter* is a device used to measure electric current. Ammeters are often used as test instruments when mechanics are troubleshooting automotive electrical systems. One type of ammeter uses a *d'Arsonval meter movement* (Fig. 3-17). It is constructed by winding a coil of fine wire on a small frame. This coil is called the *armature*, and it pivots on bearings. Adjacent to the armature is a permanent magnet.

When current flows through the armature, it becomes a small electromagnet. The magnetic poles of the electromagnet are repelled by the poles of the permanent magnet. This causes the armature to rotate against a very fine spring (Fig. 3-18). A pointer is attached to the armature and rotates with it. The greater the current flow, the stronger the magnetism and the greater the movement of the pointer. On a ammeter, the pointer swings along a scale calibrated in amperes. This makes it possible to know the amount of current flowing by reading from the scale.

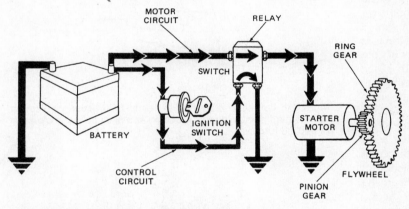

Fig. 3-15. Relay used to control the starter motor current. *(Chevrolet Division of General Motors Corporation)*

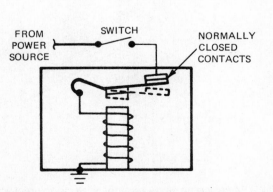

Fig. 3-16. Construction of a buzzer. *(Ford Motor Company)*

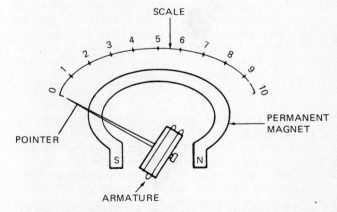

Fig. 3-17. d'Arsonval meter movement. *(Ford Motor Company)*

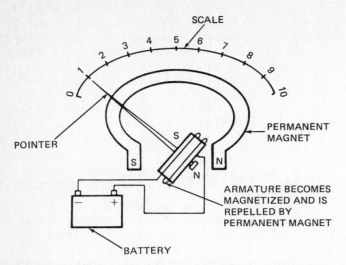

Fig. 3-18. Current flowing through the armature of a d'Arsonval meter movement. *(Ford Motor Company)*

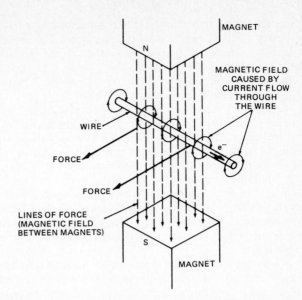

Fig. 3-19. Force on a conductor carrying electric current when it is placed in a magnetic field.

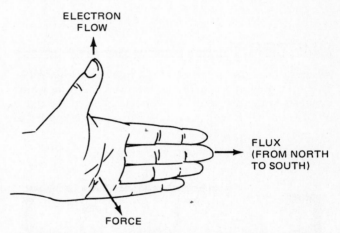

Fig. 3-20. Left-hand rule. Thumb points in direction of electron flow, fingers point in direction of flux, and palm points in direction of applied force.

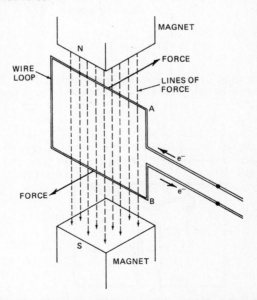

Fig. 3-21. Forces acting on a loop carrying electric current when it is placed in a magnetic field. The force tends to rotate the loop.

MOTORS

A *motor* is a device that converts electric energy into mechanical energy, usually as rotary motion. Motors perform many functions in an automobile. Starter motors, power window motors, and power seat motors are three examples. The operation of a motor is described below.

If a conductor which has current flowing in it is placed in a magnetic field, there will be a force on the conductor (Fig. 3-19). When electric current flows through a wire, a magnetic field is present around the wire. The force is caused by the interaction of this magnetic field with the magnetic field between the permanent magnets. In effect, the field is cancelled on one side of the wire and strengthened on the other side. The result is that the wire moves in the direction of the weaker field.

The *left-hand rule* can help you determine the direction of the applied force (Fig. 3-20). Hold your left hand so that your thumb points along the wire in the direction of electron flow and your fingers point in the direction of flux (from north to south). Then your palm points in the direction of the applied force. The force is perpendicular to both the current flow and the magnetic flux. Suppose that instead of a single wire, there is a wire loop in the magnetic field. Figure 3-21 shows a loop with electrons flowing into side A of the loop. The left-hand rule shows that the force on the upper conductor of the loop is going away from you and the force on the lower conductor is coming toward you. These forces produce a *torque,* or twisting action, that can be used to rotate the loop.

When the loop rotates to the position shown in Fig. 3-22, the forces on the conductors no longer produce rotation. Instead, the forces tend to spread the loop apart, and the loop will remain in this position.

If the motion of the loop carried it slightly beyond this position, and if the direction of current flow through the loop could be reversed, the motion would continue. Electrons would now flow into side B of the loop (Fig. 3-23). The left-hand rule shows that the forces act in the same direction as in Fig. 3-21.

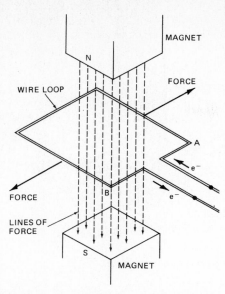

Fig. 3-22. Loop shown in a position in which the forces do not tend to rotate the loop.

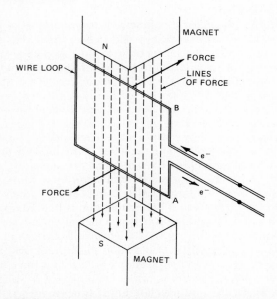

Fig. 3-23. Electrons flowing into side B of the loop. Forces on the loop act to continue rotation in the same direction.

This can be done by connecting the ends of the loop to circular electric contacts as shown in Fig. 3-24. This arrangement of contacts is called a *commutator,* and each contact is a segment of the commutator. Current is applied to the commutator through sliding contacts called *brushes.* As the commutator rotates past the brushes, the direction of current flow through the loop reverses each time the loop makes a half-rotation. Therefore, the forces on the loop wires always act to keep the loop rotating in the same direction.

This is the basic principle of electric motor operation. Because there is only one loop, this motor does not operate very smoothly. If two loops are used (Fig. 3-25), the motor operation will be a little smoother. Two loops require four commutator segments. In a starter motor, the commutator may have as many as 40 segments (20 loops) to achieve smooth motion. The rotating part of a motor which consists of the wire loops is called the *armature.*

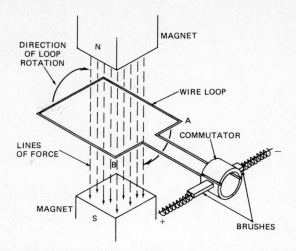

Fig. 3-24. Method of applying voltage to the loop through brushes and a commutator.

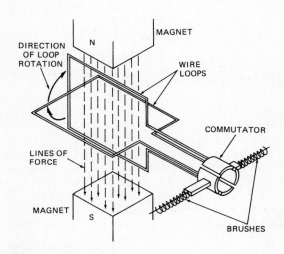

Fig. 3-25. Two-loop motor.

GENERATING AN ELECTRIC CURRENT

When Oersted made his discovery that electricity produces magnetism, it was regarded as one of the greatest scientific achievements of its day. Scientists then began to wonder if magnetism could produce electricity.

In 1831, Michael Faraday demonstrated that magnetism *could* produce electricity. But energy had to be supplied in the form of mechanical motion.

Figure 3-26 shows a conductor being moved through a magnetic field. Electromagnets are used to produce a strong magnetic field. At the ends of the wire, a very sensitive ammeter is connected. When the wire is moved so that the wire cuts across the magnetic lines of force, the needle of the ammeter deflects. Therefore, electric current (and voltage) is generated when a conductor is moved through a magnetic field.

Two conditions are required to generate a voltage in a conductor:
- A magnetic field
- Relative motion between the conductor and the magnetic field

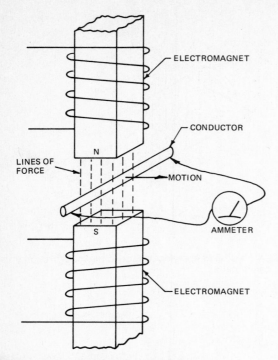

Fig. 3-26. Simple electric current generator.

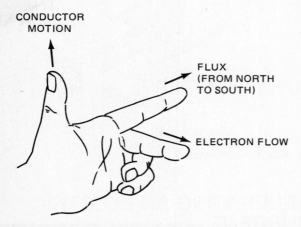

Fig. 3-27. Left-hand rule. Thumb points in direction of conductor motion, forefinger points in direction of flux, and third finger points in direction of current flow.

The conductor or magnetic field must move so that lines of force are cut. The direction of current flow can be found from another left-hand rule (Fig. 3-27). If your thumb points in the direction of conductor motion and your forefinger points in the direction of flux (from north to south), the third finger will point in the direction of electron flow. The amount of voltage generated can be increased by increasing the strength of the magnetic field and by increasing the speed of the motion. If the conductor moves in the same direction as the lines of force (parallel to the lines), no voltage is generated.

Faraday's discovery led to the development of the *generator*. A generator is a device that converts mechanical energy into electric energy. A simple generator is shown in Fig. 3-28. A wire loop is rotated in a magnetic field. If the loop is turned in the direction shown, current is generated

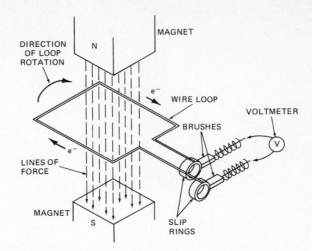

Fig. 3-28. Electric current generator.

in the upper wire in the right-hand direction and in the lower wire in the left-hand direction. Therefore, current flows around the loop.

If you connected a voltmeter across the ends of the loop, the voltmeter needle would deflect upscale as the loop cut through the magnetic field. In Fig. 3-28, a voltmeter is shown connected to the wire loop. Each end of the wire loop is attached to a small, round conductor called a *slip ring*. The voltmeter is electrically connected to the slip rings through the brushes. This arrangement prevents the wires from becoming tangled as the loop is rotated.

Figure 3-29 shows the voltage generated at various positions of the loop. When the wires of the loop are moving with (or parallel to) lines of force, no voltage is generated (Fig. 3-29, position a). When the loop wires cut directly across the lines of force, as in position c, the voltage generated is greatest. When the loop is between positions a and c, the voltage is between maximum and zero.

When the loop rotates 180° (one half-turn), the current flows in the opposite direction in the loop and the voltage reverses *polarity* (position e). Polarity is the direction of voltage (meaning which terminal of a voltage source is positive and which terminal is negative). In this example, the loop is a source of voltage, so polarity refers to which end of the loop is positive or negative.

One complete revolution of the loop (from position a to position i) produces one complete cycle of voltage. The voltage goes from zero to maximum in one direction, through zero again to maximum in the other direction, and back to zero. This is one *cycle*. The number of cycles that occur in 1 second is called *frequency*.

This type of changing voltage (and current) is called *alternating current (ac)*. Alternating current is electric current that flows first in one direction and then in the opposite direction. The shape of the voltage is called a *sine wave*. Alternating current is a common type of electric current that is used in radio, television, and most other electronic circuits. The electric power supplied for home lighting is ac. The power companies supply an ac for home usage that has a frequency of 60 cycles per second. One cycle per second is given the name *hertz* (Hz).

An ac generator is also called an *alternator*. Chapter 11 describes alternators.

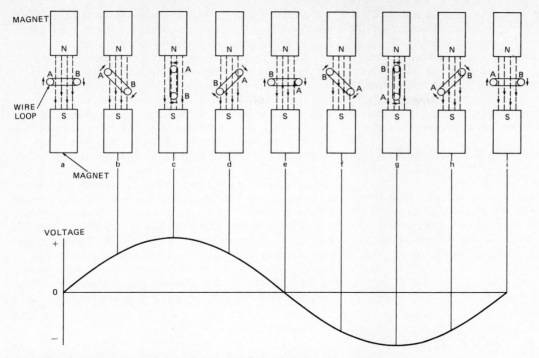

Fig. 3-29. Voltage generated in the loop for a complete rotation of the loop.

CHANGING ALTERNATING CURRENT TO DIRECT CURRENT

The generator shown in Fig. 3-28 generates ac. It is possible to generate direct current (dc) if more loops are used and if a different method is used to connect the loops to the outside circuit. Figure 3-30 shows a commutator and brushes similar to those of Fig. 3-24. However, this commutator has eight segments, which means there are four loops. The generator is designed so that when each loop passes directly through the magnetic field, the segments of the commutator connected to that loop are in contact with the brushes. This means maximum voltage is connected to the external circuit. As the loops turn, the next loop reaches the maximum position, and its commutator segments are under the brushes.

Therefore, each loop is connected to the brushes only when the loop has the maximum voltage generated in it. The voltage output from the brushes would look like that shown in Fig. 3-31. Although the voltage is not perfectly smooth, as dc should be, it is still dc because it only flows in one direction. To provide a much smoother output, many more turns of wire are needed, and many more segments are used on the commutator. The rotating loops of wire are called the *armature*. This type of generator is called a *dc generator*.

Notice the similarity between the generator of Fig. 3-30 and the motor of Fig. 3-25. In fact, they can both be the same device. A generator can be a motor, and a motor can be a generator. If the motor is driven, it will generate electric current. If the generator has voltage applied to its armature, it will turn as a motor.

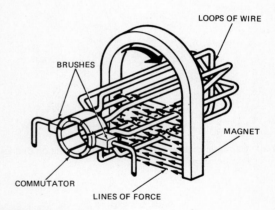

Fig. 3-30. DC generator.

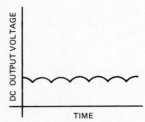

Fig. 3-31. Voltage output of a dc generator. (*Delco-Remy Division of General Motors Corporation*)

MAGNETIC TRIGGERING DEVICES

Magnetic triggering devices are used in the automobile to provide information on the position of a rotating part. Two common uses are the magnetic-pickup coil in electronic ignition distributors and the crankshaft-position sensor used in some engine control systems.

The operation of these devices is based on the principle that the reluctance in a magnetic circuit controls the flux. The lower the reluctance, the stronger the flux.

Figure 3-32 shows the magnetic-pickup coil in an electronic ignition distributor. A toothed wheel called an *armature,* or *reluctor,* is attached to the distributor shaft. A pickup-coil assembly is located close to the reluctor. The pickup-coil assembly consists of a permanent magnet, two pole pieces (which act as north and south poles), and a pickup coil.

The pickup coil is positioned around the extension of the north pole piece. The pole piece extends slightly beyond the coil in the form of a small tooth.

Figure 3-33 shows the reluctor positioned so that a reluctor tooth is lined up with the pickup-coil tooth. The dotted line shows the path of magnetic flux (which is through the pickup coil). Because the air gap is small when the teeth are lined up, the reluctance is low and the flux is strong.

In Fig. 3-34, the reluctor is positioned so that the teeth are not aligned. In this position, because the air gap is large, the reluctance is high and the flux is weak.

As the reluctor rotates, the flux is being alternately strengthened and weakened. Each time a reluctor tooth lines up with the pickup-coil tooth, there is a sharp increase in the flux. The rapid change in flux generates a voltage pulse in the pickup coil. The voltage pulse is shown in Fig. 3-35. Note that there is an upward (positive) part and a downward (negative) part. This is because an increasing flux (reluctor tooth approaching the pickup-coil tooth) generates a positive voltage. A decreasing flux (reluctor tooth leaving the pickup-coil tooth) generates a negative voltage. This voltage pulse is amplified and then used to trigger the spark in an electronic ignition system.

Another device which operates in a similar manner is the crankshaft-position sensor (Fig. 3-36). The crankshaft-position sensor is a coil mounted near the crankshaft. A toothed wheel on the crankshaft generates voltage pulses in the coil. The voltage pulses signal the position of the crankshaft for use with electronic engine control systems.

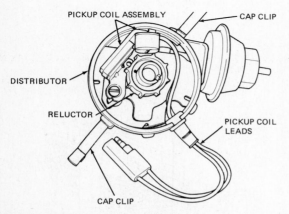

Fig. 3-32. Magnetic-pickup coil in an electronic ignition distributor. *(Chrysler Corporation)*

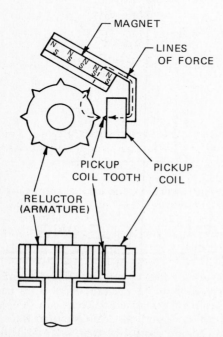

Fig. 3-33. Reluctor tooth aligned with pickup-coil tooth.

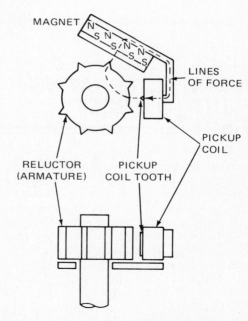

Fig. 3-34. Reluctor tooth not aligned with pickup-coil tooth.

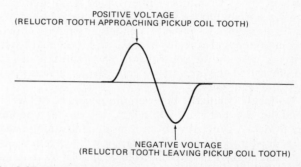

Fig. 3-35. Voltage generated in the pickup coil as reluctor tooth passes the pickup coil.

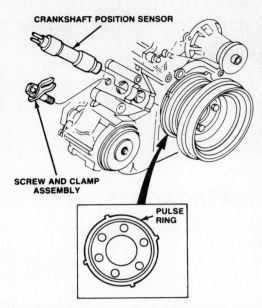

Fig. 3-36. Crankshaft-position sensor. *(Ford Motor Company)*

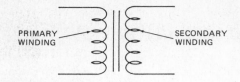

Fig. 3-37. Transformer symbol.

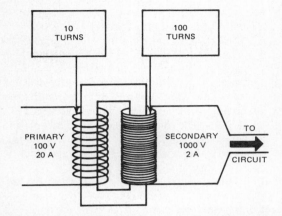

Fig. 3-38. Voltage and current in a transformer having a turns ratio of 1 to 10. *(Ford Motor Company)*

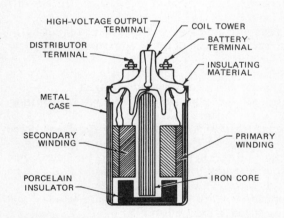

Fig. 3-39. Automotive ignition coil. *(Ford Motor Company)*

TRANSFORMERS

A *transformer* is an electrical device with two windings. It transfers electric energy from one winding to the other by *electromagnetic induction*. A transformer is made by winding two coils of wire over the same iron core. One coil is wound over the other, but they are electrically insulated from each other. One winding, the input side, is called the *primary winding*. The other winding (the output side) is called the *secondary winding*. Figure 3-37 shows the electrical symbol for a transformer.

If a changing current (like ac) flows through the primary winding of a transformer, a changing magnetic field is produced around both windings. This changing magnetic field creates, or *induces*, a voltage in the secondary winding. This is called electromagnetic induction.

Most transformers have different numbers of turns, or loops of wire, in each winding. The ratio of the number of secondary turns to the number of primary turns is called the *turns ratio*. If the turns ratio is 1 to 10, for example, there are 10 times as many secondary turns as there are primary turns. This is called a *step-up transformer*. This type of transformer is used to increase voltage. A transformer that decreases voltage is called a step-down transformer.

With a turns ratio of 1 to 10, the secondary voltage will be 10 times greater than the primary voltage (Fig. 3-38). This is because a changing primary voltage creates a changing magnetic field. Since this changing magnetic field cuts across 10 times as many turns in the secondary winding as there are in the primary winding, 10 times as much voltage is induced in the secondary winding.

The power in an electric circuit is equal to the voltage multiplied by the current (Chap. 2). In transformers, the power out of the secondary cannot be greater than the power supplied to the primary. Therefore, in a transformer,

$$\text{Power in} = \text{power out}$$

However, there is actually a small power loss due to the effects of the wire heating up as current passes through it. This is an example of the I^2R heat loss described in Chap. 2.

Power equals voltage times current. Therefore, if voltage is increased in the secondary winding, the current decreases. As a result, the power remains the same. If the voltage is 10 times higher in the secondary winding, then the current is only one-tenth as great.

Transformers will only operate with a changing voltage. If a steady dc voltage is applied to a transformer, the transformer will overheat.

The automobile ignition coil is a transformer (Fig. 3-39). The voltage in the secondary winding may be increased to 40,000 V or higher to cause a spark to jump the gap at the spark plug.

VOCABULARY REVIEW

Alternating current (ac)   Electric current that flows first in one direction and then in the opposite direction.

Armature   The part of a magnetic device that moves in a magnetic field. In a relay, the moveable arm; in a d'Arsonval meter movement, the rotating coil; in a motor, the rotating loops of wire; and in a pickup-coil, the toothed wheel.

Brush   A block of conducting material (usually carbon) which contacts a commutator or slip ring in a motor, a generator, or an alternator.

Commutator   The series of electric contacts which are located around one end of an armature and which connect to the armature conductors.

Cycle   A change of voltage (or current) from zero to maximum in one direction, through zero again to maximum in the other direction, and back to zero.

Electromagnet   A magnet made by passing an electric current through a coil of wire.

Electromagnetic induction   The relative motion of a wire or coil and a magnetic field, causing a voltage to be produced in a wire or coil.

Flux   The flow of lines of force.

Frequency   The number of cycles that occur in 1 second.

Induce   To produce a voltage in a wire or coil by the relative motion of the wire or coil and a magnetic field.

Line of force   The imaginary line which joins the north and south poles of a magnet.

Magnetic field   All the lines of force of a magnet taken together as a whole.

Magnetomotive force   The magnetic driving force that causes flux to flow through a reluctance.

Motor   A device that changes electric energy into mechanical energy in the form of a rotating motion.

Permanent magnet   A magnetic material that retains its magnetism.

Permeability   Magnetic conductivity, or the ease with which a substance concentrates and increases the number of lines of force.

Polarity   The direction of voltage (which terminal of a voltage source is positive and which terminal is negative).

Pole   The part of a magnet where there is the greatest concentration of magnetism.

Primary   The input winding of a transformer.

Relay   A magnetic device that switches current in an electric circuit.

Reluctance   The opposition to flow of lines of force.

Reluctor   The toothed wheel which is part of a magnetic triggering system.

Secondary   The output winding of a transformer.

Sine wave   The shape of the voltage produced by an ac generator.

Slip ring   The circular contact which connects electric current to the rotating part of an alternator.

Solenoid   A magnetic device that produces a force to move an object.

Transformer   An electrical device with two windings that transfers electric energy from one winding to the other by electromagnetic induction.

Turns ratio   The ratio of the number of secondary turns to the number of primary turns in a transformer.

REVIEW QUESTIONS

Select the *one* correct, best, or most probable answer to each question.

1. What parts of a dc generator permit the current generated in the armature to be connected to an external circuit?
   a. brushes and slip rings
   b. brushes and commutator
   c. armature and magnetic field
   d. commutator and armature

2. In the secondary winding of a transformer,
   a. if the voltage is doubled, the current is halved
   b. if the voltage is doubled, the current is doubled
   c. if the voltage is halved, the power is doubled
   d. if the voltage is halved, the current is halved

3. Ohm's law for magnetic circuits relates
   a. reluctance, reactance, and resistance
   b. magnetomotive force, flux, and reactance
   c. flux, resistance, and magnetomotive force
   d. magnetomotive force, flux, and reluctance

4. In a magnetic circuit,
   a. decreasing the reluctance increases the flux
   b. increasing the magnetomotive force decreases the flux
   c. increasing the reluctance decreases the magnetomotive force
   d. decreasing the reluctance decreases the flux

5. What two conditions are required to generate a voltage?
   a. magnetic field and electric current
   b. magnetic field and motion of a conductor
   c. electric current and motion of a conductor
   d. a conductor and an insulator

6. When energized, the moveable core of a solenoid or a relay always moves in the direction that
   a. reduces the flux
   b. increases the magnetomotive force
   c. increases the reluctance
   d. decreases the reluctance

7. Mechanic A says that alternators have slip rings. Mechanic B says that dc generators have a commutator. Who is right?
   a. A only
   b. B only
   c. both A and B
   d. neither A nor B

8. An electromagnet can be made stronger by
   a. increasing the number of turns of wire
   b. increasing the current flow
   c. placing an iron core inside the coil of wire
   d. all of the above

9. Which of the following statements is true?
   I. An alternator produces a sine wave.
   II. A dc generator can operate as a motor.
   a. I only
   b. II only
   c. both I and II
   d. neither I nor II

10. A starter relay is useful because
    a. a small current controls a large current
    b. it engages the starter motor pinion gear into the flywheel ring gear
    c. it eliminates the need for an ignition switch
    d. the starter motor draws a small amount of current

11. A transformer
    a. transfers power from one winding to another winding
    b. increases power
    c. increases both the voltage and the current in a circuit
    d. all of the above

12. What parts of an ac generator permit the current generated to be connected to an external circuit?
    a. brushes and slip rings
    b. brushes and armature
    c. commutator and brushes
    d. commutator and slip rings

13. All of the following statements are true of a buzzer *except*
    a. a buzzer is similar in operation to a relay
    b. a buzzer is operated by a dc voltage
    c. the moving armature produces the sound of a buzzer
    d. a buzzer has a set of normally open contacts

14. When a compass is placed near a wire in which there is a flow of electric current, the compass needle
    a. points in a direction which is parallel to the flow of current
    b. points in a direction which is perpendicular to the flow of current
    c. is not affected by the current flow
    d. points to the positive voltage

15. All of the following statements are true of relays and solenoids *except*
    a. solenoids are generally used to apply a force to move an object
    b. the normal position of a relay is the energized position
    c. relays are generally used to switch current to a circuit
    d. the moveable core of a solenoid moves to decrease reluctance

CHAPTER 4

INDUCTANCE AND CAPACITANCE

OBJECTIVES

After you have studied this chapter, you should be able to:

1. Discuss the basic principles of inductance and capacitance.

2. Explain the effect of inductance and capacitance in dc and ac circuits.

3. Describe some applications of coils and capacitors in automotive electrical systems.

There are three basic elements in electric circuits, in addition to the voltage source and connecting wiring. These elements are *resistance, inductance,* and *capacitance.* Resistance has been covered in Chap. 2. Inductance and capacitance are covered in this chapter.

Inductance is provided by components known as *inductors* (or *coils*), capacitance by components known as *capacitors* (or *condensors*). Both inductance and capacitance affect direct current (dc), pulses of direct current, and alternating current (ac).

RESISTANCE

Figure 4-1 shows an electric circuit which includes a battery, a switch, and a resistor. The effect of the resistor on current flow is described below.

Direct Current

When dc (Fig. 4-2) flows through a resistor, the resistor limits the current flow (Chap. 2). Ohm's law can be used to determine the current flow.

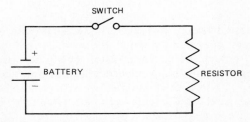

Fig. 4-1. Electric circuit with a battery, a switch, and a resistor.

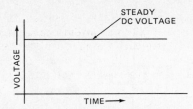

Fig. 4-2. Graph of voltage against time for a steady dc.

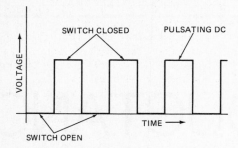

Fig. 4-3. Graph of voltage against time for a pulsating dc.

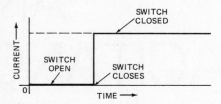

Fig. 4-4. Graph of current against time in a circuit with a resistor when the switch is closed.

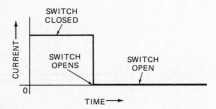

Fig. 4-5. Graph of current against time in a circuit with a resistor when the switch is opened.

Pulsating Direct Current

Direct current may not always flow continuously. It may be repeatedly switched on and off (Fig. 4-3). This is called *pulsating dc*. An example of this is the current flow through the primary winding of the ignition coil in a breaker-point ignition system. As the points (switch contacts) alternately close and open, the current flow to the coil is turned on and off. The switch in Fig. 4-1 is repeatedly closed and opened. The effect on the current flow is described below.

Switch Closes   As long as the switch is open, no current flows. But when the switch is closed, current instantly begins to flow through the resistor. This is shown as the abrupt step in the graph of current against time shown in Fig. 4-4. The amount of current flow is determined by battery voltage and the circuit resistance. Ohm's law can be used to determine current flow.

Switch Opens   When the switch is opened, the current instantly drops to zero (Fig. 4-5).

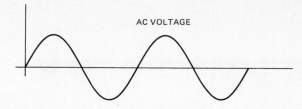

Fig. 4-6. Graph of voltage against time for an ac voltage.

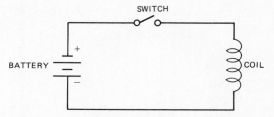

Fig. 4-7. Electric circuit with a battery, a switch, and a coil.

Alternating Current

Alternating current is an electric current that flows first in one direction and then in the opposite direction. The generator that produces ac is continually changing in voltage level and polarity. An ac voltage is shown in Fig. 4-6. A resistor opposes the flow of ac in the same manner as it opposes the flow of dc.

INDUCTANCE

Inductance is the effect of the action of a coil (inductor) on the flow of current in a circuit. Figure 4-7 shows an electric circuit which includes a battery, a switch, and a coil. The effect of the inductance of the coil on current flow is described below.

Direct Current

Whenever electric current flows through a wire, a small magnetic field is created around that wire (Chap. 2). When the wire is wound into a coil, the magnetic field is greatly increased because the individual magnetic fields add up. Direct-current flow is not opposed by a coil unless the wire used to wind the coil is small and has resistance. Therefore, a coil is said to "pass" dc. The only opposition to the flow of current is the resistance of the wire in the coil.

Pulsating Direct Current

The switch in Fig. 4-7 is repeatedly closed and opened. The effect on the current flow is described below.

Switch Closes   As long as the switch is open, no current flows. But when the switch is closed, the current gradually builds up to its full value (Fig. 4-8*a*). This will be very large, because the current is limited only by the resistance of the wire in the coil. Usually, the wire resistance is very low. The actual current flow may be found by using Ohm's law (Chap. 2) if the wire resistance is known.

As holes enter the N region, they combine with electrons to form a slight positive charge in the N region along the junction. This positive charge prevents more holes from entering the region. Now there is a small voltage across the junction.

Applying a voltage to a diode is called *biasing*. Figure 5-6 shows a battery connected to a diode with the positive terminal connected to the N region. The negative terminal is connected to the P region. This is called *reverse bias*. Reverse bias increases the voltage across the junction and prevents any current flow through the junction. Therefore, a diode does not conduct electric current when it is reverse-biased.

Figure 5-7 shows a battery connected to a diode with the positive terminal connected to the P region and the negative terminal connected to the N region. This is called *forward bias*. Forward bias decreases the voltage at the junction. This allows electrons to pass into the P region and holes to enter the N region. Therefore, a diode conducts current through the junction when it is forward-biased.

Figure 5-8 shows the current flow through a diode. Starting at the positive terminal of the battery, electrons are attracted to the positive terminal from the P region of the diode. As electrons leave the P region, holes are created which travel through the P region toward the PN junction. At the junction, the holes combine with the electrons which are being supplied by the negative battery terminal. Holes flow to the right in the P region, and electrons flow to the left in the N region. This is the way electric current flows through a diode.

A diode can be thought of as a one-way check valve. It allows current to flow through in one direction only. Figure 5-9 shows a diode and its electrical symbol. The arrow shows the direction of positive current flow through a diode. Diodes are used in alternators (ac generators) to change ac into dc to charge the battery. Alternators are covered in Chap. 11.

ZENER DIODES

When a diode is reverse-biased, it does not conduct electric current. However, if the reverse voltage is increased, a voltage level will be reached at which the diode will conduct in the reverse direction. This voltage is called the *zener voltage*. Zener breakdown (or reverse conduction) occurs when the high voltage across the junction begins to produce large amounts of ions. The ions are produced because the high voltage causes many collisions of free electrons with other electrons in the crystal structure.

A *zener diode* (Fig. 5-10) is designed to operate in the breakdown region. Once the breakdown voltage (zener voltage) is reached, a large current flows, which prevents the voltage from going any higher. Therefore, a zener diode can be used as a voltage-limiting device.

For example, if a zener diode is rated at 10 V, it will conduct in the forward direction, just as any other diode. It will not conduct in the reverse direction if the voltage is below 10 V. But as soon as the voltage reaches 10 V, it begins to conduct in the reverse direction. This prevents the voltage from going above 10 V.

Zener diodes can be used as protective devices. They are often used in electronic circuits to protect transistors from high voltage pulses.

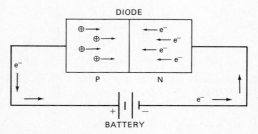

Fig. 5-8. Electric current through a diode, showing holes moving to the right and electrons moving to the left.

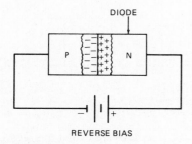

Fig. 5-6. Reverse-biased diode.

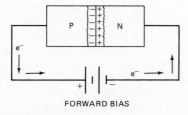

Fig. 5-7. Forward-biased diode.

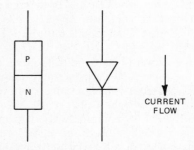

Fig. 5-9. Diode and its symbol. (The arrow shows the direction of positive current flow.)

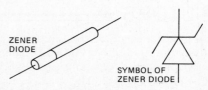

Fig. 5-10. Zener diode and its symbol.

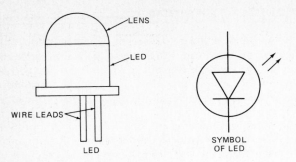

Fig. 5-11. LED and its symbol.

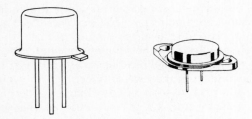

Fig. 5-12. Two types of transistors.

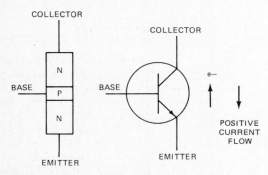

Fig. 5-13. NPN transistor and its symbol.

LIGHT-EMITTING DIODES

A *light-emitting diode (LED)* (Fig. 5-11) is similar in operation to the diode described earlier. Both types permit current to flow in only one direction. An LED emits light when it is forward-biased. A small lens is built into the diode so that the light can be seen.

During the forward-bias condition, holes from the P region combine with electrons from the N region at the PN junction. When the holes and electrons combine, energy is released in the form of light. Gallium arsenide is a chemical compound which is commonly used to make LEDs. When gallium arsenide is used, the light emitted is red. Other LEDs have been developed which emit light in other colors. LEDs are used on instrument-panel displays and in digital clocks.

TRANSISTORS

A *transistor* is a device made by combining P-type and N-type materials in groups of three (Fig. 5-12). There are two possible combinations: the NPN transistor (Fig. 5-13) and the PNP transistor (Fig. 5-14). The symbols for the two types of transistors are shown in the illustrations.

A transistor has two PN junctions separating the three

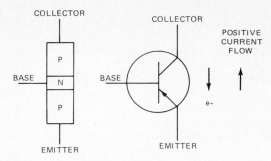

Fig. 5-14. PNP transistor and its symbol.

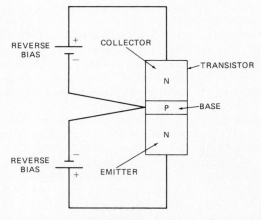

Fig. 5-15. NPN transistor with the emitter-base junction reverse-biased (no electron flow).

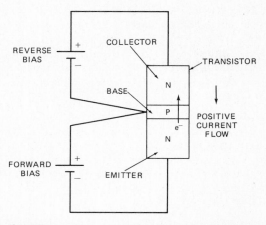

Fig. 5-16. NPN transistor with the emitter-base junction forward-biased (electrons flow).

regions. The three regions are called the *emitter,* the *base,* and the *collector.* The base is a very thin layer sandwiched between the emitter and the collector.

When a transistor is normally used in a circuit, a reverse bias is applied to the base-collector junction. If the emitter-base junction is also reverse-biased (Fig. 5-15), no current will flow through the transistor. But when the emitter-base junction is forward-biased (Fig. 5-16), electrons flow from the emitter to the base. Because the base is a thin layer and a positive voltage is applied to the collector, electrons flow from the emitter to the collector. Therefore, the voltage applied to the emitter-base junction can determine whether or not the transistor passes electric current.

The transistor shown in Figs. 5-15 and 5-16 is an NPN transistor. In a PNP transistor, the operation is the same,

54

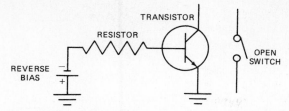

Fig. 5-17. Reverse-biased switching transistor. The transistor does not conduct electric current, acting like an open switch.

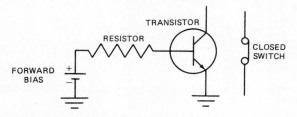

Fig. 5-18. Forward-biased switching transistor. The transistor conducts electric current, acting like a closed switch.

but the current flow is hole current.

The direction of positive current flow in the two types of transistors is shown in Figs. 5-13 and 5-14. In the NPN transistor of Fig. 5-13, positive current flow is from the collector to the emitter. In the PNP transistor of Fig. 5-14, positive current flow is from the emitter to the collector. The arrows on the transistor symbols show the direction of positive current flow.

Transistor Switches

A transistor can be used as a switch. Figure 5-17 shows an NPN transistor with a reverse bias applied to the base-emitter junction. Because collector-emitter current cannot flow, the transistor acts like an open switch.

In Fig. 5-18, a forward bias is applied to the base-emitter junction. Now collector-emitter current can flow, and the transistor acts like a closed switch.

There are many transistor switches used in the electronic circuits in an automobile. A transistor is used in electronic ignition systems to switch the ignition-coil primary current on and off. Many thousands of transistor switches are used in the microcomputers which control engine operation in late-model cars.

Transistor Amplifiers

A transistor can act as an amplifier. In a transistor amplifier circuit, a small variation in base voltage (or base current) can cause a large variation in collector-emitter current. In an amplifier circuit, the transistor is almost always conducting current: It does not stop conducting, as an open switch does.

Figure 5-19 shows the voltage pulse from a magnetic-pickup coil in an electronic distributor. This small voltage pulse is applied to the base of a transistor amplifier. It is then amplified in the collector circuit to a much larger voltage pulse. The voltage pulse still looks the same, but it has been amplified to a higher voltage. A series of transistor amplifiers may be used to provide a greater amplification. Transistors used as amplifiers are found in electronic ignition systems, radios, tape players, and many other electronic circuits in the automobile.

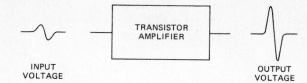

Fig. 5-19. Transistor used as an amplifier.

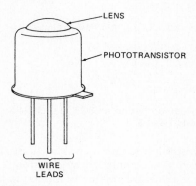

Fig. 5-20. Phototransistor.

PHOTOTRANSISTORS

A *phototransistor* is a transistor that is sensitive to light (Fig. 5-20). A small lens in the housing focuses light on the sensitive portion of the transistor. When light strikes the transistor, free electrons and holes are formed, which increases current flow through the transistor. More light causes more current to flow. Phototransistors are used in automotive headlamp dimmer circuits. When light from an approaching vehicle strikes the phototransistor, it conducts current to operate the dimmer circuit. Automatic headlamp dimmer circuits are covered in Chap. 12.

SILICON CONTROLLED RECTIFIERS

A *silicon controlled rectifier (SCR)* is a semiconductor device made with two P regions and two N regions (Fig. 5-21). An SCR has three PN junctions. If voltage is applied across an SCR as shown in Fig. 5-22, the SCR will not conduct. This is because junctions 1 and 3 are reverse-biased.

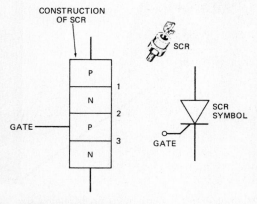

Fig. 5-21. SCR and its symbol.

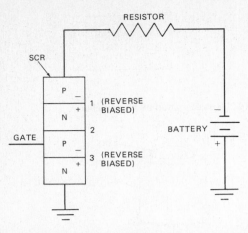

Fig. 5-22. Voltage applied to an SCR in a direction that reverse-biases junctions 1 and 3.

If voltage is applied to an SCR as shown in Fig. 5-23, the SCR will still not conduct. Now junction 2 is reverse-biased. But if a positive voltage is applied to the P region of the reverse-biased junction (Fig. 5-24), the SCR will conduct. The connection to the P region is called the *gate terminal.*

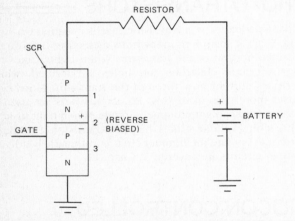

Fig. 5-23. Voltage applied to an SCR in a direction that reverse-biases junction 2.

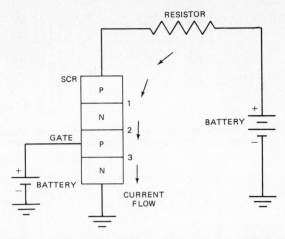

Fig. 5-24. Positive voltage applied to the gate of an SCR to allow current to flow through the SCR.

When an SCR begins to conduct current, the gate loses control. If the voltage is removed from the gate, the SCR will continue to conduct current. If the voltage is momentarily removed from across the SCR, the SCR will return to its original nonconducting state. Then the gate will again be able to control current flow. SCRs are used as switches in some circuits that control a large amount of electric current.

INTEGRATED CIRCUITS

Diodes and transistors can be made in a very small size. Thousands of transistors can be placed on a small surface called a *chip*. As many as 30,000 transistors can be placed on a chip that is only ¼ inch (in.) [6.35 millimeters (mm)] square (Fig. 5-25). In addition to transistors and diodes, resistors and capacitors are also placed on chips. In fact, entire functional circuits can be made. Because the components are all integrated together on a single chip, the

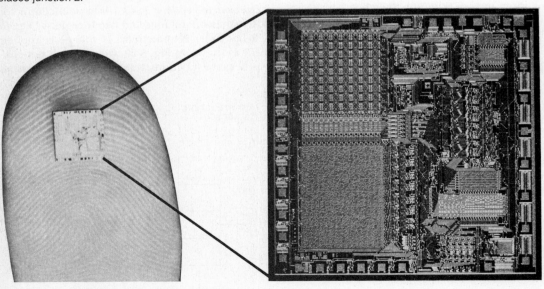

Fig. 5-25. Photograph of a chip, showing its relative size. *(Texas Instruments Incorporated)*

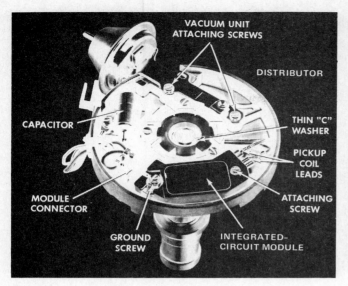

Fig. 5-26. Electronic ignition distributor, showing IC ignition module. *(Delco-Remy Division of General Motors Corporation)*

Phototransistor A transistor in which the current flow is controlled by the amount of light that strikes the transistor.

Reverse bias The bias on a PN junction which prevents current flow through the junction.

Semiconductor A material that conducts electric current under certain conditions.

Silicon controlled rectifier (SCR) A semiconductor device used as a switch.

Solid-state devices Components made from a solid material.

Transistor A semiconductor device which can be used as a switch or as an amplifier.

Zener diode A diode designed to operate in the region of reverse conduction.

Zener voltage The voltage at which a diode will conduct in the reverse direction.

resulting circuit is called an *integrated circuit (IC)*. Integrated circuits are used in electronic ignition systems (Fig. 5-26) and in the microcomputers used in other ignition and engine control systems. Microcomputers are covered in Chap. 15.

VOCABULARY REVIEW

Biasing Applying a voltage to the PN junction of a semiconductor.

Chip A small surface on which transistors and integrated circuits are placed.

Covalent bonding The sharing of electrons between adjacent atoms.

Crystal A material that has its atoms arranged in a pattern.

Diode A semiconductor device which acts as a one-way current valve.

Doping Adding impurity atoms to a crystal.

Forward bias The bias on a PN junction which allows current to flow through the junction.

Hole The absence of an electron.

Impurity atoms Atoms which are added to a crystal to produce a semiconductor.

Integrated circuit (IC) An electronic circuit made from a number of different types of components placed on a single chip.

Light-emitting diode (LED) A diode that emits light when it is forward-biased.

N-type material A semiconductor material in which the electrical conduction is electron flow.

PN junction The boundary between a P-type material and an N-type material which have been joined together.

P-type material A semiconductor material in which the electrical conduction is hole flow.

REVIEW QUESTIONS

Select the *one* correct, best, or most probable answer to each question.

1. Which of the following is *not* a semiconductor?
   a. resistor
   b. diode
   c. transistor
   d. LED

2. Applying voltage to a PN junction is called
   a. doping
   b. a diode
   c. biasing
   d. covalent bonding

3. How does a diode affect the flow of electric current?
   a. it allows the current to flow in both directions
   b. it allows the current to flow in one direction only
   c. it prevents the flow of electric current
   d. it has no effect on the flow of electric current

4. Adding impurity atoms to a silicon crystal is called
   a. doping
   b. a diode
   c. biasing
   d. covalent bonding

5. When an N-type material and a P-type material are joined together, the result is
   a. transistor
   b. covalent bonding
   c. an insulator
   d. a diode

6. Which of the following statements is true?
   I. Electric current in an N-type material is electron flow.
   II. Electric current in a P-type material is hole flow.
   a. I only
   b. II only
   c. both I and II
   d. neither I nor II

7. An element with only 1 or 2 electrons in the outer orbits of its atoms is called
   a. a conductor
   b. P-type material
   c. an insulator
   d. N-type material

8. N-type materials are
   a. negatively charged
   b. electrically neutral
   c. positively charged
   d. none of the above

9. Light-emitting diodes are made of
   a. germanium
   b. silicon
   c. gallium arsenide
   d. arsenic

10. Which of the following statements is true for a transistor?
    a. positive current flow in a PNP transistor is from the emitter to the collector
    b. positive current flow in an NPN transistor is from the emitter to the collector
    c. collector-base junctions are usually forward-biased
    d. the collector is a very thin layer

CHAPTER **6**

AUTOMOTIVE WIRING, COMPONENTS, AND CIRCUIT DIAGRAMS

OBJECTIVES

After you have studied this chapter, you should be able to:

1. Describe the types of wire and how wire sizes are specified.

2. Explain the operation of circuit protection devices.

3. Explain the meaning of the various electrical symbols.

4. Use a wiring diagram to locate a circuit or a component.

AUTOMOTIVE WIRING

Automotive wiring is either solid or stranded (Fig. 6-1). Stranded wire is made of a number of small solid wires (strands). Solid wire is used in the automobile in magnetic devices such as relays, solenoids, alternators, and motors.

However, solid wire is not flexible enough for vehicle wiring. Under severe vibration, solid wire can break. Stranded wire is more flexible. Therefore, it is used for most vehicle wiring. Because a stranded wire is made of a number of small wires, it is a *cable*. However, only large-diameter stranded wires are commonly called cables. Most automotive wire is made of copper.

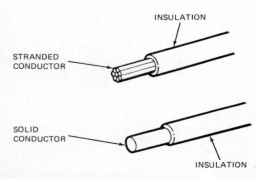

Fig. 6-1. Stranded wire and solid wire. *(Chrysler Corporation)*

Wire Size

The size of a wire determines how much current it can safely carry without overheating. The larger the wire diameter, the less resistance the wire offers to the flow of current and, therefore, the greater the current-carrying capacity. The size of a wire is called its *gauge*. The American Wire Gauge (AWG) system of wire measurement is shown in Fig. 6-2. This table is for copper wire and lists wire gauge, wire diameter, cross section of the wire in *circular mils,* and resistance of the wire in ohms per thousand feet.

A *mil* is 0.001 inch (in.) (one-thousandth of an inch). A circular mil is the square of the diameter of the wire. (The *square* of a number is the number multiplied by itself.) If the wire has a diameter of 5 mils, for example, the cross-sectional area of the wire is 5 times 5, or 25 circular mils. Note that the circular mil is not a true calculation of cross-sectional area. It is only a representation of the current-carrying capacity of the wire.

As wire diameter decreases, the wire gauge numbers increase. Therefore, a 20-gauge wire is smaller than a 5-gauge wire. The wire used in automotive wiring is usually between 10 and 18 gauge. Battery cables are between 2 and 6 gauge.

In the metric system, wire size is expressed as the cross-sectional area of the wire in square millimeters (mm^2). This designation is a true measurement of area. A table comparing metric size and AWG size is shown in Fig. 6-3.

Aluminum Wire

Aluminum wire is used in some cars. It is usually solid wire. Aluminum is a poorer conductor of electricity than copper. Therefore, to carry the same current, a larger gauge of aluminum wire is required. In addition, because alumi-

Metric wire size (mm^2)	AWG size (gauge)
.22	24
.5	20
.8	18
1.0	16
2.0	14
3.0	12
5.0	10
8.0	8
13.0	6
19.0	4
32.0	2

Fig. 6-3. Metric wire size compared with AWG size.

num wire is not as flexible as copper wire, aluminum wire is used in applications where it remains stationary.

Printed-Circuit Wiring

Many cars have *printed-circuit* wiring for instrument-panel wiring (Fig. 6-4). A printed circuit is a thin plastic base upon which strips of copper foil are bonded. The copper foil takes the place of many of the wires under the instrument panel. Another layer of plastic covers the foil to act as an insulator. Printed circuits simplify the wiring and make it easier to trace wires and to troubleshoot.

Resistance Wire

Resistance wire is wire that is made to have a certain amount of resistance per foot. It is used in some ignition systems to limit current flow through the ignition-coil primary winding. The wire is used instead of a fixed resistor and is called the *ballast resistance*. It is located between the ignition switch and the ignition coil and is included in the vehicle *wiring harness.* A wiring harness is a group of wires wrapped together in a bundle. The resistance of the ballast resistance is usually from 0.8 to 1.2 ohms (Ω).

Another type of resistance wire is used for spark plug wires (often called cables). These wires carry the high-voltage current from the distributor cap to the spark plugs.

Whenever a spark occurs, energy is radiated from the spark. This energy is called *electromagnetic energy*. Radio waves are also electromagnetic energy. A radio can receive the energy from sparks in addition to radio signals. The energy from sparks can cause interference in the vehicle radio and in other nearby radios and televisions. This is called *spark interference*. When the spark jumps the gap of a spark plug, the ignition-system wiring radiates electromagnetic energy. Spark interference from the ignition system can be heard as a buzzing sound in the radio that increases in frequency as engine speed increases.

Limiting the spark current reduces the radiated energy. Therefore, using resistance spark plug wires minimizes radio interference. Spark plug wires are made with a large amount of resistance per foot of length. A typical spark plug wire resistance can be from 10,000 to 15,000 Ω. The conductor in these wires is a carbon-impregnated linen core or a fiberglass core saturated with graphite (Fig. 6-5). These wires are called *television-radio-suppression (TVRS)* wires.

AWG size (gauge)	Wire diameter (mils)	Cross-sectional area (circular mils)	Resistance (Ω per 1000 ft)*
24	20.1	404	25.7
22	25.3	640	16.2
20	32.0	1,020	10.1
18	40.3	1,620	6.39
16	50.8	2,580	4.02
14	64.1	4,110	2.52
12	80.8	6,530	1.59
10	101.9	10,380	.9988
8	128.5	16,510	.6281
6	162.0	26,240	.3952
4	204.3	41,740	.2485
2	257.6	66,360	.1563
1	289.3	83,690	.1239
2/0	364.8	133,100	.0779
4/0	460.0	211,600	.0490

*@ 20°C

Fig. 6-2. AWG system of wire measurement for copper wire. This table is for solid, bare copper wire. Stranded-wire diameters, areas, and resistances are similar, but they may vary slightly among different wire manufacturers and in the method of stranding.

60

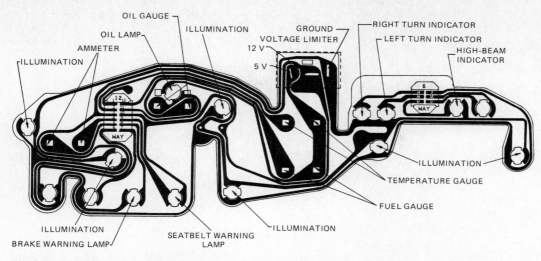

Fig. 6-4. Printed-circuit instrument-panel wiring. (*Chrysler Corporation*)

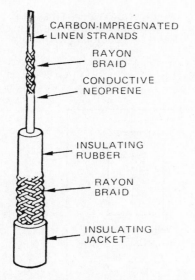

Fig. 6-5. TVRS spark plug wire. (*AC-Delco Division of General Motors Corporation*)

Shielded Wire

A *shielded wire* (Fig. 6-6) is a wire with a center conductor, a layer of insulation, and a braided conductive shield. The shield is also covered with insulation. When shielded wire is used, the shield is grounded at both ends of the wire. Shielded wire is used to connect the radio antenna to the radio and to interconnect such units as radios, tape players, and citizens band (CB) radios. This type of wire is also called *coaxial cable,* or "coax." Coax is used in radios because the grounded shield helps prevent spark interference from reaching the center conductor of the wire and being received by the radio.

SYMBOLS AND COMPONENTS ====

Symbols are used to represent components in electrical diagrams. In general, the symbols that are used resemble the components they represent. Not all manufacturers use

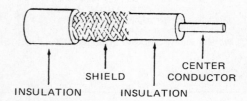

Fig. 6-6. Shielded wire.

the same symbols on their diagrams. Figures 6-7 through 6-9 show examples of symbols found in electrical diagrams. In addition, there are many different types of some components, such as switches, relays, and connectors. Many different symbols are used to represent them.

Resistors, Capacitors, and Coils

Resistors, capacitors, and coils have been discussed in previous chapters. Their symbols are shown in Fig. 6-10. The symbols are for components that have fixed values. They are manufactured to have a certain value of resistance, capacitance, or inductance. Variable resistors, capacitors, and inductors are also made. These components are adjustable, and their values can be changed. The variable feature is shown by drawing an arrow across the symbol (Fig. 6-11).

Variable resistors have a sliding wiper arm that moves along a length of resistance wire. There are two types of variable resistors: *potentiometers* and *rheostats.* A potentiometer has three terminals (Fig. 6-12a). One application of a potentiometer is a radio volume control. A rheostat has two terminals (Fig. 6-12b). Rheostats are used in headlamp switches to vary the brightness of the dash lamps. In a potentiometer, current flows through the entire length of the resistance wire. In a rheostat, current flows only through a portion of the resistance wire. A potentiometer can be used as a rheostat if only two of its terminals are connected.

In variable capacitors, the plates of the capacitor are moved to vary the capacitance. Variable inductors have a moveable core that can be moved into and out of the coil. This changes its inductance.

61

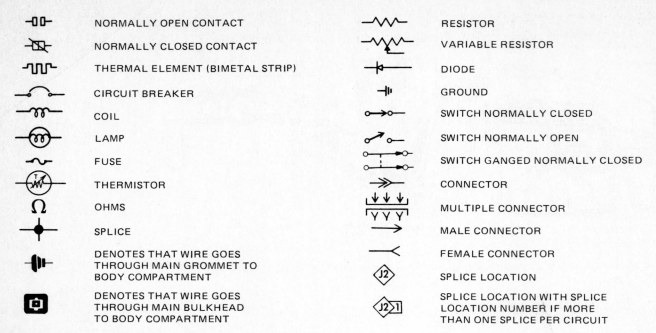

NORMALLY OPEN CONTACT	RESISTOR
NORMALLY CLOSED CONTACT	VARIABLE RESISTOR
THERMAL ELEMENT (BIMETAL STRIP)	DIODE
CIRCUIT BREAKER	GROUND
COIL	SWITCH NORMALLY CLOSED
LAMP	SWITCH NORMALLY OPEN
FUSE	SWITCH GANGED NORMALLY CLOSED
THERMISTOR	CONNECTOR
OHMS	MULTIPLE CONNECTOR
SPLICE	MALE CONNECTOR
DENOTES THAT WIRE GOES THROUGH MAIN GROMMET TO BODY COMPARTMENT	FEMALE CONNECTOR
	SPLICE LOCATION
DENOTES THAT WIRE GOES THROUGH MAIN BULKHEAD TO BODY COMPARTMENT	SPLICE LOCATION WITH SPLICE LOCATION NUMBER IF MORE THAN ONE SPLICE PER CIRCUIT

Fig. 6-7. Chrysler wiring diagram symbols. *(Chrysler Corporation)*

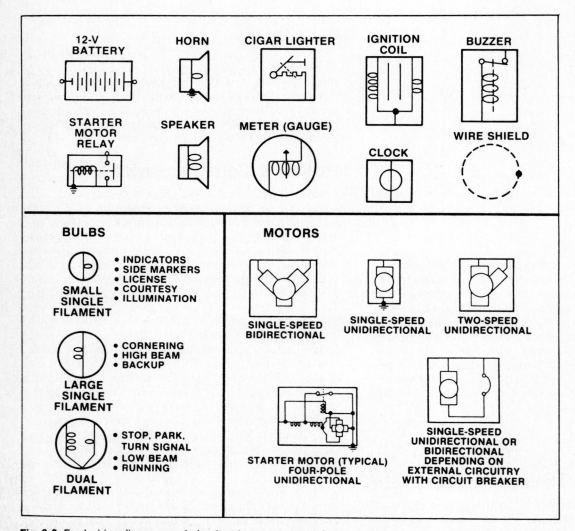

Fig. 6-8. Ford wiring diagram symbols. *(Ford Motor Company)*

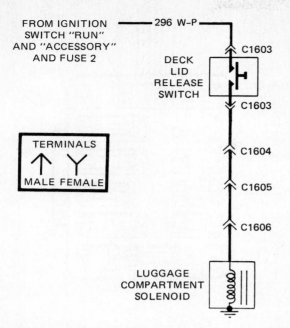

FROM IGNITION SWITCH "RUN" AND "ACCESSORY" AND FUSE 2 — 296 W-P

DECK LID RELEASE SWITCH

C1603

C1603

C1604

C1605

C1606

TERMINALS

MALE FEMALE

LUGGAGE COMPARTMENT SOLENOID

Fig. 6-28. Connector terminals as shown in a wiring diagram. *(Ford Motor Company)*

a diagram to help you locate it (Fig. 6-29). Note that the connector is shown as if it were pulled apart and you were looking into the two open ends. The two mating halves are placed side by side, pin 1 mating with pin 1, pin 2 mating with pin 2, and so on.

Weather-Resistant Connectors

Many automobiles have electronic engine control systems which include a microcomputer. Computer signals have very low voltage and current levels. Therefore, dirt or moisture entering a connector can disrupt the operation of the circuit. For this reason, special connectors are used with computer-controlled circuits to seal out dirt and moisture and prevent terminal corrosion. General Motors calls its connectors Weather Pack connectors (Fig. 6-30).

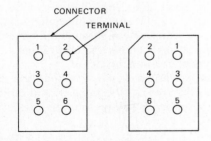

CONNECTOR
TERMINAL

1 2
3 4
5 6

2 1
4 3
6 5

Fig. 6-29. Two halves of a mating connector.

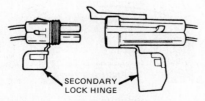

SECONDARY LOCK HINGE

Fig. 6-30. Weather Pack connector. *(Chevrolet Division of General Motors Corporation)*

CIRCUIT PROTECTION DEVICES

Automotive wiring and components are protected from possible electric overloads by the use of fuses, fusible links, and circuit breakers. An overload occurs when more current flows through a wire or component than it was designed to carry. Overloads can overheat wires, burn insulation, and cause fires.

Fuses

A *fuse* is a protective device that opens the circuit when excessive current flows. All fuses have a rated current. The rated current is the maximum current that can flow through a fuse before the fuse opens. A cartridge-type fuse is shown in Fig. 6-31. It is made of a thin metal strip supported by a glass tube. Any current that is less than rated current can flow through the fuse. However, when the rated current is exceeded, heat from the excess current flow melts the metal strip and opens the circuit. As a result, the circuit is broken before the wires can overheat. This prevents damage to the wiring. When a fuse has melted, or "blown," it must be replaced with a new fuse of the proper rating. Use of a fuse with a rating higher than that specified for the circuit can damage the wiring and may cause a fire.

Figure 6-32 shows a blade-type fuse. Blade-type fuses are smaller than cartridge-type fuses.

Most fuses are mounted in the *fuse block* (Fig. 6-33). In some cars, in-line fuse holders are used to place a cartridge fuse into a circuit (Fig. 6-34).

Fusible Links

A *fusible link* (or *fuse link*) is a short length of wire that is four sizes smaller in diameter than the wire it is designed to protect (Fig. 6-35). If there is an overload, the fusible link will melt and break the circuit before the rest of the circuit can be damaged.

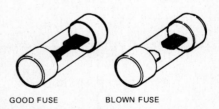

GOOD FUSE   BLOWN FUSE

Fig. 6-31. Cartridge-type fuse. *(Ford Motor Company)*

GOOD FUSE   **BLOWN FUSE**

Fig. 6-32. Blade-type fuse. *(Ford Motor Company)*

1. 20-A FUSE—HORNS AND CIGAR LIGHTER
2. 15-A FUSE—TAIL LAMP
3. 15-A FUSE—COURTESY LAMPS
4. 4-A FUSE—INSTRUMENT PANEL ILLUMINATION
   LAMPS
5. 15-A FUSE— EMERGENCY WARNING LAMPS,
   STOP LAMPS
6. 14-A FUSE—WARNING LAMPS, ENGINE, BRAKES,
   FASTEN BELTS, EMISSION CONTROL
   SOLENOID
7. BLANK
8. 15-A FUSE—WASHER/WIPER, ACCESSORY
   AIR CONDITIONER CLUTCH
9. 7.5-A FUSE—RADIO
10. 15-A FUSE— TURN SIGNAL AND BACKUP LAMPS
11. 15-A FUSE—HEATER BLOWER MOTOR
    35-A FUSE—AIR CONDITIONER BLOWER MOTOR
12. BLANK

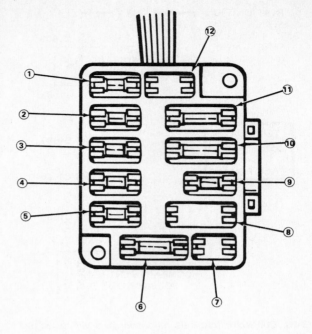

Fig. 6-33. Fuse block. *(Ford Motor Company)*

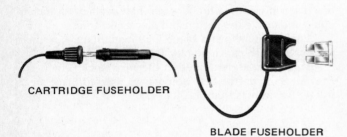

CARTRIDGE FUSEHOLDER

BLADE FUSEHOLDER

Fig. 6-34. In-line fuse holders. *(Cole Hersee Company)*

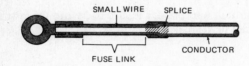

SMALL WIRE   SPLICE

CONDUCTOR

FUSE LINK

Fig. 6-35. Fusible link. *(Ford Motor Company)*

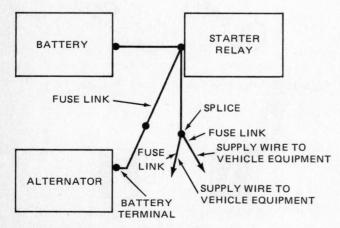

BATTERY

STARTER RELAY

FUSE LINK

SPLICE

FUSE LINK

SUPPLY WIRE TO VEHICLE EQUIPMENT

FUSE LINK

ALTERNATOR

SUPPLY WIRE TO VEHICLE EQUIPMENT

BATTERY TERMINAL

Fig. 6-36. Fusible-link locations. *(Ford Motor Company)*

Fusible links are used to protect the underhood wiring from overloads (Fig. 6-36). The main power leads from the battery to the ignition switch, and from the battery to the headlamp switch may have fusible links. The fusible link is covered with insulation. If there is an overload, the link will melt and the insulation will bubble and blister from the heat. The fusible link will then have to be cut from the circuit, and a new one installed.

Circuit Breakers

In some circuits (headlamps, for example), a fuse is undesirable. If a fuse blows, the headlamps will go out immediately. For this reason, *circuit breakers* are used in headlamp circuits. A circuit breaker opens the circuit when excess current flows.

A circuit breaker is shown in Fig. 6-37. It consists of two contacts, which are normally closed. One contact is fixed. The other is at the end of a bimetallic strip. With the contacts closed, current flows through the bimetallic strip. When too much current flows, the heat causes the bimetallic strip to bend, opening the circuit.

As soon as current flow stops, the strip cools and straightens. This "resets" the breaker, and current again flows. If the overload is still present, the cycle will repeat

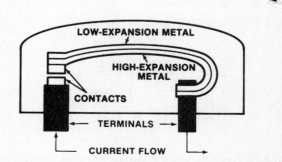

LOW-EXPANSION METAL

HIGH-EXPANSION METAL

CONTACTS

TERMINALS

CURRENT FLOW

Fig. 6-37. Circuit breaker. *(Ford Motor Company)*

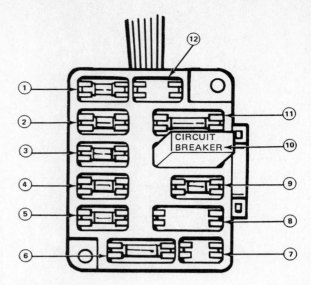

1. 20-A FUSE—ELECTRIC CHOKE
2. 15-A FUSE—TAIL LAMPS
3. 15-A FUSE—COURTESY LAMPS
4. 30-A FUSE—CIGAR LIGHTER AND HORNS
5. 20-A FUSE—STOPLAMPS AND EMERGENCY WARNING LAMPS
6. 14-A FUSE—WARNING LAMPS
7. 15-A FUSE—RADIO
8. 35-A FUSE—AIR CONDITIONER BLOWER MOTOR
9. 15-A FUSE—TURN SIGNAL FLASHER AND BACKUP LAMPS
10. 6-A CIRCUIT BREAKER—WINDSHIELD WIPER AND WASHER
11. 20-A FUSE—ACCESSORIES
12. 4-A FUSE—INSTRUMENT PANEL ILLUMINATION

Fig. 6-38. Circuit breaker mounted in a fuse block. *(Ford Motor Company)*

continuously until the fault is found and repaired. Because of this automatic resetting feature, this unit is called a *self-resetting circuit breaker*.

The circuit breaker for the headlamp circuit is built into the headlamp switch (Fig. 6-18). Circuit breakers are sometimes used in windshield wiper, windshield washer, power window, and power door lock circuits. These breakers are mounted in the fuse block (Fig. 6-38).

Some circuit breakers must be reset manually. When the breaker opens the circuit, a small button pops up. It then has to be depressed to reset the breaker. However, the self-resetting breaker is the most common type in automotive circuits.

Figure 6-40 shows a wiring diagram that includes all the lamps at the rear of the vehicle. In this diagram, the wire from the headlamp switch goes to a *splice*. A splice is a junction where two or more wires are joined together. This splice connects to a number of different circuits. From the splice, wires go to each lamp and then from each lamp to ground. Some lamps are grounded directly. Others are grounded through another splice to a location some distance away from the lamps. This is called a **remote ground**.

A complete wiring diagram covers the entire vehicle electrical system. This type of diagram can be large, and it is often provided as a series of foldout pages. Figure 6-41 shows part of a complete wiring diagram.

CIRCUIT DIAGRAMS

A *circuit diagram* is a drawing of an electric circuit. In the drawing, the components are represented by symbols, and the wires are represented by lines. Various types of drawings are used. These different types of drawings are described below.

Schematic Diagrams

A *schematic diagram* is a diagram that has electrical symbols for the components. It shows the wires and connections in their simplest form. Because of this, schematic diagrams make it easy to visualize the operation of the circuit. Figure 6-39 shows a schematic diagram of a lamp circuit. However, this type of diagram is not very useful for tracing or locating a specific part of the wiring.

Wiring Diagrams

A *wiring diagram* is a diagram that has symbols for the components and shows the wiring in its actual form. All connections are included to show the actual routing of the wires. Wiring diagrams are used to troubleshoot automotive electrical systems.

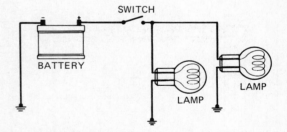

Fig. 6-39. Schematic diagram of a lamp circuit. *(Ford Motor Company)*

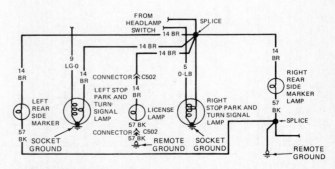

Fig. 6-40. Wiring diagram of rear lighting. *(Ford Motor Company)*

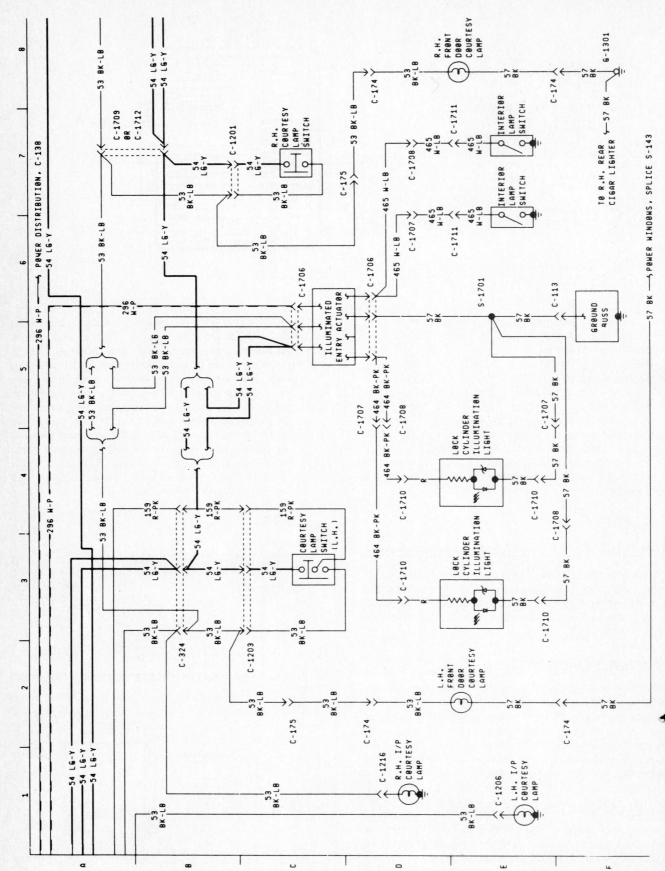

Fig. 6-41. Portion of a page of a complete wiring diagram. *(Ford Motor Company)*

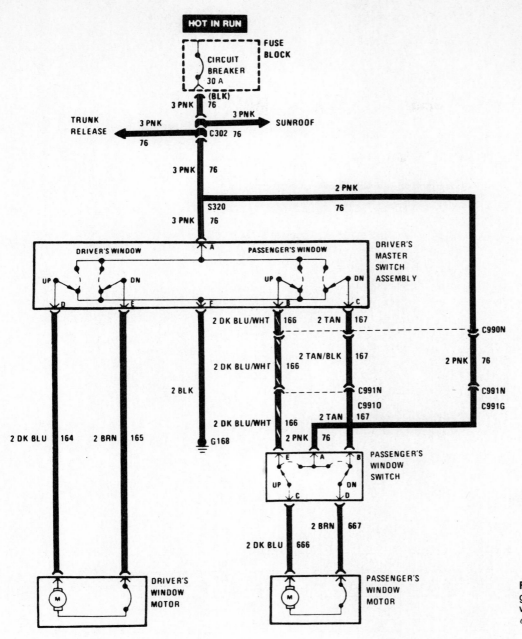

Fig. 6-42. Functional wiring diagram, showing power window wiring. *(Cadillac Motor Division of General Motors Corporation)*

Sometimes, functional wiring diagrams are provided in addition to the complete wiring diagram. This type of diagram covers one functional circuit only. Figure 6-42 shows a diagram of a power window wiring system. A functional diagram is easier to use because it is less crowded and only shows the wires in the circuit you are working on.

Block Diagrams

A *block diagram* is a diagram in which portions of an electric circuit are represented by blocks. A block diagram does not show individual components. Figure 6-43 shows a block diagram of a stereo radio system. In this diagram, the tuner is represented by one block, and the amplifiers are represented by additional blocks. A block diagram shows the relation of a portion of a system to the rest of the system. It is useful in helping you visualize how a system operates.

AUTOMOTIVE CURRENT FLOW

All modern automotive electrical systems are designed to have a negative ground. In this system, the battery negative terminal is connected to the engine block. Therefore, current flow to the vehicle electrical system begins at the positive terminal of the battery. A simplified current-flow diagram of a typical automobile is shown in Fig. 6-44. This diagram shows only the major parts of the electrical system.

Current flows from the positive terminal of the battery through the *bulkhead connector* to the headlamp switch, fuse block, and ignition switch. The bulkhead connector is the large multiwiring connector on the fire wall that connects the underhood wiring to the passenger-compartment wiring (Fig. 6-45). When the headlamp switch is closed, current flows from the headlamp switch, back through the

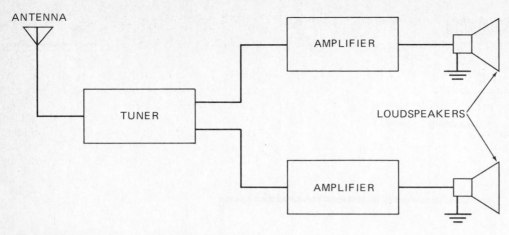

Fig. 6-43. Block diagram of a stereo radio receiver.

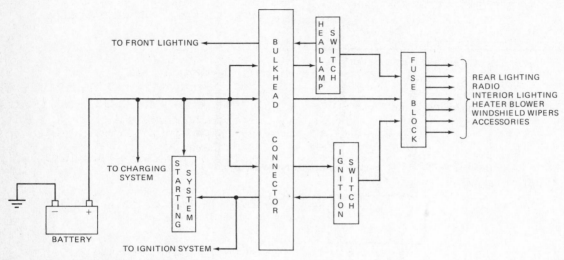

Fig. 6-44. Current flow in an automobile.

CAVITY	COLOR	DESCRIPTION
1	BK/R	HEATED REAR WINDOW (OVERLAY)
2	DBL	IGNITION RUN
3	R	BATTERY
4	BK/R	CONCEALED HEADLAMPS (OPEN)
5	DBL/Y	CONCEALED HEADLAMPS (CLOSE)
6	DGN	IN TANK FUEL PUMP (EFM)
7	BR	WINDSHIELD WASHER
8	BK/T	LOW WASHER FLUID LEVEL
9	P	HAZARD FLASHER
10	DBL	A/C CLUTCH
11	Y	STARTER
12	BK	BRAKE, WARNING LAMP
13	DBL	WINDSHIELD WIPER
14	DGN	WINDSHIELD WIPER
15	GY	OIL GAUGE
16	GY	OIL LAMP
17	BR	WINDSHIELD WIPER
18	R	WINDSHIELD WIPER
19	V	TEMPERATURE
20		
21	DGN/R	HORN
22	LBL	WINDSHIELD WIPER DWELL SWITCH
23	W	BACKUP LAMP
24	V/BK	BACKUP LAMP
25	W/R	SPEED CONTROL
26		
27	T	RIGHT TURN SIGNAL LAMP

CAVITY	COLOR	DESCRIPTION
28	LGN	LEFT TURN SIGNAL LAMP
29	DBL/R	SPEED CONTROL
30	BR/R	SPEED CONTROL
31	R	AMMETER (BATTERY)
32	BK	AMMETER (ALTERNATOR)
33		
34	BK/Y/Y	PARKING LAMPS
35		
36	R	IGNITION SWITCH
37	P	IGNITION SWITCH
38	BK	HEADLAMP SWITCH
39	R	HIGH BEAM
40	V	LOW BEAM

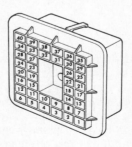

Fig. 6-45. Bulkhead connector. *(Chrysler Corporation)*

bulkhead connector, to the front lighting. In addition, current flows through the fuse block to the interior and rear lighting. When the ignition switch is closed, current from the ignition switch goes through the bulkhead connector to the ignition system and starting system. The ignition switch also supplies current to the fuse block to operate the radio, windshield wipers, and other accessory, safety, and warning devices. Wires from the battery also connect to the charging and starting systems.

All return currents flow through the frame and body of the vehicle, through the engine block, to the negative terminal of the battery.

USING SERVICE MANUAL WIRING DIAGRAMS

Vehicle service manuals usually provide information on how to use the wiring diagrams. Each manufacturer uses slightly different symbols and methods to designate wires, components, and connectors. Therefore, always study the explanatory information before you begin to work from the wiring diagram. This will save time and enable you to obtain the greatest amount of information from the diagram (Fig. 6-46).

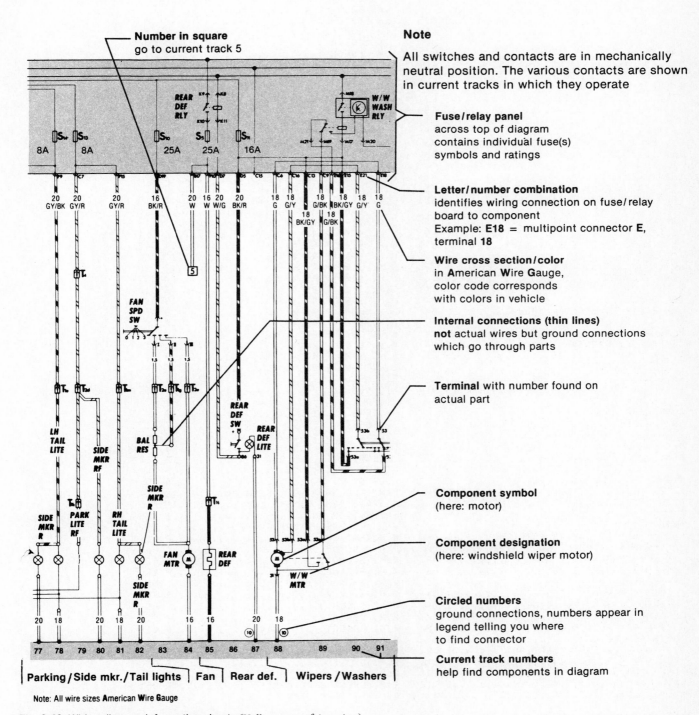

Fig. 6-46. Wiring diagram information sheet. *(Volkswagen of America)*

Some diagrams provide an index (Fig. 6-47) to help you locate a component. Suppose, for example, that you wanted to find the ignition coil. The index shows that the ignition coil is at location C14 on page 2. The diagram has a grid pattern superimposed on it with letter locations in the vertical direction and number locations in the horizontal direction (Fig. 6-48). The ignition coil will be near the intersection of the lines from the C and the 14.

Circuits are numbered to aid in tracing them and following the wires from one diagram page to another. Figure 6-49 shows a portion of a Ford diagram. Circuit 140 carries current to the backup lamp, circuit 14 is the parking lamp circuit, circuit 5 is the stoplamp and turn signal circuit, and circuit 57 is the ground circuit.

CØMPØNENT	PAGE	LØC
ACTUATØR		
ILLUMINATED ENTRY	11	C5
ALTERNATØR		
60 AMP	2	B2
100 AMP	2	A5
AMPLIFIER		
SPEED CØNTRØL	16	E6
BACKLITE		
HEATED	16	E2
HEATED	16	E3
BATTERY		
12 VØLT	1	A5
12 VØLT	2	B9
CAPACITØR		
RADIØ IGNITIØN INTERFERENCE	2	F5
RADIØ IGNITIØN INTERFERENCE	2	B13
CHØKE		
ELECTRIC	2	E9
RADIØ RECEIVER SUPPRESSIØN	3	B15
CØIL		
IGNITIØN	2	C14
CØNTRØL		
AM RADIØ RR SPEAKER VØLUME	12	D6
FLASHER		
EMERGENCY WARNING	5	C7
TURN SIGNAL	5	B7
GAUGE		
FUEL	3	B14
GØVERNØR		
W/S WIPER	14	C4
HEATER		
ENGINE BLØCK	12	D13
HØRN		
HIGH PITCH	16	B8
LØW PITCH	16	B7
LAMP		
A/C & HEATER CØNTRØLS ILLUM	17	C6
ALTERNATØR WARNING INDICATØR	3	B2
BRAKE WARNING INDICATØR	3	B9
CLØCK ILLUMINATIØN	17	C5
CLUSTER ILLUMINATIØN (4)	17	C2
CLUSTER ILLUMINATIØN (6)	17	B4
DØME	11	D9
ENGINE CØMPARTMENT	10	D7
GLØVE BØX SWITCH	10	C8
HI BEAM INDICATØR	5	E5
I/P ASH TRAY ILLUMINATIØN	17	C8
L.H. BACKUP	6	E11
L.H. BACKUP	7	E2
L.H. BACKUP	7	E10
L.H. BACKUP	8	E3
LAMP		
CØNTINUED...		
L.H. BACKUP	8	E10
L.H. BACKUP	9	E2
L.H. CØACH	7	C1
L.H. CØACH	7	C9
L.H. CØACH	8	C9
L.H. CØACH	9	C1
L.H. CØRNERING	5	E9
L.H. DRIVING	5	D13
L.H. FRØNT DØØR CØURTESY	11	D2
L.H. FRØNT SIDE MARKER	5	D11
L.H. HI BEAM HEAD	5	D15
L.H. LØ BEAM HEAD	5	D14
L.H. REAR RUNNING	7	D3
L.H. REAR RUNNING	8	D11
L.H. REAR SIDE MARKER	6	D10
L.H. REAR SIDE MARKER	7	D11
L.H. REAR SIDE MARKER	8	D2
L.H. REAR SIDE MARKER	9	D3
L.H. FRØNT PARK & T/S	5	D10
L.H. FRØNT RUNNING	5	D12
L.H. I/P CØURTESY	11	E1
L.H. STØP PARK & T/S	6	D11
L.H. STØP PARK & T/S	6	D12
L.H. STØP PARK & T/S	7	D1
L.H. STØP PARK & T/S	7	D2
L.H. STØP PARK & T/S	7	D9
L.H. STØP PARK & T/S	7	D10
L.H. STØP PARK & T/S	8	D3
L.H. STØP PARK & T/S	8	D4
L.H. STØP PARK & T/S	8	D9
L.H. STØP PARK & T/S	8	D10
L.H. STØP PARK & T/S	9	D1
L.H. STØP PARK & T/S	9	D2
L.H. TURN INDICATØR	5	E6
LICENSE	6	E12
LICENSE	6	E13
LICENSE	7	E5
LICENSE	7	E12
LICENSE	7	E13
LICENSE	8	E4
LICENSE	8	E5
LICENSE	8	E13
LICENSE	9	E4
LICENSE	9	E5
LØW FUEL WARNING INDICATØR	3	E14
LUGGAGE CØMPARTMENT	11	E15
MAP SWITCH AND	11	B16
ØIL PRES /TEMP WARNING IND	3	B12
R.H. BACKUP	6	E14
R.H. BACKUP	7	E6
R.H. BACKUP	7	E14
R.H. BACKUP	8	E6
R.H. BACKUP	8	E14
R.H. BACKUP	9	E6
R.H. CØACH	7	C8
R.H. CØACH	7	C16
R.H. CØACH	8	C16
R.H. CØACH	9	C8
R.H. CØRNERING	6	E8
R.H. DRIVING	6	D5
R.H. FRØNT DØØR CØURTESY	11	D8
R.H. FRØNT SIDE MARKER	6	D5
R.H. HI BEAM HEAD	6	D2

Fig. 6-47. Wiring diagram index. *(Ford Motor Company)*

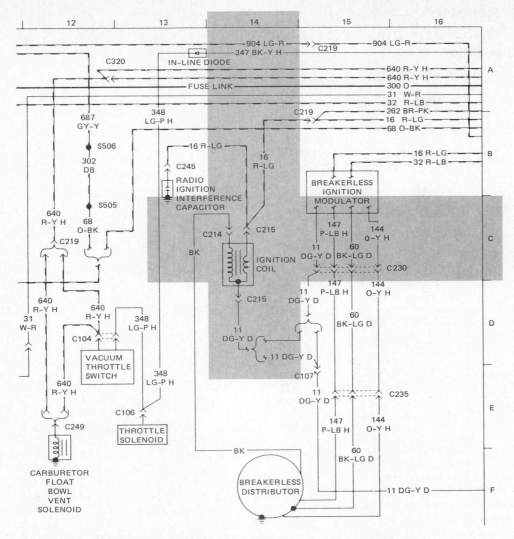

Fig. 6-48. Using the grid pattern to locate a component. *(Ford Motor Company)*

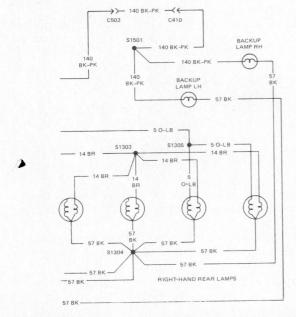

Fig. 6-49. Portion of a wiring diagram, showing the method of numbering circuits. *(Ford Motor Company)*

BK	black
BR	brown
GY	gray
O	orange
P	purple
PK	pink
R	red
T	tan
W	white
Y	yellow
DB	dark blue
LB	light blue
DG	dark green
LG	light green

Fig. 6-50. Color codes used in automotive electrical wiring diagrams. *(Ford Motor Company)*

The wire color is also shown in the diagram. Color abbreviations are listed in Fig. 6-50. Ford color-codes its wires by four methods: solid color, base color with a stripe, base color with hash marks, and base color with dots. Figure 6-51 shows the type of marking and the way the marking is indicated on the wiring diagram.

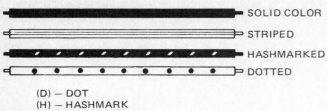

(D) — DOT
(H) — HASHMARK
STRIPE IS UNDERSTOOD

EXAMPLES:
BK — SOLID BLACK
BR-Y —BROWN WITH YELLOW STRIPE
BK-Y H — BLACK WITH YELLOW HASHMARKS
O-BK D — ORANGE WITH BLACK DOTS

Fig. 6-51. A method of wire color coding. (*Ford Motor Company*)

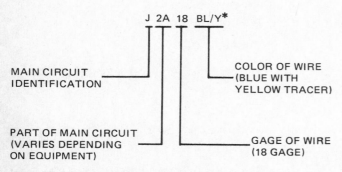

J 2A 18 BL/Y*

MAIN CIRCUIT
IDENTIFICATION

COLOR OF WIRE
(BLUE WITH
YELLOW TRACER)

PART OF MAIN CIRCUIT
(VARIES DEPENDING
ON EQUIPMENT)

GAGE OF WIRE
(18 GAGE)

Fig. 6-52. Circuit identification codes. (*Chrysler Corporation*)

Chrysler uses a different wire-numbering scheme (Fig. 6-52). The circuit identification, wire gauge, and color of the insulation are all included in the wire number. Abbreviations of the colors are shown in Fig. 6-53.

General Motors wire numbers include the wire size in square millimeters, the color of the insulation, and the circuit number. In Fig. 6-54, the wire size is 0.8 mm², the color of the insulation is black, and the wires are part of circuit 150. The splice is numbered S211, and the ground is numbered G117.

Connectors are also numbered for identification. Figure 6-55 illustrates a Ford connector (C407) as shown in a wiring diagram. The illustration shows the terminal pattern and gives the actual location of the connector. The circuit numbers and colors of the wires connecting to each terminal are also provided.

Terminals on the wiring diagram are labeled with the number of the connector in which they are located. In Fig. 6-49, terminals that are part of connectors C503 and C410 are included in the diagram.

BK	black	P	pink
BR	brown	R	red
DBL	dark blue	T	tan
DGN	dark green	V	violet
GY	gray	W	white
LBL	light blue	Y	yellow
LGN	light green	*	with tracer
O	orange		

Fig. 6-53. Color abbreviations. (*Chrysler Corporation*)

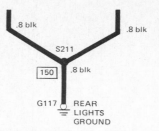

Fig. 6-54. Wire identification. (*Chevrolet Division of General Motors Corporation*)

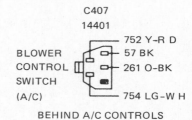

Fig. 6-55. Connector as shown on a wiring diagram. (*Ford Motor Company*)

VOCABULARY REVIEW

Ballast resistance   The resistance used in the ignition-system primary circuit to limit current flow through the ignition coil.

Bimetallic strip   A strip made of two different metals bonded together that bends when heated.

Block diagram   A diagram in which portions of an electric circuit are represented by blocks.

Bulkhead connector   The large multiwiring connector on the fire wall that connects the underhood wiring to the passenger-compartment wiring.

Cable   A wire which is made of a number of small solid wires. A stranded wire.

Circuit breaker   A device that opens the circuit when excess current flows. It is used to protect the circuit from overloads.

Circular mil   The square of the diameter of a wire.

Connector   A device that connects pairs of terminals together.

Electromagnetic energy   Energy which is radiated, such as radio waves or the energy radiated from a spark.

Fuse   A device that opens a circuit when excess current flows. It is used to protect the circuit from overloads.

Fusible link   A type of fuse made from a short length of wire that is smaller in diameter than the wire it is designed to protect.

Pole   In a switch, the "input" side, or the wiper arm.

Potentiometer   A variable resistor that has three terminals.

Printed circuit   An electric circuit made from conductive copper foil bonded to a thin plastic base.

Rheostat A variable resistor that has two terminals.

Schematic diagram A diagram that has electrical symbols for the components and shows the wires and connections in their simplest form.

Splice The junction formed when two or more wires are joined together.

Switch A device that opens or closes a circuit.

Terminal A small metal device attached to the end of a wire. It allows a wire to be connected to another wire or to a component.

Throw In a switch, the "output" side, or the fixed contact.

TVRS wires Television-radio-suppression wires. Resistance spark plug wires that are used to prevent radio interference.

Wire gauge A system of measurement of wire size.

Wiring diagram A diagram that has electrical symbols for the components and shows the wiring in its actual form.

Wiring harness A group of individual wires wrapped together in a bundle.

REVIEW QUESTIONS

Select the *one* correct, best, or most probable answer to each question.

1. What type of switch is shown below?

   a. single-pole four-position
   b. SPDT
   c. double-pole four-position
   d. four-pole two-position

2. In the connector shown below, which terminals mate together?

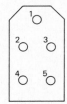 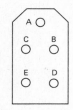

   a. terminal 1 with terminal A, and terminal 3 with terminal B
   b. terminal 2 with terminal B, and terminal 4 with terminal E
   c. terminal 3 with terminal B, and terminal 4 with terminal D
   d. terminal 4 with terminal D, and terminal 5 with terminal E

3. A General Motors wire designation is .5 BK 20. This means the wire is
   a. a 20-gauge wire
   b. a 0.5-gauge wire
   c. 0.5 mm² in cross-sectional area
   d. 20 mm² in cross-sectional area

4. A 12-gauge wire is equivalent to how many circular mils?
   a. 6530
   b. 80.8
   c. 16,510
   d. 1020

5. Which of the following statements is (are) true of aluminum wire?
   a. it is usually stranded
   b. it is not flexible
   c. it conducts as well as copper wire
   d. all of the above

6. A Chrysler wire number is D2 12 BR. This means the wire
   a. is 12 mm²
   b. is part of circuit 12
   c. is made of 12-gauge wire
   d. has 12 circular mils

7. An 18-gauge wire is equivalent to how many square millimeters?
   a. 0.22
   b. 0.8
   c. 2
   d. 8

8. Which of the following statements is (are) true about circuit protection?
   a. a fusible link is a smaller-gauge wire than the wire it is designed to protect
   b. most automotive circuit breakers need to be reset manually
   c. if a fuse keeps blowing, replace it with one of a larger value
   d. all of the above

9. Resistance spark plug wires are used to
   a. increase engine performance
   b. decrease spark plug voltage
   c. increase spark plug current
   d. eliminate radio interference

10. The illustration below shows a

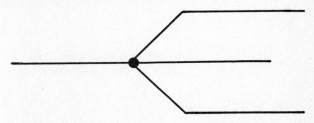

   a. bulkhead connector
   b. splice
   c. connector
   d. switch

11. Which of the following statements is true of wire sizes?
    a. a wire with a diameter of 3 mils has a cross-sectional area of 6 circular mils
    b. a circular mil is a true measurement of area
    c. a 12-gauge wire is larger than a 14-gauge wire
    d. a wire with a cross-sectional area of 3 mm^2 is equivalent to a 16-gauge wire

12. A Ford wire number is 297 BK-LG H. Which of the following statements is true?
    a. the wire is black with a light-green stripe
    b. the wire has a cross-sectional area of 297 circular mils
    c. the wire is light green with a black stripe
    d. the wire is part of circuit 297

13. What is meant by an electric overload?
    a. excess voltage
    b. excess current flow
    c. a large increase in resistance
    d. an open circuit

14. Solid wire is used in which of the following?
    a. headlight wiring
    b. alternator magnetic field
    c. power window wiring
    d. all of the above

15. What is the resistance per 1000 feet of 12-gauge wire?
    a. 0.1563 Ω
    b. 4.02 Ω
    c. 1.59 Ω
    d. 0.9988 Ω

CHAPTER 7

BATTERIES

OBJECTIVES

After you have studied this chapter, you should be able to:

1. Discuss the operation of a lead-acid storage battery.

2. Describe the construction of a lead-acid storage battery.

3. Explain the difference between chemical actions in a battery during charge and discharge.

4. Describe the various battery rating methods.

A *battery* is a device that converts chemical energy into electric energy. The battery supplies electric current to the starter motor and to the ignition system while the engine is being cranked. While the engine is running, if there is a greater demand for current than the alternator can supply, the battery will provide the additional current. In addition, the battery stabilizes the charging-system voltage by preventing any rapid changes in voltage that may tend to occur.

The first battery was built in 1800 by Alessandro Volta. Volta's battery consisted of a zinc plate and a silver plate separated by a cloth soaked with acid (Fig. 7-1). The output of the battery was weak, so Volta increased the number of plates. He called this stack of plates a pile, and it became known as a *voltaic pile* (Fig. 7-2).

Volta discovered that two dissimilar metals separated by an acid (called the *electrolyte*) would produce electricity. However, as the acid evaporated and the cloths dried out, the battery would no longer produce a voltage. He had to dismantle the stack of plates, replace the acid-soaked cloths, and reassemble the stack again.

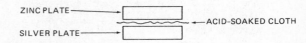

Fig. 7-1. Volta's first battery.

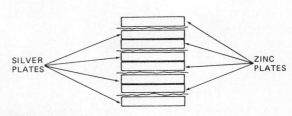

Fig. 7-2. Voltaic pile.

As batteries were developed, one of the improvements over Volta's battery was to use a wooden tray to hold the plates in a vertical position (Fig. 7-3). This design allowed the electrolyte to be maintained at the desired level. In general, this is the same type of battery used in the automobile today.

Some batteries have an electrolyte that is a liquid, and other batteries use an electrolyte that is a paste. The batteries which use a paste are called *dry-cell* batteries. Dry-cell batteries are used in flashlights, cameras, and portable radios. Batteries which use a liquid electrolyte are called *wet-cell* batteries. Automotive batteries are wet-cell batteries. They are also called *lead-acid storage* batteries. This is because the plates used in the automotive battery are lead and lead peroxide, and the electrolyte is a mixture of sulfuric acid and water.

CONSTRUCTION OF AN AUTOMOTIVE BATTERY

There are two types of automotive batteries: maintenance-free, or sealed, batteries (Fig. 7-4) and nonsealed batteries (Fig. 7-5). Sealed batteries have vent caps which cannot be removed. On nonsealed batteries, the vent caps can be removed. Both types of batteries are similar in internal construction, but they differ slightly in materials. The purpose of the vent caps, and the construction of these batteries, is described below.

Each plate of an automotive battery is made by applying a paste of a chemically active material (lead oxide) to

a *grid* (Fig. 7-6). Each grid is a rectangular framework which is made of lead mixed with a small percentage of antimony (on nonsealed batteries). The antimony stiffens and adds strength to the grids. Sealed batteries use calcium or strontium instead of antimony. The grids have a small projection at the top called a *grid lug*. A number of plates are joined together in a row by welding the grid lugs to a *plate strap* (Fig. 7-7). The joined plates in Fig. 7-7 are called a *group*. Each plate in a group is spaced some distance from the next plate. The plate strap has a projection, called a *terminal*, which allows an electrical connection to be made to the group.

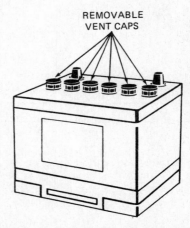

Fig. 7-5. Battery with removable vent caps. *(Battery Council International)*

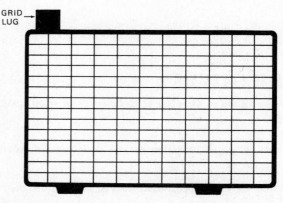

Fig. 7-6. Grid construction.

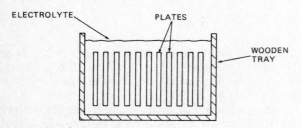

Fig. 7-3. Battery in a wooden tray.

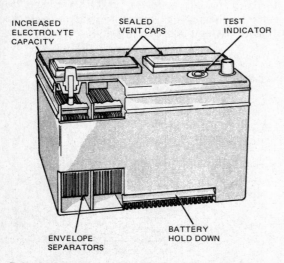

Fig. 7-4. Maintenance-free, or sealed, battery. *(Chrysler Corporation)*

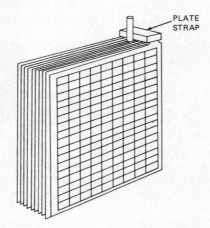

Fig. 7-7. Plate group.

Two groups are placed so that the plates mesh together, with the plates of one group and the plates of the other group alternating in position (Fig. 7-8). *Separators* are placed between the plates to keep them from touching. In the finished battery, if adjacent plates were to touch, the battery would become short-circuited. The separators are made of a porous material, usually plastic or rubber. The separator material must be porous to allow the electrolyte to flow freely to all portions of the plate surfaces. The separators used in sealed batteries are often in the form of envelopes which fit around each plate. These envelopes are sealed at the bottom and sides but are open at the top. The assembly of the two groups of plates and separators is called an *element* (Fig. 7-9).

When an element is placed in a container and the container is filled with electrolyte, the assembly is called a *cell*. The container must be acid-proof. It is usually made of hard rubber or plastic. The terminals on the plate straps of each group become the terminals of the cell. After the battery is completed, a "forming" process is performed. This makes one group of plates positive and the other group negative. Therefore, one terminal of the cell is positive, and the other terminal is negative. The forming process is described later.

The terminal voltage of a cell is approximately 2.1 V. This voltage depends on the kinds of materials used in the cell, not on the quantity or size of the materials. An automotive battery is made up of six cells (Fig. 7-10). The cells are connected in series, so that the terminal voltages of the cells add together (Fig. 7-11). Because the cell voltages are approximately 2.1 V, the terminal voltage of a fully charged battery is approximately 12.6 V. However, the automotive battery is referred to as a 12-V battery.

Cell *connectors* are used to connect the positive terminal of one cell to the negative terminal of the next cell. Because six cells are used, five connectors are needed. The negative terminal of the first cell and the positive terminal of the last cell connect to the main battery terminals. The battery shown in Fig. 7-10 has top-mounted terminals (or posts). The positive post is larger than the negative post to help prevent incorrect installation of the battery cables.

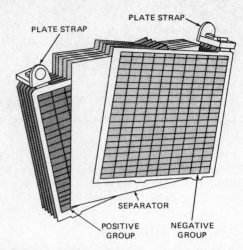

Fig. 7-8. Plate groups and separators, partially assembled. *(Ford Motor Company)*

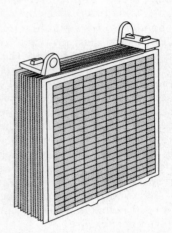

Fig. 7-9. Assembled element. *(Ford Motor Company)*

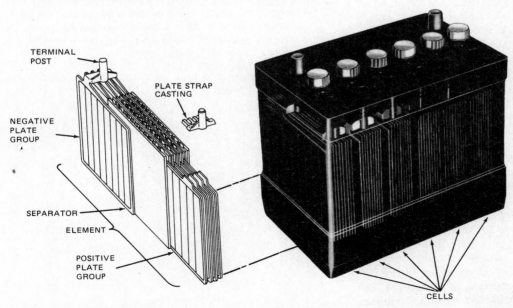

Fig. 7-10. Construction of a battery. *(Deere and Company Technical Services)*

81

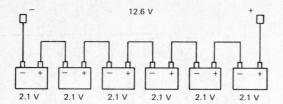

Fig. 7-11. Method of connecting cells in series to produce a 12-V battery.

Other automotive batteries have side terminals (Fig. 7-12). By moving the terminals away from the cell-vent area, corrosion on the terminals is reduced.

The Forming Process

Plates of two different metals are needed to make a battery. When the battery is assembled, all the plates are lead oxide. A forming process is then used to change some of the plates into lead peroxide and some of the plates into spongy lead. Spongy lead is a porous form of lead. In the forming process, a weak electrolyte is placed in the cells, and a voltage is applied to the battery. The voltage causes a chemical reaction to take place and the content of the plates to change. In each cell, the plates in the group that is closest to the positive voltage become lead peroxide plates. The plates in the group that is closest to the negative voltage become spongy lead plates. Therefore, in each cell, lead peroxide plates alternate with spongy lead plates.

The weak electrolyte is then removed, and normal-strength electrolyte (approximately 35 percent sulfuric acid and 65 percent water) is added. Because the plates in the cells are now two dissimilar metals, the cells produce a voltage. The lead peroxide plates are positive, and the spongy lead plates are negative.

DRY-CHARGED BATTERIES

A battery that is in storage or is not being used will slowly become discharged. The action which takes place is called *self-discharge*. This occurs when a battery slowly discharges while no electric current is being drawn from its terminals. Self-discharge is caused by chemical reactions within the battery and is encouraged by antimony in the grids, impurities in the materials, and high temperatures. Sealed batteries have a much longer storage life than nonsealed batteries. This is because antimony is not used in sealed batteries. Also, these batteries use materials of a higher purity.

To prevent self-discharge, nonsealed batteries are often manufactured as *dry-charged* batteries. Dry-charged batteries do not have electrolyte in them at the time of shipment. The electrolyte is added just before installation in the vehicle. During the manufacture of a dry-charged battery, after the forming process has taken place, the electrolyte is removed from the cells. The plates are then washed and dried, and the battery is sealed. In one method, the forming process is performed before the battery is assembled. Then the battery is assembled and sealed. Because dry-charged batteries are stored without electrolyte in them, they have a longer storage life.

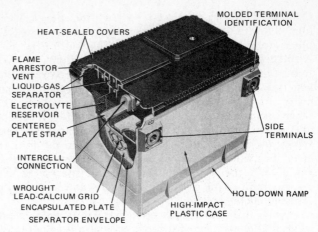

Fig. 7-12. Battery with side terminals. (*Delco-Remy Division of General Motors Corporation*)

BATTERY OPERATION— DISCHARGE AND CHARGE

The term *discharge* means to use a battery to provide electric energy. In Fig. 7-13, a lamp is used to illustrate that when a battery is being discharged, electrons (given the symbol e^-) leave the negative terminal. The battery produces electrons by means of chemical reactions. In these reactions, the following changes take place:

- Sulfuric acid breaks down into ions: positive hydrogen ions and negative sulfate ions.

- Lead molecules change into positive lead ions and, in doing so, release electrons. The electrons build up on the spongy lead plates, which become the negative plates of the battery.

- Lead peroxide also breaks down into positive lead ions and, in addition, into oxygen. The oxygen reacts with the positive hydrogen ions to form water. When water is formed, the positive charges of the hydrogen ions draw electrons away from the lead peroxide plates. Because electrons are removed from the lead peroxide plates, they become positively charged and become the positive plates of the battery.

- The positive lead ions react with the sulfate ions to form lead sulfate.

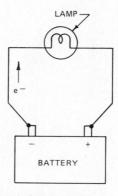

Fig. 7-13. Electron flow during discharge.

82

Figure 7-14 summarizes the effect of the chemical reactions on the quantities of the chemicals. As the battery discharges, the plate materials and the sulfuric acid are decreasing in quantity. The amount of water is increasing. If the discharge reactions were allowed to continue, the battery would become completely discharged. Much of the active material in the positive and negative plates would become lead sulfate. The electrolyte would become very weak in acid. The lead sulfate coats the plates and becomes a barrier to further chemical action. When the electrolyte is weak in acid, it is no longer effective as a supply of ions. Therefore, the battery no longer produces electric current.

To charge a battery, electrons must be made to flow into the negative terminal (Fig. 7-15). This reverses the chemical reactions. In the automobile, the alternator charges the battery by forcing a flow of electrons into the negative terminal of the battery. In the charging reactions, the following changes occur:

- Lead sulfate on the plates reacts with the water in the electrolyte to form sulfuric acid.

- Lead sulfate on the plates is also converted into spongy lead on the negative plates and lead peroxide on the positive plates.

- Water is used up.

Figure 7-16 summarizes the effect of the charging reactions on the quantities of the chemicals. As the battery charges, the plate materials are regained. At the same time, the electrolyte is increasing in acid content and decreasing in water content. A battery cannot last indefinitely, being alternately discharged and charged. Some traces of lead sulfate remain after the charging reactions are completed. These traces are slight, but they may spread across the plates to reduce the usable surface area of the plates. In time, the battery becomes ineffective.

As part of the chemical reactions during charging,

Materials	Effect of discharge
Spongy lead	Decreasing
Lead peroxide	Decreasing
Sulfuric acid	Decreasing
Water	Increasing
Lead sulfate	Increasing

Fig. 7-14. Effect of discharge on the chemicals in a battery.

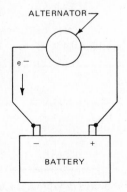

Fig. 7-15. Electron flow during charge.

Materials	Effect of charge
Spongy lead	Increasing
Lead peroxide	Increasing
Sulfuric acid	Increasing
Water	Decreasing
Lead sulfate	Decreasing

Fig. 7-16. Effect of charge on the chemicals in a battery.

hydrogen gas is liberated at the negative plates, and oxygen gas is liberated at the positive plates. This is known as *gassing*, and it causes water loss in the battery. The higher the rate of charge, the greater the amount of gassing. Vents are provided to prevent pressure buildup in the battery.

One of the factors that affects gassing is the material used in the grids. Nonsealed batteries use lead mixed with antimony to provide mechanical strength in the grids. However, antimony encourages gassing. Batteries that have a high rate of gassing use vent caps in each cell. The caps either push into openings or screw into threaded openings in the top of the battery case. The vent caps have a baffle arrangement to prevent small droplets of electrolyte from being released with the escaping gases. Any electrolyte that reaches the baffle is returned to the cell. The vent caps may be removed to add water. Some vent caps are flame-arrestor caps. These caps are designed to vent the gases and prevent a flame from entering the cell. If a flame were to enter the cell and ignite the hydrogen gas, the battery could explode.

Sealed batteries do not use antimony in the grids. Instead, either calcium or strontium is mixed with the lead. The calcium or strontium provides the needed strength in the grids and, in addition, greatly reduces gassing. Because the gassing rate is so low, these batteries can be "sealed." Water loss is so slight that openings are not provided for the addition of water. However, one or more small vent openings are provided to release any pressure formed by gassing (Fig. 7-17). The vents have baffles which do not allow droplets of electrolyte to pass through.

CHARGING A BATTERY

Charging a battery means causing electrons to flow into the negative terminal. On the car, this job is performed by the alternator. A battery may also be charged with a *battery*

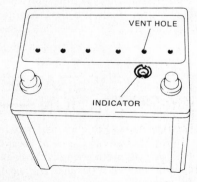

Fig. 7-17. Sealed battery having six vent holes. (*Chrysler Corporation*)

charger. A battery charger is usually powered by 117 V ac. The charger converts the ac into the proper dc voltage to charge the battery. To charge a battery, the charger produces a slightly higher voltage (approximately 13.5 to 15 V) than the battery. Therefore, electrons flow from the higher voltage (charger) to the lower voltage (battery).

A battery has a certain internal resistance. It includes the resistance of the plates and connectors and the resistance of the electrolyte. The resistance of the electrolyte is greater at lower temperatures. Therefore, at low temperature, a battery offers a greater resistance to charging current.

In a schematic diagram, a battery may be represented by an internal voltage in series with an internal resistance (Fig. 7-18). When a battery charger is connected to a battery, the charger voltage (which is applied to the battery terminals) is equal to the internal voltage plus the voltage drop across the internal resistance. This can be stated:

Charger (battery terminal) voltage
$$= \text{internal voltage} + \text{voltage drop}$$

The voltage drop (IR_b) is caused by the charging current I flowing through the internal resistance R_b. This is found by using Ohm's law.

The internal voltage of the battery varies with the state of charge. When the state of charge is low, the internal voltage is low. When the state of charge is high, the internal voltage is high. Therefore, when a battery is low in charge, it will accept more charging current because of the greater voltage difference between the charger and the internal voltage. When the battery is fully charged, it will accept only a small amount of charging current because of the smaller voltage difference. Therefore, a battery tends to self-regulate its charging current.

NOTE Internal voltage is sometimes called counter electromotive force (cemf) because it opposes the voltage supplied by the battery charger. However, it is really not a cemf because a cemf opposes the voltage that produces it (Chap. 4). The internal voltage is not produced by the battery charger, but by the chemical action within the battery.

Because of the internal resistance of the battery, heat is produced when a battery is charged ($P = I^2 R_b$). If the charging current is too high, the battery can be damaged by overheating. When a battery is being charged, the temperature of the electrolyte should never go above 125°F [51.7°C]. Battery charging procedures are covered in the shop manual.

EFFECT OF TEMPERATURE ON BATTERY OPERATION

High temperatures increase the chemical activity in a battery. In high-temperature areas (tropical areas), batteries are manufactured with an electrolyte that is weaker in acid. The battery life is lengthened because the weaker acid is less deteriorating to plates and separators.

At low temperatures, the effectiveness of a battery is

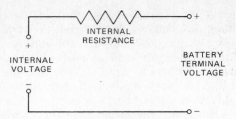

Fig. 7-18. Schematic representation of a battery.

greatly reduced. The internal resistance of a battery is higher at low temperatures. Because the viscosity of the electrolyte is higher, the chemical activity is retarded. Therefore, a battery is unable to supply full cranking power at low temperatures. At 0°F [−17.8°C], the cranking power available from a battery is only 40 percent of the power available at 80°F [26.7°C] (Fig. 7-19).

Freezing of the electrolyte may occur at very low temperatures. A discharged battery has a greater risk of freezing because its electrolyte contains more water. Freezing can crack the battery case or damage the plates.

BATTERY RATINGS

Cell voltage depends on the types of materials used in the battery, not on the quantity or size of materials. However, the size of the plates does affect the current capacity of the battery. The greater the surface area of the plates, the more chemicals enter into reactions and the more electric charge is produced. Because the flow of electrons is electric current, the greater the available charge, the more current that may be drawn from the battery.

Batteries are manufactured in different sizes, with different numbers of plates, and with different current capacities. Various rating methods are used so that one battery may be compared with another. An old method was the *ampere-hour rating.* This has been replaced by the *cold cranking rating* and the *reserve capacity rating.*

Ampere-Hour Rating

The ampere-hour rating (expressed in ampere-hours, or Ah) is the amount of current a fully charged battery can supply for 20 hours without having the terminal voltage fall below 10.5 V. This test is made at a temperature of 80°F [26.7°C]. If a battery can deliver 4 A under these conditions, it is an 80-Ah battery (4 A × 20 hours = 80 Ah).

Cold Cranking Rating

The cold cranking rating is also called the *cold cranking amps (CCA) rating.* This rating indicates the ability of a

Temperature	Cranking power (percent)
80°F [26.7°C]	100
32°F [0°C]	65
0°F [−17.8°C]	40

Fig. 7-19. Cranking power available from a fully charged battery, based on temperature.

battery to deliver a specified current at low temperature. The rating is determined by the amount of current a fully charged battery can supply for 30 seconds at 0°F [−17.8°C] without having the terminal voltage fall below 7.2 V. In addition, there is usually a second cold cranking rating for a temperature of −20°F [−28.9°C].

Large engines require that a starter motor deliver a large amount of cranking torque. Smaller engines require less torque. The greater the torque supplied by a starter motor, the more current it draws from the battery. As a rough guide, a starter motor requires approximately 1 A of current for each cubic inch (in.³) of engine displacement. Therefore, a 350-in.³ engine would require a battery with a cold cranking rating of approximately 350 amperes.

Reserve Capacity Rating

The reserve capacity rating is the time in minutes a vehicle can be driven after the charging system fails. This is roughly equivalent to the conditions after the alternator fails while the vehicle is being driven at night with the headlights on. The battery alone must supply current to the headlights and the ignition system. The assumed battery load is a constant discharge current of 25 A. The reserve capacity rating is the length of time a fully charged battery can supply 25 A before the terminal voltage falls below 10.5 V.

BATTERY INSTALLATIONS AND CABLE CONNECTIONS

Figure 7-20 shows a typical battery installation. The battery fits into a tray and is held in position by mounting hardware. The mounting hardware varies from vehicle to vehicle, but it usually consists of straps, brackets, or bolts which hold the battery in the tray. The mounting components are called *hold-downs*. The battery must be held securely to prevent loss of electrolyte and damage from shock or vibration. Most vehicles have the battery mounted in the engine compartment. A few vehicles have the battery located under a seat or in the trunk area.

Some vehicles use heat shields to protect the battery from engine heat (Fig. 7-21). The heat shield is positioned over the top of the battery and often functions as part of the hold-down (Fig. 7-22). Heat shields usually have an opening to allow a flow of cooling air to be directed past the battery.

Connections to the battery are made with large wires called *battery cables*. On batteries with the terminals (or posts) on the top of the battery, the cables connect to the terminals with battery cable clamps (Fig. 7-23). On side-

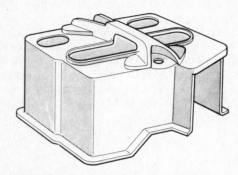

Fig. 7-21. Battery heat shield. *(Chrysler Corporation)*

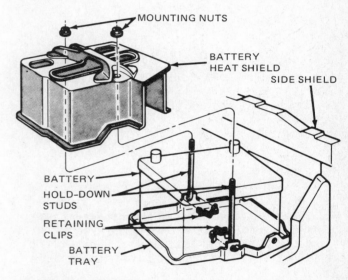

Fig. 7-22. Battery and heat-shield mounting. *(Chrysler Corporation)*

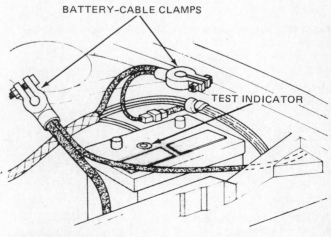

Fig. 7-23. Battery cable clamps. *(Chrysler Corporation)*

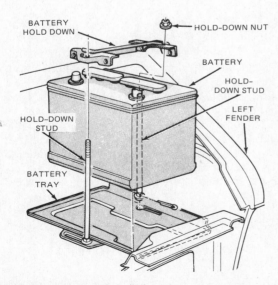

Fig. 7-20. Typical battery installation. *(Chrysler Corporation)*

terminal batteries, the cables are bolted to the battery terminals (Fig. 7-24). On most cars, the cable which connects to the negative terminal of the battery is connected to the engine or the frame of the vehicle. Therefore, the return current back to the battery flows through the frame of the vehicle. This is called a *negative ground* system. Older American cars and some imported cars have positive ground systems.

Many vehicles with diesel engines use two batteries. This is because the cranking torque that a starter motor must supply to a diesel engine is higher than that of an equivalent size spark-ignition engine. Because the cranking torque is high, the current drawn by the starter motor is high. A single battery may not be able to provide the cranking current required under all vehicle operating conditions. For this reason, two batteries are connected in parallel (Fig. 7-25). The voltage remains the same, but the current capacity is doubled. An installation which uses two batteries is shown in Fig. 7-26.

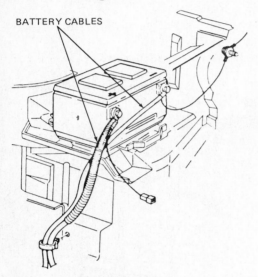

Fig. 7-24. Battery cables connected to a side-terminal battery. *(Oldsmobile Division of General Motors Corporation)*

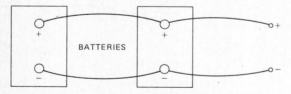

Fig. 7-25. Two 12-V batteries connected in parallel.

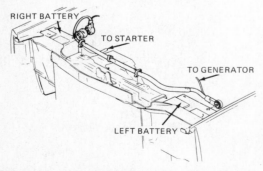

Fig. 7-26. Diesel-engine application which uses two batteries connected in parallel. *(Oldsmobile Division of General Motors Corporation)*

On some heavy-duty engines, switching circuits allow the two batteries to be connected in series to provide 24 V for cranking. After the engine has started, the batteries are switched to a parallel connection for 12-V operation.

VOCABULARY REVIEW

Ampere-hour rating A battery rating that indicates the amount of current a fully charged battery can supply for 20 hours without having the terminal voltage fall below 10.5 V.

Battery A device which converts chemical energy into electric energy.

Cell A battery element in an electrolyte-filled container.

Charge To apply voltage to a battery to increase its electric energy.

Cold cranking rating A battery rating that indicates the ability of a battery to deliver a specified current at low temperature.

Discharge To use a battery to provide electric energy.

Dry-cell battery A battery which uses a nonliquid electrolyte.

Dry-charged battery A new battery from which the electrolyte has been removed. The electrolyte must be added at the time of installation.

Electrolyte The mixture of sulfuric acid and water used in an automotive battery.

Element The assembly of two groups of plates and separators. When an element is placed in a container of electrolyte, it becomes a cell.

Gassing The liberation of hydrogen and oxygen gases from a battery while it is being charged.

Grid A rectangular framework which holds the active material in a battery plate.

Group A number of plates of a battery which are joined together by a plate strap.

Nonsealed battery A battery with removable vent caps.

Plate strap A strap that joins the plates of a group together.

Reserve capacity rating A battery rating that indicates the time in minutes a vehicle can be driven after the charging system fails.

Sealed battery A battery which does not have removable vent caps. Also called a *maintenance-free battery*.

Separator A porous rubber or plastic material that is placed between adjacent plates of a battery to keep them from touching.

Wet-cell battery A battery which uses a liquid electrolyte.

REVIEW QUESTIONS

Select the *one* correct, best, or most probable answer to each question.

1. A number of battery plates joined together by a plate strap is called a
   a. group
   b. element
   c. cell
   d. dry cell

2. Separators are used in a battery to
   a. keep positive and negative plates from touching
   b. separate the cells of a battery
   c. separate the terminals
   d. prevent the flow of electrolyte between the plates of a battery

3. Which of the following statements is true of an automotive battery?
   a. electrons gather on the surface of the lead peroxide plates
   b. a cell usually produces 1.9 V
   c. zinc and silver are the plate materials used in an automotive battery
   d. the electrolyte is a mixture of sulfuric acid and water

4. During discharge, which of the following statements is true?
   a. spongy lead is increasing in quantity
   b. water is increasing in quantity
   c. sulfuric acid is increasing in quantity
   d. lead sulfate is decreasing in quantity

5. During charge, which of the following statements is true?
   a. lead peroxide is increasing in quantity
   b. sulfuric acid is decreasing in quantity
   c. lead sulfate is increasing in quantity
   d. water is increasing in quantity

6. A battery becomes hot when it is charged because
   a. gassing produces heat
   b. the charging current flows through the internal resistance
   c. a stronger concentration of acid has a higher temperature
   d. none of the above

7. When a battery is being charged, the terminal voltage is *not* the same as the internal voltage because
   a. the internal voltage is low when a battery needs charging
   b. the electrolyte is weak in acid
   c. a voltage drop is created across the internal resistance of the battery
   d. the battery is hot

8. A sealed battery does not require the addition of water because
   a. the grids are an antimony-lead mixture
   b. there are fewer grids
   c. there is no vent
   d. the grid composition minimizes gassing

9. What is the percentage of available cranking power from a battery at 0°F [−17.8°C] compared with the same battery at 80°F [26.7°C]?
   a. 80 percent
   b. 60 percent
   c. 40 percent
   d. 20 percent

10. Which battery rating method refers to the ability of a battery to supply current under low-temperature conditions?
    a. cold cranking
    b. ampere-hour
    c. reserve capacity
    d. none of the above

11. Which battery rating method refers to the ability to maintain vehicle operation with a charging-system failure?
    a. ampere-hour
    b. cold cranking
    c. reserve capacity
    d. none of the above

12. When a battery is manufactured, the forming process
    a. shapes the plates
    b. changes the lead oxide into two dissimilar metals
    c. increases the electrolyte level in the cells
    d. forms the battery terminals into the proper shape

13. If an automotive battery has a cold cranking rating of 300, it can deliver
    a. 300 A for 30 seconds at 0°F [−17.8°C]
    b. 300 A for 300 minutes at 0°F [−17.8°C]
    c. 25 A for 300 minutes at −20°F [−28.9°C]
    d. 300 A for 30 minutes at −20°F [−28.9°C]

14. Which of the following statements is true with respect to the charge and discharge of an automobile battery?
    a. during charge, electrons flow into the negative terminal
    b. a battery charger must have a higher voltage than the battery
    c. as the state of charge of a battery increases, the internal voltage also increases
    d. all of the above

15. All of the following statements are true *except*
    a. most cars have negative ground electrical systems
    b. most diesel-engine vehicles which have two batteries have the batteries connected in parallel
    c. the electrolyte level in a nonsealed battery should be checked periodically
    d. when batteries are connected in parallel, the current capacity remains the same but the voltage is doubled

CHAPTER

THE STARTING SYSTEM

OBJECTIVES

After you have studied this chapter, you should be able to:

1. Describe the operation of the starting system.

2. Describe the operation of starter relays and solenoids.

3. Explain the function of the neutral safety switch.

4. Describe some common starting systems.

5. Name the components used in the starting system.

The *starting system* is the part of the vehicle electrical system that cranks the engine when it is being started. The starting system includes the battery, the ignition switch, the starter solenoid or relay, the neutral safety switch, and the starter motor (Fig. 8-1). An engine cannot start if the pistons are not moving. The moving pistons cause a vacuum in the intake manifold, which draws air and fuel into the cylinders. In a diesel engine, only air is drawn into the cylinders. Fuel is injected into the cylinders after the air is compressed. The air and fuel are ignited in the cylinders,

and the engine starts. Early cars were cranked by hand, but as engines became larger, the starting system replaced the hand crank.

The starting system can be separated into two circuits: the *control circuit* and the *motor circuit* (Fig. 8-2). The motor circuit is the direct circuit path from the battery positive terminal to the starter motor. The motor circuit carries the starter motor current draw, which can be approximately 150 to 200 A. The wiring in this circuit consists of large, heavy-gauge cables. This current is too large to be carried by the small ignition switch contacts. Solenoids, and some relays, have large contacts capable of carrying a large amount of current. The control circuit controls the operation of the solenoid (or relay), which in turn switches current to the starter motor. The control circuit includes the ignition switch, the neutral safety switch, and their associated wiring.

THE BATTERY

The battery supplies the energy required by the starting system to crank the engine. Some starting systems used with diesel engines have two batteries. The batteries are connected in parallel to provide the higher current required to crank a diesel engine. Batteries are covered in Chap. 7.

89

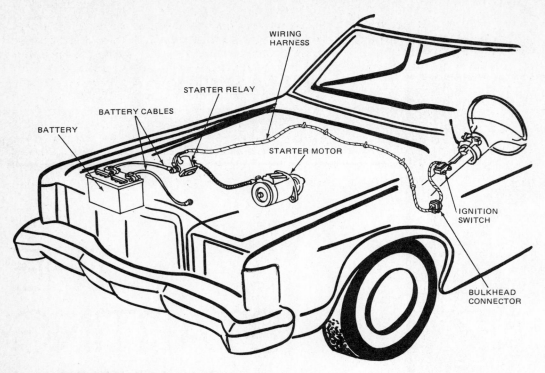

Fig. 8-1. Typical automotive starting system. *(Courtesy of Sun Electric Corporation)*

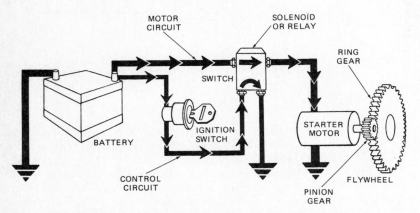

Fig. 8-2. The starting system, showing the motor circuit and the control circuit. *(Chevrolet Division of General Motors Corporation)*

THE STARTER MOTOR

The *starter motor* is a small, but powerful, electric motor which operates when the ignition switch is turned to the START position. A starter motor has an electrical winding assembly which rotates inside a magnetic field. Starter motor operation is covered in Chap. 9. The magnetic field is produced by field coils which are located around the inside of the motor housing. The rotating winding assembly is called the armature. The armature is mounted on a shaft which is supported by bearings. The starter motor has a small gear, called a *pinion gear,* mounted on the end of the armature shaft (Fig. 8-2). The pinion gear engages a large *ring gear* mounted on the outside edge of the flywheel.

A typical ratio of ring-gear teeth to pinion-gear teeth is 20 to 1. This gear ratio means that the starter motor rotates 20 times faster than the flywheel (and engine crankshaft). This ratio also means that there is a mechanical advantage of 20. It is 20 times easier for the motor to turn the crankshaft by driving the flywheel gear than for the motor to turn the crankshaft directly. This feature permits a relatively small starter motor to crank the engine.

Because the starter motor turns 20 times faster than the engine, the pinion and ring gears cannot be meshed together permanently. At high engine speeds, the starter motor shaft would be driven so fast that the armature windings would be thrown outward and the motor would be damaged. Therefore, provision must be made to engage the pinion gear into the ring gear when the engine is being cranked and to disengage the gears after the engine has started. This function is performed by the starter *drive mechanism.* The drive mechanism includes the starter solenoid, the shift lever (or shift fork), the overrunning-clutch assembly, and the pinion gear (Fig. 8-3). An *overrunning clutch* is a device that transmits torque (a twisting force) in one direction only. When turned in the other direction, the overrunning clutch slips on its shaft. Starter motor drive mechanisms are covered in Chap. 9.

SOLENOID

A *solenoid* is a device having a moveable plunger surrounded by a coil of wire (Fig. 8-3). Solenoids are used to apply a force to move an object. The coil of wire is called the *solenoid winding*. When voltage is applied to the solenoid-winding terminal, current flows through the coil and energizes the solenoid. When the solenoid is energized, the coil becomes an electromagnet and pulls the plunger into the coil. The motion of the plunger moves the shift lever, which engages the pinion gear into the ring gear (Fig. 8-4).

The solenoid performs another function. If the pinion gear were spinning when it engaged the ring gear, tooth damage would occur. Therefore, the starter motor is turned on only after the gears are fully engaged. A set of switch contacts is located inside the solenoid. When the plunger

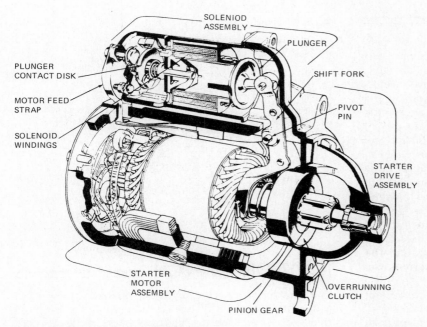

Fig. 8-3. Starter motor and solenoid components (solenoid not energized). *(Ford Motor Company)*

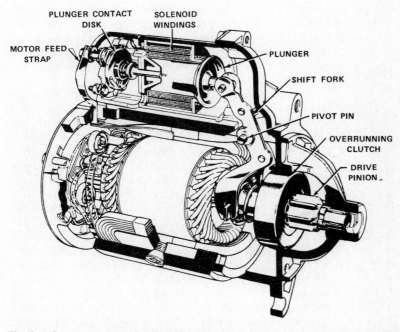

Fig. 8-4. Starter motor and solenoid components (solenoid energized). *(Ford Motor Company)*

moves to engage the gears, the switch contacts close to supply current to operate the starter motor.

Once the engine has started, the overrunning clutch slips. This permits the pinion gear to be driven faster than the motor shaft. Therefore, the engine cannot turn the motor shaft at an excessive speed. When the driver releases the ignition switch to the RUN position, the starter motor turns off and the solenoid is deenergized. A spring returns the solenoid plunger to its deenergized position. The shift lever pulls back the overrunning clutch and pinion gear to disengage the pinion gear from the ring gear.

RELAY

A *relay* is a magnetically operated switch. A relay differs in construction from a solenoid in that the moving part (called an armature) is hinged (Fig. 8-5). When voltage is applied to the relay winding, the winding becomes an electromagnet and pulls the armature. The main function of a relay is to provide a switching operation in an electric circuit.

As the relay armature moves, electric contacts are either opened or closed to control the flow of current in an external circuit. Relays are used in starting circuits because of the large starter motor current draw. The ignition switch contacts are not large enough to carry the starter motor current. They would overheat and burn. To design an ignition switch to carry this current would be impractical; the switch would be too large. Instead, the relay contacts are made large enough to carry the starter motor current. The small ignition switch contacts control the low current necessary to operate the starter relay.

Chrysler uses a relay in this manner to control current flow to the starter motor (Fig. 8-6). The Ford "starter relay" is actually a solenoid. It has a moveable plunger inside an electromagnet (Fig. 8-7). Because its only purpose is to control starter motor current, and not to perform a mechanical operation, it is called a relay.

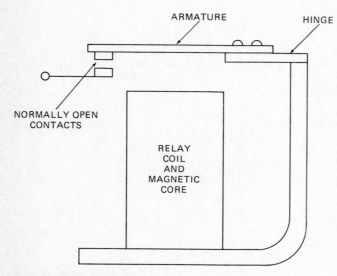

Fig. 8-5. Construction of a relay.

92

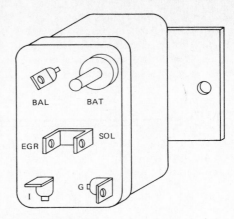

Fig. 8-6. Chrysler starter relay.

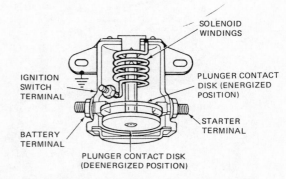

Fig. 8-7. Ford starter relay. *(Ford Motor Company)*

IGNITION SWITCH

The *ignition switch* is the key switch operated by the driver to start the engine. A typical ignition switch has five positions: ACCESSORY, LOCK, OFF, RUN, and START. In the RUN position, current is supplied to the ignition system and is available to operate the other circuits in the vehicle (Fig. 8-8). In the START position, current is supplied to the ignition system and to the starting system to operate the starter motor. The START position of the ignition switch is a momentary contact. In the START position, battery voltage is switched to the starter relay or solenoid to operate the starter motor. When the engine starts, the driver releases the key and the switch automatically returns to the RUN position.

Most vehicles with the ignition switch mounted in the steering column have a steering-column lock. On some vehicles, a *rotary switch* is located directly behind the key cylinder. A rotary switch is a switch that has contacts which are opened or closed by a rotary motion. Other vehicles have a *slide switch* mounted partway down (or at the base of) the steering column (Fig. 8-9). A slide switch is a switch that has contacts which are opened or closed by a straight-line motion. An actuator rod connects the slide switch to the key cylinder.

Another rod, or lock pin, is actuated by the motion of the key cylinder. This lock pin is spring-loaded and fits between the teeth of a lock plate (Fig. 8-10) when the key cylinder is in the LOCK position. When the rod is positioned between the teeth, the steering wheel cannot be turned. Turning the ignition switch from the LOCK position removes the rod from the lock plate. This allows the steering wheel to be turned.

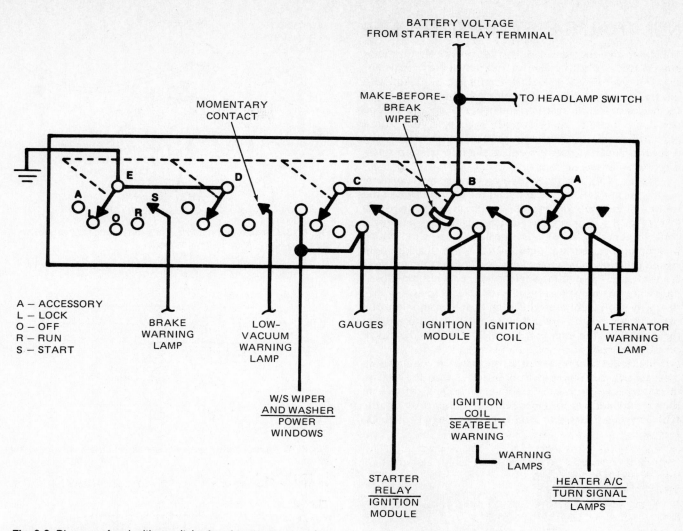

BATTERY VOLTAGE
FROM STARTER RELAY TERMINAL

MAKE–BEFORE–
BREAK
WIPER

MOMENTARY
CONTACT

TO HEADLAMP SWITCH

A – ACCESSORY
L – LOCK
O – OFF
R – RUN
S – START

BRAKE
WARNING
LAMP

LOW-
VACUUM
WARNING
LAMP

GAUGES

IGNITION
MODULE

IGNITION
COIL

ALTERNATOR
WARNING
LAMP

W/S WIPER
AND WASHER
POWER
WINDOWS

IGNITION
COIL
SEATBELT
WARNING

WARNING
LAMPS

STARTER
RELAY
IGNITION
MODULE

HEATER A/C
TURN SIGNAL
LAMPS

Fig. 8-8. Diagram of an ignition switch. *(Ford Motor Company)*

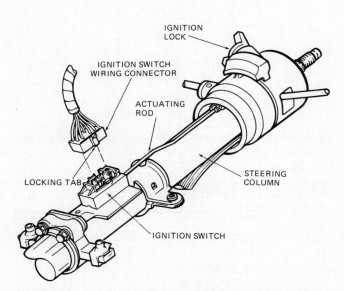

IGNITION
LOCK

IGNITION SWITCH
WIRING CONNECTOR

ACTUATING
ROD

STEERING
COLUMN

LOCKING TAB

IGNITION SWITCH

Fig. 8-9. Slide-type ignition switch. *(Ford Motor Company)*

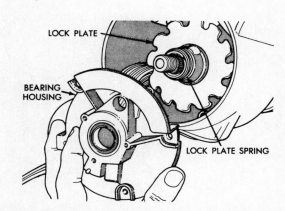

LOCK PLATE

BEARING
HOUSING

LOCK PLATE SPRING

Fig. 8-10. Steering-wheel lock plate. *(Chrysler Corporation)*

NEUTRAL SAFETY SWITCH

The *neutral safety switch* is a switch in the starter motor control circuit that prevents cranking when the transmission is in gear (Fig. 8-11). If the engine were cranked with the transmission in gear, the vehicle could jump forward (or backward) and cause serious injury. Many vehicles do not use a neutral safety switch. Instead, a mechanical blocking device prevents the ignition switch from being turned to the START position unless the transmission selector lever is in PARK or NEUTRAL.

Neutral safety switches used on vehicles with an automatic transmission are located near the shift linkage of the transmission. The switch can be mounted on the transmission (Fig. 8-12) or on the linkage inside the passenger compartment (Fig. 8-13). Some designs use a switch which incorporates a backup-light switch. The backup-light switch functions when the transmission gear selector lever is in REVERSE. The neutral safety switch contacts are closed only when the transmission selector lever is in PARK or NEUTRAL. On some vehicles with a manual transmission, the neutral safety switch is attached to the clutch linkage. On these vehicles, the engine will not crank unless the clutch pedal is depressed.

Figure 8-14 shows a neutral safety switch connected in a starting circuit. The switch is in series with the wire to the starter relay. In Fig. 8-15, the neutral safety switch is in the ground side of the starter relay. In either position, the switch will prevent operation of the relay when the vehicle is in gear.

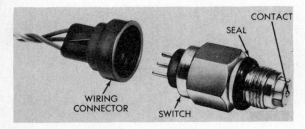

Fig. 8-11. Neutral safety switch and backup-lamp switch. *(Chrysler Corporation)*

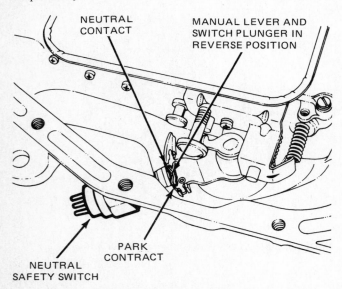

Fig. 8-12. Transmission-mounted neutral safety switch. *(American Motors Corporation)*

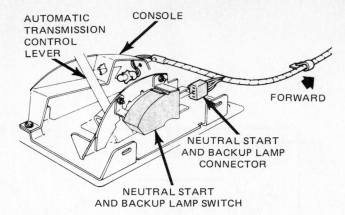

Fig. 8-13. Console-mounted neutral safety switch. *(Pontiac Division of General Motors Corporation)*

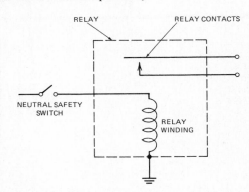

Fig. 8-14. Neutral safety switch in series with the feed wire to the relay.

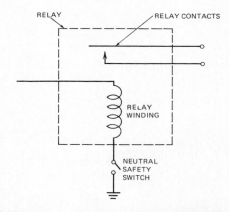

Fig. 8-15. Neutral safety switch in the ground circuit of the relay.

TYPICAL STARTING SYSTEMS

This section describes four common starting systems.

American Motors

A starting system used by American Motors is shown in Fig. 8-16. The system includes the battery, the ignition switch, the neutral safety switch, the starter solenoid, and the starter motor. In addition, two fusible links are used as circuit protection devices. The neutral safety switch is only used on vehicles equipped with an automatic transmission.

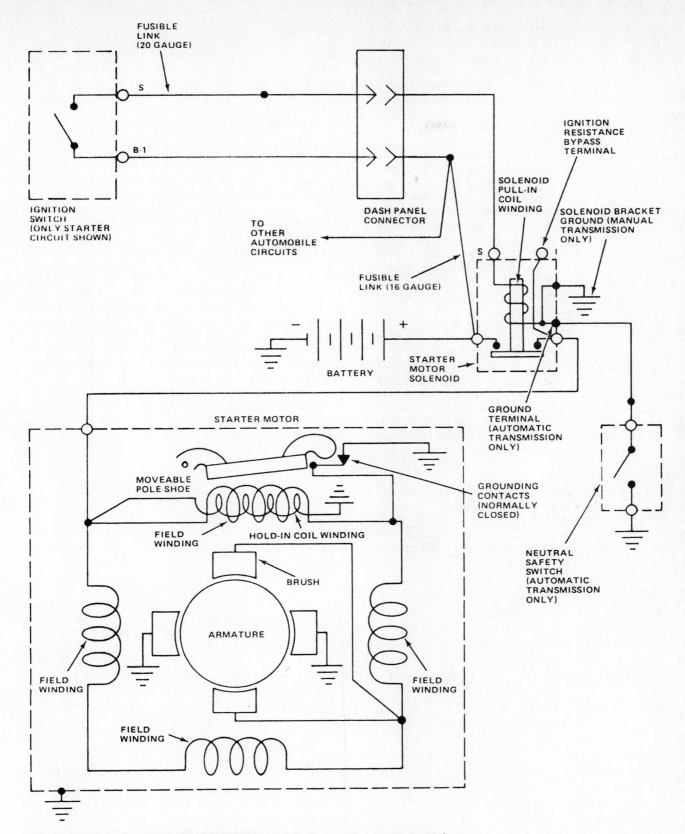

Fig. 8-16. American Motors starting-system diagram. *(American Motors Corporation)*

There are two different starter solenoids used with this system. The solenoid used on manual-transmission vehicles has an internally grounded winding. The ground circuit is completed through the mounting bracket (Fig. 8-17). The solenoid used on automatic-transmission vehicles has an additional terminal. This terminal is the solenoid-winding ground lead (Fig. 8-18). The ground terminal is connected to the neutral safety switch and is grounded only when the safety switch contacts are closed.

When the ignition switch is turned to the START position, battery voltage is applied to the solenoid-winding terminal. The solenoid will be energized on manual-transmission vehicles. On automatic-transmission vehicles, the solenoid will be energized only if the transmission selector lever is in PARK or NEUTRAL. When the starter solenoid is energized, a plunger moves a contact disk to connect the battery and starter terminals of the relay together. This completes the circuit from the battery to the starter motor. In addition, there is another contact on the starter solenoid. This contact supplies voltage directly to the ignition coil. This connection is called the *bypass circuit.* This circuit bypasses the ignition resistor to apply full battery voltage to the ignition coil while the engine is cranking. This provides a stronger spark for easier starting.

When battery voltage is connected to the starter motor, another solenoid (located inside the starter motor) is energized. This solenoid is a moveable pole shoe surrounded by a coil of wire. A pole shoe is the iron core around which a field coil is wound. Moveable-pole-shoe starter motors are described in Chap. 9. When this solenoid is energized, it performs two functions. It engages the pinion gear into the ring gear, and it switches current to the field and armature windings to operate the motor.

When the engine starts, the driver releases the key and the ignition switch returns to the RUN position. The starter solenoid deenergizes and stops the current flow to the starter motor. The moveable-pole-shoe solenoid also deenergizes, and the pinion gear disengages from the ring gear.

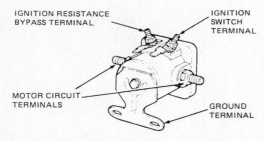

Fig. 8-17. Internally grounded starter solenoid. *(American Motors Corporation)*

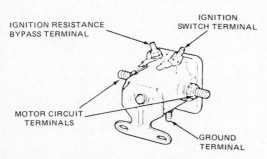

Fig. 8-18. Externally grounded starter solenoid. *(American Motors Corporation)*

96

Chrysler

The Chrysler starting system is shown in Fig. 8-19. The system includes the battery, the ignition switch, the neutral safety switch, the starter relay (Fig. 18-20), and the starter motor. There are two terminals on the starter relay, which connect to the ends of the relay winding (Fig. 8-19). One terminal receives battery voltage from the ignition switch when the switch is in the START position. The other terminal is grounded through the neutral safety switch. Therefore, both switches must be closed for the relay to be energized. The ignition switch must be turned to the START position, and the transmission selector lever must be in PARK or NEUTRAL. On some vehicles with a manual transmission, the clutch pedal must be depressed to close the neutral safety switch contacts.

When the starter relay is energized, contacts in the relay close and apply battery voltage to the starter solenoid winding. The starter solenoid is built into the starter motor. When battery voltage is applied to the solenoid, the solenoid plunger moves a shift lever, which in turn engages the pinion gear into the ring gear. In addition, when the gears are engaged, the plunger closes a set of switch contacts. The contacts switch current from the starter motor battery terminal to the field and armature windings to operate the motor.

After the engine starts, the driver releases the key and the ignition switch returns to the RUN position. The starter relay deenergizes and stops the current flow to the starter solenoid. The starter solenoid deenergizes, the motor stops, and the pinion gear disengages from the ring gear.

Ford

The Ford starting system is shown in Fig. 8-21. The system includes the battery, the ignition switch, the starter relay (actually a solenoid), and the starter motor. Vehicles with a floor-mounted transmission selector lever use a neutral safety switch. The ignition switch and the neutral safety switch are in series with the starter relay coil. Both switch contacts must be closed before the starting system can operate. The ignition switch must be turned to the START position, and the transmission selector lever must be in PARK or NEUTRAL. Vehicles with a steering-column selector lever use a mechanical blocking device on the key cylinder. The blocking device prevents the ignition switch from being turned to START unless the selector lever is in PARK or NEUTRAL.

Figure 8-22 shows the Ford starter relay with the contacts open (deenergized). When battery voltage is applied to the starter relay, a plunger and contact disk move to complete the circuit from the battery to the starter motor (Fig. 8-23). In addition, on some vehicles, when the relay is energized, battery voltage is also connected to another contact. This contact supplies voltage directly to the ignition coil. This connection is called the bypass circuit. The bypass circuit bypasses the ignition resistor to apply full battery voltage to the ignition coil while the engine is cranking. This provides a stronger spark for easier starting. On some vehicles, the bypass circuit is completed through a contact of the ignition switch.

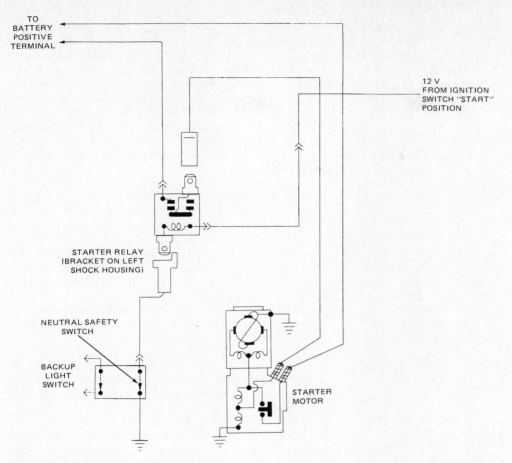

Fig. 8-19. Chrysler starting-system diagram. *(Chrysler Corporation)*

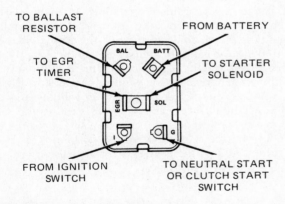

Fig. 8-20. Starter relay terminals. *(Chrysler Corporation)*

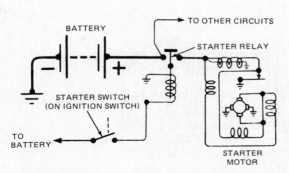

Fig. 8-21. Ford starting-system diagram. *(Ford Motor Company)*

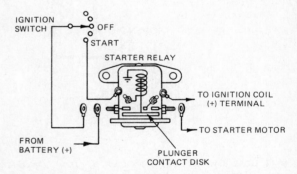

Fig. 8-22. Ford starter relay in the deenergized position.

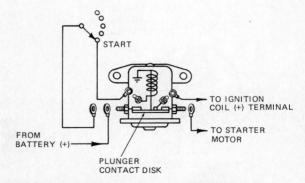

Fig. 8-23. Ford starter relay in the energized position.

When battery voltage is connected to the starter motor, the starter solenoid is energized. The solenoid used with this starter motor is a moveable pole shoe surrounded by a coil of wire. When the solenoid is energized, it performs two functions. It engages the pinion gear into the ring gear, and it switches current to the field and armature windings to operate the motor. Moveable-pole-shoe starter motors are described in Chap. 9.

When the engine starts, the driver releases the key and the ignition switch returns to the RUN position. The starter relay deenergizes and stops the current flow to the starter motor. The starter solenoid deenergizes, the motor stops, and the pinion gear disengages from the ring gear.

General Motors

The General Motors starting system is shown in Fig. 8-24. The system includes the battery, the ignition switch, the neutral safety switch, the starter solenoid, and the starter motor. The starter solenoid is mounted on the outside of the starter motor. The solenoid terminals are shown in Fig. 8-25. The battery terminal connects to the battery positive terminal, and the motor (M) terminal connects to the motor field and armature windings.

The ignition switch and the neutral safety switch are in series with the magnetic winding of the solenoid (S terminal). Therefore, the starter solenoid will not operate unless both switches are closed. The ignition switch must be turned to the START position, and the transmission selector lever must be in PARK or NEUTRAL. On some vehicles with a manual transmission, the clutch pedal must be depressed to close the neutral safety switch contacts. Many vehicles do not use a neutral safety switch. Instead, a mechanical blocking device prevents the ignition switch from being turned to the START position unless the selector lever is in PARK or NEUTRAL.

When battery voltage is applied to the S terminal, the solenoid is energized. The solenoid has two windings: a pull-in winding and a hold-in winding (Fig. 8-26). The hold-in winding is connected from the S terminal to ground. The pull-in winding is connected from the S terminal to the M terminal and is grounded through the starter motor. The magnetic field produced by the combination of both windings pulls the solenoid plunger in. This moves a shift lever, which in turn engages the pinion gear into the ring gear. Both the hold-in and the pull-in windings are needed to move the starter drive mechanism quickly. This ensures rapid gear engagement.

In addition, when the gears are engaged, the solenoid plunger closes a set of switch contacts. The contacts switch current to the field and armature windings to operate the motor. These contacts bypass the pull-in coil winding. The pull-in coil is not needed after the solenoid is energized. The hold-in coil is sufficient to hold the solenoid in its energized position. If current were permitted to flow in the pull-in coil after the solenoid was energized, the solenoid would overheat.

When the engine starts, the driver releases the key and the ignition switch returns to the RUN position. This disconnects battery voltage from the S terminal. When this occurs, current flows briefly from the solenoid battery terminal through the switch contacts, through the pull-in winding, and through the hold-in winding to ground (Fig. 8-27). Current flow through the pull-in winding is in the reverse direction from normal pull-in-winding current flow. Therefore, the magnetic fields of the pull-in winding and the hold-in winding cancel each other. This causes the solenoid to quickly deenergize. The return spring returns the solenoid plunger to its deenergized position. This stops the current flow to the starter motor and disengages the pinion gear from the ring gear.

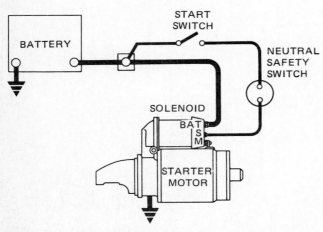

Fig. 8-24. General Motors starting-system diagram. *(Delco-Remy Division of General Motors Corporation)*

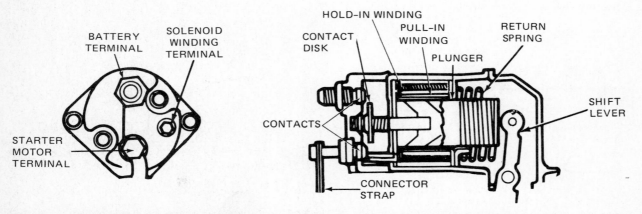

Fig. 8-25. General Motors starter solenoid terminals. *(Delco-Remy Division of General Motors Corporation)*

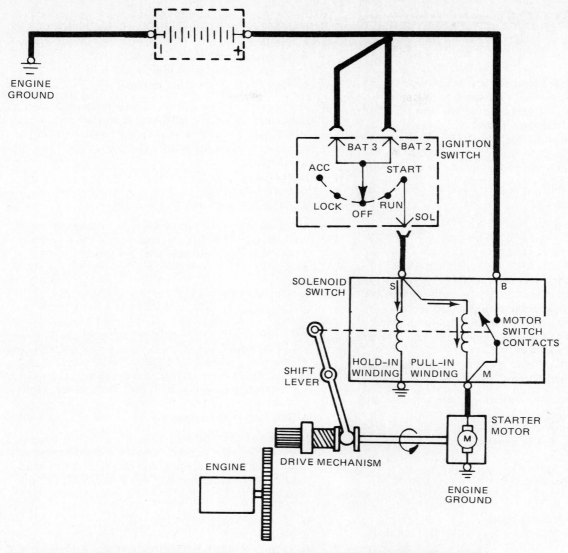

Fig. 8-26. General Motors starting-system diagram, showing solenoid hold-in winding and pull-in winding. *(Chevrolet Division of General Motors Corporation)*

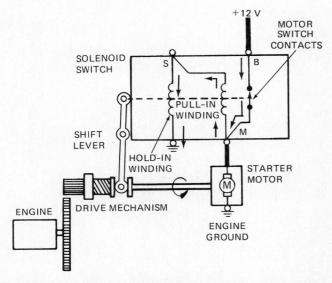

Fig. 8-27. General Motors starter solenoid, showing current flow the instant after the ignition switch is released. *(Chevrolet Division of General Motors Corporation)*

VOCABULARY REVIEW

Hold-in coil   The part of a solenoid winding that has only enough magnetic strength to hold a solenoid plunger in its energized position.

Neutral safety switch   A switch in the starter motor control circuit that prevents cranking when the transmission is in gear.

Overrunning clutch   A device that transmits torque in only one direction.

Pinion gear   The small gear mounted on the end of the starter motor armature shaft.

Pole shoe   The iron core around which a field coil is wound.

Pull-in coil   The part of a solenoid winding that has sufficient magnetic strength to pull a solenoid plunger into its energized position quickly.

Ring gear   The large gear mounted on the outside edge of the flywheel.

Torque   A twisting or turning force.

REVIEW QUESTIONS

Select the *one* correct, best, or most probable answer to each question.

1. All of the following statements are true *except*
   a. the main purpose of a solenoid is to produce a force to perform a mechanical operation
   b. a solenoid switches an electric circuit only
   c. a relay can control the operation of the starter motor
   d. relays can switch large amounts of electric current

2. The ratio of flywheel ring-gear teeth to pinion-gear teeth is approximately
   a. 5 to 1
   b. 10 to 1
   c. 20 to 1
   d. 30 to 1

3. All of the following statements are false *except*
   a. the starter motor must begin operating before the pinion gear engages the ring gear
   b. relays are used to apply a force to move an object
   c. while cranking, the engine turns 20 times faster than the starter motor
   d. the overrunning clutch prevents the starter motor shaft from being driven at an excessive speed

4. The main difference between the control circuit and the motor circuit is
   a. the length of the wire
   b. that there are fewer components in the control circuit
   c. the amount of voltage present in the circuit
   d. the gauge of the wire

5. A neutral safety switch is
   a. located in the motor circuit
   b. not required on vehicles with an automatic transmission
   c. in series with the control circuit
   d. operated by the ignition switch

6. In the American Motors starting system described in this chapter, the neutral safety switch connects to the
   a. ignition switch
   b. solenoid located in the starter motor
   c. starter solenoid ground terminal
   d. starter solenoid battery terminal

7. Mechanic A says the Chrysler starter relay switches the starter motor current. Mechanic B says the relay operates the starter solenoid and the solenoid switches the starter motor current. Who is correct?
   a. A only
   b. B only
   c. both A and B
   d. neither A nor B

8. Mechanic A says the Ford starter relay is actually a solenoid. Mechanic B says the Ford starter relay performs a switching function only. Who is correct?
   a. A only
   b. B only
   c. both A and B
   d. neither A nor B

9. What function(s) does the General Motors starter solenoid perform?
   a. switches current to the starter motor only
   b. engages the pinion gear into the ring gear only
   c. engages the gears and switches starter motor current
   d. disengages the gears only

10. Mechanic A says the pull-in winding on the General Motors solenoid is needed to ensure a rapid movement of the pinion gear. Mechanic B says the pull-in winding helps to deenergize the solenoid quickly. Who is correct?
    a. A only
    b. B only
    c. both A and B
    d. neither A nor B

CHAPTER 9

STARTER MOTORS

OBJECTIVES

After you have studied this chapter, you should be able to:

1. Describe how starter motors are constructed.

2. Describe how starter motors operate.

3. Explain the operation of starter motor drive mechanisms.

4. Name the component parts of a starter motor.

Motors are devices that convert electric energy into mechanical energy. Starter motors are built for a specific application. They are not designed for continuous operation. Instead, they are designed to produce a large amount of torque for a short period of time. The starter motor (Fig. 9-1) is a small, but powerful, electric motor that operates when the ignition switch is turned to the start position. Its purpose is to crank the engine for starting.

MOTOR OPERATION

A simple motor can be constructed by placing a loop of wire in a magnetic field (Fig. 9-2). The motor shown has two magnetic poles: a north pole and a south pole. When an electric current is passed through the loop of wire, an additional magnetic field is created around the loop (Chap. 3). The two magnetic fields interact, and a torque is produced which causes the loop to rotate. The two basic parts of a motor are called the *armature* and the *field*.

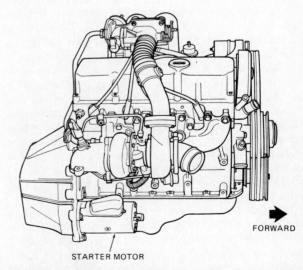

STARTER MOTOR

FORWARD

Fig. 9-1. Starter motor mounted on an engine. *(Ford Motor Company)*

101

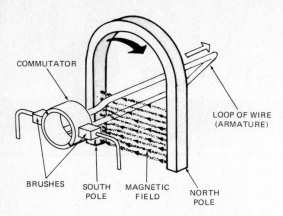

Fig. 9-2. Simple motor. *(Courtesy of Sun Electric Corporation)*

ARMATURE

Instead of having one rotating loop of wire, actual motors have many loops assembled onto an iron core. This assembly is called the armature (Fig. 9-3). The armature core is made of a number of thin iron stampings which are attached together (Fig. 9-4). The stampings are attached to a steel shaft. The type of construction which uses thin layers is called *laminated construction*. Therefore, the stampings are called *laminations*. A laminated construction is needed because if the core were solid iron, the magnetic fields would generate currents in the core. Electric currents that flow in the core are called *eddy currents*. Eddy currents are not desirable because they cause heating in the core and waste energy. Because the laminations are thin and separate the core into thin layers, eddy currents are minimized.

The outer edges of the laminations are slotted, and the armature wires are placed in the slots. The ends of the armature wires are connected to segments of a *commutator* (Fig. 9-3). The commutator is a series of conducting segments located around one end of the armature. Each segment is insulated from the adjacent segment and from the armature shaft by strips of mica. *Brushes* contact the commutator and provide a means of electrically applying a voltage to the loops of wire in the armature. The brushes are small blocks of carbon which conduct electric current to the armature. They are held against the commutator by spring tension (Fig. 9-5). The armature shown in Fig. 9-5 has four loops of wire. Two brushes and eight commutator segments are used. Automotive starter motors have four brushes: two insulated brushes and two ground brushes. A typical commutator may have 30 or more segments.

There are two types of armature winding patterns: lap winding and wave winding. Figure 9-6 shows a lap-winding pattern for a two-pole motor. This illustration shows the position of the conductors in the armature slots in relation to the poles of the motor. The winding begins and ends on adjacent commutator segments. With the lap-winding pattern, the wires passing under a pole all have current flowing in the same direction. Figure 9-7 shows a wave-winding pattern for a four-pole motor. The beginning and end of the winding are on commutator segments which are 180° apart (on opposite sides of the commutator). With the wave-winding pattern, some conductors have no current flow at certain armature positions because their ends are connected to brushes having the same polarity.

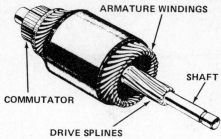

Fig. 9-3. Armature assembly. *(Courtesy of Sun Electric Corporation)*

Fig. 9-4. Armature laminations. *(Delco-Remy Division of General Motors Corporation)*

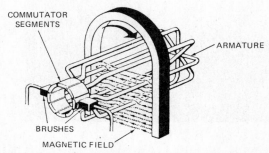

Fig. 9-5. Armature with four loops of wire and an eight-segment commutator. *(Courtesy of Sun Electric Corporation)*

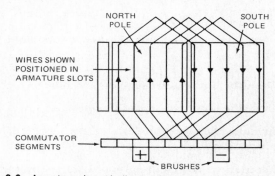

Fig. 9-6. Armature lap-winding pattern of a two-pole motor. *(Delco-Remy Division of General Motors Corporation)*

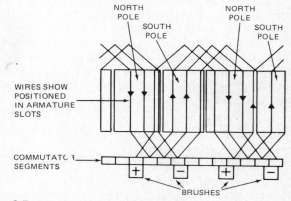

Fig. 9-7. Armature wave-winding pattern of a four-pole motor. *(Delco-Remy Division of General Motors Corporation)*

FIELD

Automotive starter motors are four-pole motors. They have four magnetic poles (two north poles and two south poles). The poles are electromagnets, and they are constructed by winding a coil of wire around a heavy piece of iron called a *pole shoe* (Fig. 9-8). The pole shoes are supported around the inside of the motor housing. The magnetic-field pattern is shown in Fig. 9-9. Notice that the starter motor housing forms part of the magnetic path.

MOTOR CONNECTIONS

Voltage is applied to both the field and the armature windings of a motor through the single terminal on the motor housing. This means the windings are connected internally. The way in which these windings are connected will affect the operating characteristics of the motor. Three common motor connections are series, shunt, and compound.

Series Motor

In a series motor, the field and armature windings are connected in series (Fig. 9-10). This means that all the armature current must pass through the field winding. When the armature of a motor is rotating, a voltage (called a counter electromotive force, or cemf) is induced in the armature. This occurs because whenever a conductor moves through a magnetic field, a voltage (and current) is generated in the conductor. This is the basic principle of electric current generation.

The cemf opposes the voltage that is being applied to the armature. Because the armature and field are in series, the effect of the cemf is to reduce the field and armature current. The faster the motor armature rotates (measured in revolutions per minute, or rpm) the greater the cemf. Therefore, at low rpm, the field current is high (low cemf), and at high rpm, the field current is low (high cemf). The torque produced by a motor is directly related to its magnetic-field strength. A series motor can produce a large torque at low rpm because this is when its field current and magnetic-field strength are greatest. At higher speeds, the torque output of the motor is reduced. This is an ideal characteristic for a starter motor. When the starter motor first begins to crank the engine, a large amount of torque is required to overcome the inertia of the engine at rest. Series motors are commonly used as automotive starter motors.

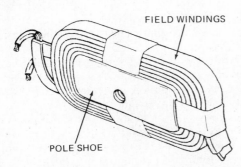

Fig. 9-8. Construction of a field coil. (*Ford Motor Company*)

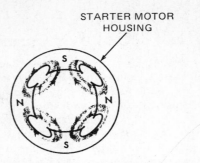

Fig. 9-9. Magnetic-field pattern of a four-pole motor. (*Delco-Remy Division of General Motors Corporation*)

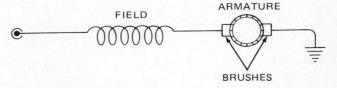

Fig. 9-10. Series-connected motor. (*Ford Motor Company*)

Shunt Motor

In a shunt motor, the armature and field are connected in parallel (Fig. 9-11). This means the cemf which is generated in the armature does not affect the field current. The magnetic-field strength is constant as motor speed changes. A shunt motor tends to regulate its own speed. If the load on the motor increases, the motor slows down and the cemf is reduced. A reduced cemf causes an increase in armature current which, in turn, increases the motor speed. These motors are used if constant speed is more important than starting torque.

Compound Motor

In a compound motor, some of the field windings are in series, and some of the windings are in parallel, or shunt (Fig. 9-12). This type of motor combines the characteristics of the series motor and the shunt motor. The compound motor has a high starting torque and a fairly constant speed. Compound motors are also used as automotive starter motors.

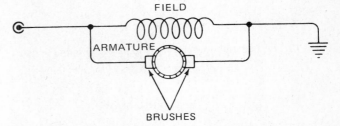

Fig. 9-11. Shunt-connected motor. (*Ford Motor Company*)

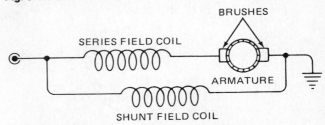

Fig. 9-12. Compound-connected motor. (*Ford Motor Company*)

CONSTRUCTION OF A STARTER MOTOR

The outer portion of a starter motor is called the *starter housing* (or *starter frame*). The pole shoes and field coils are mounted around the inside of the starter housing (Fig. 9-13). The armature rotates inside the housing. For the armature to receive maximum torque, it should fit very closely inside the pole shoes. For this reason, the pole shoes are contoured to fit the shape of the armature. This provides a very small, even gap between the armature and the pole shoes.

The armature is supported by bearings (or *bushings*) at each end. The bushings are mounted in the end frames (Fig. 9-14). The end frames attach to the ends of the housing. Often, the brushes are mounted in the end frame at the commutator end of the housing. The other end frame has provision for the starter drive mechanism. A single terminal provides the electrical connection to the motor, and the starter housing is the ground connection.

STARTER MOTOR DRIVE MECHANISMS

The starter motor *drive mechanism* is the part of the starter motor that connects the motor armature to the flywheel ring gear. The drive mechanism consists of the starter solenoid, the shift lever (or shift fork), the overrunning-clutch assembly, and the pinion gear (Fig. 9-15). The drive mechanism is required because the gear ratio of the pinion gear

to the ring gear is approximately 20 to 1. If the gears were permanently meshed together, when the engine started, the starter motor armature would be driven at an excessive speed. The armature windings would be thrown outward, and the motor would be damaged. The drive mechanism engages the pinion gear into the ring gear when the engine is being cranked and disengages the gears after the engine has started.

The overrunning-clutch assembly and the pinion gear fit over, and slide along, the motor armature shaft. The shift lever transfers the motion of the solenoid to the clutch assembly. The starter solenoid is either attached to or built into the starter motor. The solenoid has a moveable plunger which is surrounded by a coil of wire. When the driver turns the ignition switch to the START position, the starting system supplies battery voltage to the starter motor. This energizes the starter solenoid. When the solenoid is energized, the coil becomes an electromagnet and pulls the plunger (Fig. 9-16). The plunger is attached to a shift lever which pivots to force the overrunning-clutch assembly to slide along the armature shaft. This moves the drive pinion into mesh with the ring-gear teeth.

The solenoid performs another function. If the armature is spinning when the pinion gear engages the ring gear, tooth damage will occur. Therefore, the armature should begin to spin only after the teeth are fully engaged. A set of switch contacts in the solenoid (or starter motor) controls current flow to the starter motor. As the plunger begins to move (after the solenoid is energized), the drive pinion is moved into mesh with the ring gear. Then, at the end of plunger travel, the contact disk connects the battery to the starter motor. Now current flows through the disk, and the starter motor cranks the engine.

Overrunning-Clutch Operation

The overrunning-clutch assembly is a device that transmits torque in only one direction. It turns freely in the other direction. Some clutch assemblies differ slightly in construction, but they are similar in operation.

Figure 9-17 shows a typical overrunning-clutch assembly. Part of the clutch assembly is a sleeve which fits around, and is splined to, the armature shaft. The clutch housing and shell are attached to this sleeve. An extension of the pinion gear fits into the clutch housing. Spring-loaded rollers are placed between the clutch housing and the pinion-gear extension. The rollers are loosely positioned in tapered slots in the housing. When the motor operates, the sleeve is driven and the rollers are forced into the tapered slots in the clutch housing. This causes a wedging action that locks the pinion gear to the clutch housing. Torque is transmitted through the clutch assembly to the pinion gear, and the pinion gear drives the ring gear to crank the engine.

When the engine starts, the ring gear quickly begins to turn faster than the pinion gear. This releases the force on the rollers, and the pinion gear turns freely inside the clutch housing. In this way, the ring gear cannot drive the motor armature at an excessive speed. The driver then releases the key, and the ignition switch returns to the RUN position. The solenoid is deenergized and the motor turns off. A spring returns the solenoid plunger to its deenergized position. This pulls the overrunning clutch and

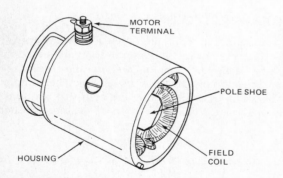

Fig. 9-13. Starter motor housing. (*Delco-Remy Division of General Motors Corporation*)

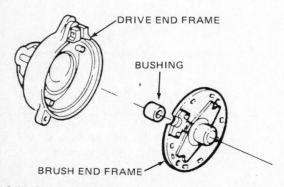

Fig. 9-14. Starter motor end frames. (*Ford Motor Company*)

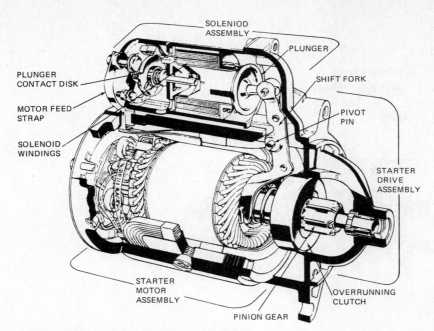

Fig. 9-15. Starter motor and drive assembly shown with solenoid deenergized. *(Courtesy of Sun Electric Corporation)*

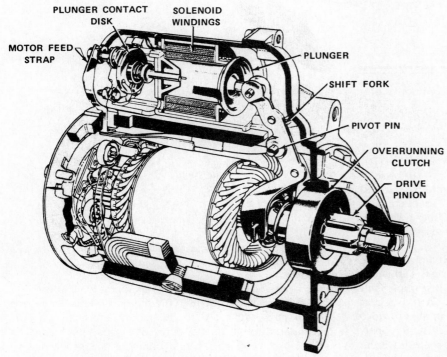

Fig. 9-16. Starter motor and drive assembly shown with solenoid energized. *(Courtesy of Sun Electric Corporation)*

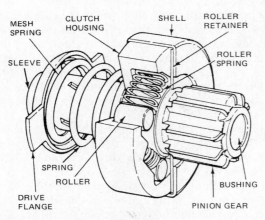

Fig. 9-17. Overrunning-clutch assembly. *(Ford Motor Company)*

pinion gear back along the armature shaft to disengage the pinion gear from the ring gear.

The large spring on the overrunning-clutch sleeve cushions the shock when the pinion gear engages the ring gear. This is especially important if the teeth do not mesh immediately, and clash on contact. In addition, if the teeth clash, the spring compresses and allows the solenoid plunger and lever to complete their movement. This closes the solenoid switch contacts, and the starter armature will begin to rotate. When the teeth line up, the spring force will push the pinion gear into mesh with the ring gear.

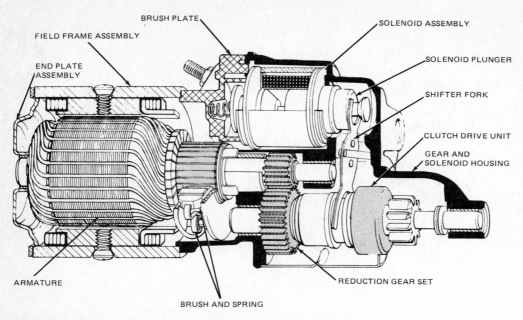

FIELD FRAME ASSEMBLY
BRUSH PLATE
END PLATE ASSEMBLY
SOLENOID ASSEMBLY
SOLENOID PLUNGER
SHIFTER FORK
CLUTCH DRIVE UNIT
GEAR AND SOLENOID HOUSING
ARMATURE
BRUSH AND SPRING
REDUCTION GEAR SET

Fig. 9-18. Chrysler gear-reduction starter motor. *(Chrysler Corporation)*

TYPICAL STARTER MOTORS

This section describes three of the most common starter motors.

Chrysler

Chrysler uses a gear-reduction starter motor which is internally connected as a compound motor (Fig. 9-18). A solenoid and shift lever are used to engage the pinion gear into the ring gear. In addition, the solenoid has a set of contacts that switch current to the motor when the gears are engaged. The solenoid is internally mounted in the drive-end housing.

The drive assembly uses a roller-type clutch. The drive assembly and pinion gear are not mounted on the armature shaft. Instead, they are mounted on a separate pinion shaft which is gear-driven by the armature shaft. There is a gear ratio of 3.5 to 1 between the pinion shaft and the armature shaft. This allows a smaller motor to be used (which operates at a higher speed) than if the armature shaft drove the pinion gear directly.

The commutator is on the drive end of the armature shaft. Therefore, the brushes are located in the center of the starter motor assembly.

Ford

The Ford *positive-engagement* starter motor is shown in Fig. 9-19. This motor uses a moveable pole shoe to engage the pinion gear into the ring gear. One of the four field-pole shoes is moveable and is attached to one end of a lever. The lever is pivoted, and its other end attaches to the drive assembly. The drive assembly consists of a roller-type overrunning clutch.

The moveable pole shoe (also called a *plunger*) is positioned inside a coil having two separate windings. The windings are called the *drive coil* and the *holding coil*. The

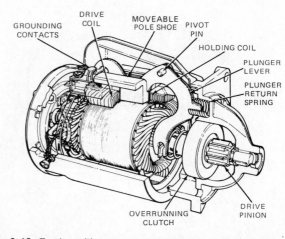

GROUNDING CONTACTS
DRIVE COIL
MOVEABLE POLE SHOE
PIVOT PIN
HOLDING COIL
PLUNGER LEVER
PLUNGER RETURN SPRING
OVERRUNNING CLUTCH
DRIVE PINION

Fig. 9-19. Ford positive-engagement starter motor. *(Ford Motor Company)*

pole shoe and coils form a type of solenoid. The holding coil is connected directly to the motor terminal. The drive coil is also connected to the motor terminal, but it is grounded through a set of normally closed switch contacts (Fig. 9-19). When the switch contacts are closed, the drive coil is connected in parallel with the armature and field windings (Fig. 9-20). Therefore, when the switch contacts are closed, current flows through the drive coil and the motor cannot operate. When battery voltage is applied to the starter motor terminal, current flows through both the holding coil and the drive coil. The magnetic field produced by the combination of both coils pulls the moveable shoe downward (Fig. 9-21). The shoe is pulled into a seat in the starter frame.

The motion of the shoe causes the lever to slide the drive assembly and pinion gear along the armature shaft to engage the ring gear. Both the drive coil and the holding coil are needed to move the shoe quickly. This ensures rapid movement of the drive assembly. Once the shoe has moved into its seat, the attraction of the holding coil alone is enough to hold the shoe in position. The drive coil is no longer needed for this purpose.

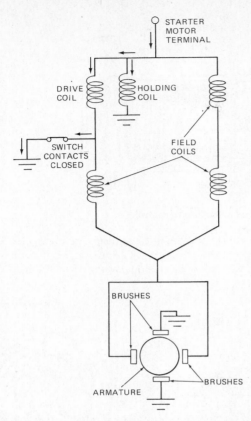

Fig. 9-20. Ford positive-engagement starter motor with switch contacts closed. Drive coil and holding coil both function to pull the moveable pole shoe into its seat.

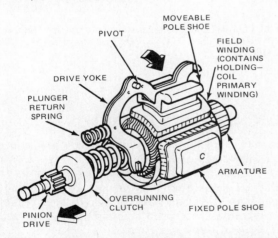

Fig. 9-21. Operation of the Ford positive-engagement starter motor. *(American Motors Corporation)*

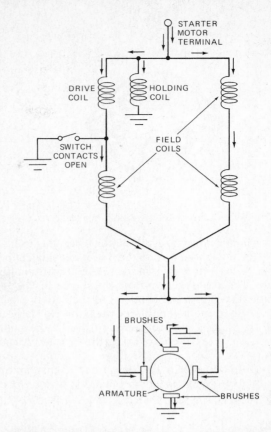

Fig. 9-22. Ford positive-engagement starter motor with switch contacts open. The holding coil holds the pole shoe in its seat, and the drive coil functions as a field coil.

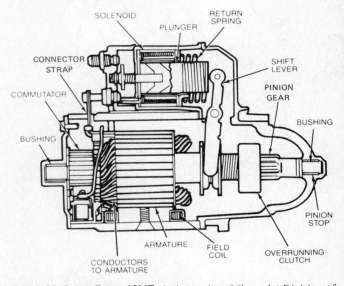

Fig. 9-23. Delco-Remy 10MT starter motor. *(Chevrolet Division of General Motors Corporation)*

When the moveable shoe is pulled into its seat, an arm on the shoe pushes open the switch contacts (Fig. 9-22). This breaks the ground connection to the drive coil. Current now flows through the field and armature windings, and the motor operates. The drive coil now functions as a normal field winding, and the motor operates as a four-pole motor. The holding coil continues to hold the moveable shoe in its seat.

When the engine starts, the overrunning clutch prevents the ring gear from driving the motor armature. The driver releases the key, which stops the current flow to the starter motor. The magnetic field collapses (which releases the moveable shoe), and the lever spring pushes the move-able shoe to its normal position. This pulls the drive assembly back along the armature shaft, and the pinion gear disengages from the ring gear.

General Motors (Delco-Remy)

The Delco-Remy starter motor is shown in Fig. 9-23. A solenoid attached to the outside of the motor housing performs two functions. It engages the pinion gear into the ring gear,

107

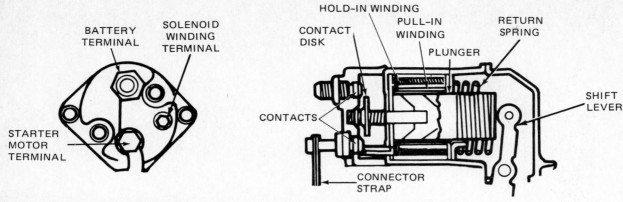

Fig. 9-24. Delco-Remy starter solenoid terminals. (*Delco-Remy Division of General Motors Corporation*)

and it switches current to the motor when the gears are engaged. A single terminal on the motor housing connects to the large lower terminal on the solenoid with a connector strap. The solenoid terminals are shown in Fig. 9-24. The large upper terminal connects to the battery positive terminal. When the solenoid operates, the two large terminals are connected together internally by the contact disk. This supplies battery voltage to the field and armature windings. The solenoid-winding terminal connects to the solenoid winding. When 12 V is applied to this terminal, the solenoid operates. Solenoid operation is described in Chap. 8.

The field and armature windings are connected differently on motors used on different engines. Figures 9-25 through 9-27 show the various motor connections.

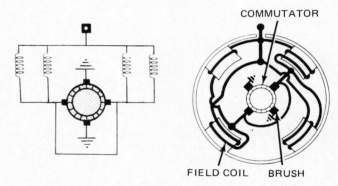

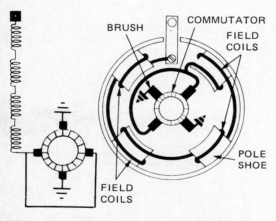

Fig. 9-25. Internal connections for starter motors used on GM V-6 and V-8 gasoline engines. (*Oldsmobile Division of General Motors Corporation*)

Fig. 9-27. Internal connections for starter motors used on GM V-6 and V-8 diesel engines. (*Oldsmobile Division of General Motors Corporation*)

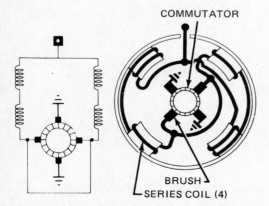

Fig. 9-26. Internal connections for starter motors used on GM V-8 diesel engines. (*Oldsmobile Division of General Motors Corporation*)

VOCABULARY REVIEW

Brushes   Small blocks of carbon which contact the commutator and conduct electric current to the armature.

CEMF   Counter electromotive force.

Commutator   The series of electric contacts located around one end of an armature which connect to the armature conductors.

Eddy currents   Electric currents that flow in the core of a motor armature or in the core of any magnetic device.

Laminated construction   A type of construction which uses thin layers.

Laminations   The thin steel stampings of which the armature core is made.

REVIEW QUESTIONS ═══════════════

Select the *one* correct, best, or most probable answer to each question.

1. All of the following statements are true *except*
   a. a laminated construction minimizes eddy currents
   b. laminations increase current flow in the armature core
   c. eddy currents waste energy
   d. eddy currents cause heating in the armature

2. All of the following statements describe motor operation *except*
   a. the field winding rotates
   b. the armature rotates within the field winding
   c. brushes supply current to the commutator
   d. the armature rotates because of the interaction of two magnetic fields

3. The brushes and the commutator
   a. conduct electric current to the field winding
   b. are connected in the field circuit
   c. conduct electric current to the laminations
   d. conduct electric current to the armature winding

4. Which type of motor produces high torque at low speed?
   a. series
   b. shunt
   c. compound
   d. parallel-connected

5. In a series motor, what limits field and armature current?
   a. cemf
   b. armature insulation
   c. motor torque
   d. the brushes

6. All of the following statements are true *except*
   a. the starter motor should begin to operate after the pinion gear has engaged the ring gear
   b. the overrunning clutch has spring-loaded rollers between the clutch housing and the pinion-gear extension
   c. the overrunning clutch is splined to the armature shaft
   d. automotive starter motors are two-pole motors

7. Which of the following devices transmits torque in only one direction?
   a. solenoid
   b. shift lever
   c. starter relay
   d. overrunning clutch

8. All of the following statements concerning the Ford positive-engagement starter motor are true *except*
   a. part of the solenoid is a moveable pole shoe
   b. the switch contacts are closed when the solenoid is engaged
   c. the solenoid has a drive coil and a holding coil
   d. the drive coil is not needed when the solenoid is energized

9. All of the following statements are true concerning starter motor drive mechanisms *except*
   a. the drive mechanism engages the pinion gear into the ring gear
   b. the drive mechanism transmits torque in only one direction
   c. the drive mechanism allows the solenoid to engage and disengage the pinion gear
   d. the drive mechanism does not transmit torque after the engine starts

10. Mechanic A says that the Ford positive-engagement starter motor does not use a solenoid. Mechanic B says the moveable pole shoe is the solenoid plunger. Who is correct?
    a. A only
    b. B only
    c. both A and B
    d. neither A nor B

CHAPTER 10

THE CHARGING SYSTEM

OBJECTIVES

After you have studied this chapter, you should be able to:

1. Describe the operation of electromechanical and electronic regulators.

2. Explain the function of charge indicators.

3. Describe the operation of typical charging systems.

The charging system includes the battery, the alternator, the regulator, the wiring harness that joins these components, and the charge indicator (Fig. 10-1). The alternator is belt-driven by the crankshaft. When an engine is started, the battery supplies energy to the starter motor to crank the engine. After the engine has started, the alternator generates current to charge the battery and to supply the vehicle electrical system (Fig. 10-2). The alternator charges the battery because it produces a higher voltage than the battery. The *regulator* controls the alternator voltage to prevent overcharging and to maintain the voltage at the proper level.

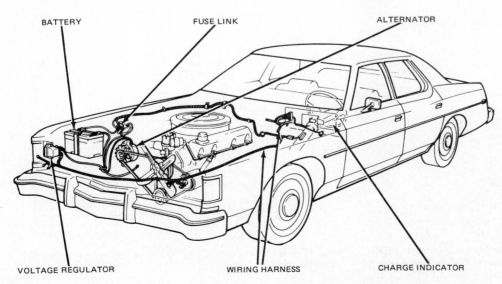

BATTERY   FUSE LINK   ALTERNATOR

VOLTAGE REGULATOR   WIRING HARNESS   CHARGE INDICATOR

Fig. 10-1. Components of a charging system. *(Ford Motor Company)*

111

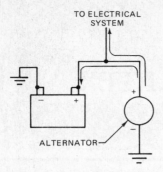

Fig. 10-2. Charging-system current flow with the engine running.

ALTERNATOR

In an alternator, a magnetic field rotates inside a stationary winding (Fig. 10-3). The rotating part of an alternator is called the *rotor*. The stationary winding is called the *stator*. The field winding is wound on the rotor. The field of an alternator is an electromagnet. As it rotates, it induces a voltage (and current) in the stator winding. The stronger the magnetic field in the field winding, the greater the induced voltage (and current) in the stator winding.

Controlling the magnetic-field strength of the field winding is a way of controlling the output of the alternator. The field strength is controlled by varying the current supplied to the field winding. The greater the current flow, the stronger the magnetic field.

To supply current to the field, electric contact must be made to the moving rotor. Brushes and slip rings (Chap. 3) are used for this purpose (Fig. 10-4). An alternator rotor has two slip rings. Each slip ring connects to one end of the field winding. A brush contacts each slip ring and voltage is applied to the brushes. One brush carries current to the field, and the other brush carries the return current from the field.

The regulator controls the amount of current supplied to the alternator field winding. There are two basic ways of connecting a regulator to an alternator. Figure 10-5 shows the regulator connected between the battery and the alternator. The battery positive terminal connects directly to the regulator. A wire from the regulator leads to one of the alternator field brushes. The other field brush is grounded. This is a grounded-field system.

Figure 10-6 shows the regulator connected between the alternator and ground. The battery positive terminal connects directly to one of the alternator field brushes. A wire from the other field brush leads to the regulator, which is grounded. This is a grounded-regulator system.

Both systems operate in the same manner. However, they require different testing procedures.

REGULATOR

The regulator senses the charging-system voltage, and on the basis of the voltage level it senses, it controls the output of the alternator. The charging-system voltage is the voltage measured at the battery or at the alternator output

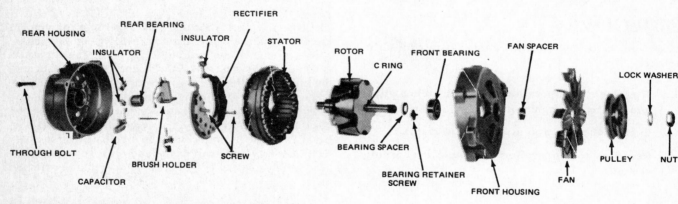

Fig. 10-3. Disassembled alternator. (*Ford Motor Company*)

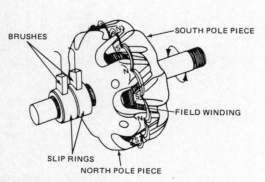

Fig. 10-4. Rotor assembly, with brushes shown in contact with the slip rings. (*Delco-Remy Division of General Motors Corporation*)

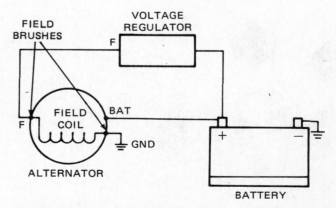

Fig. 10-5. Grounded-field charging system. (*Courtest of Sun Electric Corporation*)

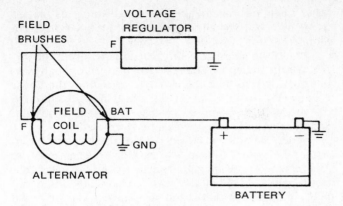

Fig. 10-6. Grounded-regulator charging system. *(Courtesy of Sun Electric Corporation)*

terminal while the engine is running. The voltage should be the same at the battery and the alternator; however, the voltage measured at the battery may be slightly lower because of voltage drops in wires and connections. The regulator can react to small changes [tenths of a volt (V)] in charging-system voltage.

The regulator is designed to sense and react to voltage, because the actual value of the charging-system voltage is a measure of the conditions in the charging system. The amount of current drawn from an alternator has an effect on the alternator output voltage. The current drawn from an alternator is referred to as the load on the alternator. A small current is called a *light load,* and a large current is called a *heavy load.* When little current is drawn from the alternator (light load), the output voltage is relatively high. When a high current is drawn from the alternator (heavy load), the alternator output voltage is reduced. Therefore, by reacting to changes in voltage, the regulator is reacting to changes in current load.

Regulators can be either electromechanical or electronic. An *electromechanical regulator* uses relays to control current flow to the field winding. *Electronic regulators* use transistors to control current flow to the field winding.

Electromechanical Regulator

An electromechanical regulator includes a field relay and a voltage regulator (Fig. 10-7).

Field Relay   The field relay is used to apply battery voltage to the field winding of the alternator after the engine has started. In some applications, this relay only serves to control the operation of a charge indicator lamp. In these applications, it may be called a *charge relay.* Field relay operation in specific charging systems is described later in this chapter.

Single-Contact Voltage-Regulator Units   A voltage-regulator unit which is connected into a charging system is shown in Fig. 10-8. It consists of a single-pole single-throw relay and a resistor. The resistor is connected in parallel with the relay contacts. The relay coil is connected between the output of the alternator and ground. The magnetic-field strength in the relay coil is affected by the system voltage. The higher the system voltage, the stronger the magnetic field. The relay contacts are normally closed.

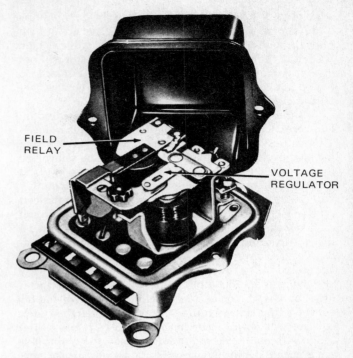

Fig. 10-7. Electromechanical regulator with a field relay and a voltage regulator. *(Delco-Remy Division of General Motors Corporation)*

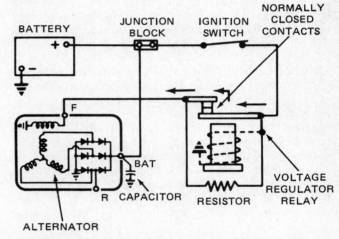

Fig. 10-8. Single-contact regulator when the system voltage is low and the contacts are closed. *(Courtesy of Sun Electric Corporation)*

When the relay is energized, the armature is pulled toward the relay coil and the contacts are opened.

> **NOTE**   The voltage-regulator relay is often called the *regulator.* The unit which contains the voltage-regulator relay and the field relay is also called the *regulator.*

After cranking the engine, the battery needs to be charged. This is because cranking the engine removes energy from the battery. In Fig. 10-8, the voltage-regulator relay is not energized because the system voltage is low. The magnetism in the relay coil is not strong enough to pull the armature of the relay. Therefore, the relay contacts

113

are closed. System voltage is applied to the field winding of the alternator through the closed relay contacts. Therefore, the current output of the alternator will be high. While the battery is being charged, the alternator will produce maximum current. Because of the high current load, the output voltage will be low, and the relay contacts will remain closed.

As the battery becomes charged, and accepts less and less current, the current load on the alternator is reduced. This causes the alternator output voltage to rise. (An increase in engine speed will also cause the output voltage to rise.) When the voltage rises to a high enough level, the magnetism in the relay coil will become strong enough to pull the armature of the relay. This will open the relay contacts (Fig. 10-9), and field current must now pass through the resistor. Now less voltage is applied to the field winding, which results in a reduced field current, less magnetism in the field winding, and a reduced output from the alternator.

If the reduced output causes the system voltage to drop too low, the relay contacts close again, applying full voltage to the field winding. This will increase the system voltage, which will again open the relay contacts. This action will repeat over and over to regulate the system voltage to the proper level. The switching action can take place hundreds of times a second. The regulator maintains the system voltage at the specified level, regardless of the current load on the system or the engine speed.

The regulator shown in Figs. 10-8 and 10-9 is a single-contact regulator. It is used with alternators having a low current output.

Double-Contact Voltage-Regulator Units

The double-contact regulator (Fig. 10-10) provides better regulation over a wider range of output currents than the single-contact regulator described above. The double-contact regulator has a relay with single-pole double-throw contacts. Contacts on the armature swing upward to touch an upper contact and downward to touch a lower contact.

When the current load is high, the system voltage is low and the armature contact is against the upper relay contact (Fig. 10-11). This is because the relay coil does not have enough magnetic strength to move the armature.

When the upper contacts are closed, full voltage is applied to the field winding and the alternator produces its maximum current.

When the alternator current load is reduced, the system voltage increases. The relay coil now has enough magnetic strength to hold the armature away from the upper contact (Fig. 10-12). Current to the field must pass through the 10-ohm (Ω) resistor. Less voltage is applied to the field, and the alternator output current is decreased.

When the alternator current load is reduced to a minimum, the system voltage is at its highest. Therefore, the relay coil holds the armature contact against the lower contact (Fig. 10-13). When the lower contacts are closed, the field winding is grounded and no voltage is applied to the field. Alternator output current is zero.

In actual operation, the contacts do not remain in one position. They are continually opening and closing to maintain the system voltage at the proper level. When the current load is high, the armature is vibrating against the upper contact. When the current load is low, the armature is vibrating against the lower contact.

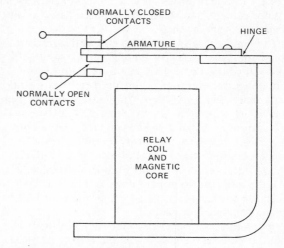

Fig. 10-10. Double-contact regulator.

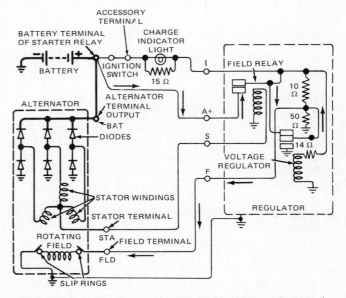

Fig. 10-11. Double-contact regulator when the system voltage is low. The armature contact is against the upper relay contact. *(Ford Motor Company)*

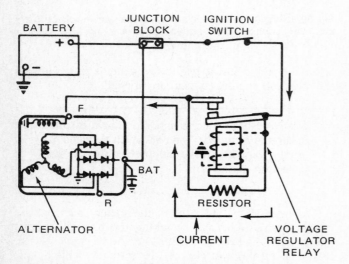

Fig. 10-9. Single-contact regulator when the system voltage is high and the contacts are open. *(Courtesy of Sun Electric Corporation)*

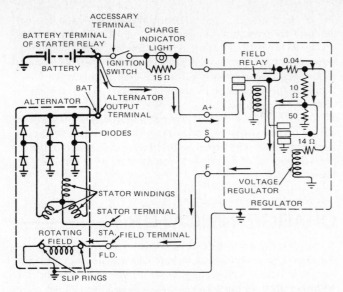

Fig. 10-12. Double-contact regulator when the system voltage is higher. The armature is not in contact with either relay contact. *(Ford Motor Company)*

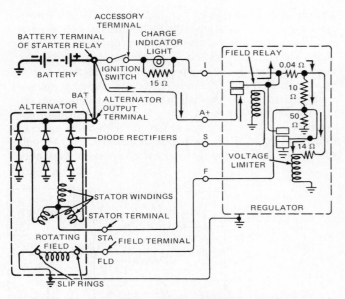

Fig. 10-13. Double-contact regulator when the system voltage is high. The armature contact is against the lower relay contact. *(Ford Motor Company)*

Temperature Compensation

The internal resistance of a battery is greater when it is cold. Therefore, the battery requires a higher charging voltage. To provide a higher charging voltage, most regulators are temperature-compensated. This allows the regulated voltage to increase as the temperature decreases. Figure 10-14 is a table listing typical charging voltages at various temperatures.

Three devices are used to temperature-compensate an electromechanical regulator, and many regulators use all of them. The devices are the bimetallic hinge, the magnetic shunt, and the ballast resistor.

Bimetallic Hinge The *hinge* is the part of the relay that allows the armature to move (Fig. 10-10). The hinge is made of a bimetallic strip that can bend and is similar to a

Air temperature near voltage regulator	Voltage range
−20°F [−29°C]	14.9 to 15.9
80°F [27°C]	13.9 to 14.6
140°F [60°C]	13.3 to 13.9
Above 140°F [60°C]	Less than 13.60

Fig. 10-14. Charging-system voltage settings for various temperatures. *(Chrysler Corporation)*

flat spring. The spring tension in the hinge affects the voltage that is required to move the armature. If the tension in the hinge is increased, a higher voltage is required to move the armature. If the tension is decreased, a lower voltage is required. Because the relay hinge is made from a bimetallic strip, the spring tension in the hinge changes with temperature. Therefore, the regulated-system voltage is compensated for temperature changes.

Magnetic Shunt A *magnetic shunt* is a bypass, or parallel path, for the magnetic field in the relay (Fig. 10-15). The relay armature forms part of the magnetic path, and the shunt bypasses a portion of the field past the armature. The shunt is made of a magnetic material that changes in permeability with temperature. Depending on the temperature, more or fewer lines of magnetic force bypass the armature. Therefore, as temperature changes, the pull on the armature varies. The result is a regulated voltage that changes with temperature.

Ballast Resistor As temperature increases, the resistance of the relay coil increases. More voltage is required to cause the same current to flow and to produce the same magnetic-field strength. This is undesirable because the regulated voltage will increase as temperature increases.

To minimize this effect, the relay is designed to have a low resistance, and a ballast resistor is placed in series with the coil. In Fig. 10-11, the 14-Ω resistor is the ballast resistor. The relay coil is designed to have a small percentage of the total series resistance. Any change in coil resistance has very little effect on the total series resistance. Therefore, a change in relay-coil resistance does little to affect the system voltage.

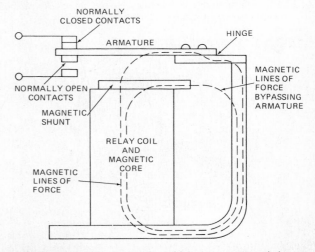

Fig. 10-15. Voltage-regulator relay which uses a magnetic bypass.

Electronic Regulators

An electronic regulator (Fig. 10-16) operates in the same manner as an electromechanical regulator. Both control alternator output by varying the voltage applied to the alternator field winding. Electronic regulators use transistors to switch the field current on and off. In addition, resistors, diodes, and zener diodes are used in regulator circuits. Electronic regulators can be made of individual components or can be made in a single chip called an integrated circuit (Fig. 10-17). These regulators are so small that they are built into some alternators (Fig. 10-18). Regulators that are built into an alternator are called *integral regulators*.

Electronic regulators have several advantages over electromechanical regulators:

- Small size
- No moving parts to wear
- More accurate sensing of the system voltage
- Faster switching for more accurate control of the system voltage

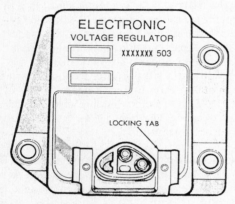

Fig. 10-16. Electronic regulator. *(Chrysler Corporation)*

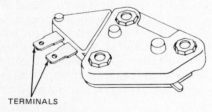

Fig. 10-17. Integrated-circuit regulator. *(Delco-Remy Division of General Motors Corporation)*

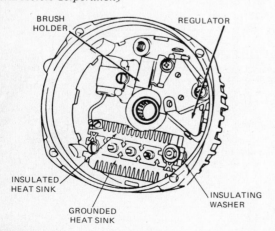

Fig. 10-18. Integral regulator mounted in the rear housing of an alternator. *(Chevrolet Division of General Motors Corporation)*

A diagram of a Delco-Remy alternator which has an integral regulator is shown in Fig. 10-19. This is a grounded-regulator circuit. Transistor TR1 is the switching transistor that controls the field current. When TR1 is ON, its collector is effectively grounded and field current flows through the transistor to ground. When TR1 is OFF, field current cannot flow.

The regulator senses system voltage, and transistor TR1 is turned on and off to control the alternator field current. Transistor TR1 can turn on and off thousands of times per second to regulate the system voltage to the proper level.

CHARGE INDICATORS

A charge indicator is a device that shows the driver whether the charging system is operating. The charge indicator can be an indicator lamp, an electronic voltage monitor, an ammeter, or a voltmeter.

Indicator Lamp

The charging-system indicator lamp (located on the instrument panel) is lighted any time the ignition switch is in the RUN position and the alternator is not producing voltage. When the ignition switch is turned to RUN before the engine is started, the lamp is lighted. This serves as a prove-out circuit for the lamp. Once the engine starts and the alternator produces charging voltage, the lamp goes off.

Figure 10-20 shows a Ford charging system with the ignition switch in the RUN position and the engine not running. Battery voltage is applied to one terminal of the indicator lamp through the ignition switch contacts. The other

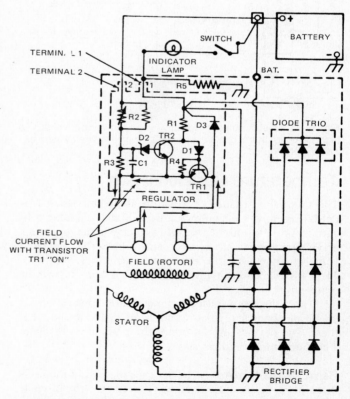

Fig. 10-19. Schematic diagram of a Delco-Remy 1OSI alternator. *(Chevrolet Division of General Motors Corporation)*

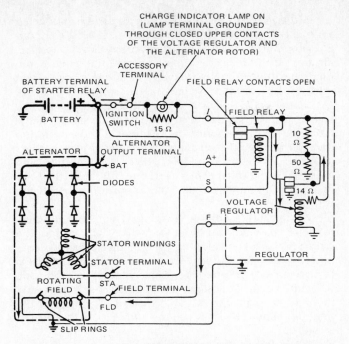

CHARGE INDICATOR LAMP ON
(LAMP TERMINAL GROUNDED
THROUGH CLOSED UPPER CONTACTS
OF THE VOLTAGE REGULATOR AND
THE ALTERNATOR ROTOR)

Fig. 10-20. Ford charging system with ignition switch on and engine not running (indicator lamp on). *(Ford Motor Company)*

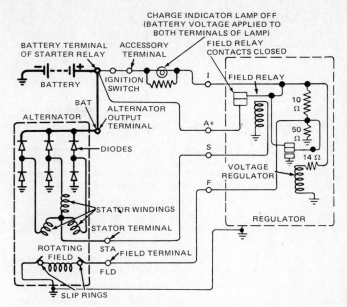

Fig. 10-21. Ford charging system with engine running and alternator generating voltage (indicator lamp off). *(Ford Motor Company)*

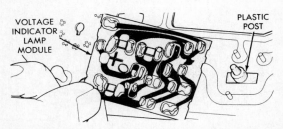

Fig. 10-22. Voltage indicator lamp-module assembly. *(Chrysler Corporation)*

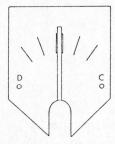

Fig. 10-23. Ammeter used as a charge indicator. *(Chrysler Corporation)*

terminal of the lamp is grounded through the upper contacts of the voltage-regulator relay and the alternator rotor. Therefore, the indicator lamp is on. When the engine is started, the alternator begins to generate voltage (Fig. 10-21). The voltage energizes the field relay and causes its contacts to close. With the field relay contacts closed, battery voltage is applied to both sides of the indicator lamp and the lamp goes off. The lamp does not indicate that the regulated voltage is to specification. When the lamp is on with the engine running, the alternator is not charging the battery. An indicator lamp will not detect an overcharge condition.

Electronic Voltage Monitor

Another type of charge indicator lamp is controlled by an electronic voltage-sensing module (Fig. 10-22). A *module* is a functional electronic circuit that is packaged as a single unit. The module monitors the system voltage. When the system voltage is above 11.2 V, the lamp is off. When the system voltage drops below 11.2 V, a transistor amplifier in the module turns on the lamp. A lamp or a light-emitting diode (LED) can be used with this type of system. The module shown in Fig. 10-22 controls a lamp.

Ammeter

An ammeter is a device that is used to measure electric current flow. When an ammeter is used as a charge indicator, it is connected between the battery and the alternator. This type of ammeter has the zero in the middle of the scale (Fig. 10-23). The meter needle moves in either direction, depending on which direction current is flowing in the circuit. When current is flowing from the alternator to the battery, the needle deflects to the right. This direction is labeled CHARGE or C on the meter. When current flows from the battery to the alternator, the needle deflects to the left. This direction is labeled DISCHARGE or D on the meter.

When the engine is running and the alternator output voltage is greater than the battery voltage, current will flow from the alternator to the battery. The ammeter will deflect to the right and indicate that the battery is being charged. If the engine is running and the alternator output voltage is zero, or is lower than the battery voltage, the battery will supply current to the vehicle electrical system through the ammeter. Then the ammeter will deflect to the left to show that the battery is being discharged.

Voltmeter

Some vehicles use a voltmeter as a charge indicating device. The voltmeter is connected to measure the system voltage (Fig. 10-24). If the voltage drops below specification, something is wrong. A voltmeter can indicate an overcharge condition if the voltage reading is above the specified level.

EXAMPLES OF CHARGING-SYSTEM CIRCUITS

Figure 10-11 shows a charging system with an electromechanical regulator and an indicator lamp. When the ignition switch is turned to RUN with the engine off, the lamp is lighted. When the engine starts and the alternator generates a voltage, the lamp goes off. This operation has been described previously.

The indicator lamp performs another function. It provides a current path to the alternator field winding while the engine is cranking. This allows enough voltage to be generated in the stator to energize the field relay when the engine starts. A 15-Ω resistor is connected across the lamp to provide the current path if the bulb is burned out. When the field relay is energized, battery voltage is applied to the field winding of the alternator through the field relay and regulator contacts.

If the indicator lamp is off, the alternator is producing sufficient voltage to close the field relay. However, this does not indicate that the regulated voltage level is to specification. If the indicator lamp is on with the engine running, the alternator output is too low to energize the field relay. This indicates that something is wrong.

Figure 10-25 shows a schematic diagram of a similar system which uses an electronic regulator and a charge indicator lamp. The stator (STA) terminal is connected to the S terminal of the regulator. When the voltage at the S terminal is below a certain level, the charge indicator lamp is on. When the voltage increases above this level, the lamp goes off. This indicates that the alternator is producing voltage.

Figure 10-19 shows a charging system with an electronic regulator and an indicator lamp. When the ignition switch is closed, one terminal of the indicator lamp is connected to the battery positive terminal. While the engine is being cranked, the alternator stator winding is producing very little voltage. Terminal 1 is then effectively grounded through the regulator. With 12 V on one terminal of the indicator lamp and ground on the other terminal, the lamp is lighted.

When the engine starts and the alternator stator produces voltage, 12 V is applied to terminal 1. With 12 V on both terminals of the indicator lamp, the lamp goes off.

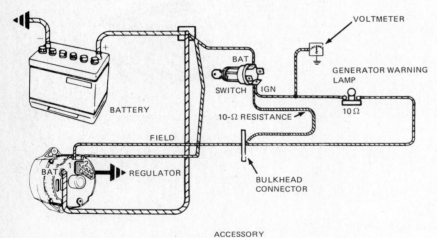

Fig. 10-24. Voltmeter used as a charge indicator. *(Chevrolet Division of General Motors Corporation)*

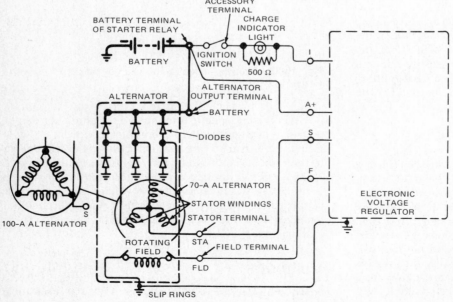

Fig. 10-25. Charging system with electronic regulator and indicator lamp. *(Ford Motor Company)*

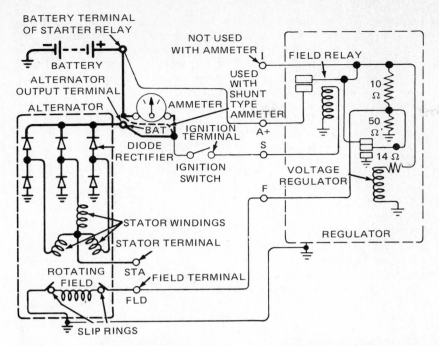

Fig. 10-26. Charging system with electromechanical regulator and ammeter. *(Ford Motor Company)*

When the lamp goes off, the alternator is producing voltage. However, as in the previous example, this is not an indication that the regulated voltage level is to specification. If the indicator lamp is on with the engine running, there is a malfunction in the charging system.

Figure 10-26 shows a charging system with an electromechanical regulator and an ammeter. In this circuit, the battery connects to the field relay through the ammeter and the ignition switch. When the ignition switch is turned to RUN, the field relay is energized. Therefore, battery voltage is applied to the alternator field winding through the field relay contacts and the regulator contacts. The ammeter is connected between the output terminal of the alternator and the battery.

When the alternator is charging the battery, the ammeter needle deflects to the right (CHARGE). If the alternator is not charging the battery, current flows through the ammeter in the opposite direction. Then the needle deflects to the left (DISCHARGE).

The ammeter shown in Fig. 10-26 uses a shunt, which bypasses a portion of the current past the meter. In this way, full charging-system current does not flow through the ammeter. This minimizes the voltage drop across the ammeter so that the ammeter does not affect the operation of the circuit.

VOCABULARY REVIEW

Charge indicator A device that shows the driver whether the battery is being charged.
Electromechanical regulator A regulator which uses relays to control current flow to the alternator field winding.
Electronic regulator A regulator which uses transistors to control current flow to the alternator field winding.
Field relay A device used to switch battery voltage to the field winding of the alternator when the engine has started.
Heavy load A large current draw.
Integral regulator A regulator built into an alternator.
Light load A small current draw.
Regulator The unit that controls the alternator field current to regulate the charging-system voltage. Also, the voltage-regulator relay in an electromechanical regulator.

REVIEW QUESTIONS

Select the *one* correct, best, or most probable answer to each question.

1. Which of the following statements is true?
   I. A grounded-field system has one grounded stator terminal.
   II. Grounded-field systems produce a higher charging voltage than grounded-regulator systems.
   a. I only
   b. II only
   c. both I and II
   d. neither I nor II

2. In the double-contact regulator, when the armature is not touching either contact,
   a. the field current must flow through a resistor
   b. the field current is zero
   c. full voltage is applied to the field
   d. the alternator output current is at a minimum

3. After the engine has started, which of the following statements is true?
   a. the system voltage is high
   b. the battery acts as a light load to the alternator
   c. the magnetism in the voltage-regulator relay coil is strong
   d. full voltage is applied to the field winding by the regulator

4. The regulator senses and reacts to changes in
   a. charging current
   b. system voltage
   c. alternator field current
   d. alternator stator current

5. Which of the following statements is true when the battery is fully charged and the electrical load is small?
   a. the system voltage is low
   b. the battery acts as a light load
   c. the magnetism in the voltage-regulator relay coil is weak
   d. full voltage is applied to the field winding by the regulator

6. In the double-contact regulator, when the armature is touching the upper contact,
   a. the field current must flow through a resistor
   b. the alternator output current is at a minimum
   c. full voltage is applied to the field
   d. the field current is zero .

7. Which statement is true regarding regulator temperature compensation?
   a. a regulator with a bimetallic hinge provides a higher charging voltage when the weather is cold
   b. when the temperature is low, the battery requires a lower charging voltage
   c. the battery offers a lower resistance to charging current when the weather is cold
   d. a magnetic shunt bypasses some of the field current through a resistor

8. Mechanic A says that electronic regulators provide a higher charging voltage than electromechanical regulators. Mechanic B says the main difference is that electronic regulators use transistors to control the field current and electromechanical regulators use relay contacts. Who is correct?
   a. A only
   b. B only
   c. both A and B
   d. neither A nor B

9. Which charge indicator can indicate an overcharge condition?
   a. indicator light
   b. voltmeter
   c. electronic voltage monitor
   d. none of the above

10. Mechanic A says that a charge indicator lamp goes off because the same voltage is applied to both sides of the lamp. Mechanic B says that electronic voltage monitors turn on the lamp only when the system voltage drops below a preset level. Who is correct?
    a. A only
    b. B only
    c. both A and B
    d. neither A nor B

CHAPTER 11

ALTERNATORS

OBJECTIVES

After you have studied this chapter, you should be able to:

1. Describe how alternators are constructed.

2. Explain the operation of alternators and the functions of the various components.

3. Describe the basic types of automotive alternators.

An *alternator* is a device that converts mechanical energy into electric energy. It is part of the vehicle charging system. The purpose of the alternator is to supply electrical energy to charge the battery and to supply energy to the electrical components in the vehicle. The alternator is belt-driven by the crankshaft. Therefore, the engine supplies the mechanical energy to the alternator. The alternator is controlled by the regulator (Chap. 10).

CONSTRUCTION

Figure 11-1 shows the construction of an alternator. The main components are the stator and the rotor. Other parts include the pulley and fan, the front and rear housings, and the rectifier assembly or diodes.

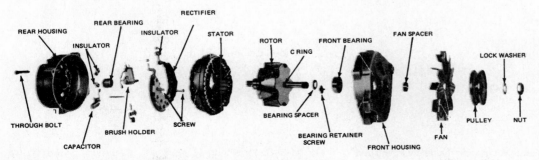

Fig. 11-1. Disassembled alternator. *(Ford Motor Company)*

Pulley and Fan

The pulley and fan are attached to the rotor shaft with a lock washer and nut. A V belt runs in grooves in the pulleys on the alternator and on the engine crankshaft. The crankshaft drives the belt, and it drives the alternator pulley. A fan is located behind the pulley to provide a flow of cooling air through the alternator.

Rotor Assembly

The rotor assembly is shown in Fig. 11-2. It includes the rotor shaft, the field winding, and the north and south pole pieces. Two copper *slip rings* are located at the end of the rotor shaft. The slip rings connect to each end of the field winding. Contact with the slip rings is made by *brushes.* The brushes are small blocks of carbon that conduct electric current. Springs hold the brushes in light contact with the slip rings. When the rotor is turning, one brush conducts electric current through a slip ring to the field winding. The other brush conducts return current from the field winding through the other slip ring.

The field winding consists of a single coil wound with many turns of wire. When current flows through the winding, it becomes an electromagnet (Chap. 3). Pole pieces are located at the ends of the electromagnet. The pole piece on one end becomes a north pole, and the one on the other end becomes a south pole. The pole pieces have projections, or "fingers," which interleave when the rotor is assembled. The pole pieces form alternating north and south poles around the center of the rotor assembly (Fig. 11-3).

Front and Rear Housings

Bearings in the front and rear housings support the ends of the rotor shaft (Fig. 11-1). The rear housing holds the brush assembly, the rectifier, and the capacitor (Fig. 11-4). In some alternators, the regulator is built into and attached to the rear housing.

The brush assembly consists of the brush holder, the brushes, and the springs. The rectifier changes (or rectifies) the alternating current (ac) of the alternator into direct current (dc) for charging the battery. The capacitor acts as a filter. It bypasses to ground any voltage pulses produced by the alternator that may cause static or interference in the radio. In addition, the capacitor acts as a protective device by bypassing to ground any high voltage pulses which may damage the rectifier.

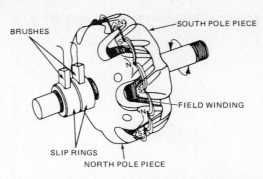

Fig. 11-3. Assembled rotor, showing alternating north and south poles.

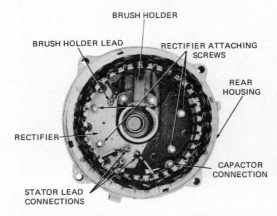

Fig. 11-4. Rear housing, showing brush holder and rectifier assembly. *(Ford Motor Company)*

Stator Winding

The *stator assembly* is the stationary part of the alternator. The electrical winding which is part of the stator assembly is called the *stator winding.* It has three windings wound around an iron core (the stator core) (Fig. 11-5). When the alternator is assembled, the rotor fits inside the stator core. As the rotor turns, the field winding generates voltage (and current) in the stator windings.

The stator core is made from thin steel stampings which are riveted together. This is called a *laminated construction,* and the stampings are called *laminations.* A laminated construction prevents the flow of eddy currents in the core. If the core were solid, the field would generate currents in the core in addition to the current in the stator

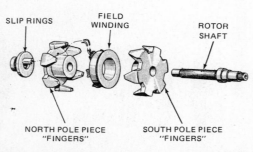

Fig. 11-2. Alternator rotor assembly, showing the field winding and pole pieces. *(Ford Motor Company)*

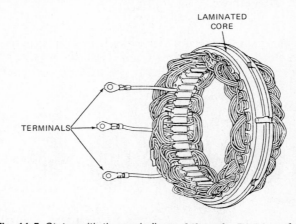

Fig. 11-5. Stator with three windings. *(Chevrolet Division of General Motors Corporation)*

winding. Eddy currents cause heating in the core, which wastes energy.

There are three windings, or sets of wire coils, in the stator. The coils in each winding are connected in series. Each winding has as many coils as there are pairs of poles in the rotor. The rotor shown in Fig. 11-2 has six pairs of poles. Therefore, each stator winding has six coils of wire connected in series.

Figure 11-6 shows a three-winding stator which has only a single winding installed in the core. The winding has seven coils of wire and is used with a rotor having seven pairs of poles. The coils for the other two windings will be installed in the slots in the stator.

When a stator is shown in a wiring diagram, the number of coils of wire in each winding is ignored and the windings are shown as single coils of wire. The windings can be connected together in either of two ways: Y or delta.

Y Connection   In a Y connection (Fig. 11-7), one end of each of the three windings is connected together. The connection is called the *stator neutral junction*. The other ends of the windings are the three stator output wires. The Y connection is the most common connection used in automotive alternators. Four connections are made to a Y-connected stator.

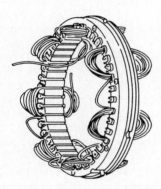

Fig. 11-6. Stator with only the coils making up one winding installed in the core. *(Delco-Remy Division of General Motors Corporation)*

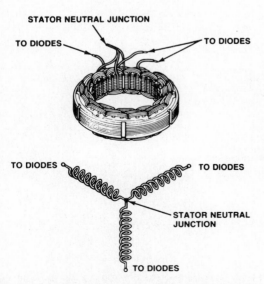

Fig. 11-7. Y-connected stator. *(Ford Motor Company)*

Delta Connection   The delta connection (Fig. 11-8), named for the Greek letter delta, is represented by a triangle. In a delta connection, one end of a winding is connected to one end of another winding, and the junction forms a stator output wire. The other two junctions and output wires are formed in the same manner. Three connections are made to a delta-connected stator.

Rectifier Assembly

The current produced in the stator winding of an alternator is ac. Because ac cannot be used to charge a battery, the ac must be changed into dc. A *rectifier* is an electric circuit which changes ac into dc. A typical alternator rectifier consists of six diodes. On early alternators, individual diodes were pressed into the rear housing (Fig. 11-9). On later alternators, the diodes are part of a rectifier assembly which is located in the rear housing (Fig. 11-10).

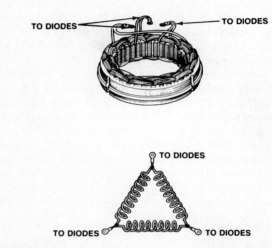

Fig. 11-8. Delta-connected stator. *(Ford Motor Company)*

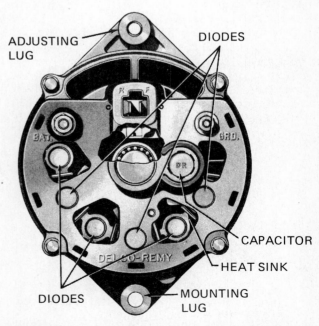

Fig. 11-9. Alternator with individual diodes pressed into the rear housing. *(Pontiac Division of General Motors Corporation)*

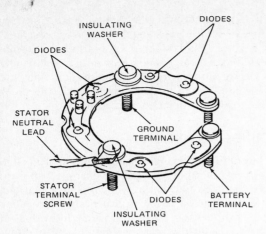

Fig. 11-10. Rectifier assembly. *(Ford Motor Company)*

An alternator diode is shown in Fig. 11-11. The semiconductor material (PN junction) is a silicon-crystal wafer. A wire attached to one side of the wafer forms one terminal of the diode. The outer case serves as the other terminal. If the wafer is positioned so that the N-type material is in contact with the outer case, the diode is called a *negative diode*. If the wafer is positioned so that the P-type material is in contact with the case, the diode is called a *positive diode*. Some rectifier assemblies have diodes that are built into the assembly (Fig. 11-10). There are three positive and three negative diodes in a typical alternator rectifier.

Current flow through a diode produces heat. Excessive heat can quickly destroy a diode. To prevent this, the alternator diodes are mounted in a *heat sink* (Fig. 11-12). This device transfers heat from the diodes to the surrounding air. Some heat sinks have cooling fins to help dissipate heat.

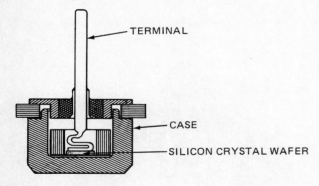

Fig. 11-11. Alternator diode.

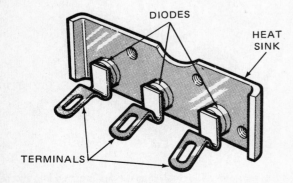

Fig. 11-12. Diodes mounted in a heat sink. *(Chrysler Corporation)*

OPERATION OF THE ALTERNATOR

As the alternator rotor spins, current (and voltage) is generated in the three windings of the stator. Consider only one of the stator windings. Assume that the rotor has six pairs of poles. This means the stator will have six coils in each winding. There are certain rotor positions where the poles of the rotor line up exactly with the coils of wire in the stator. When a north pole passes the right side of a coil as in Fig. 11-13, current is induced (generated) in the coil. At the same time, the adjoining south pole is passing the left side of the coil and generating a current in it. The arrows in Fig. 11-13 show the direction of induced current, which is counterclockwise in this position of the rotor. The polarity of the voltage generated to produce this direction of current flow is shown below the diagram and is assumed to be positive.

When the rotor has turned slightly and the north pole passes the left side of the coil, current is generated in the opposite direction. At the same time, another south pole is passing the right side of the coil (Fig. 11-14). The direction of the induced current is now clockwise. Now a negative voltage is generated.

This type of current is called ac because the direction of current flow is constantly changing. The shape of the voltage as it rises and falls is called a *sine wave*. There are other poles passing five other coils at the same time. Therefore, the same voltage is generated in each coil. With the coils connected in series, the voltages across the coils add together to form the total voltage from the winding. With each revolution of the rotor, six complete sine waves are generated in the winding (Fig. 11-15).

The same action takes place in the other windings. However, the coils of those windings are in different positions around the stator. Therefore, their sine waves occur at different times. Figure 11-16 shows the voltages produced in the three windings of the stator. The voltages are labeled V_a, V_b, and V_c.

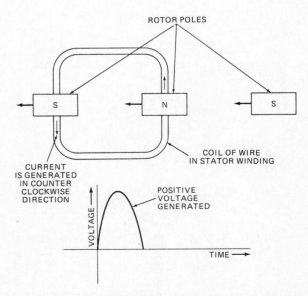

Fig. 11-13. Rotor field poles passing a stator coil, generating a counterclockwise current flow.

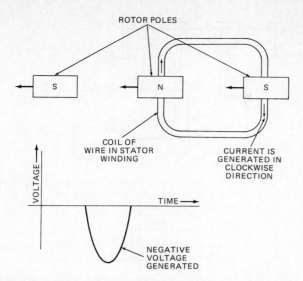

Fig. 11-14. Rotor field poles passing a stator coil, generating a clockwise current flow.

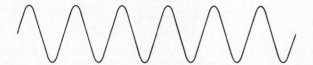

Fig. 11-15. Sine wave generated in a stator winding with one revolution of the rotor.

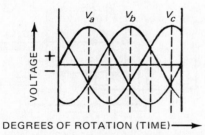

Fig. 11-16. The voltages produced in the three windings. (Delco-Remy Division of General Motors Corporation)

The output terminals of the Y-connected stator are attached to the diode rectifier (Fig. 11-17). The capacitor shown helps reduce static in the radio.

In Fig. 11-17, the stator windings are labeled a, b, and c, and the output terminals are labeled A, B, and C. The voltages applied to the rectifier are the voltages from one winding terminal to another. Therefore, the voltages applied to the rectifier are the voltages from points A to B, B to C, and C to A. These voltages are called V_{ab}, V_{bc}, and V_{ca}.

To find V_{ab}, for example, first find the voltage difference between point A and point B. This is done by subtracting the voltage at point B from the voltage at point A. Because alternating current is constantly changing, this subtraction must be done at many different times. Figure 11-18a shows the individual winding voltages V_a, V_b, and V_c. Figure 11-18b shows the voltages across the stator output terminals: V_{ab}, V_{bc}, and V_{ca}. An example is given to show how the subtraction is done. At the instant that V_a is +8 volts (V), V_b is

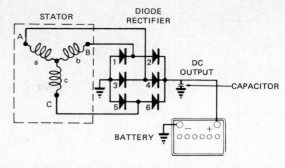

Fig. 11-17. Y-connected stator connected to the rectifier. (Courtesy of Sun Electric Corporation)

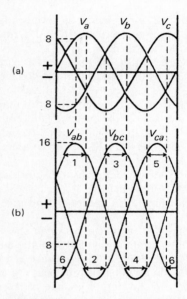

Fig. 11-18. Stator voltages. (a) Individual winding voltages. (b) Voltages across the stator terminals. (Delco-Remy Division of General Motors Corporation)

−8 V. The difference in voltage from +8 V to −8 V is 16 V. Therefore, V_{ab} at that instant is 16 V. Many such subtractions must be done to find the entire pattern of V_{ab}. Similarly, V_{cb} is found by subtracting the V_b from V_c, and V_{ca} is found by subtracting V_a from V_c.

The voltage across each pair of stator output terminals is approximately 1.7 V higher than the individual winding voltages. In addition, the voltages reach their peaks at different times than the winding voltages.

The voltages at the stator terminals are applied to the rectifier assembly. There are six possible current paths through the rectifier. Which path the current takes depends on the stator terminal voltages. This is because the voltage causes some diodes to be forward-biased and other diodes to be reverse-biased. The sequence of voltages is shown in Fig. 11-18b. Figure 11-19 shows the current flow when V_{ab} is positive. This means the voltage at A is positive with respect to B. Current is being supplied to the battery because the alternator is producing a higher voltage than the battery. The flow is from stator terminal A, through diode 2, to the positive terminal of the battery. The return current to the alternator is from the battery negative terminal, through diode 3, to stator terminal B. Diodes 2 and 3 are forward-biased because the voltage at A is positive with respect to B. Stator winding c does not conduct any

125

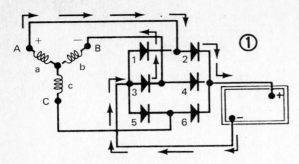

Fig. 11-19. Current flow through rectifier when V_{ab} is positive. *(Delco-Remy Division of General Motors Corporation)*

current because it is connected to reverse-biased diodes. The junction of the three diodes (D2, D4, and D6) is the alternator *output* terminal.

From Figure 11-18*b*, the next current path is the flow when V_{ca} is negative. This is when the voltage at terminal C is negative with respect to terminal A (Fig. 11-20). The current flow is from stator terminal A, through diode 2, to the positive terminal of the battery. The return current to the alternator is from the negative battery terminal, through diode 5, to stator terminal C. Stator winding b does not conduct.

The other four current paths are shown in Figs. 11-21 through 11-24. Notice that the diodes always allow a positive voltage to force current into the positive terminal of the battery.

The voltage applied to the battery is shown in Fig. 11-25. Because the current always flows in the same direction, it is called dc. The fluctuations are caused by the peaks of the sine waves and do not affect the charging of the battery. The fluctuation in the output voltage of the alternator is called the ripple.

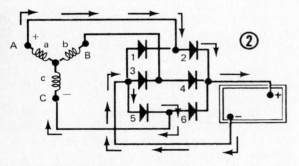

Fig. 11-20. Current flow through rectifier when V_{ca} is negative. *(Delco-Remy Division of General Motors Corporation)*

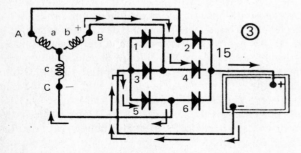

Fig. 11-21. Current flow through rectifier when V_{bc} is positive. *(Delco-Remy Division of General Motors Corporation)*

126

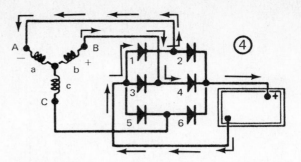

Fig. 11-22. Current flow through rectifier when V_{ab} is negative. *(Delco-Remy Division of General Motors Corporation)*

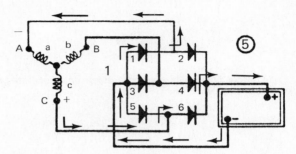

Fig. 11-23. Current flow through rectifier when V_{ca} is positive. *(Delco-Remy Division of General Motors Corporation)*

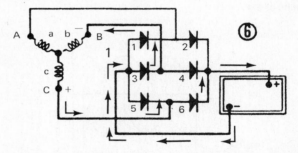

Fig. 11-24. Current flow through rectifier when V_{bc} is negative. *(Delco-Remy Division of General Motors Corporation)*

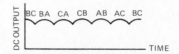

Fig. 11-25. Rectified voltage applied to the battery. *(Delco-Remy Division of General Motors Corporation)*

With a Y-connected rectifier, current flows through only two of the stator windings at a time. This is because the third winding is always connected to diodes that are reverse-biased.

Delta Connection

A delta-connected stator (Fig. 11-26) operates in a similar manner to a Y-connected stator. The six current paths through the diodes are the same, and the voltage applied to the battery has the same ripple. However, there are two differences:

- The voltages across the stator terminals are the same as the individual winding voltages.

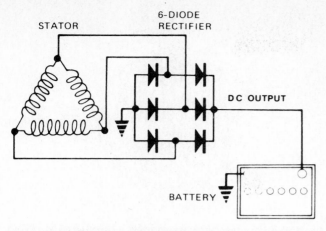

Fig. 11-26. Delta-connected stator connected to the rectifier. *(Courtesy of Sun Electric Corporation)*

- All three windings conduct current. This is because when one winding is conducting current, the other two windings are connected together in parallel with the first winding.

Brushless Alternators

Some alternators do not use brushes and slip rings to supply current to the field winding. Instead, the field winding is stationary, and screw terminals are used to make connection to it. Figure 11-27 shows the internal construction of a brushless alternator. Both the field winding and the stator winding are stationary and are attached to the alternator housing. The rotor, which has the pole pieces, fits between the field winding and the stator winding.

When current is applied to the field winding, a magnetic field builds up. Assume that the direction of current flow through the field winding produces a north pole at the right end of the coil and a south pole at the left end. Therefore, the rotor pole pieces on the right side of the diagram are north poles, and those on the left side are south poles.

The path for magnetic lines of force is as follows:

- From the right end of the field coil, across the air gap, to the rotor north pole piece

- From the rotor north pole piece, across the air gap, to the stator winding

- From the stator winding, across the air gap, to the rotor south pole piece

- From the rotor south pole piece, across the air gap, to the left end of the field coil

Notice that there are four air gaps in the magnetic path. There is another air gap from the north pole piece directly to the south pole piece. If the lines of force were to pass through this air gap, they would bypass the stator winding. Therefore, a *nonmagnetic ring* (a ring made of a high-reluctance material) is placed in this air gap. The ring diverts the lines of force into the stator winding.

The pole pieces on the rotor concentrate the magnetic field into alternating north and south poles. When the rotor is not spinning, there is no voltage induced in the stator because the magnetic field is not moving. When the rotor spins, the alternating north and south poles pass the stator winding. The moving magnetic field induces a voltage in the stator winding. Rectification and regulation in a brushless alternator are similar to that in a brush-type alternator. Because this alternator design eliminates slip rings and brushes, maintenance is greatly reduced.

SPECIFIC EXAMPLES OF ALTERNATORS

Chrysler

A Chrysler alternator is shown in Fig. 11-28. The rectifier assembly has three negative diodes and three positive diodes mounted in separate heat sinks. Both heat sinks are attached to the rear housing. The positive heat sink is insulated from the housing.

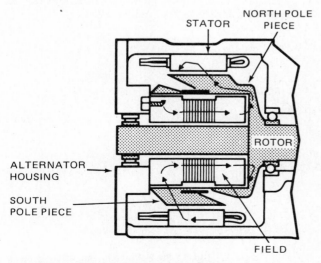

Fig. 11-27. Internal construction of a brushless alternator. *(Delco-Remy Division of General Motors Corporation)*

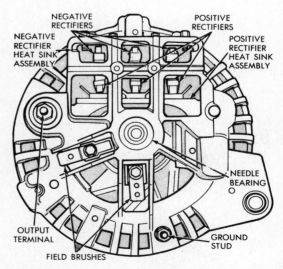

Fig. 11-28. Rear view of a Chrysler alternator. *(Chrysler Corporation)*

There are three terminals on the rear of the alternator:

- The battery (BAT) terminal is the stator output terminal. This terminal supplies the battery charging voltage.

- There are two field (FLD) terminals. Battery voltage is applied to one field terminal, and the other field terminal connects to the regulator.

The alternator is grounded through its mounting bolts.

Chrysler (Mitsubishi)

The Mitsubishi alternator is shown in Fig. 11-29. This alternator has a built-in regulator. There are two separate Y-connected stator windings, each having six diodes. In addition, three more diodes (called a *diode trio*) are used to provide rectified stator voltage to the field winding. Therefore, 15 diodes are used in this alternator (Fig. 11-30).

There are three terminals on the alternator rear housing:

- The B terminal connects to the output of both stator windings. This terminal supplies the battery charging voltage.

- The R terminal connects to the regulator. This terminal is used to supply 12 V to the internal regulator.

- The L terminal connects to the output of the diode trio. This terminal provides rectified stator voltage for use in certain circuits. This voltage is available only when the engine is running.

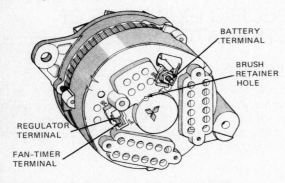

Fig. 11-29. Mitsubishi alternator. *(Chrysler Corporation)*

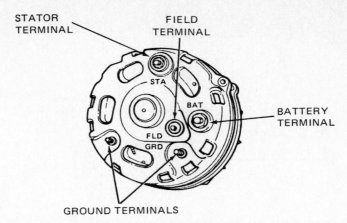

Fig. 11-31. Ford rear-terminal alternator. *(Ford Motor Company)*

Ford Rear-Terminal Alternator

The Ford rear-terminal alternator is shown in Fig. 11-31. There are two types of rectifiers used with this alternator. One rectifier has a single plate with the six diodes built into the plate (Fig. 11-32). This is called a *flat-type rectifier*. The other rectifier consists of two plates which are mounted as shown in Fig. 11-33. This is called a *stacked-type rectifier*. One plate has three positive diodes, and the other plate has three negative diodes. With either type of rectifier, the negative diodes are grounded when the rectifier is attached to the rear housing.

The rectifier assembly also serves as a mounting for the terminals which extend through the rear housing. There are four terminals on the rear housing:

- The battery (BAT) terminal is the stator output terminal. This terminal supplies the battery charging voltage (Fig. 11-34).

- The field (FLD) terminal connects to one side of the field winding through one brush and slip ring. The other brush is internally grounded to the alternator housing.

- The stator (STA) terminal connects to the neutral point of the stator winding.

- The ground (GRD) terminal provides a connection for the ground wire from the regulator.

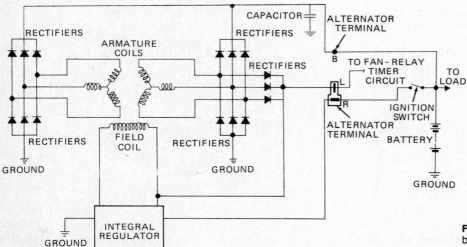

Fig. 11-30. Schematic diagram of a Mitsubishi alternator having two separate stator windings. *(Chrysler Corporation)*

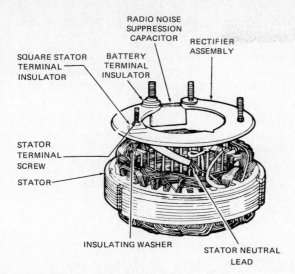

Fig. 11-32. Flat-type rectifier. *(Ford Motor Company)*

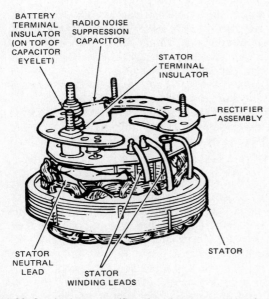

Fig. 11-33. Stacked-type rectifier. *(Ford Motor Company)*

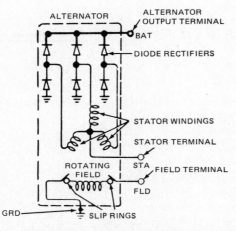

Fig. 11-34. Schematic diagram of a Ford alternator. *(Ford Motor Company)*

Ford Side-Terminal Alternator

The Ford side-terminal alternator is shown in Fig. 11-35. A flat-type rectifier is used with this alternator. The same four terminals are used as on the rear-terminal alternator. However, the terminals are arranged in a different pattern.

General Motors (Delco-Remy 10SI Series)

The Delco-Remy 10SI alternator is shown in Fig. 11-36. This alternator has a built-in electronic regulator. The regulator is located inside the rear housing (Fig. 11-37).

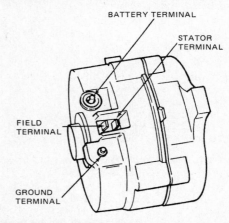

Fig. 11-35. Ford side-terminal alternator. *(Ford Motor Company)*

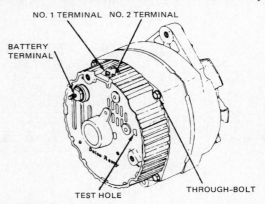

Fig. 11-36. Delco-Remy 1OSI alternator. *(Chevrolet Division of General Motors Corporation)*

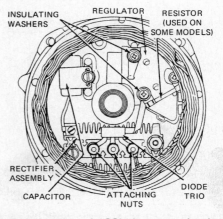

Fig. 11-37. Rear housing of 1OSI alternator, showing regulator and rectifier assembly. *(Chevrolet Division of General Motors Corporation)*

129

The rectifier assembly is also mounted inside the rear housing. There are three positive diodes and three negative diodes mounted in two separate heat sinks. Both heat sinks are joined together in a plastic holder and installed as a single unit. When installed, the negative-diode heat sink is grounded to the housing, and the positive-diode heat sink is insulated from ground.

Most 10SI models have three additional diodes, which are called the diode trio (Fig. 11-38). The diode trio is used to rectify the stator voltage that is applied to the field winding (Fig. 11-39).

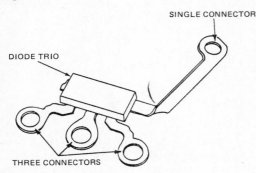

Fig. 11-38. Diode trio. (*Chevrolet Division of General Motors Corporation*)

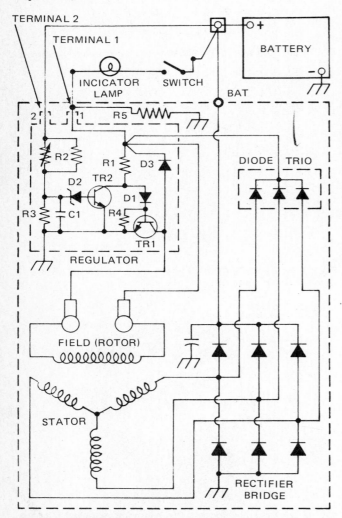

Fig. 11-39. Schematic diagram of Delco-Remy 1OSI alternator. (*Chevrolet Division of General Motors Corporation*)

130

There are three terminals on the rear housing of the alternator:

- The number 1 terminal connects to the field through one brush and slip ring and to the output of the diode trio. This terminal also connects to a portion of the regulator circuitry.

- The number 2 terminal connects to the regulator. This connection supplies battery voltage to a portion of the regulator circuitry.

- The battery (BAT) terminal is connected to the output of the stator winding. This terminal supplies the battery charging voltage.

VOCABULARY REVIEW

Alternator A device that converts mechanical energy into electric energy and is used to charge the battery.

Brushes Small blocks of carbon that conduct electric current to the slip rings of an alternator rotor.

Diode trio Three diodes assembled in one unit which provides rectified stator voltage to the field winding of certain alternators.

Heat sink A device used to absorb heat to protect the alternator diodes.

Pole piece The part of a rotor assembly that becomes a north or south pole.

Rectifier An electric circuit that changes ac into dc.

Ripple The fluctuation in the output voltage of the alternator.

Rotor The rotating part of an alternator which usually contains the field winding.

Slip rings On the alternator rotor, the two copper rings which each connect to one end of the field winding. The brushes contact the slip rings.

Stator The stationary part of an alternator which includes the stator winding and core.

Stator neutral junction The point where the three windings are connected together in a Y-connected stator.

REVIEW QUESTIONS

Select the *one* correct, best, or most probable answer to each question.

1. Which part of an alternator is an electromagnet?
   a. stator winding
   b. armature
   c. field winding
   d. slip rings

2. The capacitor in an alternator
   a. acts as a filter
   b. acts as a resistance
   c. helps rectify the voltage
   d. is used to light the indicator lamp when there is a system malfunction

3. All of the following statements are true *except*
   a. the capacitor in an alternator acts as a filter
   b. each stator winding has as many coils as there are pairs of poles in the rotor
   c. the three stator windings are connected in parallel
   d. the rotor is a rotating electromagnet

4. All of the following statements are true *except*
   a. ac is generated in the stator winding of an alternator
   b. in a diode, positive current flows from the P material to the N material
   c. the rectifier changes ac into dc
   d. in a Y-connected stator, the voltages across the stator terminals are the same as the individual winding voltages

5. The purpose of the diode trio in a Delco-Remy alternator is to provide rectified stator voltage to
   a. magnetize the field winding
   b. operate the regulator
   c. charge the battery
   d. light the indicator lamp

6. The stator core is laminated to
   a. reduce construction costs
   b. reduce eddy currents
   c. permit the stator to dissipate more heat
   d. reduce the current flow in the stator winding

7. If a rotor has six pairs of poles, how many separate coils will each stator phase have?
   a. twelve
   b. two
   c. seven
   d. six

8. All of the following statements are true *except*
   a. ac can be used to charge a battery without being rectified
   b. a rectifier can be constructed with six diodes
   c. a rectifier is an electric circuit that changes ac into dc
   d. a heat sink helps dissipate heat from a diode

9. How many current paths are there in the rectifier of a Y-connected stator if the rectifier has six diodes?
   a. one
   b. two
   c. six
   d. twelve

10. What is the main difference between a brushless alternator and a brush-type alternator?
    a. the field is stationary
    b. the stator is stationary
    c. the rotor is stationary
    d. the field winding is an electromagnet

HEADLAMPS

The construction of a headlamp is shown in Fig. 12-5. The filament is placed a certain distance in front of a reflector. The reflector directs the light from the filament through the lens. The lens focuses the light from the reflector into the desired pattern. This lamp construction is called a *sealed-beam headlamp*.

Some lamps have two filaments. One filament is focused into a low beam. The low beam produces a light pattern that illuminates the road a certain distance from the vehicle (Fig. 12-6). The low-beam pattern is low enough to prevent glare to oncoming vehicles. The high-beam filament is focused to produce a high light pattern to illuminate the road a greater distance from the vehicle (Fig. 12-7).

Headlamp terminals are shown in Figs. 12-8 and 12-9. A ground terminal is used because headlamps do not have a metal base. Therefore, a ground wire is used in the wiring harness to carry the return current from the headlamp to the vehicle ground. Headlamps with a single filament have two terminals (Fig. 12-8). Headlamps with a dual filament have three terminals (Fig. 12-9).

Headlamps are designated by a code which consists of a number and a letter. The number represents the number of filaments, and the letter represents the size and shape of the headlamp. Round-headlamp sizes are 5¾ inches (in.) [146 millimeters (mm)] and 7 in. [178 mm] in diameter. Round 5¾-in. headlamps are designated type 1C with single filaments and type 2C with dual filaments. All round 7-in. headlamps have dual filaments and are designated type 2D. Rectangular-headlamp sizes are 4 × 6½ in. [100 × 165 mm] and 5.6 × 7.9 in. [142 × 200 mm]. Rectangular 4 × 6½ in. headlamps are designated type 1A with single filaments and type 2A with dual filaments. All rectangular 5.6 × 7.9 in. headlamps have dual filaments and are designated type 2B.

Some vehicles use two headlamps; others use four headlamps. Figure 12-10 shows both rectangular and round two-headlamp systems. The lamps used are type 2 lamps. On vehicles with four-headlamp systems (Fig. 12-11), two lamps are type 1 lamps and the other two are type 2 lamps. In low-beam operation, one filament of each of the dual-filament lamps is lit. Therefore, in low-beam operation only two headlamps are illuminated. In high-beam operation, the single-filament lamps are illuminated. Only the high-beam filament is lit on the dual-filament lamps. Therefore, all four headlamps are illuminated.

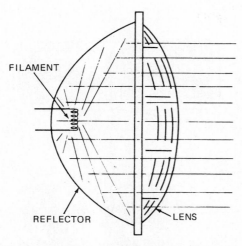

Fig. 12-5. Construction of a sealed-beam headlamp.

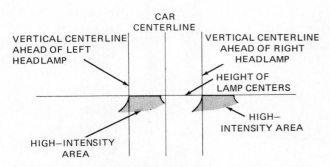

Fig. 12-6. Low-beam headlamp pattern. *(Chrysler Corporation)*

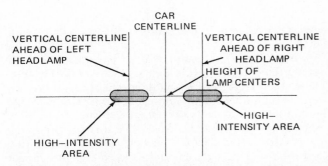

Fig. 12-7. High-beam headlamp pattern. *(Chrysler Corporation)*

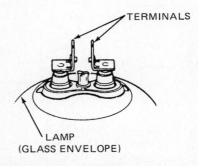

Fig. 12-8. Single-filament headlamp terminals. *(AC-Delco Division of General Motors Corporation)*

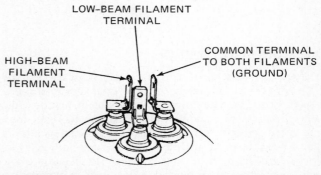

Fig. 12-9. Dual-filament headlamp terminals. *(AC-Delco Division of General Motors Corporation)*

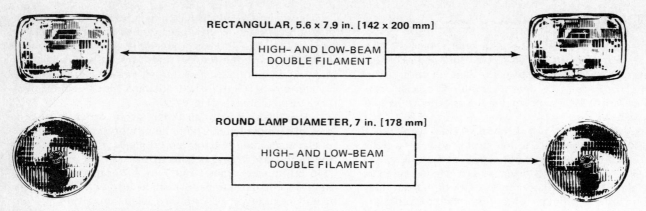

RECTANGULAR, 5.6 x 7.9 in. [142 x 200 mm]

HIGH– AND LOW–BEAM
DOUBLE FILAMENT

ROUND LAMP DIAMETER, 7 in. [178 mm]

HIGH– AND LOW–BEAM
DOUBLE FILAMENT

Fig. 12-10. Two-headlamp systems. *(AC-Delco Division of General Motors Corporation)*

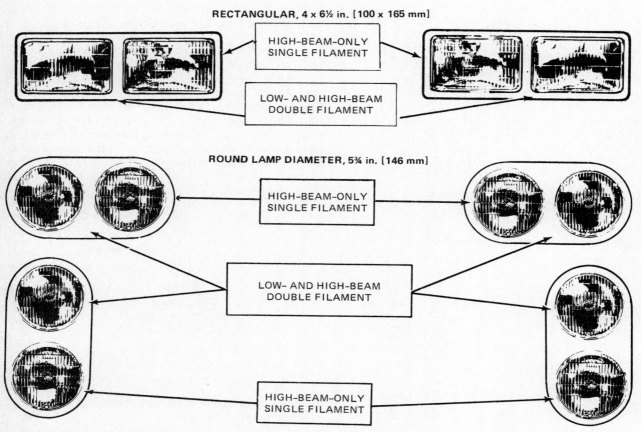

RECTANGULAR, 4 x 6½ in. [100 x 165 mm]

HIGH-BEAM-ONLY
SINGLE FILAMENT

LOW– AND HIGH-BEAM
DOUBLE FILAMENT

ROUND LAMP DIAMETER, 5¾ in. [146 mm]

HIGH-BEAM-ONLY
SINGLE FILAMENT

LOW– AND HIGH-BEAM
DOUBLE FILAMENT

HIGH-BEAM-ONLY
SINGLE FILAMENT

Fig. 12-11. Four-headlamp systems. *(AC-Delco Division of General Motors Corporation)*

Halogen Headlamps

Halogen headlamps are used on some vehicles (Fig. 12-12). *Halogen* is the name given to a certain group of chemically related nonmetallic elements which include chlorine, fluorine, and iodine. Iodine is the halogen most commonly used in automotive headlamps. A halogen headlamp consists of a small bulb filled with iodine vapor located inside the headlamp housing. The filament of the bulb is made of tungsten and is designed to operate at a higher temperature than the filaments of conventional headlamps. Therefore, the lamp produces a greater light output.

In any lamp, the heating of the filament causes atoms of tungsten to be released from the surface of the filament. These atoms are deposited on the inside of the glass envelope. This produces a blackening effect which reduces the light output of the lamp. With a halogen lamp, the iodine vapor causes the tungsten atoms to be redeposited back on the filament. This almost eliminates blackening of the lamp, allowing the light output to remain high throughout the life of the lamp.

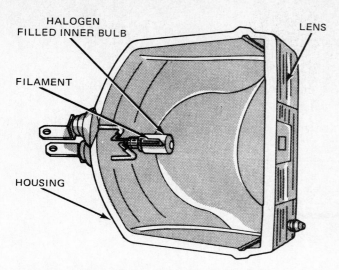

Fig. 12-12. Halogen sealed-beam headlamp. (*Chrysler Corporation*)

Headlamp Switches

The headlamp switch controls most of the vehicle lighting (Fig. 12-13). Most headlamp switches are three-position switches (OFF, PARK, and HEADLAMP). In the OFF position, the headlamp knob is pushed all the way in (Fig. 12-14). Battery voltage is supplied to two terminals of the headlamp switch. One terminal receives battery voltage from a fuse located in the fuse panel. With the knob pulled out to the PARK position, the voltage at this terminal is switched to the parking lamps, side marker lamps, license plate lamp, and dash lamps (Fig. 12-15). The other terminal receives battery voltage directly. When the knob is pulled all the way out to the HEADLAMP position, voltage at this terminal is switched to the headlamps (Fig. 12-16). The lamps that were on in the PARK position remain on in the HEADLAMP position. A circuit breaker is included in the switch to prevent a temporary overload from totally disabling the headlamps.

Other functions of the headlamp switch are to provide a variable brightness adjustment of the dash lamps and to control the courtesy lamps. These functions are covered later in the chapter.

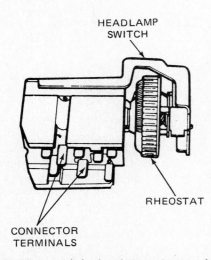

Fig. 12-13. Headlamp switch. (*Ford Motor Company*)

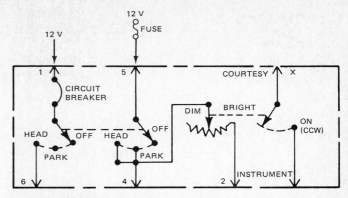

Fig. 12-14. Headlamp switch in OFF position. (*Chevrolet Division of General Motors Corporation*)

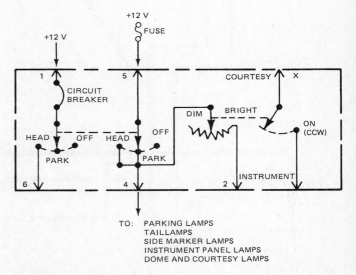

TO: PARKING LAMPS
     TAILLAMPS
     SIDE MARKER LAMPS
     INSTRUMENT PANEL LAMPS
     DOME AND COURTESY LAMPS

Fig. 12-15. Headlamp switch in PARK position. (*Chevrolet Division of General Motors Corporation*)

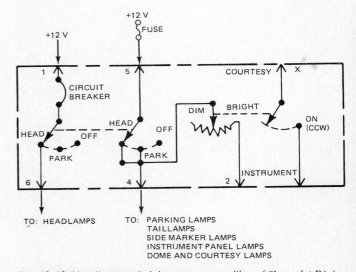

TO: HEADLAMPS   TO: PARKING LAMPS
                            TAILLAMPS
                            SIDE MARKER LAMPS
                            INSTRUMENT PANEL LAMPS
                            DOME AND COURTESY LAMPS

Fig. 12-16. Headlamp switch in HEADLAMP position. (*Chevrolet Division of General Motors Corporation*)

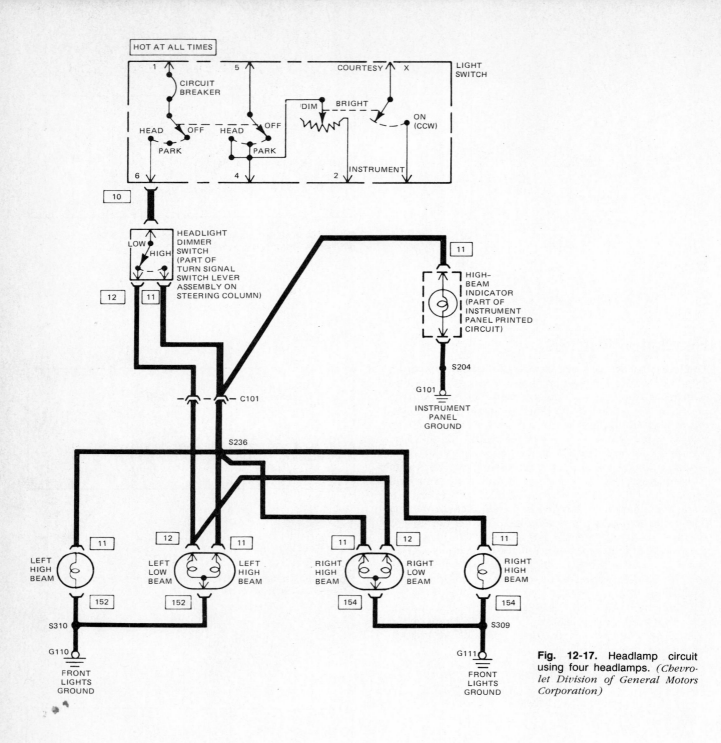

Fig. 12-17. Headlamp circuit using four headlamps. *(Chevrolet Division of General Motors Corporation)*

Headlamp Circuits

Figure 12-17 shows a diagram of a headlamp circuit having four headlamps. The circuit consists of a headlamp switch, a dimmer switch, a high-beam indicator, and the headlamps. Battery voltage is supplied to terminal 1 of the headlamp switch. When the switch is placed in the HEADLAMP position, current flows to the dimmer switch through the circuit breaker located in the switch. The dimmer switch (which is a single-pole double-throw switch) selects either low-beam or high-beam operation. Dimmer switches can be located on a lever on the steering column (Fig. 12-18)

or on the floor. A foot-operated dimmer switch is shown in Fig. 12-19.

When the dimmer switch is in the LOW-BEAM position (Fig. 12-20), battery voltage is supplied to one filament of the dual-filament lamps. When the dimmer switch is in the HIGH-BEAM position, battery voltage is supplied to the other filaments of the dual-filament lamps and to the single-filament lamps (Fig. 12-21). A high-beam indicator lamp on the instrument panel also receives battery voltage when the dimmer switch is in the HIGH-BEAM position. This lamp alerts the driver that the headlamps are operating on high beam.

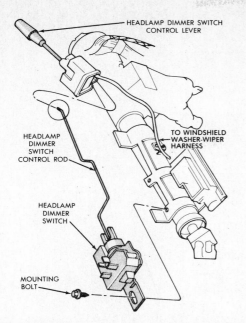

HEADLAMP DIMMER SWITCH CONTROL LEVER

HEADLAMP DIMMER SWITCH CONTROL ROD

HEADLAMP DIMMER SWITCH

MOUNTING BOLT

TO WINDSHIELD WASHER-WIPER HARNESS

WIRING ASSEMBLY

DIMMER SWITCH ASSEMBLY

SCREW

Fig. 12-19. Floor-mounted headlamp dimmer switch. *(Ford Motor Company)*

Fig. 12-18. Headlamp dimmer switch mounted on the steering column. *(Chrysler Corporation)*

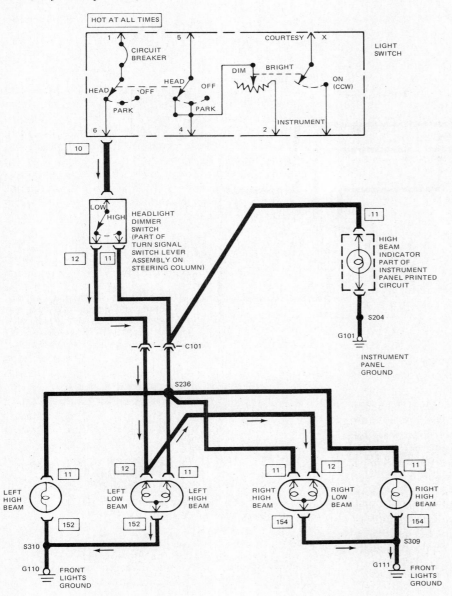

HOT AT ALL TIMES

LIGHT SWITCH

CIRCUIT BREAKER

COURTESY X

DIM BRIGHT

HEAD OFF

HEAD OFF

PARK PARK

ON (CCW)

INSTRUMENT

HEADLIGHT DIMMER SWITCH (PART OF TURN SIGNAL SWITCH LEVER ASSEMBLY ON STEERING COLUMN)

LOW HIGH

HIGH BEAM INDICATOR PART OF INSTRUMENT PANEL PRINTED CIRCUIT

S204

G101

INSTRUMENT PANEL GROUND

C101

S236

LEFT HIGH BEAM

LEFT LOW BEAM

LEFT HIGH BEAM

RIGHT HIGH BEAM

RIGHT LOW BEAM

RIGHT HIGH BEAM

S310

G110 FRONT LIGHTS GROUND

S309

G111 FRONT LIGHTS GROUND

Fig. 12-20. Headlamp circuit diagram, showing current flow with dimmer switch in the LOW BEAM position. *(Chevrolet Division of General Motors Corporation)*

139

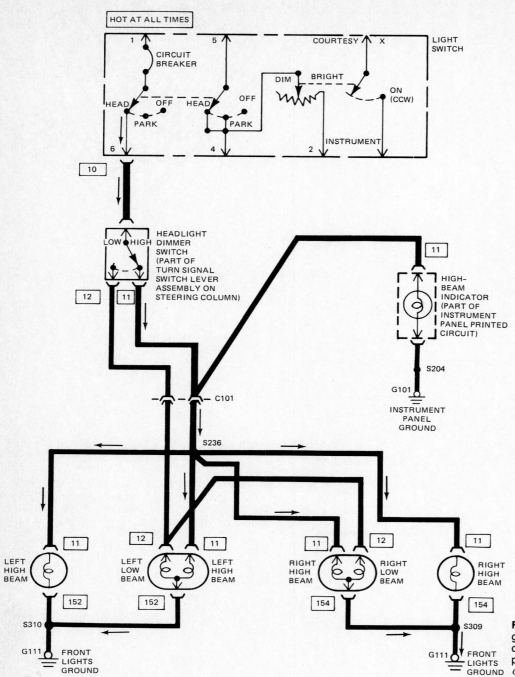

Fig. 12-21. Headlamp circuit diagram, showing current flow with dimmer switch in the HIGH BEAM position. *(Chevrolet Division of General Motors Corporation)*

Concealed Headlamps

Some vehicles have concealed headlamps. When the headlamp switch is off, the lamps are concealed. When the headlamp switch is turned on, doors open to expose the lamps. Headlamps are concealed to enhance vehicle styling and to keep dirt and debris from striking the headlamps when they are not in use. The headlamp doors can be vacuum-operated or electrically operated. Figure 12-22 shows a headlamp switch with a vacuum distribution valve. When the headlamps are turned on, intake manifold vacuum is directed to vacuum motors which control the headlamp doors (Fig. 12-23). When the switch is turned off, vacuum is released from the system and springs pull the doors closed.

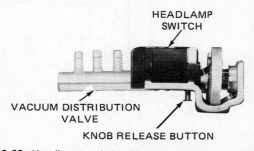

Fig. 12-22. Headlamp switch with a vacuum distribution valve. *(Ford Motor Company)*

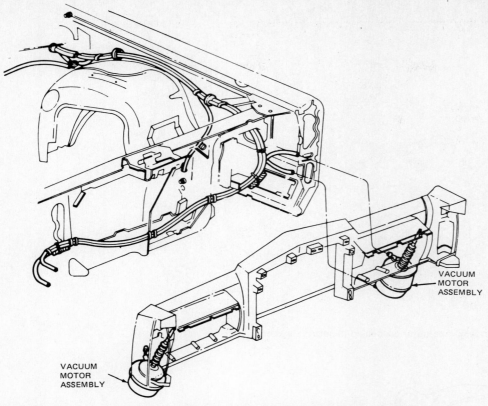

Fig. 12-23. Vacuum-operated concealed-headlamp system. (*Ford Motor Company*)

Figure 12-24 is a diagram of an electrically operated system using an electric motor and a relay. The motor opens and closes both headlamp doors by rotating a torsion bar attached to both doors (Fig. 12-25). The motor has two field windings. When current flows through one winding, the motor rotates in one direction. When current flows through the other winding, the motor rotates in the other direction. The motor rotates in one direction to open the headlamp doors and in the other direction to close the doors. Therefore, one field winding is a door-opening winding, and the other field winding is a door-closing winding.

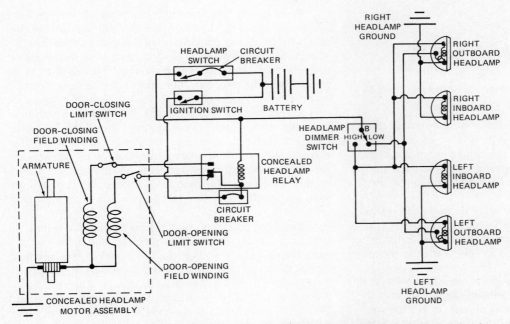

Fig. 12-24. Diagram of an electrically operated concealed-headlamp system. (*Chrysler Corporation*)

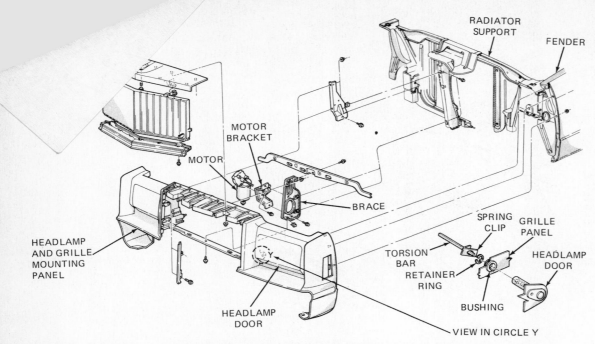

Fig. 12-25. Components of an electrically operated concealed-headlamp system. (*Chrysler Corporation*)

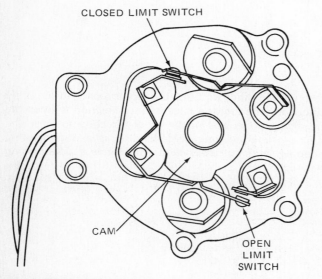

Fig. 12-26. Concealed-headlamp motor limit switches. (*Chrysler Corporation*)

The motor assembly includes a door-opening limit switch and a door-closing limit switch (Fig. 12-26). These switches limit the door travel by turning off the motor when the doors reach their open or closed position. Each limit switch is in series with one field winding and is operated by a cam in the motor assembly.

A single-pole double-throw relay controls the operation of the motor. One terminal of the relay coil is connected to the ignition switch (through a circuit breaker). The other terminal is connected to the headlamp switch and the headlamps.

Assume that the ignition switch is turned on, with the headlamp switch off and the headlamp doors closed (Fig. 12-27). When the ignition switch is turned on, battery voltage is applied to one terminal of the relay coil. When the headlamp switch is off, the coil is grounded through the

headlamp filaments. The filaments act as a ground because the filament resistance is much lower than the resistance of the relay coil. With the coil grounded, the relay is energized and voltage is applied to the door-closing field winding. Because the headlamp doors are closed, the cam on the motor has opened the door-closing limit switch. The limit switch prevents the motor from operating, and the doors remain closed. However, the cam has closed the door-opening limit switch.

When the headlamp switch is turned on, battery voltage is applied to the headlamps and to the terminal of the relay coil that had been grounded through the headlamps. Therefore, battery voltage is applied to both terminals of the relay coil. Because battery voltage is applied to both terminals of the coil, current cannot flow through the coil, and the relay deenergizes (Fig. 12-28). The relay contacts now direct battery voltage to the door-opening winding (through the closed door-opening limit switch). The motor operates to open the headlamp doors. When the doors reach the fully open position, the cam opens the door-opening limit switch. This action stops the motor. At the same time, the cam closes the door-closing limit switch to ready the system for the headlamps to be turned off.

When the headlamp switch is turned off, the relay coil is again grounded. The coil is energized, and the relay contacts direct battery voltage to the door-closing winding (through the closed door-closing limit switch) (Fig. 12-29). The motor operates to close the doors. When the doors reach the fully closed position, the cam opens the door-closing limit switch, which stops the motor. At the same time, the cam closes the door-opening limit switch to ready the system for the next time the headlamps are turned on.

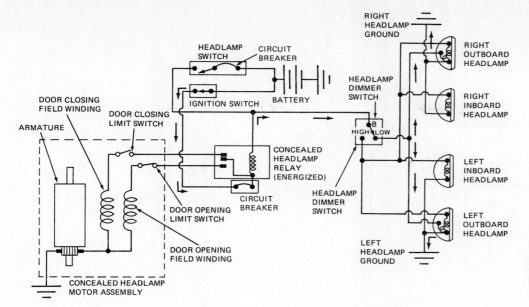

Fig. 12-27. Circuit diagram of a concealed-headlamp system with headlamps off and headlamp doors closed. *(Chrysler Corporation)*

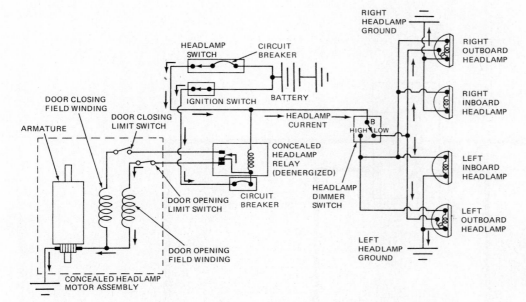

Fig. 12-28. Circuit diagram of a concealed-headlamp system with headlamps on and headlamp doors opening. *(Chrysler Corporation)*

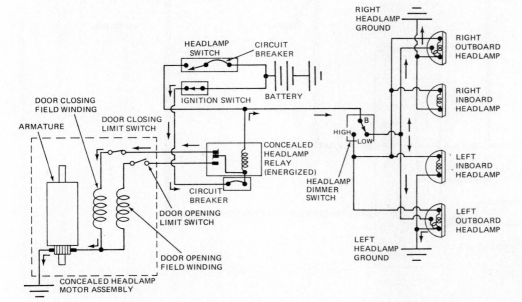

Fig. 12-29. Circuit diagram of a concealed headlamp system with headlamps off and headlamp doors closing. *(Chrysler Corporation)*

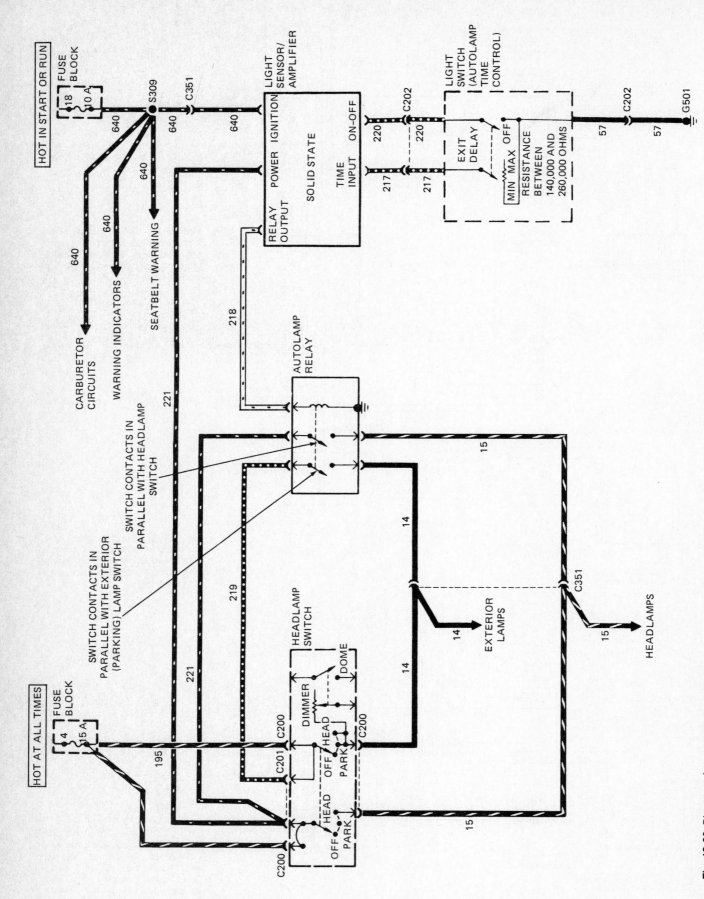

Fig. 12-30. Diagram of an automatic and delayed-exit headlamp and lighting system. *(Ford Motor Company)*

144

Automatic and Delayed-Exit Headlamp and Lighting Systems

An automatic and delayed-exit headlamp and lighting system performs two functions. It automatically switches on the headlamps when the outside light decreases below a certain level. In addition, it allows the headlamps to remain on to provide light when passengers are exiting the vehicle. In the system shown in Fig. 12-30, a photocell is used to turn on lights which are normally controlled by the headlamp switch. A *photocell* is a device that changes in resistance when exposed to light. The photocell is located above the instrument panel and is exposed to outside light (Fig. 12-31). When the light decreases below a certain level, the photocell triggers a sensor-amplifier module. The sensor-amplifier module operates a relay which is connected in parallel with the headlamp switch. In the system shown in Fig. 12-30, the relay has two sets of single-pole single-throw contacts. One set of contacts is in parallel with the headlamp switch contacts that control the headlamps. The other set is in parallel with the contacts that control the parking lamps. Therefore, when the outside light decreases, the headlamps and parking lamps are automatically switched on. If the outside light increases, the lamps will automatically turn off.

The automatic feature will only operate if the headlamp switch is in the OFF position. When the headlamp switch is pulled on, it overrides the automatic operation. When the vehicle has concealed headlamps, the automatic operation includes opening and closing the headlamp doors.

Another part of this system is the delayed-exit feature. *Delayed exit* means the headlamps remain on for a short time after the ignition switch is turned off. The driver can adjust the time delay by turning a control on the headlamp switch assembly (Fig. 12-32). The control is a *potentiometer* (a variable resistor). In the system shown, the time delay can be adjusted to as long as 4½ minutes. The delayed turn-off provides light for the occupants when they are leaving the vehicle.

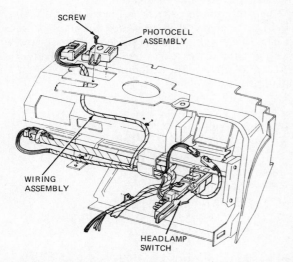

Fig. 12-31. Location of photocell assembly for an automatic headlamp system. (*Ford Motor Company*)

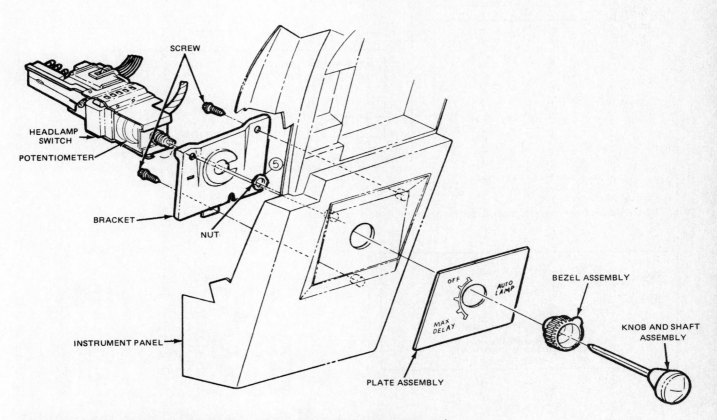

Fig. 12-32. Headlamp switch in an automatic headlamp system. (*Ford Motor Company*)

Automatic Headlamp Dimmer Circuits

Figure 12-33 shows a diagram of an automatic headlamp dimmer circuit. This system automatically switches the headlamps from high beam to low beam under either of the following conditions:

- When light from the headlights of an approaching vehicle strikes the sensor-amplifier
- When light from the taillights of a vehicle that is being overtaken strikes the sensor-amplifier

The system consists of a light sensor-amplifier unit, a high-beam–low-beam relay, a sensitivity control, and a dimmer switch. The light sensor-amplifier unit is mounted toward the front of the vehicle in a position that will receive light (Fig. 12-34). Because the sensor position is critical, a method of aligning or leveling the sensor is provided.

Battery voltage is applied to one terminal of the high-beam–low-beam relay coil through circuit 221. When the headlamp switch is on and the dimmer switch is in the LOW-BEAM position, the relay is not energized (Fig. 12-35). This is because with the dimmer switch in the LOW-BEAM position, the other terminal of the relay coil is not grounded. With the relay not energized, battery voltage is applied to the low-beam filaments of the headlamps through the normally closed contacts of the relay.

When the dimmer switch is placed in the AUTOMATIC position, the relay coil is grounded through the sensor-amplifier (if no light is being sensed) (Fig. 12-36). With the coil grounded, the relay is energized, and battery voltage is applied to the high-beam filaments of the headlamps.

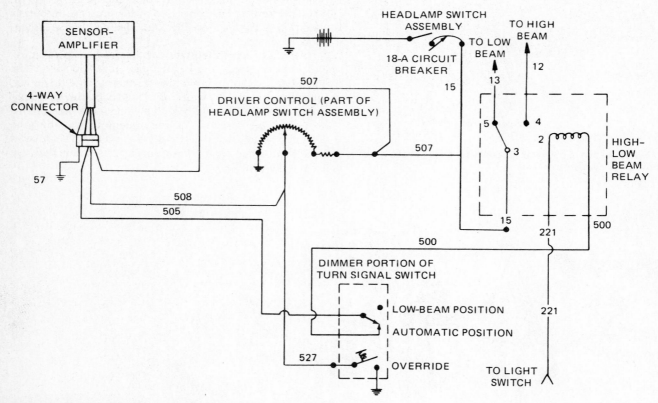

Fig. 12-33. Automatic headlamp dimmer circuit diagram. *(Ford Motor Company)*

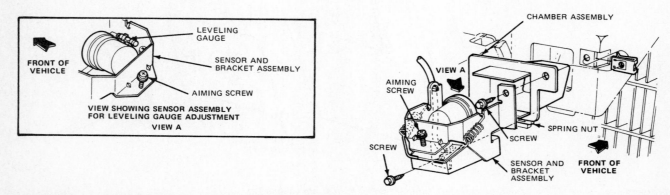

Fig. 12-34. Automatic headlamp dimmer sensor installation. *(Ford Motor Company)*

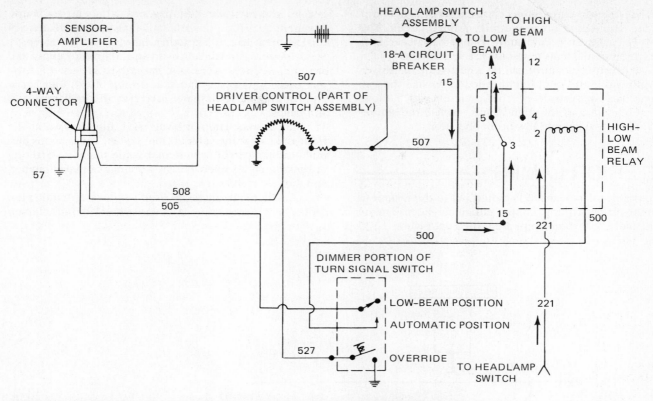

Fig. 12-35. Automatic dimmer system, showing current flow with dimmer switch in LOW-BEAM position. *(Ford Motor Company)*

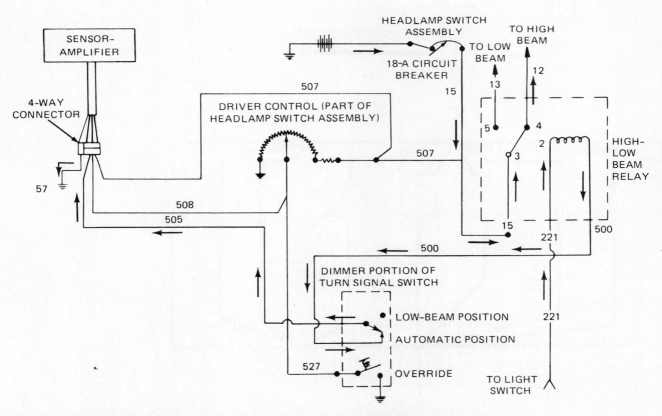

Fig. 12-36. Automatic dimmer system, showing current flow with dimmer switch in AUTOMATIC position (no light being sensed). *(Ford Motor Company)*

When the sensor receives a certain level of light, it triggers the amplifier to break the relay ground circuit. This deenergizes the relay, and battery voltage is switched from the high-beam filaments to the low-beam filaments.

The sensitivity control can be adjusted by the driver, and it adjusts the level of light needed to operate the sensor-amplifier. An override switch is provided which allows manual operation of the high beams, even if the sensor-amplifier has switched to low-beam operation.

EXTERIOR LAMPS

When the headlamp switch is pulled out to the PARK position, the front parking lamps, taillamps, license plate lamps, and side marker lamps are turned on. Figures 12-37

and 12-38 show two circuit diagrams of the exterior lamps. The front parking lamps and taillamps use one filament of dual-filament lamps. The other filament of these lamps is used for turn signal lamps, hazard warning lamps, and stoplamps. Often, more than two lamps are used for the rear taillamp-stoplamp function. In Fig. 12-37, four lamps are used. Red lenses are used for the taillamps and stoplamps.

Side marker lamps provide side illumination at the front and rear of the vehicle (Fig. 12-39). These lamps permit the vehicle to be seen from the side when it is entering or backing onto a roadway. The front marker lens is amber, and the rear marker lens is red.

License plate lamps are used to provide illumination for the rear license plate. A license plate lamp installation is shown in Fig. 12-40.

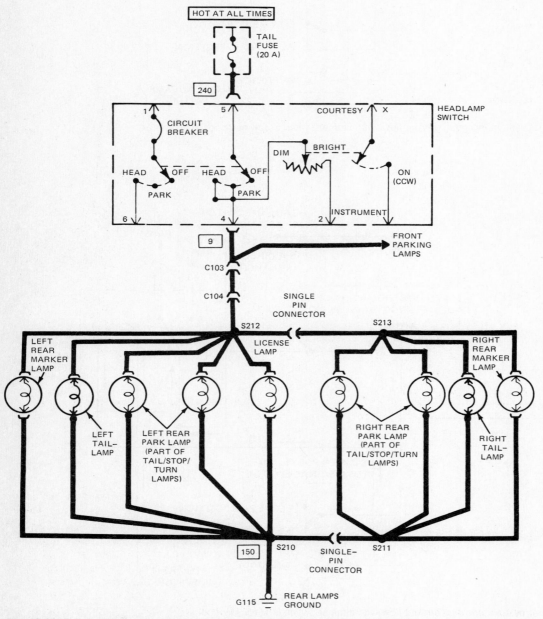

Fig. 12-37. Exterior lighting diagram. (*Chevrolet Division of General Motors Corporation*)

148

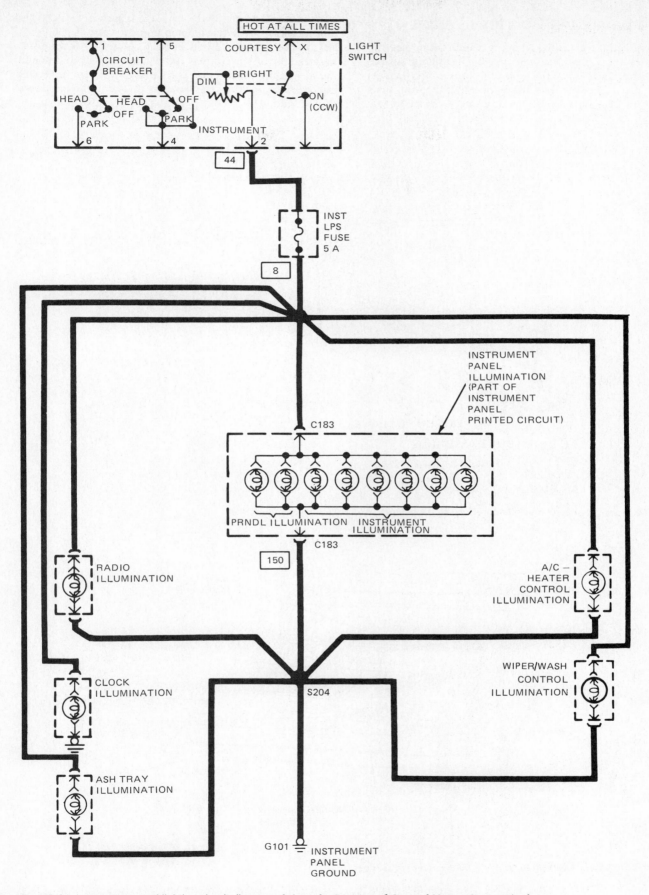

Fig. 12-61. Instrument-panel lighting circuit diagram. *(Chevrolet Division of General Motors Corporation)*

Dome Lamp and Courtesy Lamps

The dome lamp and courtesy lamps, which illuminate the vehicle interior, are controlled by the headlamp switch. Courtesy lamps are sometimes located in door-trim panels (Fig. 12-62), under the dash panel, or under the front seats (Fig. 12-63). Figure 12-64 shows an example of a courtesy lamp circuit diagram. Battery voltage is supplied directly to one terminal of the dome lamp and the courtesy lamps. A set of contacts in the headlamp switch is connected between the other terminal of the lamps and ground. When the headlamp switch knob is rotated to the extreme counterclockwise position, the contacts close and the lamps are illuminated.

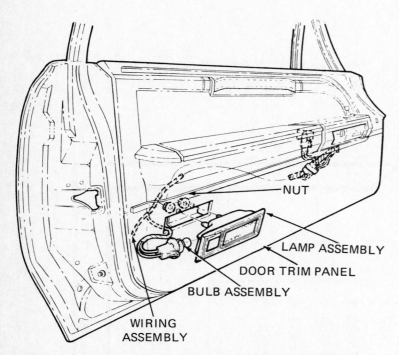

NUT

LAMP ASSEMBLY

DOOR TRIM PANEL

BULB ASSEMBLY

WIRING ASSEMBLY

Fig. 12-62. Door-mounted courtesy lamp. *(Ford Motor Company)*

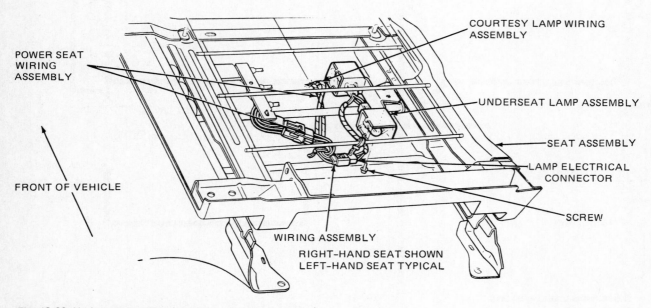

COURTESY LAMP WIRING ASSEMBLY

POWER SEAT WIRING ASSEMBLY

UNDERSEAT LAMP ASSEMBLY

SEAT ASSEMBLY

LAMP ELECTRICAL CONNECTOR

FRONT OF VEHICLE

SCREW

WIRING ASSEMBLY

RIGHT-HAND SEAT SHOWN LEFT-HAND SEAT TYPICAL

Fig. 12-63. Underseat courtesy lamp. *(Ford Motor Company)*

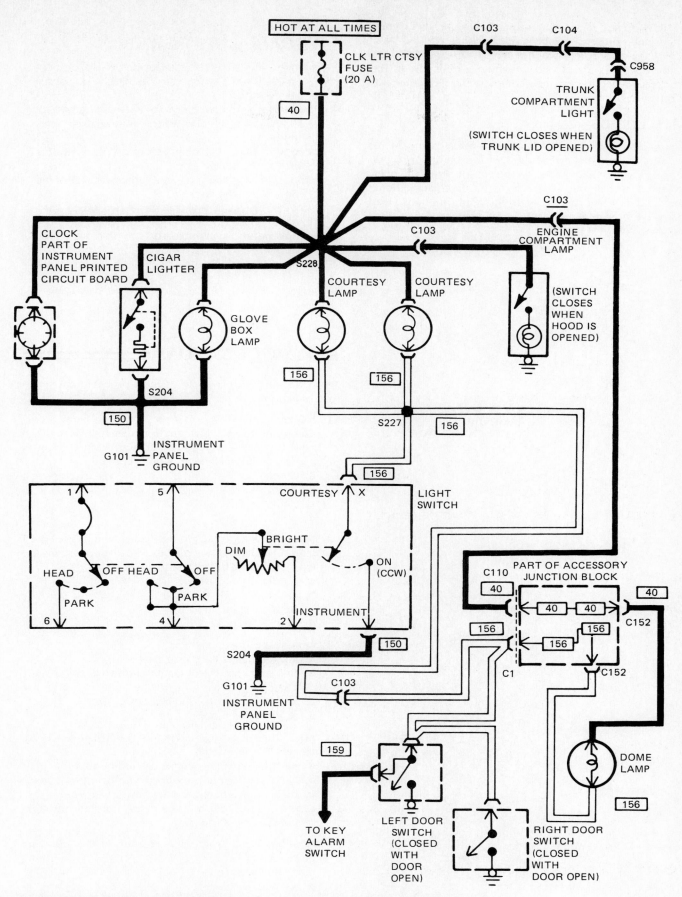

Fig. 12-64. Courtesy lamp circuit diagram. *(Chevrolet Division of General Motors Corporation)*

The dome lamp and courtesy lamps are also illuminated when either the left or right door is opened. Normally closed doorjamb switches (Fig. 12-65) are held open when the doors are closed. Opening a door allows the doorjamb switch to close and complete the ground circuit of the lamps.

Map Lamps

A *map lamp* is a lamp that is placed on the dash panel or headliner to provide a reading light for the driver or passenger. A switch is provided on the lamp assembly to operate the lamp. Figure 12-66 shows a combination dome lamp and map lamp assembly. In this application, two map lamps are provided, and each lamp is operated by a separate switch.

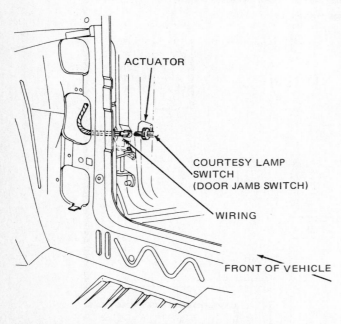

Fig. 12-65. Doorjamb switch. *(Ford Motor Company)*

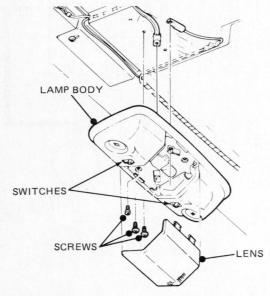

Fig. 12-66. Dome lamp and map lamp assembly. *(Ford Motor Company)*

158

REVIEW QUESTIONS

Select the *one* correct, best, or most probable answer to each question.

1. Mechanic A says the glass envelope of a lamp is only used to protect the filament from damage. Mechanic B says the glass envelope prevents air from coming in contact with the filament. Who is correct?
   a. A only
   b. B only
   c. both A and B
   d. neither A nor B

2. Mechanic A says that two-headlamp systems use type 1 lamps. Mechanic B says that two-headlamp systems use type 2 lamps. Who is correct?
   a. A only
   b. B only
   c. both A and B
   d. neither A nor B

3. On four-headlamp systems
   a. all four lamps are type 1 lamps
   b. two lamps are type 1 lamps, and two lamps are type 2 lamps
   c. all four lamps are type 2 lamps
   d. none of the above

4. All of the following statements about halogen headlamps are true *except*
   a. most halogen headlamps use iodine vapor
   b. lamp blackening is reduced with halogen lamps
   c. halogen headlamps do not have a filament
   d. the light output remains nearly constant throughout the life of the lamp

5. Most headlamp switches contain all of the following items *except*
   a. a dimmer switch
   b. a circuit breaker
   c. two-pole three-position switch contacts
   d. a rheostat

6. Concerning an electrically operated concealed-head-lamp system, Mechanic A says the limit switches limit the headlamp-door travel. Mechanic B says the limit switches are in series with the motor field windings. Who is correct?
   a. A only
   b. B only
   c. both A and B
   d. neither A nor B

7. All of the following statements are true concerning the automatic headlamp system described in this chapter *except*
   a. a photocell is used as a light sensor
   b. the relay contacts are in parallel with the headlamp switch contacts
   c. automatic operation will not occur if the headlamp switch is off
   d. the sensor-amplifier module operates the relay

8. All of the following lamps are operated when the headlamp switch is in the PARK position *except*
   a. courtesy lamps
   b. side marker lamps
   c. the license plate lamp
   d. instrument-panel lamps

9. All of the following lamps are wired through the turn signal switch *except*
   a. backup lamps
   b. turn signal lamps
   c. hazard warning lamps
   d. stoplamps

10. All of the following statements are true *except*
   a. the instrument-panel lamp brightness is controlled by a rheostat in the headlamp switch
   b. flasher units use a bimetallic strip to control a set of normally closed contacts
   c. courtesy lamps can be controlled by a doorjamb switch or the headlamp switch
   d. cornering lamps flash on and off with the turn signals

CHAPTER 13

HORN CIRCUITS AND WINDSHIELD WIPER AND WASHER CIRCUITS

OBJECTIVES

After you have studied this chapter, you should be able to:

1. Describe the operation of horn circuits.

2. Describe the operation of windshield wiper and washer circuits.

HORNS

A *horn* is a device operated by the driver to produce an audible warning signal (Fig. 13-1). Sound is produced from a horn when a column of air is caused to vibrate. This is the same way that sound is produced in many types of musical instruments. The number of vibrations per second is called the *frequency*. The quality of the sound is called the *tone*. The design and shape of the horn determine the frequency and tone of the sound. Most automotive horns have a coiled construction similar in shape to a seashell.

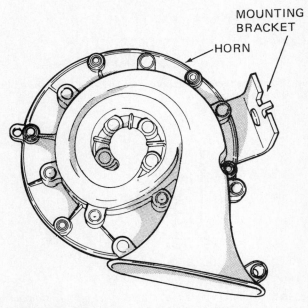

Fig. 13-1. Automotive horn. *(Chrysler Corporation)*

Horns are usually designed to produce notes of the musical scale. Horns can be used singly or in pairs. On some vehicles, three or four horns are used. When more than one horn is used, the frequencies of the sounds are chosen to produce an ear-pleasing combination. One combination of notes that is used is F and A, which have frequencies of 360 and 447 vibrations per second, respectively. Delco-Remy manufactures horns of the following frequencies:

Note	Frequency
D	300
F	360
A	447
C	524

When two horns are used, one is called the *low-note horn*. The other is the *high-note horn*.

Figure 13-2 shows the construction of a horn. A set of normally closed switch contacts is wired in series with a coil of wire (Fig. 13-3). A moveable core, called an armature, is positioned partially inside the coil. One end of the armature is attached to a *diaphragm*. The diaphragm is a thin, flexible, circular plate that is held around its outer edge by the horn housing. Because the diaphragm is flexible, the armature can move a small distance in and out of the coil. The diaphragm acts as a type of spring. When it is deflected and released, it will return to its rest position.

When voltage is applied to the horn, the coil becomes an electromagnet and attracts the armature toward it. The armature is moved against the spring tension of the diaphragm. The movement of the armature opens the switch contacts, which breaks the current flow to the coil. This releases the armature, which is then pulled back by the diaphragm. The movement allows the switch contacts to close. This action repeats itself rapidly, which causes the armature to vibrate. The diaphragm also vibrates, which causes the column of air inside the horn to vibrate. The vibration of the column of air produces the sound. The electrical operation of the horn is the same as that of the buzzer described in Chap. 3.

Some horn circuits have a relay. The relay controls the horn current. The horn switch controls the relay (Fig. 13-4). This allows the horn switch to carry the small relay current, while the relay contacts carry the larger horn current. The switch is in the relay ground circuit. The horn switch closes to operate the relay (and the horn).

Horn switches can be located on the steering wheel (Fig. 13-5) or on a lever (stalk) which attaches to the steering column (Fig. 13-6). Steering-wheel-mounted switches must operate in all positions of the steering wheel. Therefore, in a steering-wheel-mounted switch, the connection from the relay to the switch must pass through a set of sliding contacts. A circular contact in the steering wheel slides against a spring-loaded contact in the steering column. In this way, the horn switch is connected to the wire from the relay in any position of the steering wheel.

Figure 13-7 shows a horn circuit using a single horn. The switch controls the horn current directly (without a relay). In this design, the horn switch grounds the horn. In

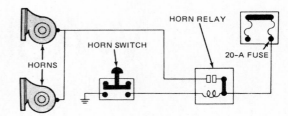

Fig. 13-4. Horn circuit which uses a relay. (*Chrysler Corporation*)

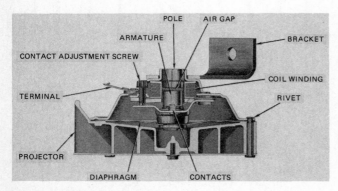

Fig. 13-2. Construction of a horn. (*Delco-Remy Division of General Motors Corporation*)

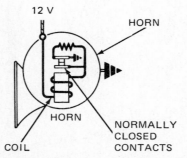

Fig. 13-3. Electrical diagram of a horn. (*Delco-Remy Division of General Motors Corporation*)

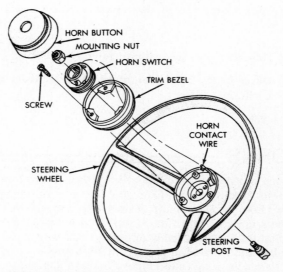

Fig. 13-5. Horn switch located in the center of the steering wheel. (*Chrysler Corporation*)

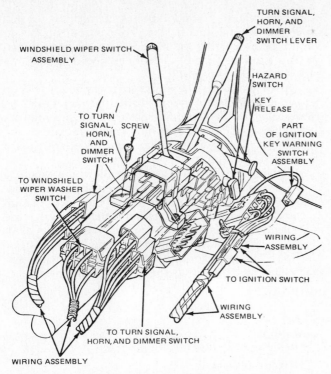

Fig. 13-6. Horn switch located on a lever (stalk) which attaches to the steering column. *(Ford Motor Company)*

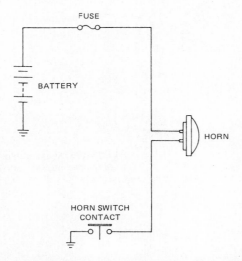

Fig. 13-7. Horn circuit which uses the horn switch to ground the horn. *(Chevrolet Division of General Motors Corporation)*

other designs, the horn is grounded, and the horn switch supplies 12 volts (V) to the horn (Fig. 13-8).

WINDSHIELD WIPERS

Windshield wipers are mechanical arms which sweep back and forth across the windshield to remove water, snow, or dirt (Fig. 13-9). The wiper arms have rubber blades which contact the windshield. Most vehicles have two wiper arms for the windshield. Some have an additional wiper arm for the rear window (Fig. 13-10). Windshield wipers are operated by a wiper switch (controlled by the driver), a wiper motor, and a mechanism which links the motor to the

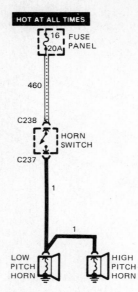

Fig. 13-8. Horn circuit which uses the horn switch to apply battery voltage to the horn. *(Ford Motor Company)*

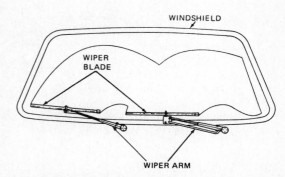

Fig. 13-9. Windshield wiper sweep pattern. *(Ford Motor Company)*

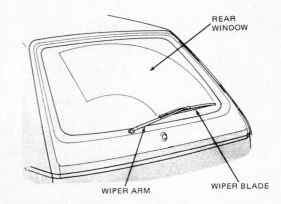

Fig. 13-10. Rear-window wiper. *(Chrysler Corporation)*

wiper arms. Wiper switches can be mounted on the dashboard or on the steering column (Fig. 13-11). The wiper mechanism includes a gear-reduction unit at the motor (Fig. 13-12). A crank and linkage connect to the wiper arms (Fig. 13-13) and convert the rotary motion of the motor into the back-and-forth movement of the wiper arms.

When windshield wipers are turned off, they assume a rest position at the lower-moulding edge of the windshield. This rest position is called the PARK position. A set

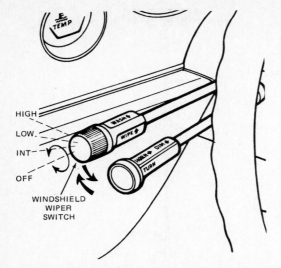

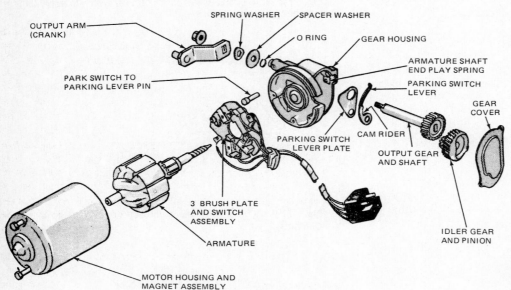

Fig. 13-11. Wiper switch mounted on the steering column. *(Ford Motor Company)*

of switch contacts, called the PARK CONTACTS, is located inside the motor assembly. The park contacts supply current to the motor after the wiper switch has been turned off. This allows the motor to continue operating until the wipers reach the PARK position.

On some vehicles, the wipers are concealed. They stop below the rear edge of the hood after they are turned off. This is called the DEPRESSED-PARK position. A depressed-park system has an additional switching circuit. It operates the wiper motor in reverse for the short time necessary to reach the DEPRESSED-PARK position.

Many vehicles have a feature that allows the wipers to be run intermittently. The wipers sweep across the windshield, pause for a certain interval, and then sweep again. A control allows the driver to select the time interval. Some systems permit time intervals of up to 25 seconds. A module or governor unit controls the switching and time-delay functions. The governor unit for some interval wiper systems is mounted on the steering column (Fig. 13-14).

Fig. 13-12. Disassembled windshield wiper motor. *(Ford Motor Company)*

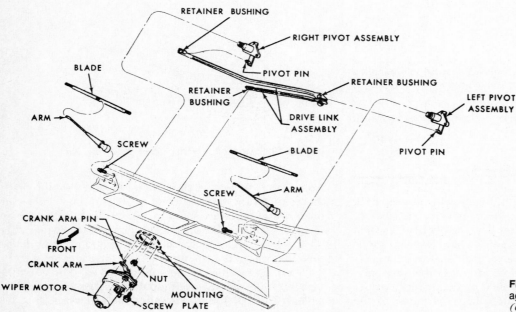

Fig. 13-13. Windshield wiper linkage and drive mechanism. *(Chrysler Corporation)*

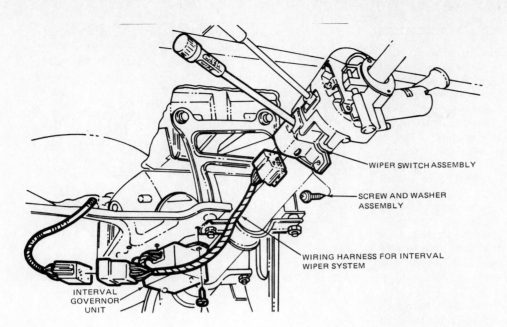

Fig. 13-14. Interval governor unit.
(Ford Motor Company)

Wiper Motors

Most windshield wiper motors are two-speed electric motors with permanent field magnets. Three brushes contact the commutator: a high-speed brush, a low-speed brush, and a common brush (Fig. 13-15). The common brush conducts current during both high-speed and low-speed operation. On most motors, the low-speed brush is positioned directly opposite the common brush, and the high-speed brush is slightly offset from the low-speed brush.

The speed of the motor is controlled by the number of armature windings that are connected in the circuit. The brushes are positioned so that fewer armature windings are connected between the high-speed brush and the common brush. More armature windings are connected between the low-speed brush and the common brush. When battery voltage is applied to fewer armature windings (from the high-speed brush to the common brush), the armature speed is high. This is because with fewer armature windings, there is less magnetism in the armature and a lower counterelectromotive force (cemf). Because the cemf opposes battery voltage, a lower cemf in the armature means there will be greater armature current. Greater armature current means a higher armature speed.

When battery voltage is applied to more armature windings (from the low-speed brush to the common brush), the armature speed is low. This is because with more armature windings, there is more magnetism in the armature and a higher cemf. A higher cemf means there will be less armature current. This results in a lower armature speed.

Motors with electromagnetic fields are sometimes used. Figure 13-16 shows a motor with a series field and a shunt field. Motor speed is controlled by switching a resistor into and out of the shunt field. The motor speed is higher with the resistor connected. With a resistor in the shunt field, there is less field current and, therefore, less magnetism in the shunt field. With less magnetism in the shunt field, there will be a lower cemf in the armature. A lower cemf means there will be greater armature current, which results in a higher motor speed. Because control of motor speed is done by changing field current, this type of motor uses only two brushes.

Many windshield wiper motors have a built-in circuit breaker. Use of a circuit breaker prevents a temporary overload from totally disabling the wipers. On some systems, the circuit breaker is located in the fuse panel.

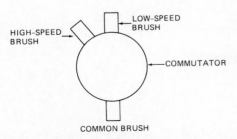

Fig. 13-15. Brush arrangement for two-speed wiper motor with permanent field magnets.

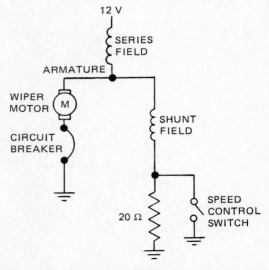

Fig. 13-16. Windshield wiper motor with electromagnetic fields.
(Chevrolet Division of General Motors Corporation)

WINDSHIELD WASHERS

Windshield washers spray washer fluid onto the windshield so that dirt may be easily removed by the wipers. A small plastic reservoir holds a supply of washer fluid. An electrically operated pump provides a supply of pressurized fluid to one or more spray nozzles. The nozzles direct small streams of fluid onto the windshield. On some systems, the washer pump is part of the wiper motor assembly (Fig. 13-17). Other systems use a pump which is located in the reservoir (Fig. 13-18).

The washer pump shown in Figure 13-17 uses a small piston to pump the washer fluid (Fig. 13-19). When the washer switch is operated, a solenoid engages a piston actuator to the wiper motor. When this occurs, the wiper motor moves the piston to operate the washer pump, which has one intake valve and two exhaust valves. On the intake stroke of the piston (Fig. 13-19*a*), fluid is drawn into the chamber. On the exhaust stroke (Fig 13-19*b*), fluid is pumped to both spray nozzles.

In another type of washer, a small electric motor drives a centrifugal pump. A centrifugal pump has an *impeller* (a disk with spiral fins or vanes) which rotates and pushes the fluid outward by centrifugal force.

CIRCUIT DESCRIPTIONS

Circuit descriptions of some common windshield wiper and washer systems follow.

Basic Two-Speed Wiper and Washer System with Permanent Field Magnets

Figure 13-20 shows an American Motors windshield wiper and washer system. The wiper motor has two speeds and

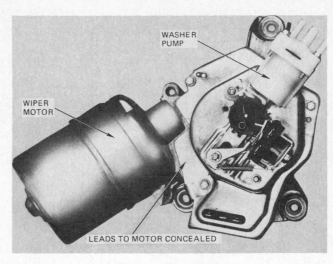

Fig. 13-17. Wiper motor and washer pump assembly. *(Chevrolet Division of General Motors Corporation)*

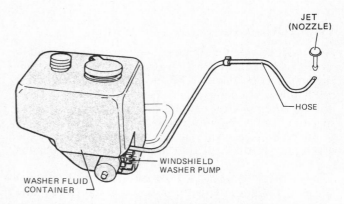

Fig. 13-18. Washer pump located in the fluid reservoir. *(Volkswagen of America)*

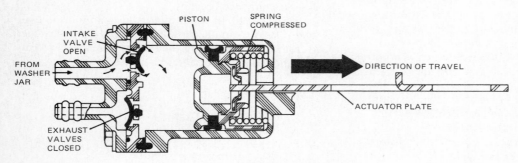

(a) INTAKE STROKE

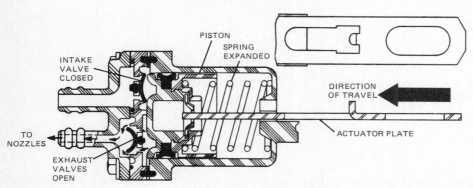

(b) EXHAUST STROKE

Fig. 13-19. Washer pump operation. *(Chevrolet Division of General Motors Corporation)*

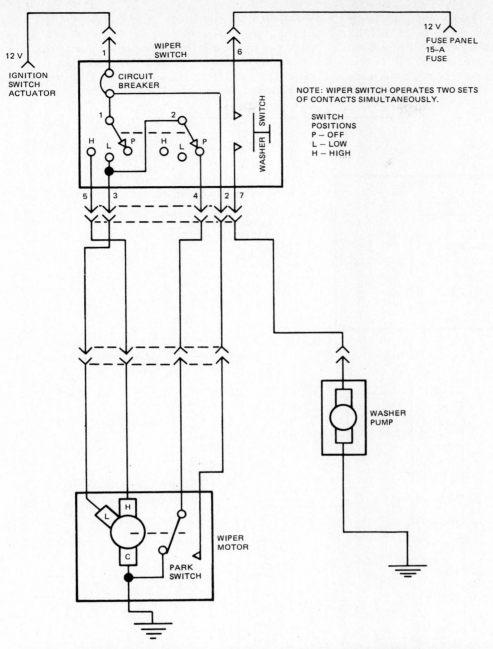

Fig. 13-20. Diagram of a two-speed wiper and washer system with permanent field magnets. *(American Motors Corporation)*

uses permanent field magnets. The wiper switch is a two-pole three-position switch. The positions are HIGH SPEED, LOW SPEED, and OFF (PARK). The washer switch is a single-pole single-throw switch. Battery voltage is supplied to the system from two sources. The ignition switch supplies battery voltage to the wiper switch through a circuit breaker located in the wiper switch. Battery voltage is supplied to the washer switch from a fuse located in the fuse panel.

A set of park contacts are included in the motor assembly. These contacts open and close with each motor rotation. For approximately nine-tenths of the wiper arm movement, the park contacts are in the position shown in Fig. 13-21a. For approximately one-tenth of the wiper arm movement, the park contacts are in the position shown in Fig. 13-21b.

The wiper switch, being a two-pole switch, has two sets of contacts which are independent of each other. Con-

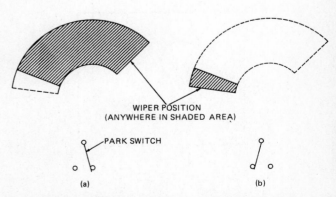

Fig. 13-21. Park switch operation. (*a*) Contact position for nine-tenths of the wiper arm movement. (*b*) Contact position for one-tenth of the wiper arm movement.

tact set 1 switches battery voltage to the wiper motor in the HIGH-SPEED and LOW-SPEED positions and is off in the PARK position. Contact set 2 does not function in the HIGH-SPEED or LOW-SPEED switch positions, but contact set 2 does connect a park switch contact to the low-speed brush in the PARK position.

Figure 13-22 shows the current flow with the wiper switch in the HIGH-SPEED position. Current flow is through the wiper switch, the high-speed brush, the armature, and the common brush to ground. The park contacts in the motor open and close as shown in Fig. 13-21, but they do not affect the circuit operation.

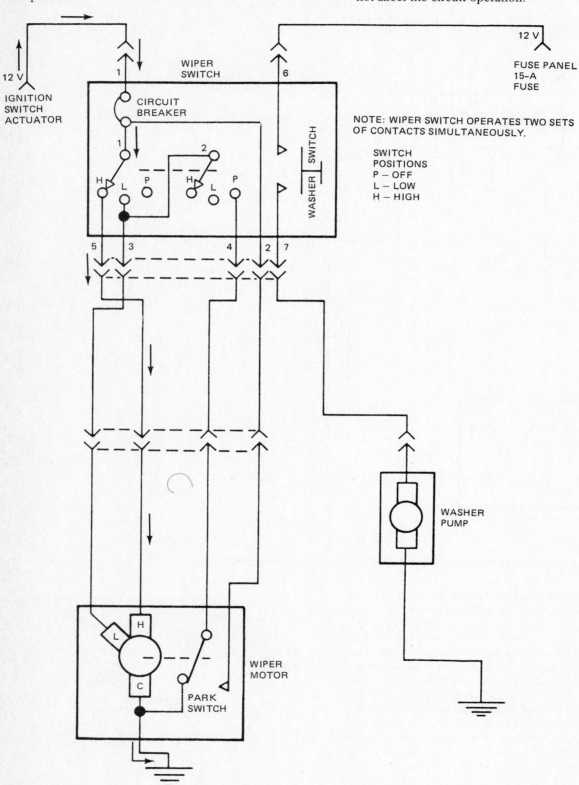

Fig. 13-22. Current flow in windshield wiper circuit of Fig. 13-20 with wiper switch in the HIGH-SPEED position. *(American Motors Corporation)*

168

Figure 13-23 shows the current flow with the wiper switch in the LOW-SPEED position. Current flow is through the wiper switch, the low-speed brush, the armature, and the common brush to ground. The park contacts open and close in this position also and do not affect the circuit operation.

Figure 13-24 shows the current flow with the wiper switch in the OFF (or PARK) position. When the wipers are turned off with the wipers in the position shown in Fig. 13-21a, the park contacts supply 12 V to the low-speed brush. Current flow is from the circuit breaker, through the park contacts, through wiper switch contact set 2, to the low-

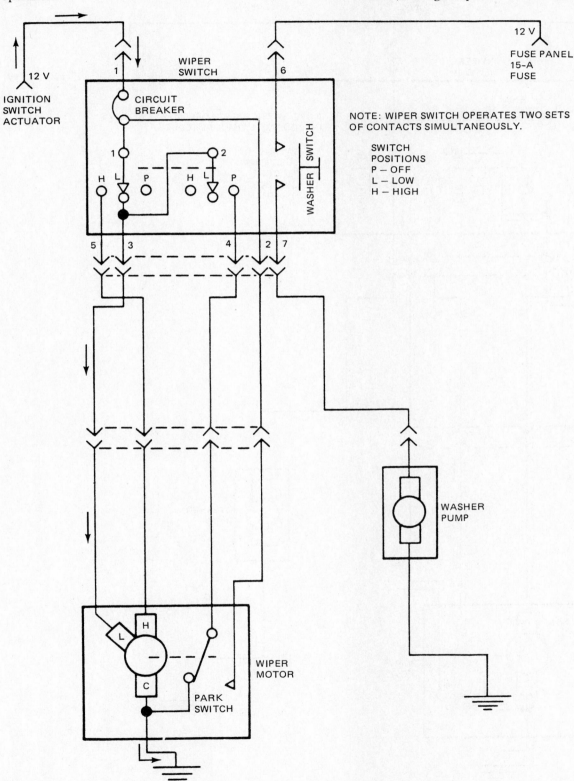

Fig. 13-23. Current flow in windshield wiper circuit of Fig. 13-20 with wiper switch in the LOW-SPEED position. *(American Motors Corporation)*

speed brush. Therefore, the wiper motor continues to operate at low speed after the wiper switch is turned off. When the wiper arms reach the PARK position (Fig. 13-21b), the park contacts break the current flow to the low-speed brush. The motor stops, and the wiper arms remain in the PARK position. The park contacts allow the wipers to stop in the PARK position no matter what position they were in when they were switched off.

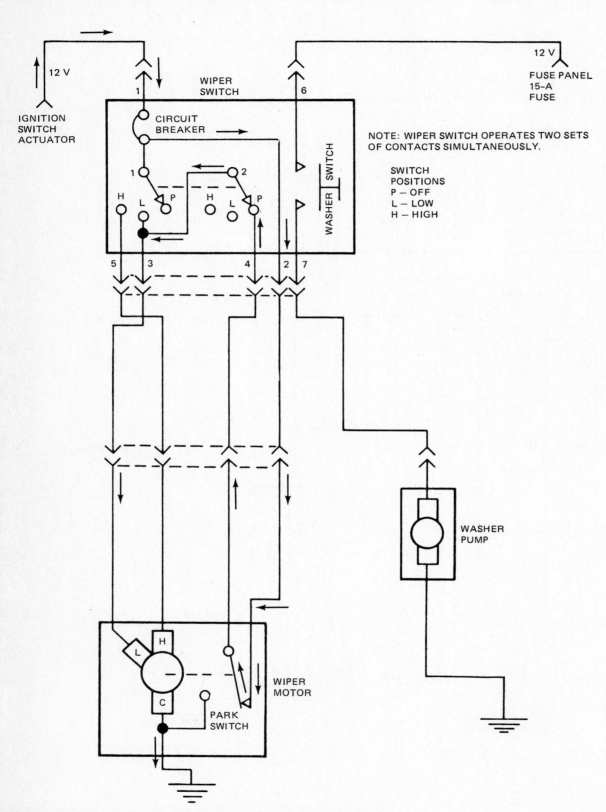

Fig. 13-24. Current flow in windshield wiper circuit of Fig. 13-20 with wiper switch in the OFF (or PARK) position. *(American Motors Corporation)*

Basic Two-Speed Wiper and Washer System with Electromagnetic Field

Figure 13-25 shows a General Motors windshield wiper and washer system which uses a two-speed wiper motor with an electromagnetic field. Battery voltage is supplied to the system through a fuse in the fuse panel. A circuit breaker is placed in series with the wiper motor to prevent a temporary overload from blowing the fuse. The wiper switch is a two-pole three-position switch. The positions are HIGH SPEED, LOW SPEED, and OFF (PARK). The wiper switch operates a relay in both the HIGH-SPEED and LOW-SPEED positions. The relay contacts control current flow to the motor. The washer pump motor is controlled by a single-pole single-throw switch.

The wiper motor has a series field and a shunt field. The motor speed is changed by changing the resistance in the shunt field. A resistor is switched into the field for high-speed operation. For low-speed operation, no resistance is used in the field. The wiper switch performs this function by switching a 20-ohm (Ω) resistor into, and out of, the field.

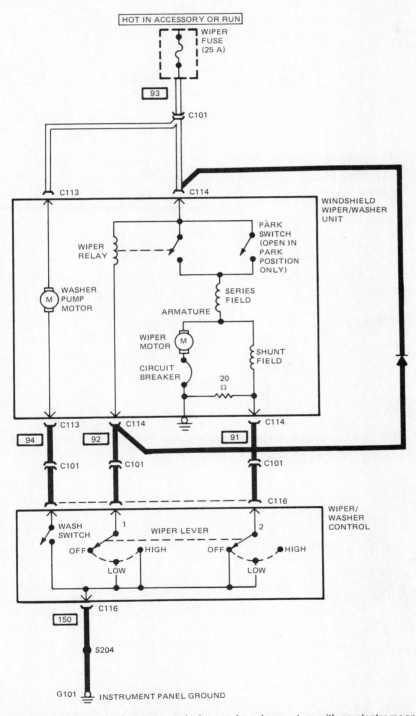

Fig. 13-25. Diagram of a two-speed wiper and washer system with an electromagnetic field. (*Chevrolet Division of General Motors Corporation*)

Because the wiper switch is a two-pole switch, there are two separate sets of switch contacts. Contact set 1 operates the relay which in turn controls current to the wiper motor. Contact set 2 controls the high and low wiper motor speeds.

A set of park contacts is included in the motor assembly. The park contacts supply current to the motor after the wiper switch has been turned off. This allows the wipers to continue to the PARK position. The circuit operation is described below.

> NOTE   Some General Motors wiper motors do not use park contacts. Instead, a small device (*pawl*) rotates with the motor shaft and latches into an arm on the relay. The latching occurs only after the wiper switch is turned off, and it opens the relay contacts to stop the motor in the PARK position (Fig. 13-26).

Figure 13-27 shows the current flow with the wiper switch in the HIGH-SPEED position. Contact set 1 grounds the wiper relay, which closes its contacts. Contact set 2 does not function in this switch position. Current flow is through the relay contacts, the series field, the shunt field, and the 20-Ω resistor to ground. The resistance in the shunt field causes the motor speed to be high. The park contacts open and close with each motor rotation, but they do not affect the circuit operation.

Figure 13-28 shows the current flow with the wiper switch in the LOW-SPEED position. Current flow is through the relay contacts, the series field, the shunt field, and con-

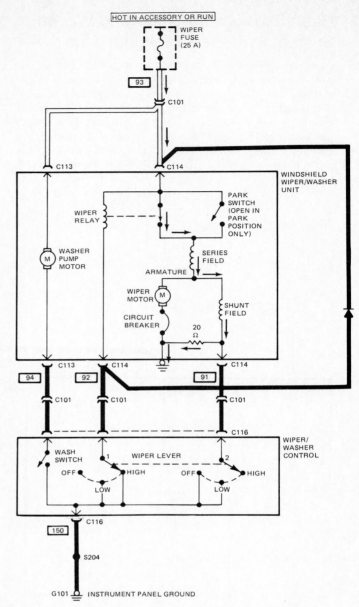

Fig. 13-27. Current flow in windshield wiper circuit of Fig. 13-25 with wiper switch in the HIGH-SPEED position. (*Chevrolet Division of General Motors Corporation*)

tact set 2 to ground. No resistance in the shunt field causes the motor speed to be low. As in the HIGH-SPEED position, the park contacts open and close but do not affect the circuit operation.

Figure 13-29 shows the current flow with the wiper switch in the OFF, or PARK, position. When the wiper switch is turned off with the wiper arms in the position shown in Fig. 13-21a, the park contacts supply current to the wiper motor. Therefore, the motor continues to operate after the wiper switch is turned off. The motor operates at low speed, because contact set 2 grounds the shunt field. With no resistance in the field, the motor speed is low.

When the wiper arms reach the PARK position (Fig. 13-21b), the park contacts open and stop the current flow to

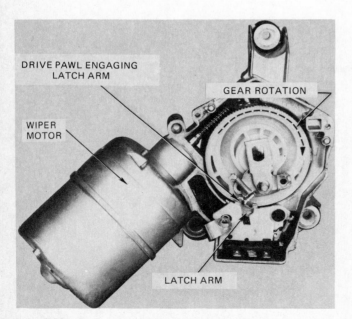

Fig. 13-26. Wiper motor about to stop in the PARK position. (*Chevrolet Division of General Motors Corporation*)

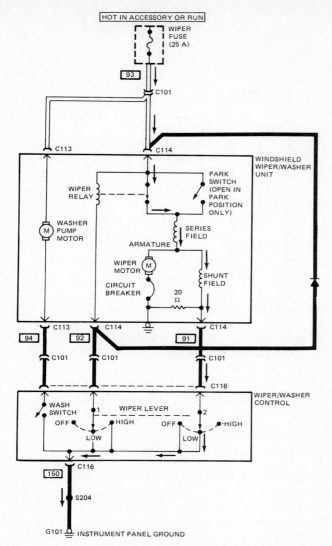

Fig. 13-28. Current flow in windshield wiper circuit of Fig. 13-25 with wiper switch in the LOW-SPEED position. *(Chevrolet Division of General Motors Corporation)*

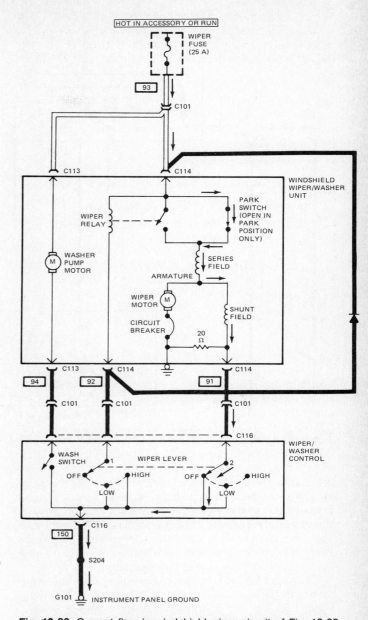

Fig. 13-29. Current flow in windshield wiper circuit of Fig. 13-25 with wiper switch in the OFF (or PARK) position. *(Chevrolet Division of General Motors Corporation)*

the motor. This stops the motor, so the wiper arms remain in the PARK position.

Depressed-Park Windshield Wiper System

Figure 13-30 shows a Ford windshield wiper and washer system which has a two-speed wiper motor and a depressed-park feature. Battery voltage is supplied to the system through a circuit breaker located in the fuse panel. The wiper switch is a three-pole three-position switch. The positions are HIGH SPEED, LOW SPEED, and OFF.

The washer pump is controlled by a single-pole single-throw switch. A washer fluid-level switch and low-fluid warning lamp are included in the system. When the washer fluid drops below a certain level, the switch closes and illuminates the warning lamp.

The wiper motor has permanent field magnets. Three brushes (a high-speed brush, a low-speed brush, and a common brush) provide the two motor speeds. Two sets of park contacts are included in the motor assembly. These contacts perform two functions:

- The park contacts supply current to the motor after the wiper switch has been turned off. This allows the wipers to continue to the conventional PARK position.

- When the wipers reach the conventional PARK position, the park contacts reverse the direction of rotation of the motor. This allows the wipers to move to the DEPRESSED-PARK position.

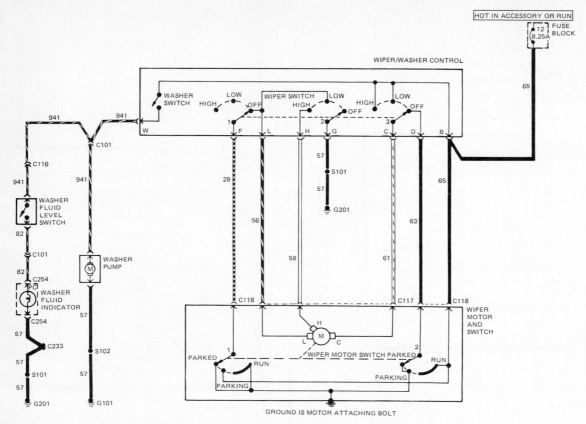

Fig. 13-30. Diagram of depressed-park windshield wiper system. *(Ford Motor Company)*

Figure 13-31 shows the current flow with the wiper switch in the HIGH-SPEED position. Current flow is through contact set 3 of the wiper switch to the common brush of the motor, through the armature to the high-speed brush, and through contact set 2 of the wiper switch to ground. Both sets of park contacts operate with each motor rotation, but they do not affect the circuit operation.

Figure 13-32 shows the current flow with the wiper switch in the LOW-SPEED position. Current flow is through contact set 3 of the wiper switch to the common brush of the motor, through the armature to the low-speed brush, and through contact set 2 of the wiper switch to ground. As in the HIGH-SPEED position, the park contacts do not affect circuit operation.

Figure 13-33 shows the current flow with the wiper switch in the OFF position. When the wiper switch is turned off with the wiper arms in the position shown in Fig. 13-21*a*, the park contacts supply current to the wiper motor. Current flow is through park contact set 2, wiper switch contact set 3, the common brush of the motor, and the armature to the low-speed brush and through wiper switch contact set 1 and park contact set 1 to ground. Therefore, the wiper motor continues to operate after the wiper switch is turned off. The wiper arms continue to the conventional PARK position.

When the wiper arms reach the position shown in Fig. 13-21*b* (with the wiper switch off), the park contacts reverse the current flow through the motor (Fig. 13-34). Current flow is through park contact set 1, wiper switch contact set 1, the low-speed brush of the motor, and the armature to the common brush and through wiper switch

contact set 3 and park contact set 2 to ground. Note that the direction of current flow through the motor armature is the opposite of the direction of normal current flow. Therefore, the motor reverses direction and operates until the wiper arms reach the DEPRESSED-PARK position. When the wipers reach the DEPRESSED-PARK position, park contact set 1 breaks the current flow to the motor and the wiper arms stop. The park contacts appear as in Fig. 13-30 when the wiper arms reach DEPRESSED PARK.

Interval Windshield Wiper System

Figure 13-35 shows a General Motors two-speed wind-shield wiper and washer system with an interval, or delay, feature. Battery voltage is supplied to the system through a fuse located in the fuse panel. The wiper switch is a double-pole five-position switch. The positions are HIGH SPEED, LOW SPEED, DELAY, OFF, and MIST. A wiper pulse module is wired between the wiper switch and the wiper motor assembly. In delay mode, the wiper arms complete one cycle and then stop and wait for the next time-delay period. The wiper pulse module determines the time delay between wiper sweeps. An adjustable control allows the driver to adjust the length of delay. The MIST position of the wiper switch is a momentary contact. The wipers operate at low speed until the driver releases the wiper control.

High-speed and low-speed operation and the action of the park contacts are similar to those in the systems described previously. Current flow for these modes is shown in Figures 13-36 through 13-38.

174

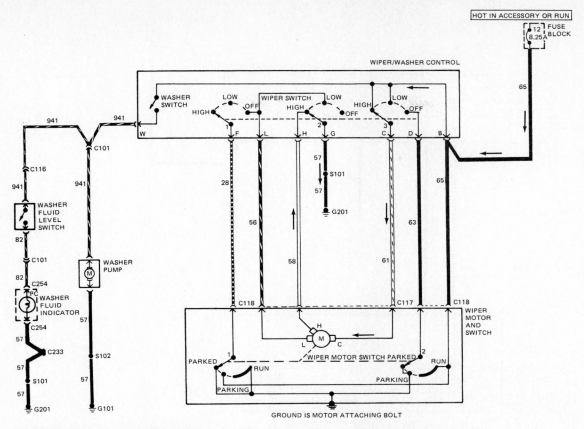

Fig. 13-31. Current flow in windshield wiper circuit of Fig. 13-30 with wiper switch in the HIGH-SPEED position. *(Ford Motor Company)*

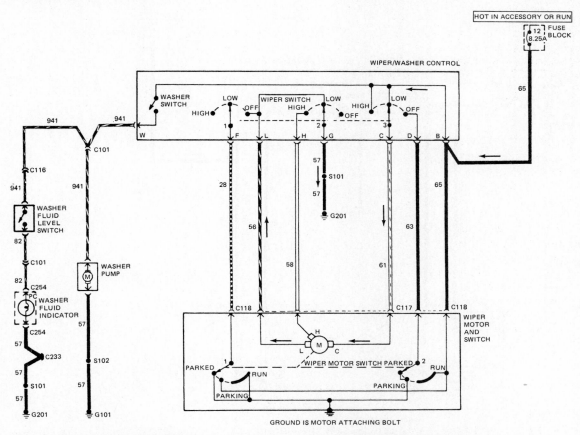

Fig. 13-32. Current flow in windshield wiper circuit of Fig. 13-30 with wiper switch in the LOW-SPEED position. *(Ford Motor Company)*

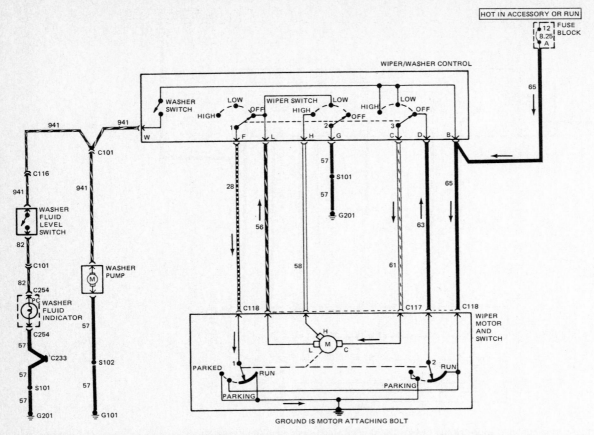

Fig. 13-33. Current flow in windshield wiper circuit of Fig. 13-30 with wiper switch in the OFF (or PARK) position. *(Ford Motor Company)*

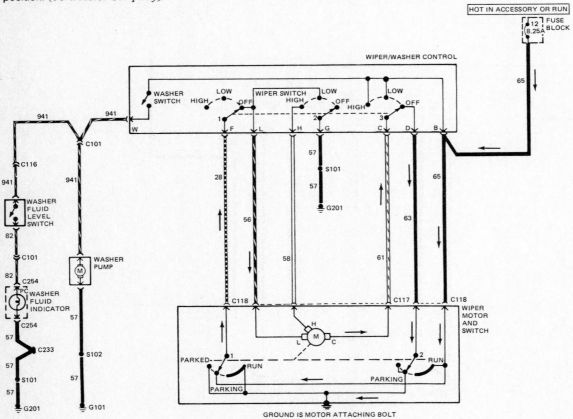

Fig. 13-34. Windshield wiper circuit of Fig. 13-30 with park contacts reversing the current flow through the motor. *(Ford Motor Company)*

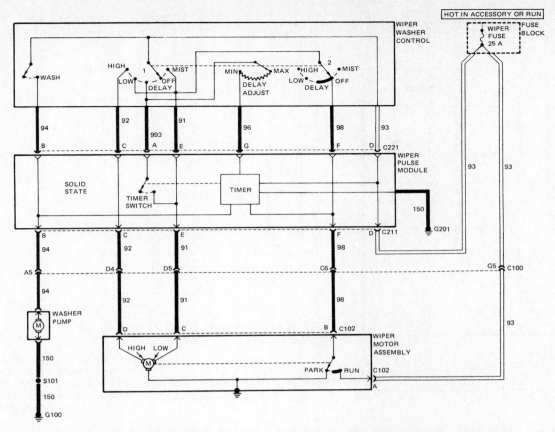

Fig. 13-35. Diagram of an interval windshield wiper system. *(Oldsmobile Division of General Motors Corporation)*

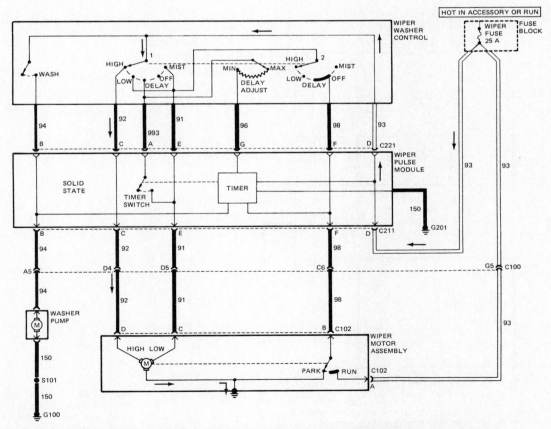

Fig. 13-36. Current flow in windshield wiper circuit of Fig. 13-35 with wiper switch in the HIGH-SPEED position. *(Oldsmobile Division of General Motors Corporation)*

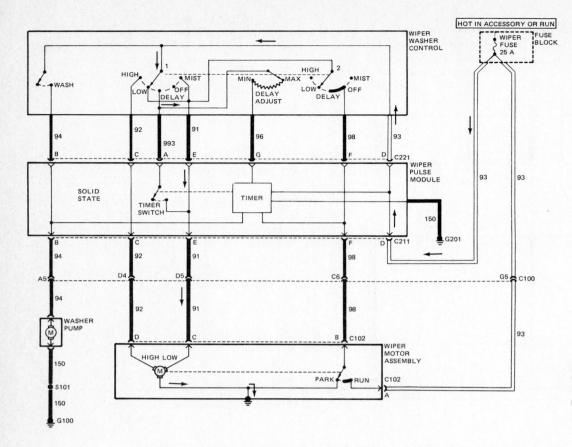

Fig. 13-37. Current flow in windshield wiper circuit of Fig. 13-35 with wiper switch in the LOW-SPEED position. *(Oldsmobile Division of General Motors Corporation)*

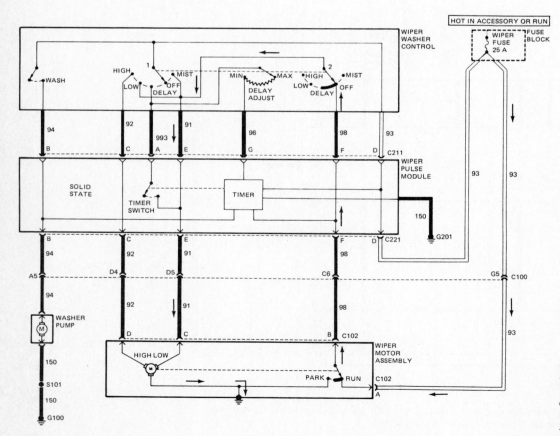

Fig. 13-38. Current flow in windshield wiper circuit of Fig. 13-35 with wiper switch in the OFF (or PARK) position. *(Oldsmobile Division of General Motors Corporation)*

Figure 13-39 shows the current flow with the wiper switch in the DELAY position. Current flow is through the wiper pulse module, contact set 1 of the wiper switch, and the delay adjust control (a variable resistor) to a *timer* in the module. The timer is an electronic circuit that closes a switch at a certain length of time after power is applied to the circuit. The timer operates when battery voltage is applied to terminal G of the module and terminal F of the module is grounded. The delay time of the timer is determined by the setting of the delay adjust control. When the delay time has elapsed, the timer switch closes. Now current flows from contact set 1 through the timer switch to the low-speed brush of the motor. Therefore, the wiper motor begins to operate at low speed. The timer switch is only closed momentarily. When the wiper arms move, the park contact supplies current to the low-speed brush through contact set 2 and contact set 1 (Fig. 13-38). Therefore, when the timer switch opens, the wiper motor continues to operate. When the wiper arms reach the PARK position, the park contact is grounded and the wiper arms stop in the PARK position.

When the park contact is grounded, the timer is also grounded. Grounding the timer again starts its operation. When the delay time is reached, the timer switch closes to start the wiper motor. This action continually repeats itself until the driver selects another wiper switch position. With this system, delay times of up to 25 seconds can be selected.

REAR-WINDOW WIPER AND WASHER SYSTEM

Figure 13-40 shows a diagram of a rear-window wiper and washer system. Battery voltage is supplied to the system through a fuse in the fuse panel and an in-line circuit breaker. The wiper and washer switch supplies battery voltage to the washer pump motor and to the wiper motor. A set of park contacts located in the motor assembly function in the same manner as the park contacts in windshield wiper systems.

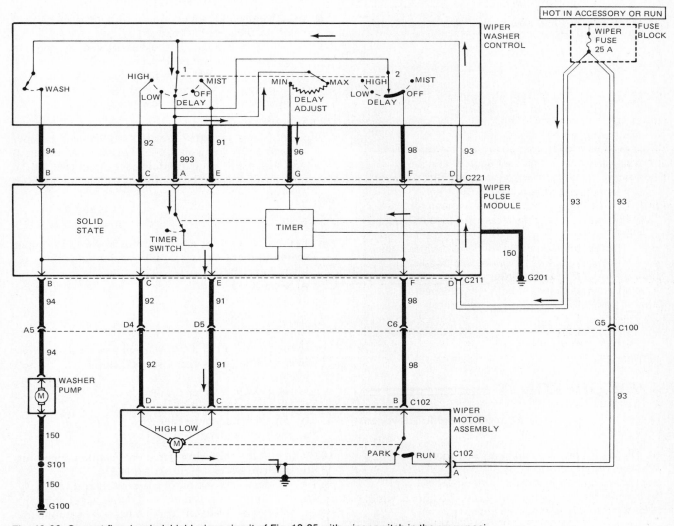

Fig. 13-39. Current flow in windshield wiper circuit of Fig. 13-35 with wiper switch in the DELAY position. *(Oldsmobile Division of General Motors Corporation)*

179

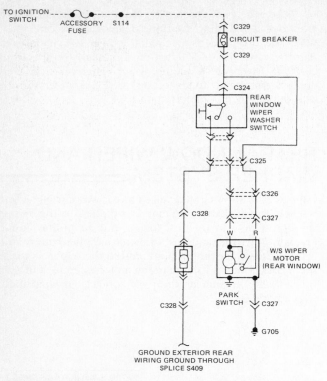

TO IGNITION SWITCH
ACCESSORY FUSE S114

C329
CIRCUIT BREAKER
C329

C324
REAR WINDOW WIPER WASHER SWITCH

C325

C326

C328   C327

W   R

W/S WIPER MOTOR (REAR WINDOW)

PARK SWITCH   C327
C328

G705

GROUND EXTERIOR REAR WIRING GROUND THROUGH SPLICE S409

Fig. 13-40. Diagram of a rear-window wiper and washer system. *(Ford Motor Company)*

VOCABULARY REVIEW

Armature The moveable magnetic core inside the electromagnet of a horn.

Depressed park The rest position of the windshield wiper arms below the rear edge of the hood.

Diaphragm The thin circular plate which vibrates to produce sound from a horn.

Impeller A disk with spiral fins or vanes used in a water pump to push fluid outward by centrifugal force.

Park The rest position of the windshield wiper arms at the lower edge of the windshield moulding.

Timer An electronic circuit that controls a function after a certain interval of time has elapsed.

Tone The quality of the sound from a horn.

REVIEW QUESTIONS

Select the *one* correct, best, or most probable answer to each question.

1. All of the following statements are true concerning horn operation *except*
   a. a column of air is caused to vibrate
   b. a set of normally open contacts in the horn is wired in series with an electromagnet
   c. a column of air is coiled into a spiral form
   d. the electromagnet moves the armature

2. Mechanic A says that a horn relay is used to allow the horn switch to carry low current. Mechanic B says the horn switch grounds the horn relay. Who is correct?
   a. A only   c. both A and B
   b. B only   d. neither A nor B

3. The moveable core in a horn is called
   a. the electromagnet
   b. the armature
   c. the diaphragm
   d. none of the above

4. What part of a windshield wiper motor assembly allows the wiper arms to stop at the lower edge of the windshield moulding?
   a. park contacts
   b. gears
   c. linkage
   d. armature

5. In a windshield wiper motor with an electromagnetic field, the speed is changed by
   a. applying voltage to brushes placed in different positions around the armature
   b. inserting a resistor into the field
   c. using fewer armature windings
   d. changing the armature resistance

6. In a windshield wiper motor with permanent field magnets, the speed is changed by
   a. applying voltage to brushes placed in different positions around the armature
   b. inserting a resistor into the field
   c. applying different voltages to the armature
   d. changing the armature resistance

7. Mechanic A says that with depressed-park wipers, the wiper motor reverses direction to enable the wiper arms to reach the DEPRESSED-PARK position. Mechanic B says that there is an additional set of contacts in the motor assembly for the depressed-park feature. Who is correct?
   a. A only   c. both A and B
   b. B only   d. neither A nor B

8. In the circuit of Fig. 13-25, current flow with the wiper switch in the LOW-SPEED position is through all the following *except* the
   a. series field
   b. wiper switch
   c. 20-Ω resistor
   d. shunt field

9. In the circuit of Fig. 13-30, current flow with the wiper switch in the HIGH-SPEED position is through all the following *except*
   a. wiper switch contact set 3
   b. the common brush
   c. wiper switch contact set 2
   d. the park contacts

10. Which of the following statements is true concerning the interval wiper system shown in Fig. 13-35?
    a. the delay adjust control is a variable resistor
    b. the timer controls the speed of the wiper arms
    c. in interval mode, the park contacts do not function
    d. current does not flow through the wiper pulse module during high-speed operation

CHAPTER 14

INSTRUMENTS, WARNING DEVICES, AND DISPLAYS

OBJECTIVES

After you have studied this chapter, you should be able to:

1. Describe the construction and operation of automotive gauges.

2. List and describe the various types of sending units and sensors.

3. List the types of electronic displays and describe their operation.

4. Describe the operation of instrument and warning circuits.

Instruments are devices that provide information to the driver on various vehicle operating conditions (Fig. 14-1). An instrument can be a gauge, an electronic display, or a light. Warning devices also provide information to the driver, but they usually do so with a light or with an audible signal. Warning devices warn the driver of a possible problem or hazardous condition. Some vehicles have a voice that alerts the driver to certain conditions. Many different types of instruments and warning devices are used.

This chapter covers the operation of gauge, warning lamp, and electronic warning circuits. In addition, the displays such as vacuum fluorescent, liquid crystal, and light-emitting diode are described in detail.

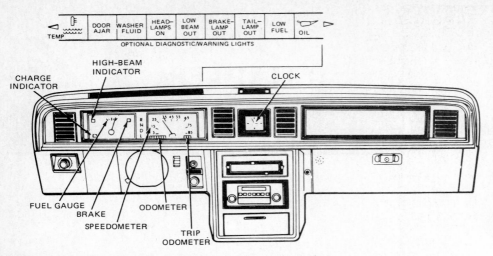

Fig. 14-1. Instrument panel, showing instruments and warning devices. *(Ford Motor Company)*

SPEEDOMETER

A *speedometer* indicates vehicle speed in miles per hour (mph) [or kilometers per hour (km/h)]. A speedometer cable connects a gear in the transmission (Fig. 14-2) to the speedometer unit in the instrument panel. The speed of rotation of the transmission gear is directly related to vehicle speed. The transmission gear rotates the speedometer cable, which in turn rotates a small magnet in the speedometer. The magnet rotates inside a small aluminum cup (Fig. 14-3). The cup is mounted on a shaft supported by bearings. The indicator pointer is attached to the cup.

The rotating magnet produces a rotating magnetic field around the cup. Aluminum is not attracted by a magnet, but it is a conductor of electric current. The rotating magnetic field generates circulating currents (called eddy currents) in the aluminum cup. The eddy currents produce a small magnetic field which interacts with the field of the rotating magnet. The interaction of the two magnetic fields causes the aluminum cup to be pulled around with the rotating magnet. The cup is held back by a fine hairspring. The faster the magnet rotates, the farther the cup is rotated against the spring. As the cup rotates, the pointer moves across the speedometer scale. The scale is calibrated in miles per hour (or kilometers per hour).

ODOMETER

The *odometer* is a mechanical counter in the speedometer unit. It is driven by the speedometer cable through a worm gear. The odometer provides a record of the total distance traveled by the vehicle. Some vehicles have a trip odometer in addition to the vehicle odometer. The trip odometer can be reset to zero, and it records distance over an interval selected by the driver.

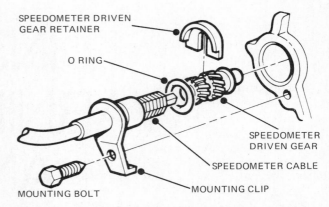

Fig. 14-2. Speedometer cable connection to the transmission. *(Ford Motor Company)*

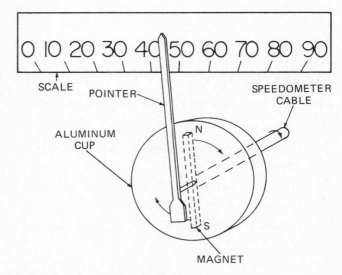

Fig. 14-3. Components of a speedometer.

TACHOMETER

A *tachometer* is an instrument that measures the speed of an engine in revolutions per minute (rpm). Tachometers can be either mechanical or electronic. A mechanical tachometer is operated by a rotating cable driven by the engine camshaft. It functions in the same manner as a speedometer. An electronic tachometer receives voltage pulses from the ignition coil. Each voltage pulse corresponds to the generation of one spark at a spark plug. The frequency of the voltage pulses is a direct measure of the speed of the engine. An electronic circuit in the tachometer converts the pulse frequency into a varying voltage. The voltage is applied to a voltmeter which serves as the speed indicator. The faster the voltage pulses occur at the ignition coil, the higher the voltage in the tachometer and the higher the rpm reading.

GAUGES

A *gauge* is a device that displays a measurement by means of a pointer which moves along a calibrated scale (Fig. 14-4). A gauge is electrically operated and functions mechanically. Therefore, it is an electromechanical device.

When a gauge is used in an indicator circuit, the gauge cannot function alone. A sensing device is needed to provide "information" to the gauge. The sensing device is often called a *sending unit*. A sending unit used with a gauge is a variable resistance that changes in resistance as some physical quantity changes. Sending units can be designed to change in resistance with changes in pressure, temperature, or fluid level.

In operation, voltage is applied to the gauge. The amount of current that flows through the gauge is determined by the resistance of the sending unit (Fig. 14-5). In this way, the sending unit controls the gauge reading. Three types of gauges are used as automotive indicating devices. These are the d'Arsonval meter movement, the bimetallic gauge, and the magnetic gauge.

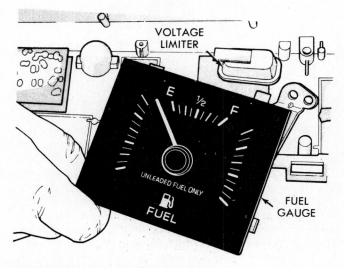

Fig. 14-4. Fuel gauge. *(Chrysler Corporation)*

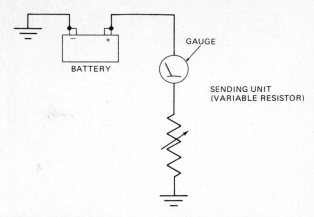

Fig. 14-5. Instrument-panel gauge controlled by a sending unit.

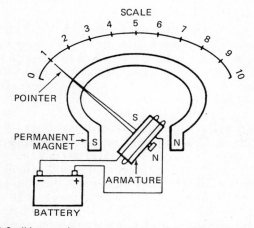

Fig. 14-6. d'Arsonval meter movement. *(Ford Motor Company)*

d'Arsonval Meter Movement

The d'Arsonval meter movement is covered in Chap. 3. When current flows through the armature, the armature becomes an electromagnet and is repelled by the permanent magnet (Fig. 14-6). The pointer is attached to the armature and swings along a calibrated scale. When the current flow through the armature is low, the pointer deflection is small. When the current is high, the deflection is large. The armature has a small spring which returns the pointer to zero when the voltage is removed from the gauge. Voltmeters and ammeters often use d'Arsonval meter movements.

Bimetallic Gauges

A bimetallic gauge has a heating coil wrapped around a small bimetallic strip (Fig. 14-7). The bimetallic strip bends when it is heated. When voltage is applied to the gauge, current flows through the heating coil and through the sending unit to ground. Current flow through the heating coil causes its temperature to increase. As the temperature of the heating coil increases, the bimetallic strip bends and moves a pointer. The pointer swings along a calibrated scale. When the current flow through the heating coil is low, the pointer deflection is small. When the current is high, the deflection is large.

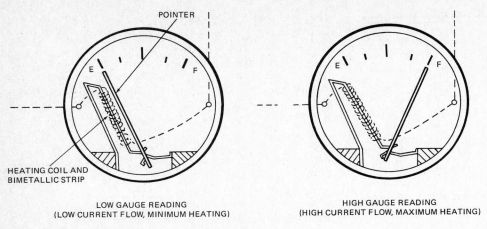

POINTER

E | I I I I F   E I I I I I F

HEATING COIL AND
BIMETALLIC STRIP

LOW GAUGE READING
(LOW CURRENT FLOW, MINIMUM HEATING)

HIGH GAUGE READING
(HIGH CURRENT FLOW, MAXIMUM HEATING)

Fig. 14-7. Bimetallic gauge. *(Ford Motor Company)*

The charging-system voltage can vary due to temperature changes and charging conditions. Any change in voltage in a bimetallic-gauge circuit affects the gauge reading. For this reason, a small voltage regulator is used with this type of gauge. The regulator is called an *instrument voltage regulator (IVR)*.

Instrument Voltage Regulator   An IVR is shown in Fig. 14-8. It consists of a set of normally closed contacts and a heating coil wrapped around a bimetallic strip. When voltage is applied to the IVR, current flows through the contacts and through the heating coil to ground. The current flow causes the temperature of the heating coil to increase. The increase in temperature causes the bimetallic strip to bend. When the strip bends, the contacts open and the current flow stops. When this occurs, the heating coil cools, and the bimetallic strip straightens and closes the contacts. This action repeats itself continuously and causes a pulsating voltage to appear at the IVR output terminal. The pulsating voltage has an average level of approximately 5 volts (V). This pulsating, or regulated, voltage is applied to the gauge. The IVR output is 5 V, regardless of the value of the charging-system voltage.

Magnetic Gauges

A magnetic gauge which is commonly used in the automobile is the three-coil magnetic gauge (Fig. 14-9). It has a low-reading coil, a bucking coil, and a high-reading coil. The bucking coil produces a magnetic field which bucks, or opposes, the magnetic field produced by the low-reading coil. The low-reading coil and the bucking coil are wound together, but in opposite directions. One coil is wound clockwise; the other is wound counter-clockwise. The high-reading coil is positioned at a 90° angle to the other two coils. A resistor, connected to two gauge terminals, is placed in parallel with the low-reading coil. The resistor bypasses a certain amount of current past the coil. When current passes through the coils, they become small electromagnets. A pointer is positioned near the coils and is affected by their magnetic fields. The magnetic field of the low-reading coil attracts the pointer and moves it to the left. The magnetic field of the high-reading coil attracts the pointer and moves it to the right.

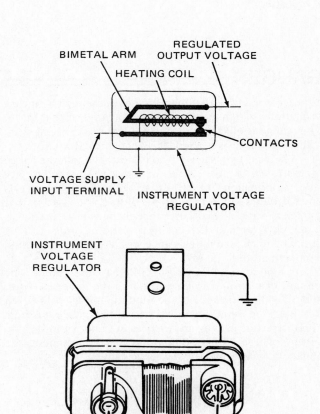

REGULATED
OUTPUT VOLTAGE
BIMETAL ARM
HEATING COIL

CONTACTS

VOLTAGE SUPPLY
INPUT TERMINAL

INSTRUMENT VOLTAGE
REGULATOR

INSTRUMENT
VOLTAGE
REGULATOR

INPUT SIDE   RADIO CHOKE   OUTPUT SIDE
12-V DC (APPROX.)   5-V AVERAGE
                                         (12 V PULSATING)

Fig. 14-8. Instrument voltage regulator. *(Ford Motor Company)*

When voltage is applied to the gauge, there are two current paths. One path is through the low-reading coil and through the sending unit to ground (Fig. 14-10). The other path is through the low-reading coil and through the bucking coil and high-reading coil to ground (Fig. 14-11). The resistance of the sending unit determines which path the current takes. When the sending-unit resistance is low, more current flows through the low-reading coil than through the bucking and high-reading coils. This causes the pointer to be attracted to the left, so the gauge reads zero.

184

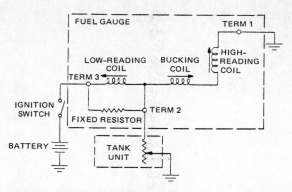

Fig. 14-9. Three-coil magnetic gauge. *(AC-Spark Plug Division of General Motors Corporation)*

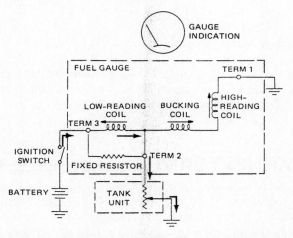

Fig. 14-10. Magnetic gauge. With sending-unit resistance low, the pointer is attracted to the left. *(AC-Spark Plug Division of General Motors Corporation)*

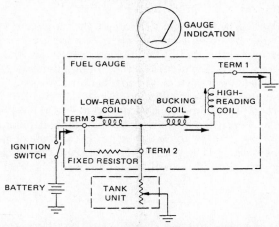

Fig. 14-11. Magnetic gauge. With sending-unit resistance high, the pointer is attracted to the right. *(AC-Spark Plug Division of General Motors Corporation)*

When the sending-unit resistance is high, very little current flows through the sending unit. The current path is through the three coils. The magnetic field of the bucking coil cancels the magnetic field of the low-reading coil. Therefore, the high-reading coil attracts the pointer to the right, so the gauge reads maximum.

At an intermediate sending-unit resistance, current flows through both paths. The pointer is attracted by both the low- and high-reading coils. The position of the pointer will depend on the relative strengths of the magnetic fields of the low- and high-reading coils.

The pointer is not spring-loaded. It is pulled to the right or left by magnetic attraction alone. Therefore, with a three-coil magnetic gauge, the pointer remains in its last position when the voltage is removed from the gauge.

Variation in charging-system voltage does not affect this type of gauge. Because current flows through both the low- and high-reading coils, any changes in system voltage affect the current flow through both coils. Therefore, any changes in magnetism caused by changes in voltage are canceled out. An IVR is not needed with a magnetic gauge.

EXAMPLES OF GAUGE CIRCUITS

Fuel Gauge Circuits

A fuel gauge circuit is shown in Fig. 14-12. The sending unit is located in the fuel tank and includes a float and a variable resistor. The float rises and falls with the level of fuel in the tank. When the fuel tank is full, the float position is high. When the fuel tank is empty, the float position is low. The float connects to a sliding contact on the variable resistor. Therefore, the value of resistance is determined by the position of the float.

A sending unit used with a bimetallic gauge has a low resistance when the float position is high. A low resistance causes a high gauge current and results in a high gauge reading. The resistance is high when the float position is low.

A sending unit used with a magnetic gauge has a high resistance when the float position is high. The resistance is low when the float position is low.

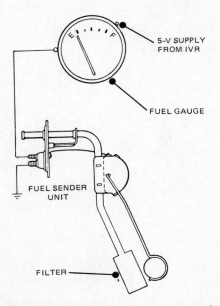

Fig. 14-12. Fuel gauge circuit. *(Ford Motor Company)*

Temperature Gauge Circuits

A coolant-temperature sending unit is shown in Fig. 14-13. The sending unit is a variable resistor which threads into the engine water jacket. The sending-unit resistance controls the current flow through the gauge. The sending unit is a thermistor, which changes resistance with temperature. Sending units used with bimetallic gauges decrease in resistance with increasing temperature. Sending units used with magnetic gauges increase in resistance with increasing temperature.

Pressure Gauge Circuits

An oil-pressure sending unit is shown in Fig. 14-14. The sending unit has a diaphragm which attaches to a sliding contact on a variable resistor. The sending unit threads into the lubrication system on the pressure side of the oil pump. Oil pressure causes the diaphragm to deflect and move the sliding contact on the variable resistor. Sending units used with bimetallic gauges decrease in resistance with increasing pressure. Sending units used with magnetic gauges increase in resistance with increasing pressure.

Multiple-Gauge Circuits

Figure 14-15 shows an indicator circuit which includes a fuel-level gauge, a coolant-temperature gauge, and an engine oil-pressure gauge. Regulated voltage for all three gauges is supplied by a single IVR. Because the IVR contacts vibrate and switch current so rapidly, radio interference is produced. For this reason, a radio-interference

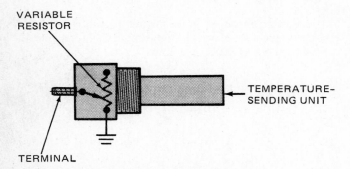

Fig. 14-13. Temperature sending unit. (*Chrysler Corporation*)

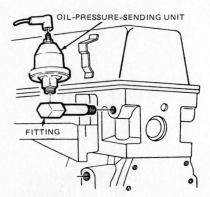

Fig. 14-14. Pressure gauge sending unit. (*Ford Motor Company*)

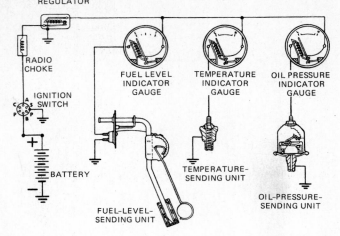

Fig. 14-15. Multiple-gauge circuit. (*Ford Motor Company*)

choke (Chap. 3) is connected in series with the IVR. The choke blocks the interference and prevents it from being carried to the radio through the vehicle wiring.

WARNING LAMPS

A *warning lamp* is a lamp that is illuminated to warn the driver of a possible problem or hazardous condition. Warning lamps are commonly used to indicate low oil pressure, a defective charging system, or an overheated engine. A warning lamp circuit can be operated by using a sending unit or by controlling the voltage applied to the lamp.

Sending-Unit-Controlled Circuit

In a warning lamp circuit, a sending unit is a switch. The switch can be either normally open or normally closed, depending on the application. Figure 14-16 shows an oil-pressure warning lamp circuit. The sending unit is a normally closed switch which threads into an oil passage on the pressure side of the oil pump (Fig. 14-17). A small diaphragm in the sending unit is exposed to engine oil pressure. The switch contacts are controlled by the diaphragm. When the ignition switch is turned to RUN (with the engine off), the warning lamp goes on. This is because the switch contacts are normally closed (with no pressure applied to

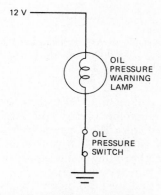

Fig. 14-16. Oil-pressure warning lamp circuit.

ELECTRONIC WARNING CIRCUITS

Many vehicles use electronic circuits to operate warning lights. Two examples are the lamp-out warning system and the low-fuel warning system. Both are described below.

Lamp-Out Warning System

Some vehicles have a warning system to indicate when a headlamp or a taillamp has burned out (Fig. 14-26). In Fig. 14-27, a resistance wire is shown placed in series with a taillamp. The resistance is small, so current flows to the taillamp through the resistance. This current flow causes a small voltage drop across the resistor. An electronic module senses this voltage drop.

Two connections are made to the module: a reference connection and a sensing connection. The reference connection supplies battery voltage to the module. The sensing connection supplies lamp voltage to the module. The lamp voltage is slightly lower than battery voltage because of the voltage drop across the resistance. When the taillamp is operating normally, the voltage drop is applied to the module. However, if the taillamp burns out, the current flow stops. Then there is no voltage drop because the lamp voltage is the same as the battery voltage. The module senses this and turns on the TAILLAMP-OUT warning lamp. Figure 14-28 is a diagram of a warning system which indicates a failure of a headlamp, taillamp, or stoplamp.

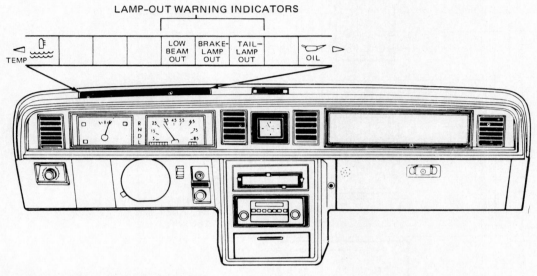

Fig. 14-26. Lamp-out warning system. *(Ford Motor Company)*

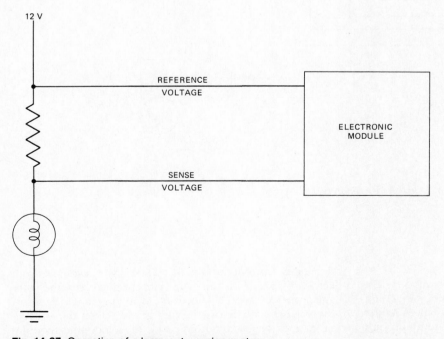

Fig. 14-27. Operation of a lamp-out warning system.

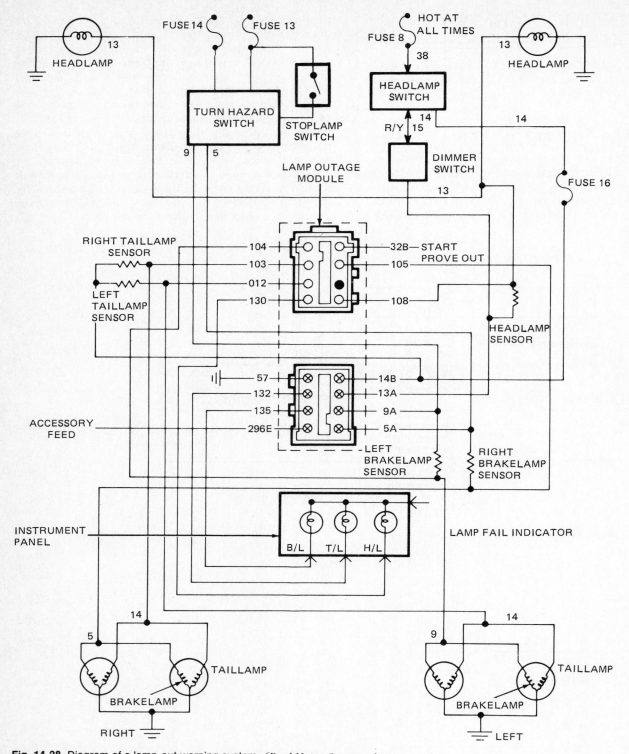

Fig. 14-28. Diagram of a lamp-out warning system. *(Ford Motor Company)*

Low-Fuel Warning System

Some vehicles use an electronic fuel-level warning system in addition to a fuel gauge (Fig. 14-29). Fuel gauge and float operation are described earlier in this chapter. As the float level drops, the resistance of the sending unit increases and the current flow through the gauge decreases. Current through the gauge causes a voltage drop across the gauge. As the gauge current decreases, the voltage drop decreases. An electronic switching module senses the voltage drop across the fuel gauge. When the voltage drop goes below a certain level, the electronic module switches voltage to the warning lamp.

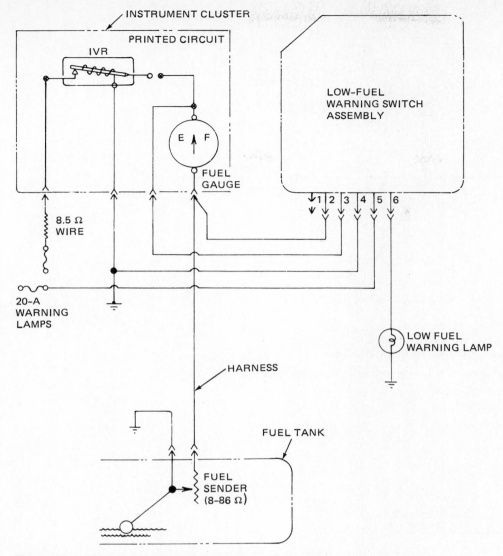

Fig. 14-29. Diagram of a low-fuel warning system. *(Ford Motor Company)*

Another low-fuel warning system is shown in Fig. 14-30. A light-emitting diode (LED) connects across the low-reading coil of a type of magnetic fuel gauge (Fig. 14-31). (LED displays are covered later in this chapter.) When the fuel level is low, the resistance of the sending unit is low, and a relatively large current flows through the low-reading coil. This current flow causes a large voltage drop across the coil. The voltage drop will increase with decreasing fuel level. When the voltage reaches a certain level, the LED will conduct and glow.

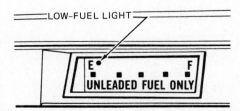

Fig. 14-30. Fuel gauge using an LED as a low-fuel warning. *(Cadillac Motor Car Divison of General Motors Corporation)*

COMPLETE INSTRUMENT AND WARNING LAMP SYSTEM

Figure 14-32 shows an example of a complete instrument and warning lamp system. All the components function together to provide the driver with complete information on the vehicle operation. A brief description of each component follows.

A voltmeter is used as a charging-system monitor, in addition to a charge indicator lamp. A tachometer is shown connected to the primary winding of the ignition coil through a resistor. Both an oil-pressure gauge and a warning lamp are used to warn the driver of low engine oil pressure. A variable resistor and a normally closed switch are used in a single sending unit. Two IVRs are used. One is used with the oil-pressure gauge, and the other is used with the coolant-temperature and fuel-level gauges. In addition to the fuel gauge, a low-fuel warning lamp is provided. A door-ajar warning lamp is used to warn the driver that a door is not securely latched. A brake warning lamp is illuminated if the parking brake is on or if the level of brake fluid is low in either section of the dual master cylinder.

LOW-FUEL-WARNING FUEL GAUGE

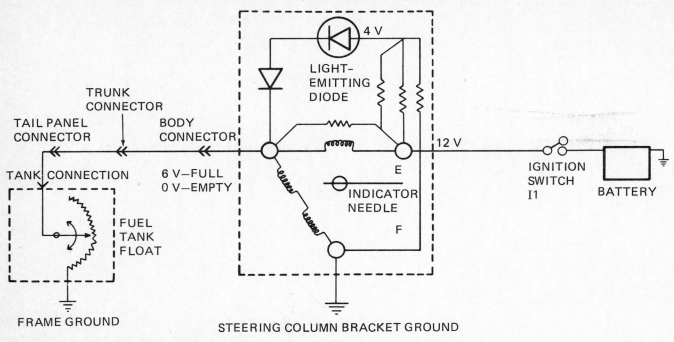

Fig. 14-31. Diagram of a fuel gauge with a low-fuel warning. *(Cadillac Motor Car Division of General Motors Corporation)*

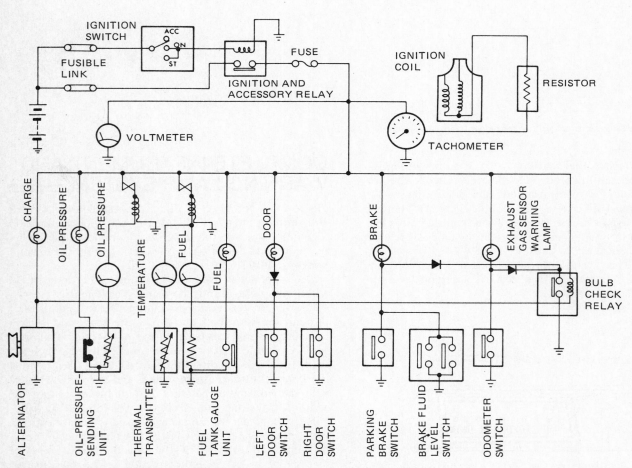

Fig. 14-32. Complete instrument and warning lamp system. *(Nissan Motor Corporation)*

The exhaust-gas-sensor warning lamp is operated by an odometer switch. The exhaust-gas sensor measures the amount of oxygen in the exhaust gas. This information is used to control the engine air-fuel ratio. The odometer switch closes after the odometer has registered 30,000 miles [48,000 kilometers (km)]. This warns the driver that the exhaust-gas sensor should be inspected.

A bulb-check relay is operated when the ignition switch is turned to RUN or START. The relay is grounded through the alternator when the engine is not running. When the relay is grounded, the contacts close and the brake lamp and exhaust-gas-sensor warning lamp are illuminated. This provides a prove-out circuit for these lamps. The diodes are needed to isolate the lamps from each other and to permit one set of relay contacts to control both lamps.

AUDIBLE WARNING SIGNALS

Buzzers

Buzzers are often used as warning devices. A buzzer is similar in construction to a relay (Fig. 14-33). However, in the buzzer, a set of normally closed switch contacts is connected in series with the buzzer coil. One contact is fixed; the other contact is located on a moveable arm, or armature. When voltage is applied to the buzzer, current flows through the switch contacts and through the buzzer coil to ground. The coil becomes an electromagnet which attracts the armature and pulls the moveable contact away from the fixed contact. This opens the circuit, the current flow stops, and the armature is released. The contacts return to their normally closed position. Current again flows, and the armature is again attracted by the buzzer coil. This action repeats itself continually, which causes the armature to vibrate rapidly. This vibration causes the buzzing sound. Buzzers are commonly used as fasten-seatbelt warnings and as key-in-ignition warnings.

Figure 14-34 shows a warning circuit which uses two buzzers. One buzzer serves as a fasten-seatbelt warning. Battery voltage is supplied to the buzzer from the ignition switch through a timer. The timer opens the buzzer circuit after 4 to 8 seconds have elapsed. The buzzer circuit is also opened when the seatbelts are engaged.

The other buzzer serves as a key-in-ignition warning. Battery voltage is supplied to the buzzer through the courtesy lamp switch on the driver's door. The buzzer is grounded when the key is in the ignition switch. Therefore, the buzzer operates when the key is in the ignition switch and the driver's door is open.

Tone Generators

Some vehicles use an electronic *tone generator* to produce an audible warning. The tone generator has an electronic circuit which produces the tone. The tone is then applied to a loudspeaker. Figure 14-35 shows a circuit which uses a tone generator. This circuit provides a warning if the door

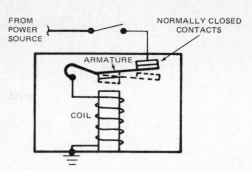

Fig. 14-33. Internal construction of a buzzer. *(Ford Motor Company)*

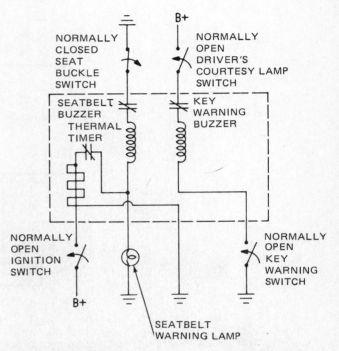

Fig. 14-34. Seatbelt and key warning-buzzer circuit. *(Ford Motor Company)*

is open and either the key is in the ignition switch or the headlights are on. This circuit also produces a tone (in addition to lighting a warning lamp) as a fasten-seatbelt warning.

Voice Warning Systems

Voice warning systems use speech that is produced by a computer to alert the driver to conditions in the vehicle. These systems are described in Chap. 15.

FIBER-OPTIC CONDUCTORS

Fiber-optic conductors are special plastic or glass strands that conduct light. The strands can be curved and used to conduct light from a source to a viewing location. One application of fiber-optic conductors is shown in Fig. 14-36. One end of the fiber-optic conductor attaches to the headlamp wiring connector and is exposed to light at the

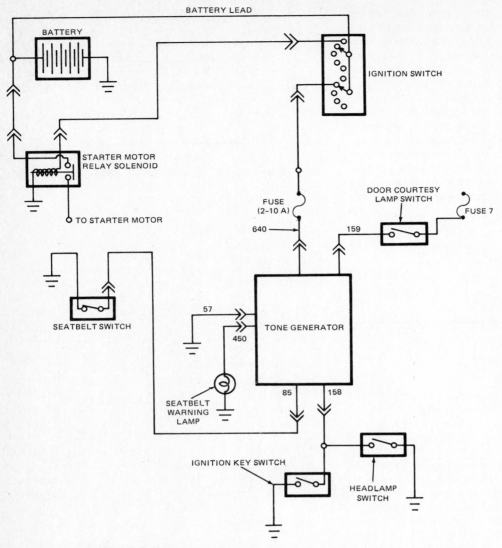

Fig. 14-35. Tone-generator warning circuit. *(Ford Motor Company)*

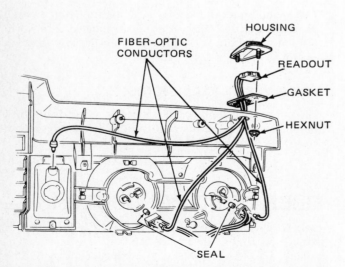

Fig. 14-36. Fiber-optic conductor used in a headlamp and parking lamp monitor. *(Cadillac Motor Car Division of General Motors Corporation)*

rear of the headlamp. The other end connects to a monitor mounted on the fender. When the headlamp is on, the driver can see the light in the monitor. Additional fiber-optic conductors are used to indicate that the headlamp high beams, parking lights, and turn signal lights are on.

ELECTRONIC DISPLAYS

An electronic display provides information to the driver in the form of numbers, words, or symbols. The most common form of automotive electronic display is the *vacuum fluorescent display*. Liquid crystal displays (LCDs) and light-emitting diodes (LEDs) are also used. Electronic displays are often used to indicate vehicle speed, engine temperature, and fuel level.

Vacuum Fluorescent Display

A vacuum fluorescent display emits light in a similar manner to a cathode ray tube (television picture tube). A filament is heated, which causes it to emit electrons. The emitted electrons are directed to strike a phosphorescent screen by applying a positive voltage to the screen (Fig. 14-37). The screen is the visible portion of the display, which emits light when it is struck by the electrons.

Liquid Crystal Display

LCDs use the principle of polarized light. Natural light is composed of waves which vibrate in many different directions (Fig. 14-38). Polarized light vibrates in only one direction. Some substances act as a type of filter and pass only light that is vibrating in one direction. These substances are called *polarizers.* Polarizers convert natural light into polarized light. Light can be polarized in any

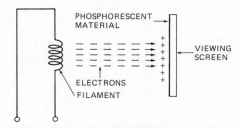

Fig. 14-37. Operation of a vacuum fluorescent display.

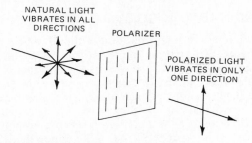

Fig. 14-38. Natural light and polarized light.

direction. However, we will only consider light that is polarized horizontally and light that is polarized vertically.

The construction of an LCD is shown in Fig. 14-39. The liquid crystal material is sandwiched between two glass plates and sealed. The liquid crystal is extremely thin. The glass plates have coatings which are transparent and electrically conductive. The front glass plate has the conductive coating in the form of a pattern or number. Ahead of the front glass plate is a vertical polarizer, and behind the rear glass plate is a horizontal polarizer and a reflector.

The display is viewed through the vertical polarizer. Light passes through the vertical polarizer to the liquid crystal. The liquid crystal has a special property. Its molecules are positioned in such a way that the direction of polarization of light is rotated 90° as it passes through the liquid. The light that is applied to the liquid is vertically polarized (because it must first pass through the front polarizer). As the light passes through the liquid, the light is rotated 90°, and it leaves the liquid as horizontally polarized light. The light then passes through the horizontal polarizer to the reflector. The light is reflected back through the horizontal polarizer, rotated 90° through the liquid crystal to vertical polarization, and passes back through the vertical polarizer. Therefore, light passes from the front of the display to the reflector and back to the front of the display. When this occurs, the display appears light and no pattern or display is seen.

If a voltage is applied to the conductive coating on the glass plates, the position of the molecules in the liquid is affected. The liquid no longer rotates the direction of polarization, and the light leaves the liquid as vertically polarized light (Fig. 14-40). Vertically polarized light cannot pass through a horizontal polarizer. Therefore, light cannot reach the reflector, and light is not reflected back through the display. When this occurs, the display appears dark.

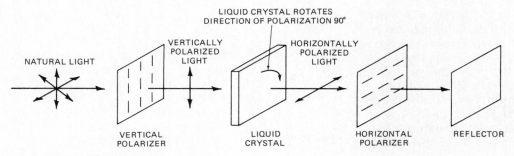

Fig. 14-39. Construction of an LCD.

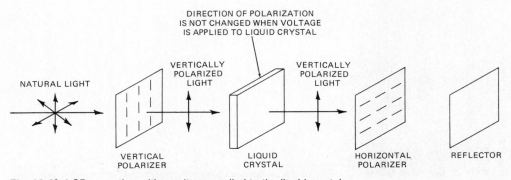

Fig. 14-40. LCD operation with a voltage applied to the liquid crystal.

Therefore, the display is normally light but can be made to appear dark by applying voltage to the liquid crystal. The part of the display that appears dark is the electrically conductive pattern on the front glass. LCDs *reflect* light; they do not produce light. To view an LCD at night, a separate light source must be provided.

Light-Emitting-Diode Display

An LED emits light when it is forward-biased (Chap. 5). Gallium arsenide is commonly used as an LED material. When gallium arsenide is used, the light emitted is red. Other LEDs emit light in other colors. The LED can be used as a single small lamp or as part of a larger display unit. Figure 14-41 shows an LED used as a warning device as part of a gauge assembly.

METHODS OF DISPLAYING INFORMATION

LCDs, LEDs, and vacuum fluorescent displays can be used to display information in several ways. Some of the most common methods are the seven-segment display, the alphanumeric display, the 5 × 7 matrix, and displays which use special symbols designed for specific applications.

Seven-Segment Display

A seven-segment display can be a vacuum fluorescent display or an LCD. A seven-segment display is a type of display that represents numbers by using seven small straight-line segments (Fig. 14-42). The digits 0 through 9 can each be represented with various combinations of these segments. Each segment can be illuminated individually, or in groups, to form the combinations. The digits 0 through 9, as represented by a seven-segment display, are shown in Fig. 14-43. When a vacuum fluorescent display is used in a seven-segment form, each segment of the display has an independently controlled screen. Therefore, each segment is illuminated by controlling the voltage applied to its screen. To display a particular digit, voltage is applied to the segments needed to represent that digit. Complex electronic circuits select the segments to be illuminated. When an LCD is used in a seven-segment form, the voltage to each segment of the LCD is controlled by electronic circuits, in a similar manner to voltage control in a vacuum fluorescent display.

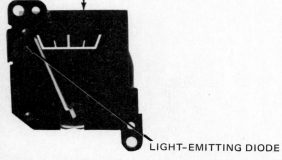

FUEL OR TEMPERATURE GAUGE

LIGHT–EMITTING DIODE

Fig. 14-41. LED used as a warning device as part of a gauge assembly. *(Chrysler Corporation)*

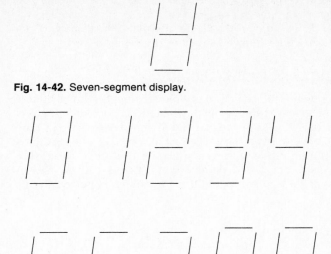

Fig. 14-42. Seven-segment display.

Fig. 14-43. The digits 0 through 9 as represented by a seven-segment display.

Alphanumeric Display

An alphanumeric display represents either numbers or letters by using small straight-line segments (Fig. 14-44). Two different types are used. One type uses a 14-segment character. The other type uses a 16-segment character. The digits 0 through 9 and the letters A through Z can each be represented with various combinations of segments. The operation is similar to that of a seven-segment display, and the display can be either an LCD or a vacuum fluorescent type. Some examples of numbers and letters represented by these types of displays are shown in Fig. 14-45.

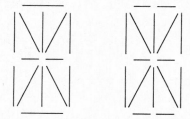

Fig. 14-44. Alphanumeric 14- and 16-segment characters.

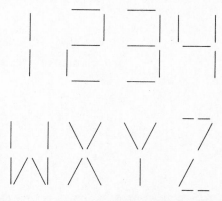

Fig. 14-45. Some examples of numbers and letters represented by 14- and 16-segment displays.

5 × 7 Matrix

A 5 × 7 matrix is shown in Fig. 14-46. A *matrix* is a group of elements arranged in columns and rows. In a 5 × 7 matrix display, there are five columns and seven rows. The elements of the matrix can be individual LEDs or LCDs or individual screens of a vacuum fluorescent display. Electronic circuits apply voltage to illuminate individual elements of the matrix. The digits 0 through 9 and the letters A through Z can be represented with various combinations of elements (Fig. 14-47).

Fig. 14-46. Example of a 5 × 7 matrix.

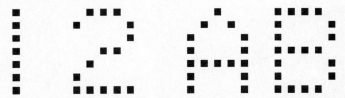

Fig. 14-47. Some examples of numbers and letters represented by a 5 × 7 matrix.

Fig. 14-48. Electronic instrument-panel display using special symbols. *(Ford Motor Company)*

Special Symbols

Vacuum fluorescent display screens and LCDs can be designed to show special symbols instead of numbers and words. Figure 14-48 shows an electronic instrument-panel display. International Standards Organization (ISO) symbols are used to represent fuel and engine coolant. Small bars are used to indicate the fuel level and coolant temperature. Other ISO symbols are shown in Fig. 14-49.

One type of fuel-level display is shown in Fig. 14-50. The level of fuel is represented by 32 bars. When the tank is full, all the bars are illuminated. When the fuel level drops to the level of three illuminated bars, the fuel symbol flashes on and off to alert the driver to a low-fuel condition. Each bar is a separate screen of a vacuum fluorescent display.

Graphic Displays

A graphic display provides information to the driver in a pictorial form. Figure 14-51 shows a graphic display that warns the driver of inoperative headlamps, taillamps, and brake lamps and low levels of windshield washer fluid and fuel. An outline of the top view of a car is shown in the display. LEDs are placed on the outline in positions which correspond to the actual positions of the components they represent. When a problem exists, the appropriate LED lights to provide a warning to the driver. Sensors provide information to an electronic module, which in turn controls voltage to the LEDs.

EXAMPLES OF ELECTRONIC DISPLAYS

Many electronic warning display circuits are computer-controlled. These warning systems monitor vehicle functions and provide audible and visual information and warning signals. Examples of this type of display system are covered in Chap. 15.

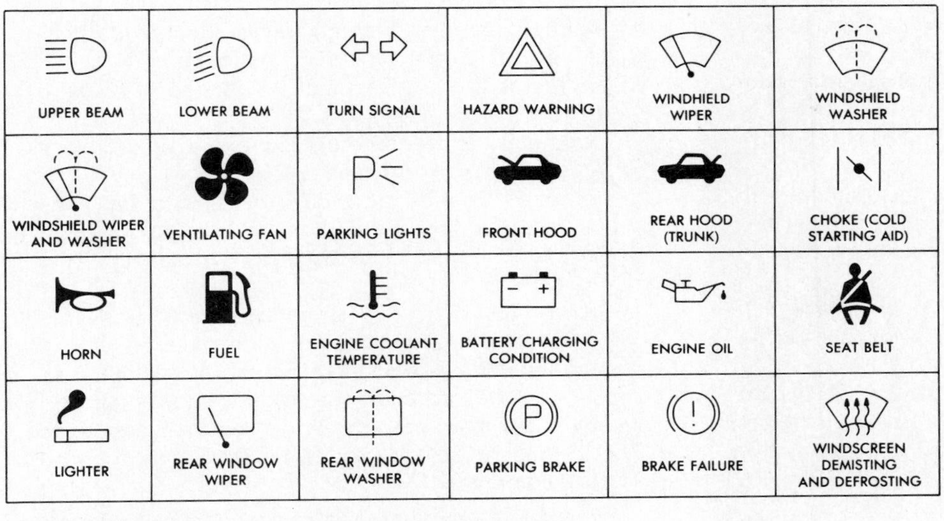

UPPER BEAM	LOWER BEAM	TURN SIGNAL	HAZARD WARNING	WINDSHIELD WIPER	WINDSHIELD WASHER
WINDSHIELD WIPER AND WASHER	VENTILATING FAN	PARKING LIGHTS	FRONT HOOD	REAR HOOD (TRUNK)	CHOKE (COLD STARTING AID)
HORN	FUEL	ENGINE COOLANT TEMPERATURE	BATTERY CHARGING CONDITION	ENGINE OIL	SEAT BELT
LIGHTER	REAR WINDOW WIPER	REAR WINDOW WASHER	PARKING BRAKE	BRAKE FAILURE	WINDSCREEN DEMISTING AND DEFROSTING

Fig. 14-49. International symbols. *(Chrysler Corporation)*

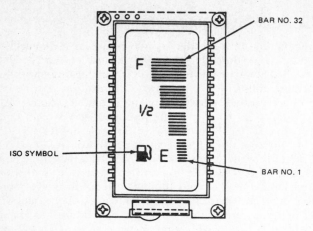

Fig. 14-50. Fuel-level display using illuminated bars. *(Ford Motor Company)*

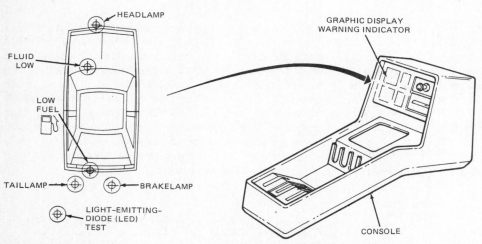

Fig. 14-51. Graphic display which uses LEDs to warn the driver of inoperative lamps and low fluid levels. *(Ford Motor Company)*

VOCABULARY REVIEW

Alphanumeric display A display that represents numbers or letters by using combinations of small straight-line segments.

Bimetallic gauge A gauge using a heating coil wrapped around a bimetallic strip.

Buzzer A warning device which produces a buzzing sound.

Fiber-optic conductors Special plastic or glass strands that conduct light.

Gauge A device that displays a measurement with a pointer which moves along a calibrated scale.

Graphic display A display that provides information in a pictorial form.

Instrument voltage regulator (IVR) A device that provides a regulated voltage of about 5 V for use with bimetallic gauges.

International Standards Organization (ISO) An organization whose symbols are used in the automobile to represent various automotive components or functions.

Light-emitting diode (LED) A diode that emits light when it is forward-biased.

Liquid crystal display (LCD) A device that conveys information by using the rotation of polarized light to produce light areas and dark areas on a viewing surface.

Magnetic gauge A gauge using coils of wire positioned at right angles to each other.

Matrix A group of elements arranged in columns and rows.

Odometer A counter that records the total distance a vehicle has traveled.

Polarized light Light which vibrates in only one direction.

Polarizer A filter that converts natural light into polarized light.

Prove-out circuit A circuit which allows the driver to check the operation of a warning device.

Sending unit A variable resistor or switch that controls the operation of a gauge or warning lamp.

Seven-segment display A display that represents numbers by using seven small straight-line segments.

REVIEW QUESTIONS

Select the *one* correct, best, or most probable answer to each question.

1. Mechanic A says that a fuel-tank sending unit will have a high resistance only when the tank is full. Mechanic B says that its resistance when the tank is full depends on whether the sending unit is designed for use with a bimetallic gauge or with a magnetic gauge. Who is correct?
   a. A only
   b. B only
   c. both A and B
   d. neither A nor B

2. An odometer
   a. measures vehicle speed
   b. measures distance traveled
   c. is usually an electronic counter
   d. uses the principle of eddy currents

3. An electronic tachometer
   a. is gear-driven by the transmission
   b. measures vehicle speed
   c. measures distance traveled
   d. receives voltage pulses from the ignition coil

4. Thermistors are used in
   a. fuel gauge sending units
   b. oil-pressure sending units
   c. coolant-temperature sending units
   d. digital speedometers

5. All of the following statements are true of automotive gauges *except*
   a. an IVR is used with a magnetic gauge
   b. a magnetic gauge remains in its last position when the voltage is removed from the gauge
   c. when the sending-unit resistance is low, a bimetallic-gauge reading is high
   d. when the sending-unit resistance is low, a magnetic gauge reading is low

6. The sending unit for an oil-pressure warning lamp circuit is a
   a. thermistor
   b. normally closed switch
   c. normally open switch
   d. variable resistor

7. All of the following statements are true *except*
   a. buzzers have a set of normally open contacts
   b. a coolant-temperature warning lamp is controlled by a normally open switch
   c. an oil-pressure gauge is controlled by a variable resistor
   d. a temperature gauge sending unit is a thermistor

8. Fiber-optic conductors
   a. produce light
   b. are powered by a 12-V battery
   c. transmit light
   d. draw a small amount of electric current

9. Which of the following operates in a similar manner to a cathode ray tube?
   a. vacuum fluorescent display
   b. LED
   c. LCD
   d. Fiber-optic conductors

10. Which of the following uses the principle of polarized light?
   a. vacuum fluorescent display
   b. LED
   c. LCD
   d. Fiber-optic conductors

11. What does a lamp-out warning system sense to detect that a lamp has burned out?
   a. current flow to the lamp
   b. light output of the lamp
   c. heat produced by the lamp
   d. a voltage drop across a resistor

12. Which of the following devices does not produce light?
   a. bulb
   b. LED
   c. LCD
   d. vacuum fluorescent display

13. Mechanic A says that an IVR is used to prevent changes in charging-system voltage from affecting the gauge readings. Mechanic B says that an IVR is not needed with a magnetic gauge. Who is correct?
   a. A only
   b. B only
   c. both A and B
   d. neither A nor B

14. A temperature warning lamp is on while the engine is cranking because the
   a. sending-unit resistance is low
   b. sending-unit contacts are closed
   c. sending-unit contacts are open
   d. prove-out circuit grounds the lamp

CHAPTER 15

COMPUTER-CONTROLLED WARNING DEVICES AND ACCESSORIES

OBJECTIVES

After you have studied this chapter, you should be able to:

1. Describe the basic operation of a micro-computer.

2. Explain the operation of computer-controlled instrument circuits.

3. Discuss the operation of a voice warning system.

4. Explain the operation of travel information systems.

5. Describe the operation of a keyless-entry system.

A *computer* is an electronic device that stores and processes data (information). In addition to this, computers can control the operation of other devices. Computers were first used on automobiles to control ignition timing. Later, their usage was expanded to include control of exhaust emissions and many other functions.

This chapter provides a brief description of the basic operation of computers. Then, four computer-controlled automotive systems are described in detail. These systems are as follows:

- Computer-controlled instruments
- Voice warning systems
- Travel information systems
- Keyless-entry systems

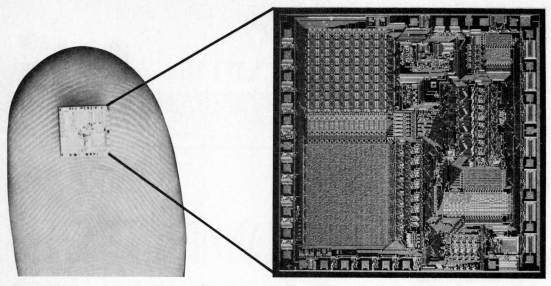

Fig. 15-1. Photograph of a chip, showing its relative size. *(Texas Instruments Incorporated)*

MICROCOMPUTERS

When computers were first developed, they were extremely large. One of the first computers used 18,000 vacuum tubes and filled an entire room. As vacuum tubes were replaced by transistors, computers became smaller. Improved manufacturing methods led to further reductions in size. Thousands of transistors can now be placed on a small surface called a chip (Fig. 15-1). The small computers which use these tiny chips are called *microcomputers.*

Figure 15-2 shows a block diagram of a typical microcomputer. The basic parts are the *microprocessor,* the *memory,* the *input device,* and the *output device.* Each part is described below.

Microprocessor

A microprocessor is also called a *central processing unit (CPU).* It contains an electronic clock which generates voltage pulses that time all the operations of the computer. In addition, the microprocessor coordinates the movement of data from one part of the computer to another, and it ties all parts of the computer together. All the calculations and processing of data take place in the microprocessor.

Memory

A memory is the part of a computer which can store data. There are two different types of memories in a computer: a read-only memory (ROM) and a random access memory (RAM). A ROM has data stored in it when it is manufactured. The data will remain in the ROM for the life of the computer. The data in the ROM can be "read out" when it is needed. Reading out the data does not remove it from the ROM; the data can be read again and again. Data cannot be added to the ROM during the operation of the computer. A RAM can also be called a *read-and-write memory* because data can be added to the memory (written into it) and then read out when needed. The ROM and the RAM serve different purposes during the operation of the computer.

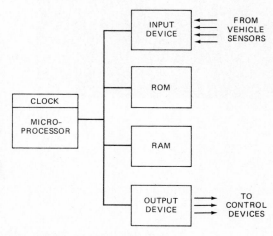

Fig. 15-2. Block diagram of a microcomputer.

Input Device

An input device is the part of the microcomputer circuit that connects a *sensor* to the microcomputer. Sensors convert some measurement of vehicle operation, such as engine speed, door open or closed, or coolant temperature, into an electric signal. Some sensors change in resistance as the function they are sensing varies. Other sensors produce a varying voltage. Switch-type sensors provide either an open circuit or a closed circuit. The input device converts the output of the sensor into the type of data that a computer can use.

Output Device

An output device connects the microcomputer to a control device on the automobile. The output device converts computer data into a signal that will control some function on the vehicle.

OPERATION OF A COMPUTER

During the operation of a microcomputer, the microprocessor controls everything. Its clock generates the voltage pulses which time all computer operations. A typical microprocessor clock rate is about 1 million clock pulses per second. This means that each separate computer operation is completed in only one-millionth of a second.

For a computer to perform any type of function, it must be programmed. A *program* is a set of instructions that tells the microprocessor what to do and when to do it. The program is stored in the ROM at the time of manufacture. The microprocessor tells the ROM to read out each program instruction in the proper sequence.

Information from the sensors is converted into computer data by the input device. This data is then supplied to the microprocessor. During the operation of the microcomputer, the microprocessor samples the input signals, performs calculations, compares numbers, and makes decisions on the basis of the program that is stored in the ROM. While the program is running, the RAM is used for temporary storage of data. When the final result of the program is reached, the data that represents the result is sent to the output device. The output device then converts the data into a signal which will operate a control device. Some common control devices are motors and solenoids. In some applications, the output of the microcomputer is presented on a visual display.

EXAMPLE OF COMPUTER OPERATION

Suppose, for example, that the computer is programmed to provide the driver with information on fuel economy. The driver must signal the computer that this information is wanted. This is done by operating a switch which signals the input device. The input device then signals the microprocessor to begin the program. To simplify the operation, the program is broken down into the four steps listed below. In an actual program, however, many steps are needed to perform a calculation.

- *Step 1*   The microprocessor samples the signal from a speed sensor after the signal has passed through the input device. The microprocessor then temporarily stores this data in the RAM (Fig. 15-3).

- *Step 2*   The microprocessor samples the signal from a fuel-flow sensor after the signal has passed through the input device. The microprocessor also stores this data in the RAM (Fig. 15-4).

- *Step 3*   The microprocessor reads out both speed data and fuel data from the RAM and performs a division calculation (Fig. 15-5). The result will be data that represents fuel economy in miles per gallon (mi/gal) or kilometers per liter (km/L)

- *Step 4*   The fuel-economy data is sent to the output device (Fig. 15-6). The output device then converts this data into a voltage signal to operate a visual display.

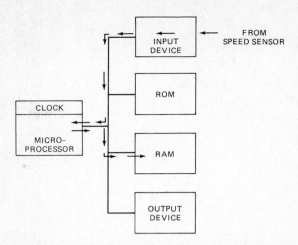

Fig. 15-3. Speed information being temporarily stored in the RAM.

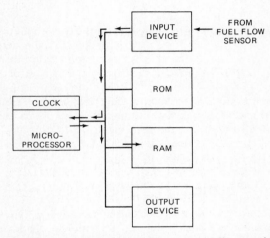

Fig. 15-4. Fuel-flow information being temporarily stored in the RAM.

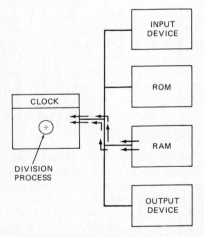

Fig. 15-5. Microprocessor performing a division calculation.

The computer can be programmed to update the fuel-economy display continually. This is done by having the program automatically repeat itself after it has reached the final step. A calculation such as the one in the previous example can be performed hundreds of times each second. However, such rapid updating may be confusing to the

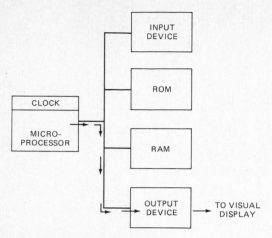

Fig. 15-6. Fuel-economy data passing through the output device to the display.

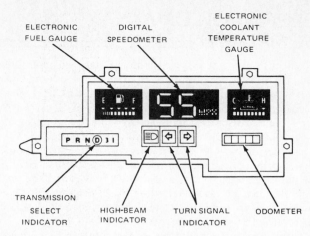

Fig. 15-7. Electronic instrument cluster. *(Ford Motor Company)*

driver. The display will change too quickly and will be difficult to read. Therefore, a program of this type may be designed to update itself only once each second or once every 2 seconds for ease of viewing. For some control operations, it may be desirable to update the control function at a rapid rate. The following examples of computer-controlled accessories describe four different applications of the microcomputer to the automobile.

COMPUTER-CONTROLLED INSTRUMENT CIRCUITS

Some vehicles use a microcomputer to operate an electronic instrument display. Figure 15-7 shows an electronic instrument cluster that includes a digital speedometer, an electronic fuel-level indicator, and an electronic coolant-temperature indicator. Sensors provide information to a microcomputer. The microcomputer is programmed to process the information and perform the required calculations. In addition, it converts the results of its calculations into voltage signals which operate the display. In the electronic instrument cluster shown in Fig. 15-7, the speedometer and the fuel and temperature indicators all share the same microcomputer. The circuits for each instrument are described below.

Digital Speedometer

A sensor for the digital speedometer is shown in Fig. 15-8. A small, slotted wheel is rotated by the speedometer cable. A light-emitting diode (LED) and phototransistor are positioned so that they face each other, separated by the slotted wheel. As the wheel rotates, light from the LED reaches the phototransistor each time a slot in the wheel lines up with the LED. The phototransistor produces a voltage pulse each time a slot passes the LED. The microcomputer receives these voltage pulses from the sensor. At the same time, the internal clock provides a time reference. The microcomputer counts the number of voltage pulses received in a certain period of time and calculates the vehicle speed in miles per hour (mph). The number calculated is converted to the voltages necessary to operate the digital display. The display is updated twice every second. A but-

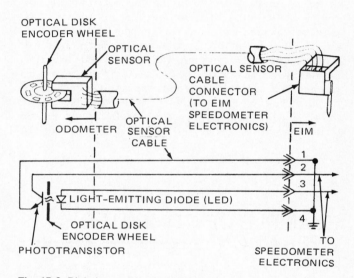

Fig. 15-8. Digital speedometer sensor. *(Ford Motor Company)*

ton is provided to allow the driver the option of selecting a readout in kilometers per hour (km/h). Then the microcomputer makes an additional calculation which converts miles into kilometers.

The microcomputer goes through a self-check routine whenever the ignition switch is turned to the ACC or RUN positions. The self-check routine lasts 3 seconds and consists of the following steps as viewed on the display: all segments on, all segments off, and zero mph or km/h (Fig. 15-9). The self-check routine advises the driver that the system is working properly.

Electronic Temperature Indicator

The electronic temperature indicator uses a thermistor temperature sensor (Fig. 15-10) which threads into the engine water jacket. The resistance of the thermistor decreases as temperature increases. In the system shown, the sensor has a resistance of approximately 250,000 ohms (Ω) at $-18°C$ [$0°F$]. The resistance decreases to approximately 1000 Ω at $126°C$ [$260°F$].

The microcomputer receives the temperature information as a resistance value. That information is converted into voltage signals to operate the display. The display has

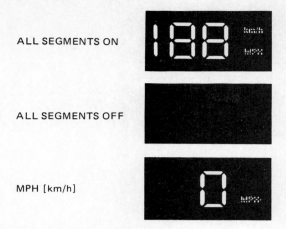

ALL SEGMENTS ON

ALL SEGMENTS OFF

MPH [km/h]

Fig. 15-9. Digital speedometer—self-check routine. *(Ford Motor Company)*

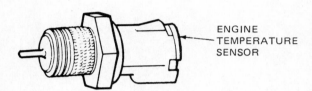

ENGINE TEMPERATURE SENSOR

Fig. 15-10. Sensor for the electronic temperature indicator. *(Ford Motor Company)*

nine bars which are illuminated to indicate the temperature. The greater the number of bars illuminated, the higher the temperature. An International Standards Organization (ISO) symbol for temperature is located above the bars. The symbol flashes when the temperature level has reached eight or nine bars. Also included in the display are a normal range indication and C (cold) and H (hot) symbols.

The computer performs a self-check routine whenever the ignition switch is turned from LOCK or OFF to the ACC or RUN position. The self-check routine lasts for 3 seconds. It consists of the following steps as viewed on the display: all segments on, flashing ISO symbol, all segments blank, and present temperature reading (Fig. 15-11).

Electronic Fuel-Level Indicator

The sensing device for fuel level is a variable resistor controlled by a float. This device is called a sending unit, and it is the same type of sending unit that is used with a fuel gauge. The resistance of the sending unit is approximately 12 Ω when the tank is empty and 166 Ω when the tank is full.

The microcomputer receives the fuel-level information (as a resistance value) and converts that information into voltage signals to operate the display. The display has eleven bars which are illuminated to indicate the fuel level. The greater the number of bars illuminated, the higher the fuel level. An ISO symbol for fuel is located above the bars. The symbol flashes to alert the driver that the fuel level is low. Also included in the display are small triangles, representing quarter-tank levels, and E (empty) and F (full) symbols.

The computer goes through a self-check routine whenever the ignition switch is turned from LOCK or OFF to the ACC or RUN position. The self-check routine lasts for 3 seconds and consists of the following steps as viewed on the display: all segments on and ISO symbol flashing, all segments off with symbol still flashing, and normal display with present fuel-level reading (Fig. 15-12).

VOICE WARNING SYSTEMS

Some warning systems use computer *synthesized speech* to alert the driver to certain conditions in the vehicle. Human speech can be broken down into simple, basic sounds called *phonemes*. There are about 50 for the English language. Synthesized speech is speech produced by combining phonemes together. An electronic circuit called a *phoneme generator* can produce sounds which duplicate these basic sounds. The phoneme generator is connected to a small loudspeaker. Human speech can be simulated by causing the generator to produce certain combinations of phonemes. The generator can do nothing more than produce sounds. A computer must be programmed to control the generator to produce phonemes in the right combinations to form words and sentences.

ALL SEGMENTS ON, THEN FLASHING ISO

FLASHING ISO, THEN ALL SEGMENTS BLANK

PRESENT TEMPERATURE READING

Fig. 15-11. Electronic temperature indicator—self-check routine. *(Ford Motor Company)*

FIRST, ALL SEGMENTS LIGHT AND ISO SYMBOL FLASHES

NEXT, ISO SYMBOL CONTINUES TO FLASH AND ALL OTHER SEGMENTS TURN OFF

FINALLY, PRESENT FUEL LEVEL IS INDICATED

Fig. 15-12. Electronic fuel-level indicator—self-check routine. *(Ford Motor Company)*

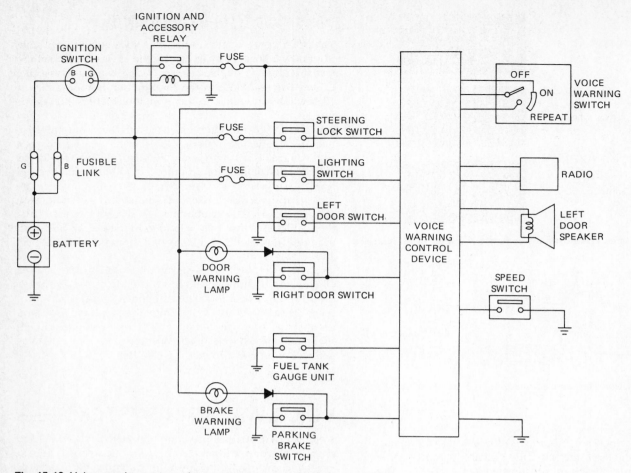

Fig. 15-13. Voice warning system. *(Nissan Motor Corporation)*

A voice warning system used by Nissan is shown in Fig. 15-13. If the ignition switch is ON and the right door is open (for example), the voice warning will be, "Right door is open." This system has six warnings. Figure 15-14 lists the warnings and describes the conditions which trigger them. Some voice warning systems say "thank you" when the computer receives the signal that the driver has remedied the fault.

Item	Condition			Voice warning
Left door	Ignition switch ON	Left door switch is ON (left door is open)	Speed switch is ON Car speed is more than 6 mph [10 km/h]	Left door is open
Right door		Right door switch is ON (right door is open)		Right door is open
Parking brake		Parking brake switch is ON		Parking brake is ON
Fuel level		Fuel level is less than 2⅝ U.S. gal, 2¼ imp gal [10 L]	—	Fuel level is low
Ignition key	Ignition switch OFF	Left door switch is ON (left door is open)	Steering lock switch is ON	Key is in the ignition
Light			Lighting switch is ON	Lights are ON

Fig. 15-14. Operation of a voice warning system. *(Nissan Motor Corporation)*

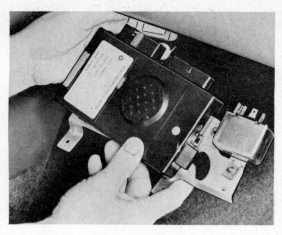

Fig. 15-15. Electronic voice-alert module. *(Chrysler Corporation)*

Chrysler uses a voice warning system that has 24 warning functions. The voice warning is part of an electronic monitor system which consists of a microcomputer, a vacuum fluorescent display, and a voice-alert module (Fig. 15-15). Sensors throughout the vehicle supply information to the microcomputer on certain conditions (Fig. 15-16). Four different types of sensors are used with this system. The sensor types are:

- Modules that detect a failure and send an alternating-current (ac) signal to the microcomputer. These sensors are used to sense headlamp, taillamp, or stoplamp failure.

- A temperature-sensitive resistor which triggers a warning in the microcomputer when its resistance reaches a certain value. This sensor is used to sense a low level of engine oil.

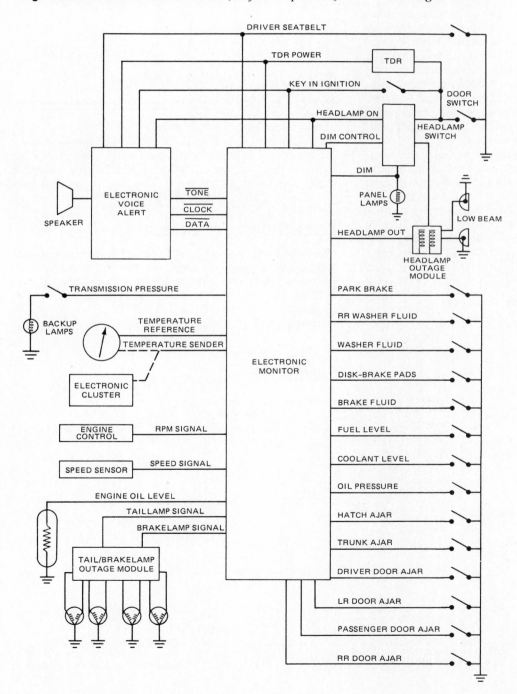

Fig. 15-16. Circuit diagram of the Chrysler 24-warning voice-alert system. *(Chrysler Corporation)*

207

- A voltage sensing device. This device is used to measure charging-system voltage.

- Sensors which act as normally open switches and provide a ground to the microcomputer when a failure has occurred or an unsafe condition exists. These sensors are used to sense door ajar, fluid level, oil pressure, and brake-pad wear.

In addition, the microcomputer receives information on coolant temperature from a temperature sensor, vehicle speed from a speed sensor, and engine speed from the ignition system.

If a sensor detects a failure or an unsafe condition, a warning is activated. When this occurs, a warning message is indicated on the display and the voice-alert module produces a short tone to alert the driver and then delivers the voice message.

The microcomputer may require more than one input signal to activate a warning. For example, the engine temperature warning is a two-part message. The first voice warning is, "Your engine temperature is above normal." To activate this message, engine coolant temperature must be too high, and engine speed must remain above 300 revolutions per minute (rpm) for longer than 30 seconds. Therefore, the microcomputer must receive temperature information, engine speed information, and time information (from its internal electronic clock). On the basis of these three inputs, the microcomputer activates the warning message if the failure conditions are met. If the engine temperature is too high for 30 seconds and if the engine speed is greater than 300 rpm for 60 seconds, then the microcomputer activates a second message: "Your engine is overheating. Prompt service is required."

The other messages provided by this system are:

- "Your keys are in the ignition."

- "Your headlamps are on."

- "Please fasten your seatbelts."

- "Your parking brake is on."

- "Please close your left rear door (driver's door) (right rear door) (passenger door) (trunk lid) (rear hatch)."

- "Your washer fluid is low."

- "Your rear washer fluid is low."

- "Please check your fuel level (engine coolant level) (brake fluid level) (transmission fluid level) (engine oil level)."

- "Please check your disk brake pads."

- "Please check your headlamps (taillamps) (brake lamps)."

- "Your engine oil pressure is critical. Engine damage may occur."

- "Your charging system is malfunctioning. Prompt service is required."

TRAVEL INFORMATION SYSTEMS

Travel information systems provide the driver with information such as the time of day, fuel economy, and estimated time of arrival. Travel information systems vary in terms of the components used and the information provided the driver. Two travel information systems are described below.

Ford Tripminder System

Figure 15-17 shows the Ford Tripminder system. A speed sensor and a fuel-flow sensor provide information to a microcomputer. The microcomputer is part of the display module. The display is the vacuum fluorescent type. Seven push buttons on the module control the operation of the system (Fig. 15-18). The RESET, SET, and ENGLISH/METRIC but-

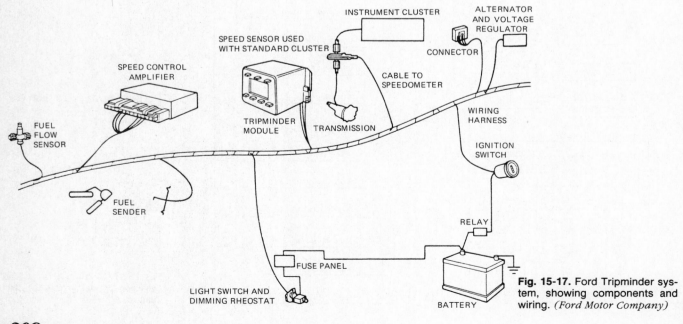

Fig. 15-17. Ford Tripminder system, showing components and wiring. (*Ford Motor Company*)

tons are used to control the various functions. Their operation is as follows:

- The RESET button resets selected functions back to zero.

- The SET button changes the date, day, and time of day.

- The ENGLISH/METRIC button selects either an English or a metric display.

When the engine is started, the display automatically indicates the date, day, and time of day (Fig. 15-19). The FUEL, ECON, TRIP, and TIME buttons operate as follows:

- The FUEL button, when depressed, displays the fuel used since the last time the RESET button was operated (Fig. 15-20).

- The ECON button, when depressed once, displays instantaneous fuel economy (Fig. 15-21). When the button is depressed twice, it displays average fuel economy since the last time the RESET button was operated (Fig. 15-22).

- The TRIP button, when depressed once, displays distance traveled (elapsed distance) since the last time the RESET button was operated (Fig. 15-23). When the button is depressed twice, it displays average speed since the last RESET (Fig. 15-24).

- The TIME button, when depressed twice, displays elapsed time since the last time the RESET button was operated (Fig. 15-25). The clock continues to run even if the ignition switch is off. If the TIME button is depressed again, the time of day, day, and date are again displayed.

The Tripminder system has a built-in diagnostic mode to check for trouble in the system. It is activated when the TIME and ENGLISH/METRIC buttons are depressed simultaneously. Then depressing the other buttons will cause the desired test information to be displayed.

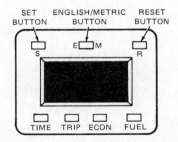

Fig. 15-18. Tripminder system display module. *(Ford Motor Company)*

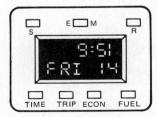

TIME, DAY, AND DATE

Fig. 15-19. Tripminder system with display showing date, day, and time of day. *(Ford Motor Company)*

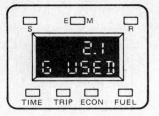

GALLONS USED

Fig. 15-20. Tripminder system with display showing fuel used since last RESET. *(Ford Motor Company)*

INSTANTANEOUS FUEL ECONOMY

Fig. 15-21. Tripminder system with display showing instantaneous fuel economy. *(Ford Motor Company)*

AVERAGE TRIP FUEL ECONOMY

Fig. 15-22. Tripminder system with display showing average fuel economy since last RESET. *(Ford Motor Company)*

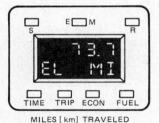

MILES [km] TRAVELED

Fig. 15-23. Tripminder system with display showing distance traveled since last RESET. *(Ford Motor Company)*

AVERAGE TRIP SPEED, MPH [km/h]

Fig. 15-24. Tripminder system with display showing average speed since last RESET. *(Ford Motor Company)*

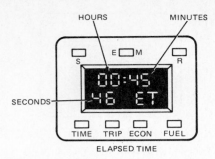

Fig. 15-25. Tripminder system with display showing elapsed time since last RESET. *(Ford Motor Company)*

warning functions. The microcomputer provides the following travel information:

- Month, date, day, and time of day
- Distance remaining before fuel tank is empty
- Estimated time of arrival at a given destination
- Average vehicle speed
- Average fuel economy
- Instantaneous fuel economy
- Distance remaining to a given destination
- Elapsed time since the system was last reset
- Elapsed distance since the system was last reset

Ford Electronic Message Center System

The Ford Electronic Message Center system is shown in Fig. 15-26. The system consists of a message center display and keyboard (Fig. 15-27), a control module (microcomputer), a tone generator, and various sensors. The sensors provide information on vehicle operation to the microcomputer.

This system combines a travel information system with an electronic instrument panel. Therefore, the system displays travel information in addition to instrument-panel

The keyboard has 12 keys. Most keys are labeled with a number and a function, as shown and described in Fig. 15-28. When the ignition switch is turned to the RUN or ACCESSORY position, the display automatically indicates the time of day, day, and date. When a key is depressed, the information selected will be shown on the message center display in place of the time. In addition, the tone generator produces a tone to advise the driver that the signal has been received by the control module. The keys with numbers are also used to enter trip information into the microcomputer. For example, the number of miles to a given destination must be entered to permit the microcomputer

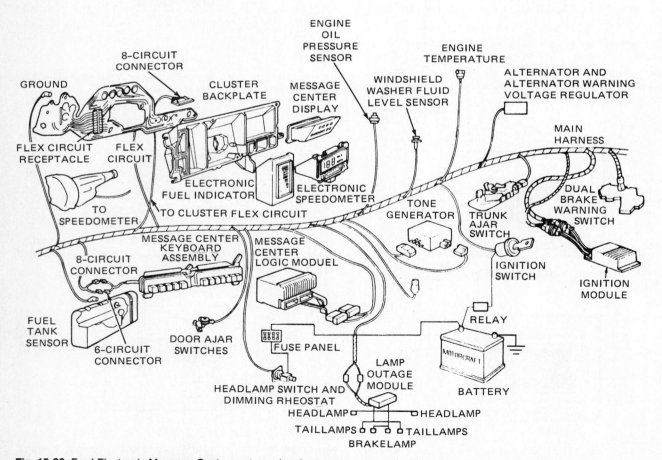

Fig. 15-26. Ford Electronic Message Center system, showing components and wiring. *(Ford Motor Company)*

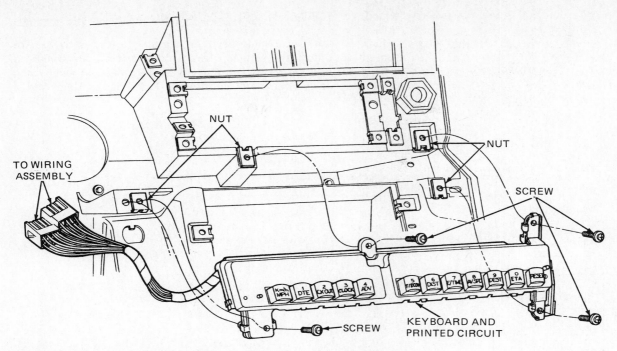

NUT

NUT

TO WIRING ASSEMBLY

SCREW

SCREW

KEYBOARD AND PRINTED CIRCUIT

Fig. 15-27. Ford Electronic Message Center keyboard. *(Ford Motor Company)*

Key	Function
mph (km/h)	Miles per hour (kilometers per hour)
1/DTE	Distance to empty fuel tank
2/CK OUT	Warning checkout
3/CLOCK	Select clock or portion to be set
4/ADV	Advance clock (only for resetting mode)
5/F/ECON	Trip average and instantaneous (5.0-L engine only) distance per gallon (fuel economy)
6/DIST	Elapsed distance
7/E/TIME	Elapsed time
8/AV SPD	Average vehicle speed
9/DEST	Distance to destination
0/ETA	Estimated time of arrival
RESET	Reset trip log functions

Fig. 15-28. Electronic Message Center keys and their functions. *(Ford Motor Company)*

to calculate the estimated time of arrival and the distance remaining until arrival.

Several devices provide input to the microcomputer as part of the vehicle warning system. These devices are:

- Engine oil-pressure sensor
- Windshield washer fluid-level sensor
- Engine temperature sensor
- Trunk-ajar switch
- Door-ajar switch
- Brake warning switch
- Lamp-out warning system
- Fuel-tank sensor

The switches are all normally open switches. One terminal of each switch is connected to vehicle ground. A warning is activated when the switch closes and provides a ground at the microcomputer. If an input to the microcomputer indicates that a failure has occurred or that an unsafe condition exists, the microcomputer provides the following warning messages:

- DOOR—indicates that a door is not closed
- TRUNK—indicates that the rear deck lid is not closed
- CHARGE SYSTEM—indicates that the charging system is not operating properly
- OIL PRESSURE—indicates that the engine oil pressure is low
- ENGINE TEMPERATURE—indicates that the engine coolant temperature is too high
- DISTANCE TO EMPTY—indicates that the fuel tank will be empty in 50 miles [80 km], based on current fuel usage
- WINDSHIELD WASHER FLUID—indicates that the washer fluid reservoir is nearly empty
- BRAKE PRESSURE—indicates there is a failure in the brake hydraulic system
- HEADLAMPS—indicates there is a failure in one or more low-beam headlamps
- TAILLAMPS—indicates there is a failure in one or more taillamps
- BRAKE LAMPS—indicates there is a failure in one or more stoplamps

When there is a warning, the warning message flashes on and off and overrides the clock display. In addition, a tone sounds to alert the driver that a warning message has been activated.

When the CK OUT button on the keyboard is depressed, the system goes into automatic checkout mode. In checkout mode, the microcomputer checks all the inputs which are part of the vehicle warning system. Then the condition of each input system is displayed. Figure 15-29 shows the checkout sequence.

KEYLESS-ENTRY SYSTEM

The keyless-entry system permits the driver to lock or unlock the vehicle doors without using a key. The Ford keyless-entry system (Fig. 15-30) includes a keypad located on the outside of the driver's door (Fig. 15-31), a micro-

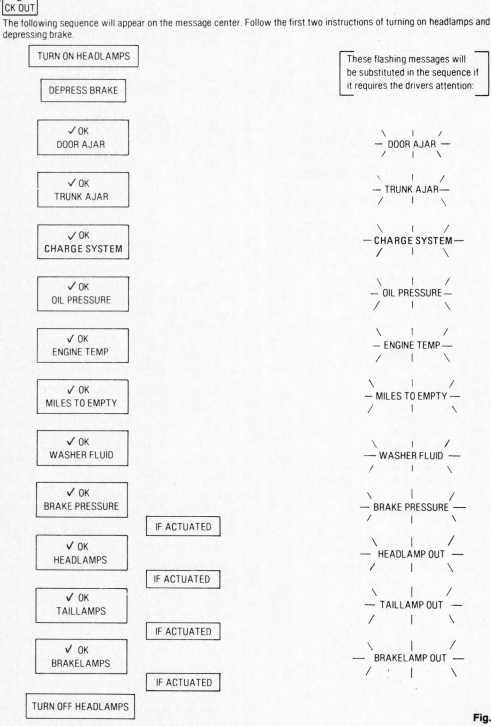

SYSTEM CHECKOUT

1. Start Engine
2. Press | 2 / CK OUT |

The following sequence will appear on the message center. Follow the first two instructions of turning on headlamps and depressing brake.

TURN ON HEADLAMPS

DEPRESS BRAKE

✓ OK
DOOR AJAR

✓ OK
TRUNK AJAR

✓ OK
CHARGE SYSTEM

✓ OK
OIL PRESSURE

✓ OK
ENGINE TEMP

✓ OK
MILES TO EMPTY

✓ OK
WASHER FLUID

✓ OK
BRAKE PRESSURE

✓ OK
HEADLAMPS   IF ACTUATED

✓ OK
TAILLAMPS   IF ACTUATED

✓ OK
BRAKELAMPS   IF ACTUATED

                     IF ACTUATED

TURN OFF HEADLAMPS

GOES BACK TO PREVIOUS DISPLAY

These flashing messages will be substituted in the sequence if it requires the drivers attention:

— DOOR AJAR —

— TRUNK AJAR—

—CHARGE SYSTEM—

— OIL PRESSURE —

— ENGINE TEMP —

— MILES TO EMPTY —

— WASHER FLUID —

— BRAKE PRESSURE —

— HEADLAMP OUT —

— TAILLAMP OUT —

— BRAKELAMP OUT —

Fig. 15-29. Ford Electronic Message Center with system in checkout mode. *(Ford Motor Company)*

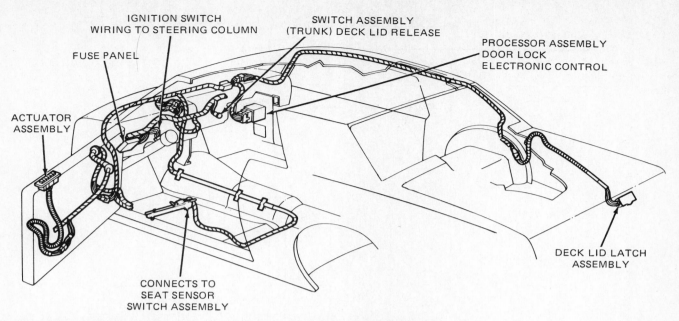

Fig. 15-30. Keyless-entry system, showing components and wiring. *(Ford Motor Company)*

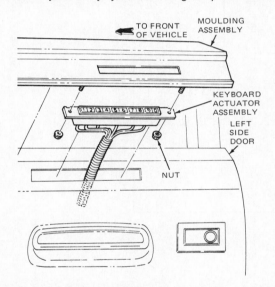

Fig. 15-31. Keyless-entry-system keypad. *(Ford Motor Company)*

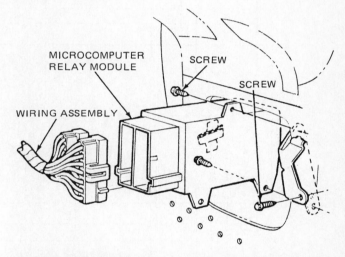

Fig. 15-32. Keyless-entry-system microcomputer-relay module. *(Ford Motor Company)*

computer-relay module (Fig. 15-32), and the door lock motors. The keypad consists of five normally open, single-pole single-throw switches. Each switch represents two digits. The switches are the 1/2 switch, the 3/4 switch, the 5/6 switch, the 7/8 switch, and the 9/0 switch. A circuit diagram is shown in Fig. 15-33.

The microprocessor is programmed to lock the doors when the 7/8 and 9/0 switch buttons are pressed simultaneously. The driver's door may be unlocked by entering a five-digit code into the microcomputer. The code is entered by depressing the switch buttons in the proper sequence. For example, a code of 36051 means the following buttons should be depressed in this sequence: 3/4, 5/6, 9/0, 5/6, and 1/2. The unlock code for each car is programmed into the microcomputer at the factory. The driver may add a second code by following instructions which are provided in the owner's manual.

In addition to locking and unlocking the doors, the microcomputer can:

- Unlock the rest of the vehicle doors if the 3/4 keypad button is depressed within 5 seconds after the driver's door has been unlocked.

- Release the rear deck lid if the 5/6 keypad button is depressed within 5 seconds after the driver's door has been unlocked.

- Turn on the courtesy lamps, keypad lamp, and door lock LEDs when any keypad button is depressed or when the front-door handle is raised.

- Automatically lock all doors when all the following conditions are met:
  - Ignition switch is in the RUN position.
  - Driver's seat is occupied (seat switch closed).
  - Doors are closed (doorjamb switches open).
  - Transmission selector lever passes through REVERSE (backup-lamp switch closed momentarily).

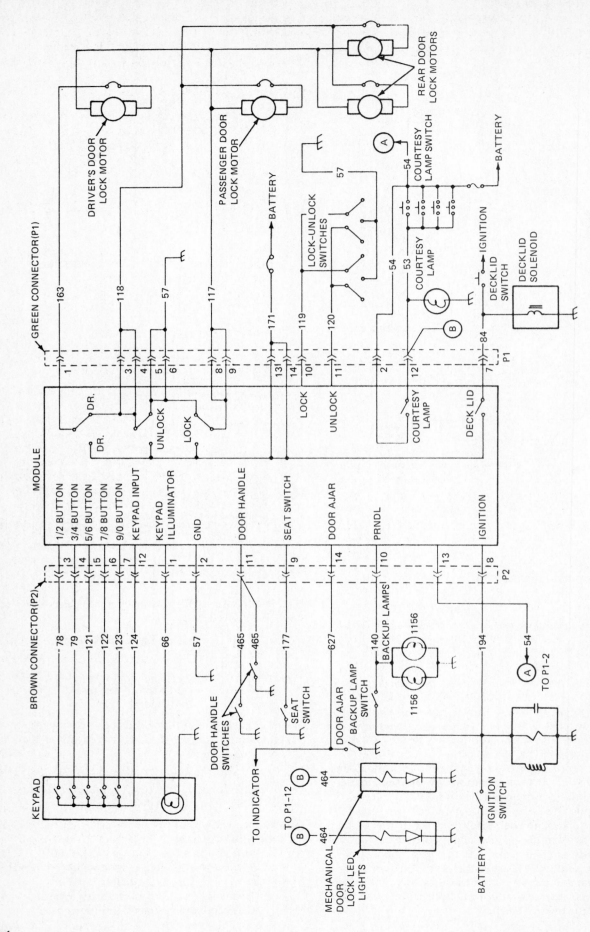

Fig. 15-33. Circuit diagram of a keyless-entry system. *(Ford Motor Company)*

The microcomputer receives inputs from the following components:

- Keypad switches (closed when switch button is depressed)
- Door handle switches (closed with door handle raised)
- Driver's seat switch (closed with seat occupied)
- Backup-lamp switch (closed with selector lever in REVERSE)
- Doorjamb switches (closed with doors open)
- Ignition switch (supplies battery voltage in RUN position)
- Door lock and unlock switches (each switch grounding a terminal of the module when operated)
- Door-ajar switch (closed when door is ajar)

Based on the inputs received, the microcomputer can:

- Operate the door lock motors
- Operate the rear deck-lid release solenoid
- Operate the keypad lamp
- Operate the door lock LEDs
- Operate the courtesy lamps

SYSTEM OPERATION

The microcomputer-relay module is connected to the circuit wiring with two 14-pin connectors: connector P1 and connector P2. Battery voltage is supplied to terminals 2, 13, and 14 of connector P1 and to terminal 13 of connector P2. The module contains the microcomputer and performs a series of relay switching functions.

Locking the Doors

When the 7/8 and 9/0 switch buttons are depressed, the microcomputer locks the doors. The lock switch closes, and the current flow is as shown in Fig. 15-34. Note that current flows through all the lock motors to lock all the doors.

Unlocking the Driver's Door

When the correct code is entered on the keypad, the microcomputer unlocks the driver's door. The driver's door switch closes and applies battery voltage to the lock motor with the proper polarity to unlock the door (Fig. 15-35). Note that the direction of current flow through the lock motor is the opposite of that in Fig. 15-34.

Unlocking the Rest of the Doors

When the 3/4 keypad button is depressed within 5 seconds after the driver's door has been unlocked, the microcom-puter unlocks the other doors. The unlock switch closes and applies battery voltage to the lock motors as shown in Fig. 15-36. The direction of current flow through the lock motors causes the rest of the doors to be unlocked.

Releasing the Rear Deck Lid

When the 5/6 keypad button is depressed within 5 seconds after the driver's door has been unlocked, the microcom-puter releases the rear deck lid. The deck-lid switch closes and applies battery voltage to the deck-lid solenoid. It then operates to release the deck lid (Fig. 15-37).

Illuminating the Courtesy Lamps and Door Lock LED

When a door handle is raised or any keypad button is depressed, the microcomputer lights the courtesy lamps and the door lock LEDs. The courtesy lamp switch closes and directs battery voltage to the courtesy lamps and the door lock LEDs (Fig. 15-38). In addition, the module supplies battery voltage to the keypad lamps from terminal 1 of connector P2.

Automatic Door Lock Function

The doors lock automatically when the following four conditions are met: the ignition switch is in RUN, the driver's seat is occupied, the doors are closed, and the transmission selector lever passes through REVERSE. When the ignition switch is in RUN, battery voltage is applied to terminal 8 of connector P2. When the driver's seat is occupied, the seat switch closes and grounds terminal 9 of connector P2. When the doors are closed, the doorjamb switches are open. As the selector lever passes through REVERSE, the backup-lamp switch closes momentarily and supplies battery voltage to terminal 10 of connector P2. The microcomputer is programmed to operate the lock switch when the above four conditions are met. The current flow is shown in Fig. 15-39. All the door lock motors are operated to lock all the doors.

In addition to being operated by computer control, the doors may be locked or unlocked with the door lock and unlock switches. When the door lock switch operates, it grounds terminal 10 of connector P1. The unlock switch grounds terminal 11. The doors may also be locked and unlocked with the key.

SERVICING COMPUTER-CONTROLLED SYSTEMS

The service and repair of keyless-entry and travel information systems require special troubleshooting procedures. Each system requires a precise sequence of tests. Some computer-controlled systems have a built-in diagnostic procedure. Follow the procedures in the manufacturer's service manual when troubleshooting computer-controlled systems.

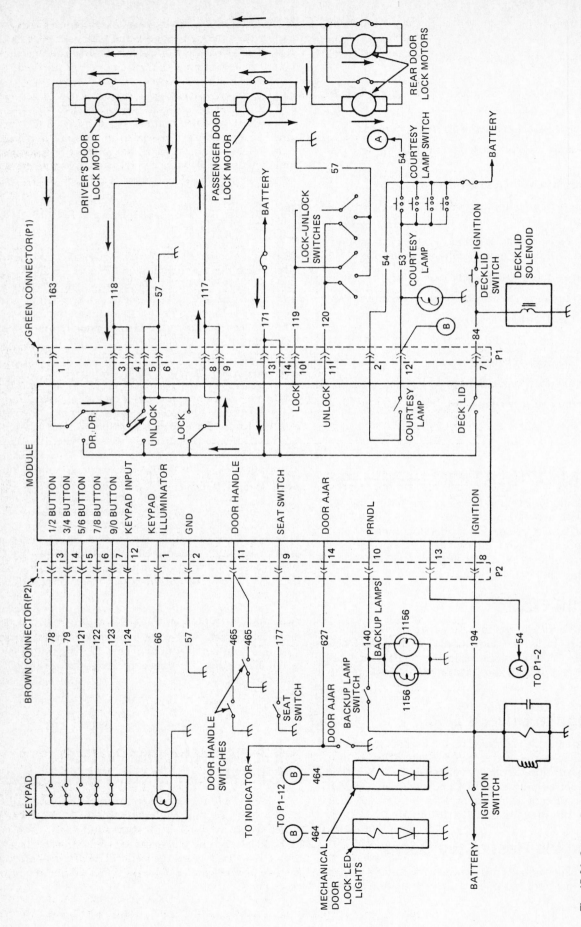

Fig. 15-34. Current flow in keyless-entry system—locking the doors. (*Ford Motor Company*)

216

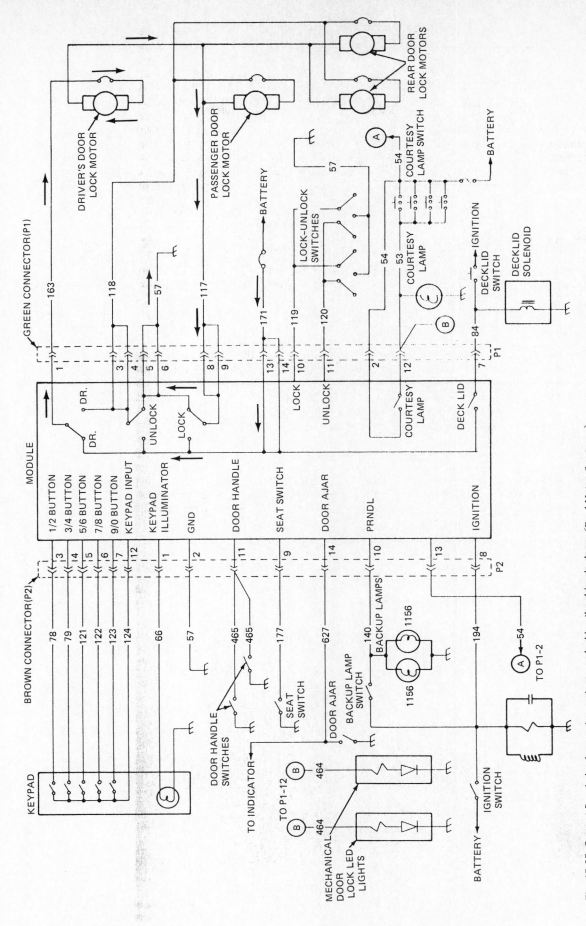

Fig. 15-35. Current flow in keyless-entry system—unlocking the driver's door. *(Ford Motor Company)*

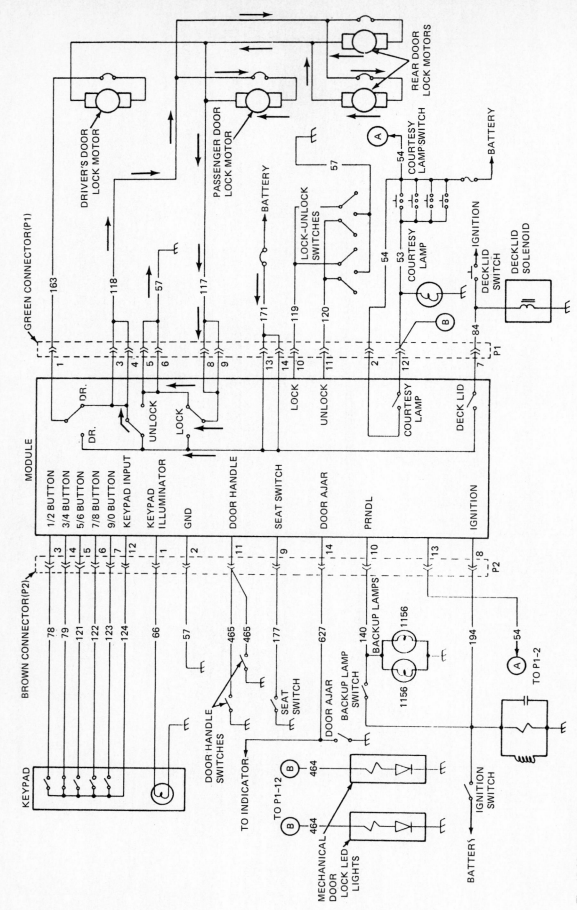

Fig. 15-36. Current flow in keyless-entry system—unlocking the other doors. *(Ford Motor Company)*

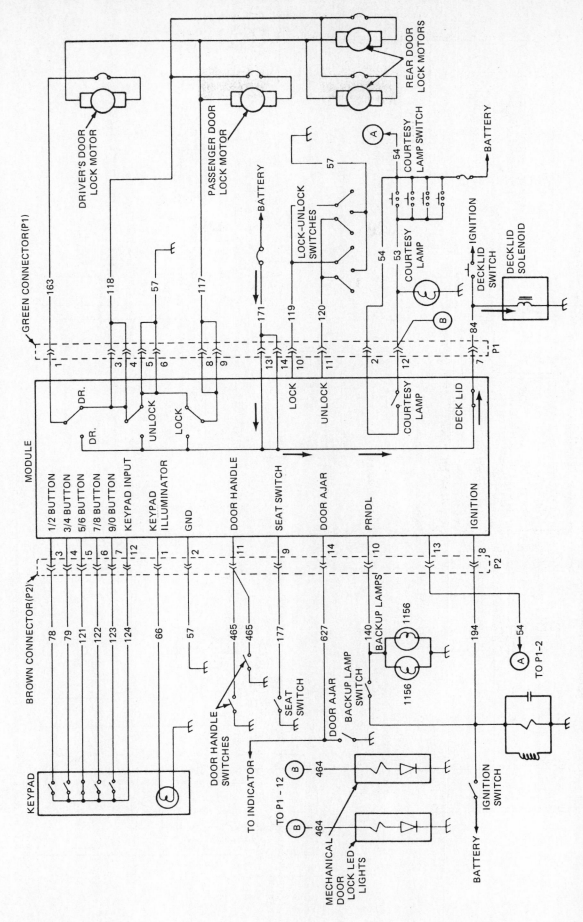

Fig. 15-37. Current flow in keyless-entry system—releasing the rear deck lid. *(Ford Motor Company)*

219

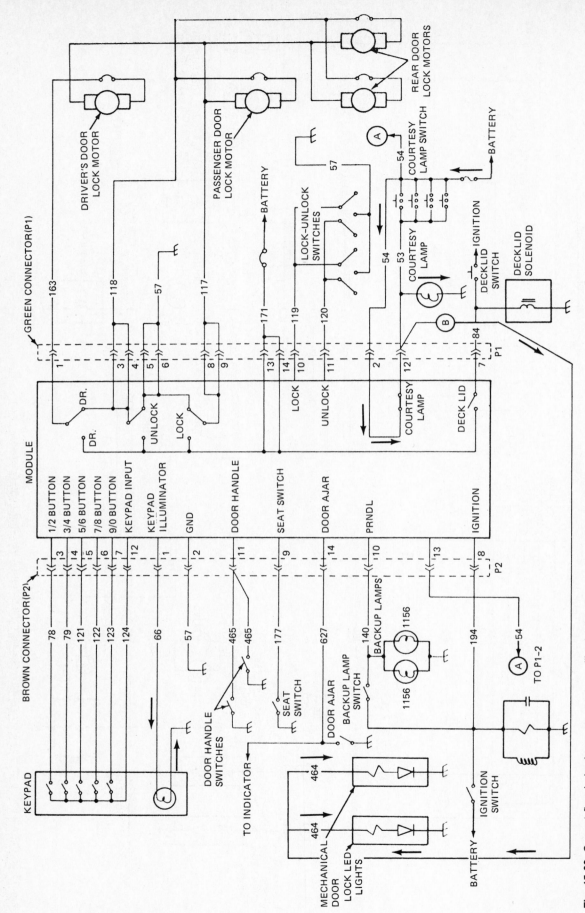

Fig. 15-38. Current flow in keyless-entry system—illuminating the courtesy lamps and door lock LED. *(Ford Motor Company)*

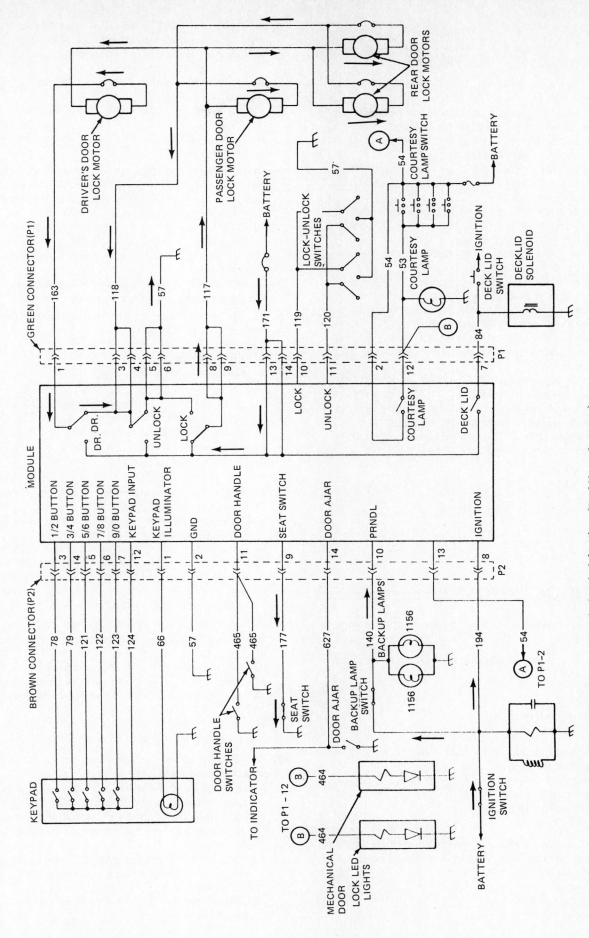

Fig. 15-39. Current flow in the keyless-entry system—automatic door lock function. *(Ford Motor Company)*

VOCABULARY REVIEW

Computer An electronic device that stores and processes data.

Input device The part of a microcomputer circuit that connects a sensor to the microcomputer.

Memory The part of a computer that stores data.

Microcomputer A miniature computer.

Microprocessor The part of a microcomputer that controls all operations. Also called a *central processing unit (CPU)*.

Output device The part of a microcomputer circuit that connects the microcomputer to a control device on the automobile.

Phoneme A basic sound of which human speech is composed.

Phoneme generator An electronic circuit which produces phonemelike sounds.

Program A set of instructions that tells the microprocessor what to do and when to do it.

Random access memory (RAM) The part of a computer where data can be added (written in) and read out.

Read-only memory (ROM) The part of a computer that contains stored data.

Sensor A device which converts some feature of vehicle operation into an electric signal.

Synthesized speech Speech produced by combining phonemes by electronic means.

REVIEW QUESTIONS

Select the *one* correct, best, or most probable answer to each question.

1. The part of a microcomputer that stores the program is called the
   a. RAM
   b. ROM
   c. microprocessor
   d. input device

2. Which part of a microcomputer controls the operation of the microcomputer?
   a. microprocessor
   b. read-only memory
   c. read-and-write memory
   d. input device

3. Which part of a computer converts computer data into a signal that can control a function on the vehicle?
   a. input device
   b. program
   c. microprocessor
   d. output device

4. In the keyless-entry system described in this chapter, how is the keypad used to lock the vehicle doors?
   a. by depressing the 5/6 button within 5 seconds after the code has been entered
   b. by depressing the 7/8 and 9/0 buttons simultaneously
   c. by entering a five-digit code into the microcomputer
   d. by depressing the 3/4 and 5/6 buttons simultaneously

5. In the keyless-entry system described in this chapter, how is the keypad used to unlock the rear deck lid?
   a. by depressing the 5/6 button within 5 seconds after the code has been used to unlock the doors
   b. by depressing the 5/6 and 9/0 buttons simultaneously
   c. by entering a five-digit code into the microcomputer
   d. by depressing the 3/4 button within 5 seconds after the code has been used to unlock the doors

6. All of the following are inputs to the keyless-entry microcomputer *except* the
   a. backup-lamp switch
   b. door lock switches
   c. door handle switches
   d. door lock motors

7. All of the following are inputs to the Ford Electronic Message Center system *except*
   a. engine temperature information
   b. fuel-economy information
   c. trunk-ajar signal
   d. brake warning switch signal

8. All of the following statements are true of the Ford Electronic Message Center system *except*
   a. the sensor switches signal a warning by providing a ground signal to the microcomputer
   b. estimated distance must be entered into the microcomputer using the numbered keyboard buttons
   c. the sensor switches are normally closed switches
   d. the automatic checkout mode is activated by depressing the CK OUT button

9. In the Nissan voice warning system, what conditions are necessary to cause the warning "Parking brake is on"?
   a. parking brake is in the engaged position
   b. ignition switch is on, and parking brake is engaged
   c. driver's door is open, and parking brake switch is on
   d. ignition switch is on, parking brake switch is on, and car speed is above 6 mph [10 km/h]

10. Which of the following statements is true of the Chrysler voice warning system?
    a. the module that detects a headlamp failure sends an ac signal to the microcomputer
    b. normally closed switches signal the microcomputer that a failure has occurred or an unsafe condition exists
    c. a sensor switch sends a ground signal to the microcomputer when a failure has occurred or an unsafe condition exists
    d. engine oil level is sensed by a temperature-sensitive resistor

CHAPTER 16

ACCESSORIES

OBJECTIVE

After you have studied this chapter, you should be able to:

1. **Describe the operation of various automotive accessories.**

Many different accessories are available on the automobile. An *accessory* is a device which adds to driver comfort and convenience. However, it is not essential to the operation of the vehicle. As the use of electronics increases on the automobile, each year the list of accessories grows longer. Many accessories are similar in operation. Therefore, only the most common accessories that represent the greatest variations in design are covered here. These are:

- Power windows
- Power seats
- Power door locks
- Heated-rear-window systems

- Rear deck-lid release and locking circuits
- Entertainment systems (radios, tape players, and citizens band, or CB, radios)
- Power antennas
- Speed control systems
- Illuminated-entry systems
- Antitheft alarm systems

POWER WINDOWS

Power windows are windows that are raised and lowered by electric motors. Manually operated windows use a crank handle to operate a *window regulator*. This device converts the rotary motion of the crank handle into the up-and-down movement of the window. With power windows, the electric motor operates the regulator. Some motors engage the window regulator directly. Others operate the regulator

223

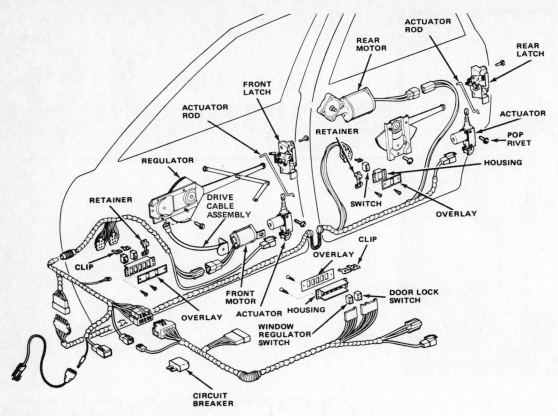

Fig. 16-1. Power window system. *(American Motors Corporation)*

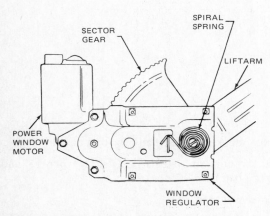

Fig. 16-2. Power window motor and regulator. *(Fisher Body Division of General Motors Corporation)*

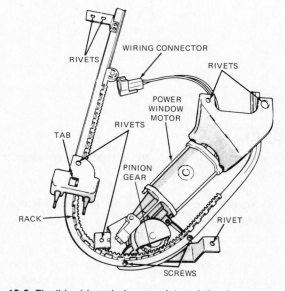

Fig. 16-3. Flexible-drive window regulator. *(Chrysler Corporation)*

through a drive cable (Fig. 16-1). When the motor is connected directly to the regulator, a gear on the end of the motor shaft engages a gear on the window regulator (Fig. 16-2).

The gear on the regulator is a section of gear teeth called a *sector gear*. As the window is lowered, a spiral spring attached to the sector gear is wound up. Energy must be supplied to the spring to wind it up. As the window is raised, the spring unwinds releasing energy which helps raise the window. The spring action helps compensate for the weight of the window. Without the spring, a small force could lower the window, but a much larger force would be required to raise it. The spring makes the

load on the motor about the same whether the window is being raised or lowered.

Another type of window regulator uses rack-and-pinion gears. The pinion gear is on the end of the motor shaft. The rack is a flexible strip of gear teeth. One end of the rack is attached to the window, as shown in Fig. 16-3. As the motor shaft rotates, the rack moves to raise or lower the window.

Two types of power window motors are commonly used. One type of motor is grounded and has two field windings. The other type of motor is not grounded, and it has a single field winding. Figure 16-4 shows a non-grounded-motor system. The direction of current flow through the motor is reversed to change the direction of rotation of the motor. This raises or lowers the window. Figure 16-5 shows a grounded-motor system. Each motor has two field windings. When voltage is applied to one winding, it causes the motor to rotate in one direction to lower the window. When voltage is applied to the other winding, it causes the motor to rotate in the other direction to raise the window.

A master switch, operated by the driver, controls the voltage applied to the window motors. In addition, each door (with the exception of the driver's door) has an individual switch to permit a passenger in the vehicle to operate the window. Some master control switches have a safety switch (sometimes called a *lock-out switch*). The safety switch disconnects voltage from the passenger switches so that only the driver can operate the windows in the vehicle. Figure 16-6 shows a master control switch with a safety switch.

Most window motors have a built-in circuit breaker to protect the motor if a switch is held too long in the UP or DOWN position.

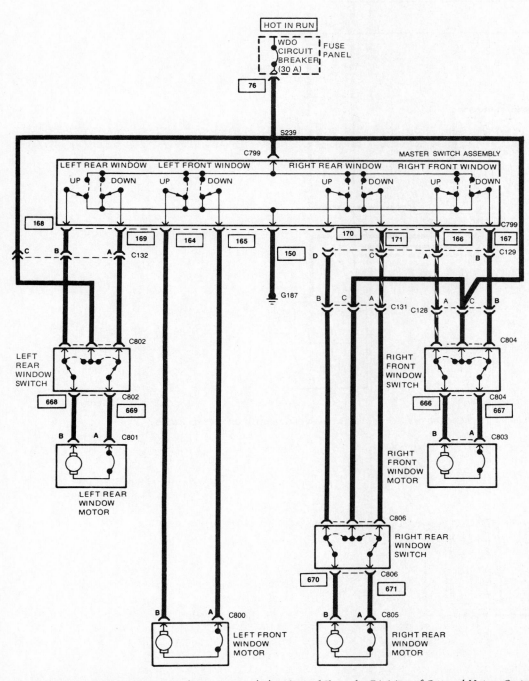

Fig. 16-4. Power window system using nongrounded motors. *(Chevrolet Division of General Motors Corporation)*

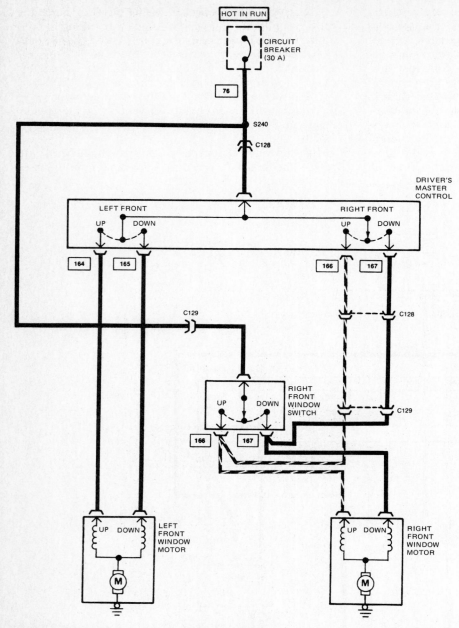

Fig. 16-5. Power window system using grounded motors. *(Chevrolet Division of General Motors Corporation)*

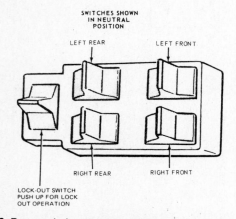

Fig. 16-6. Power window master control switch. *(Ford Motor Company)*

With the nongrounded-motor system, the switches ground the motor in addition to supplying voltage to the motor. Figure 16-7 shows the current flow with the master control switch in the DOWN position to lower the right front window. Figure 16-8 shows the current flow with the switch in the UP position. Figures 16-9 and 16-10 show the current flow with a passenger switch in the DOWN position and UP position.

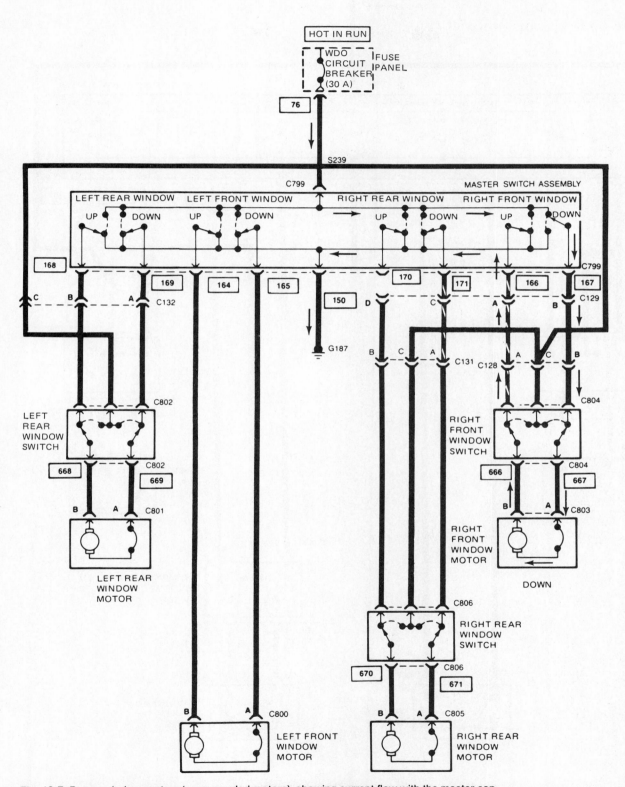

Fig. 16-7. Power window system (nongrounded motors), showing current flow with the master control switch in the DOWN position. *(Chevrolet Division of General Motors Corporation)*

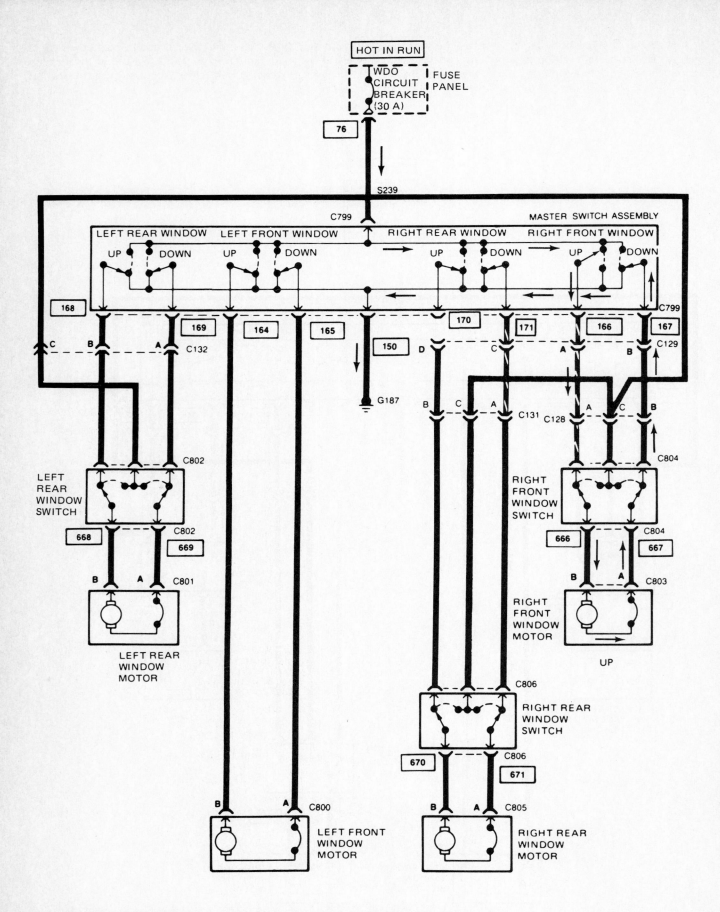

Fig. 16-8. Power window system (nongrounded motors), showing current flow with the master control switch in the UP position. *(Chevrolet Division of General Motors Corporation)*

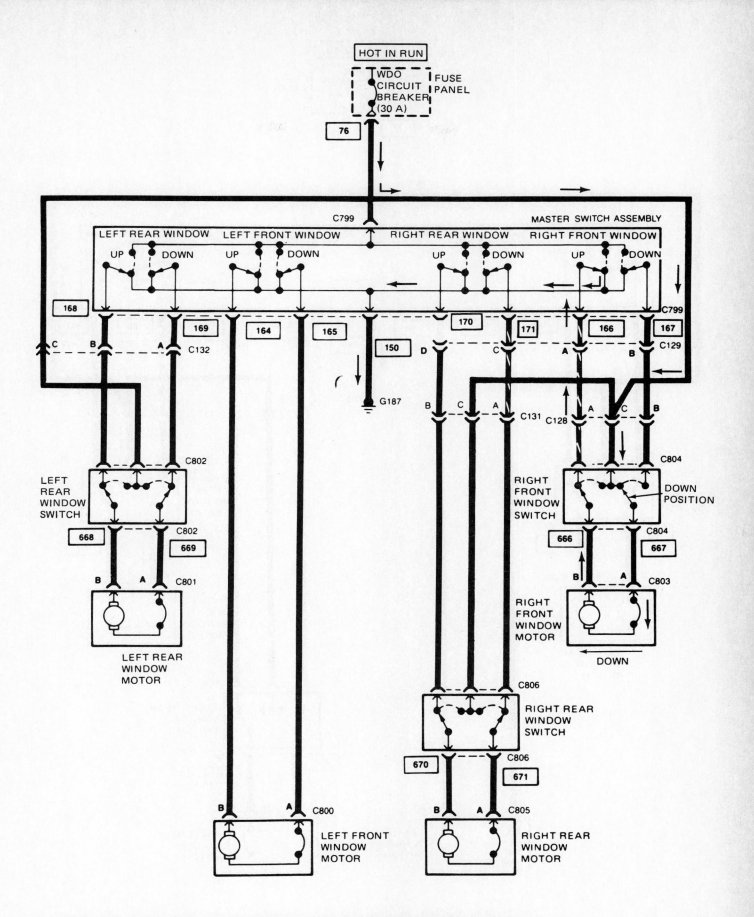

Fig. 16-9. Power window system (nongrounded motors), showing current flow with a passenger switch in the DOWN position. *(Chevrolet Division of General Motors Corporation)*

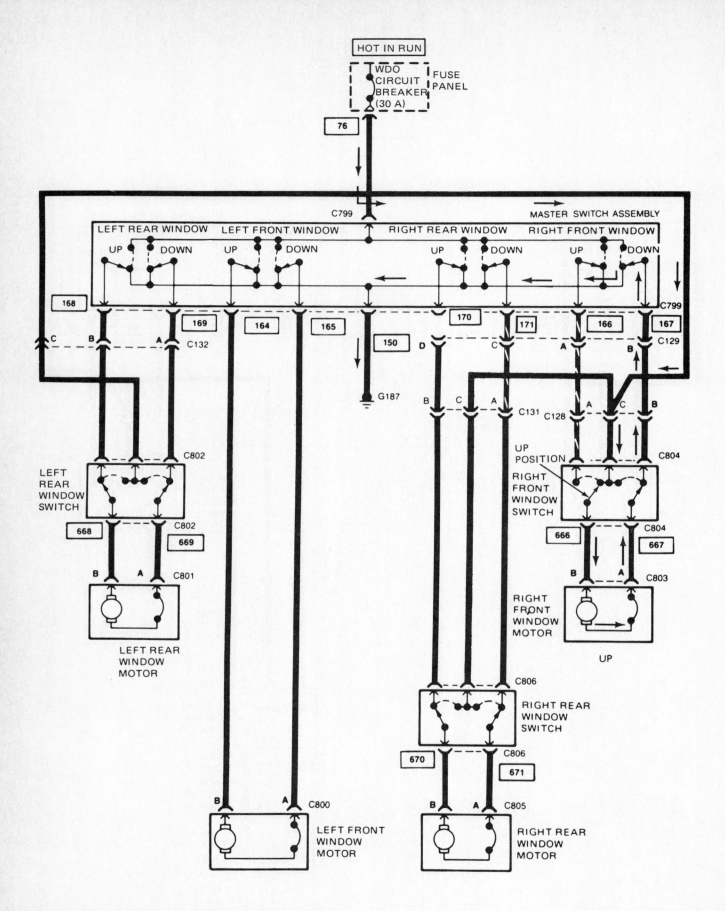

Fig. 16-10. Power window system (nongrounded motors), showing current flow with a passenger switch in the UP position. *(Chevrolet Division of General Motors Corporation)*

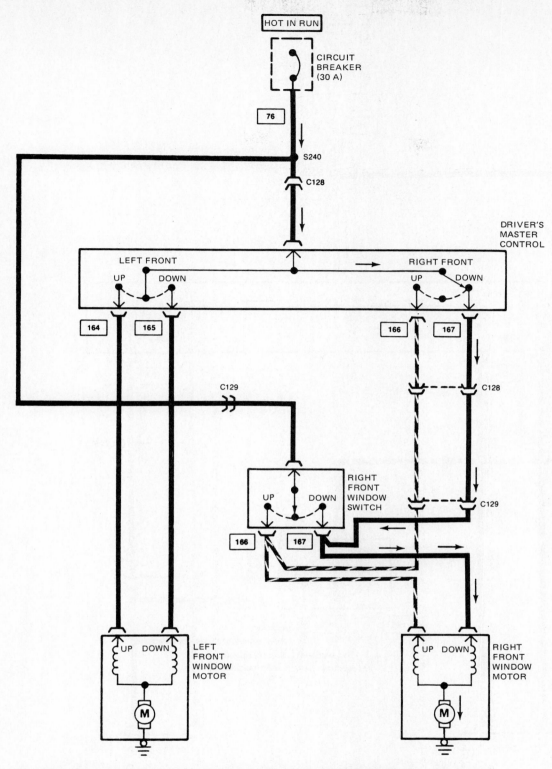

Fig. 16-11. Power window system (grounded motors), showing current flow with the master control switch in the DOWN position. *(Chevrolet Division of General Motors Corporation)*

With the grounded-motor system, the switches direct voltage to the appropriate field winding to raise or lower the window. Figure 16-11 shows the master control switch in the DOWN position to lower the right front window. In this position, voltage is applied to the DOWN field winding.

When the master control switch is moved to the UP position, voltage is applied to the UP field winding. This raises the window (Fig. 16-12). Figures 16-13 and 16-14 show the current flow with a passenger switch in the DOWN and UP positions.

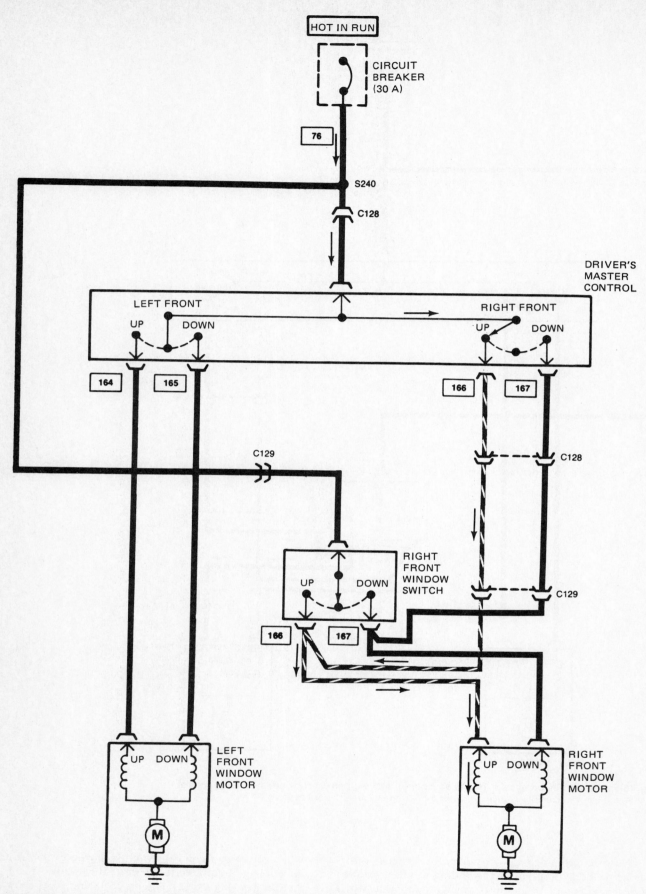

Fig. 16-12. Power window system (grounded motors), showing current flow with the master control switch in the UP position. *(Chevrolet Division of General Motors Corporation)*

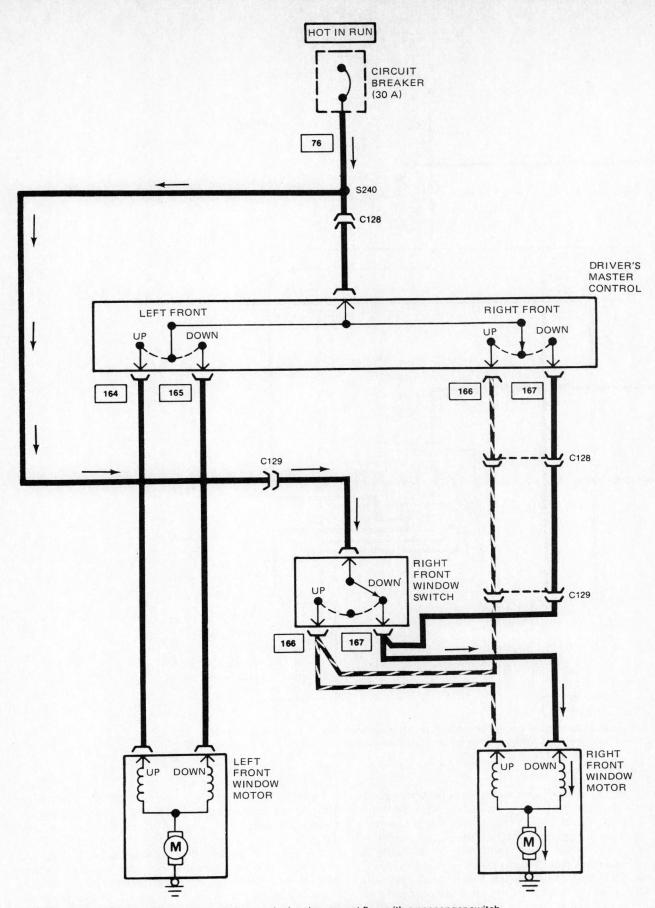

Fig. 16-13. Power window system (grounded motors), showing current flow with a passenger switch in the DOWN position. *(Chevrolet Division of General Motors Corporation)*

233

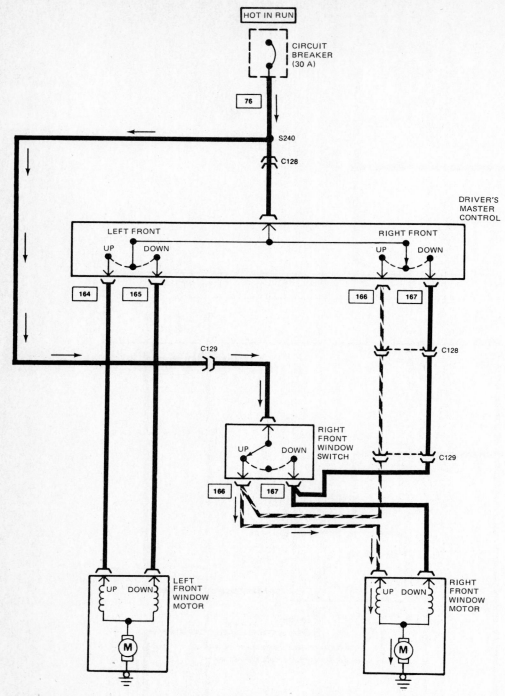

Fig. 16-14. Power window system (grounded motors), showing current flow with a passenger switch in the UP position. *(Chevrolet Division of General Motors Corporation)*

Some power window systems will operate with the ignition switch in the RUN position only. Other systems will operate in RUN or ACCESSORY. In Figs. 16-4 and 16-5, current is supplied from the ignition switch to the power window system through a circuit breaker in the fuse block. Figure 16-15 shows a circuit that uses a relay to supply power to the system. When the ignition switch is turned to ACCESSORY or RUN, the relay is energized through a circuit breaker located in the fuse block. When the relay is energized, voltage is supplied from the battery through the relay contacts

to the system. Another circuit breaker protects the power window system from overloads. With this design, the ignition switch carries only the current required to energize the relay.

Figure 16-16 shows a tailgate power window diagram. The motor can be controlled by a key cylinder switch located in the tailgate or by a driver-operated switch. A block-out switch, connected in series with the motor, is open when the tailgate is open. This switch permits motor operation only when the tailgate is closed.

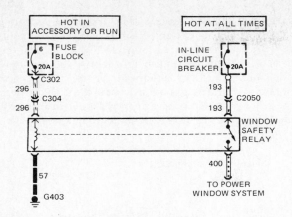

Fig. 16-15. Power window relay. *(Ford Motor Company)*

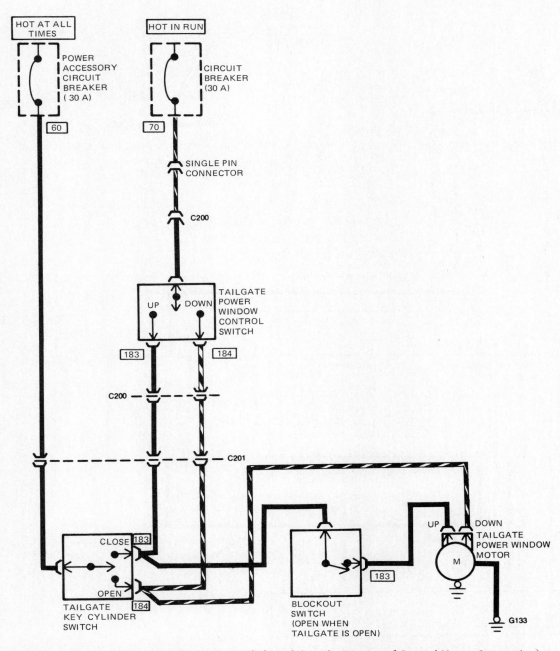

Fig. 16-16. Circuit diagram of a tailgate power window. *(Chevrolet Division of General Motors Corporation)*

POWER SEATS

Power seats are seats that are operated by electric motors. One common design uses three motors to move the seat six different ways: down, up, forward, rearward, forward tilt, and rearward tilt. Figure 16-17 shows a permanent-magnet, three-motor-drive unit. The three armatures are mounted in a single housing. The direction of rotation of each armature can be reversed by changing the direction of current flow through the armature winding. Drive cables connect the armatures to small transmissions which move the seat in the various directions, as shown in Fig. 16-18. The three motors are called the front-height motor, the rear-height motor, and the forward-rearward motor. These three motors control the height of the front of the seat, the height of the rear of the seat, and the forward and rearward movement of the seat. A power seat circuit diagram is shown in Fig. 16-19.

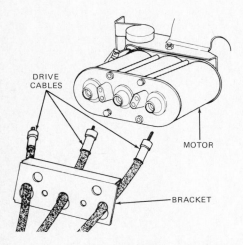

Fig. 16-17. Power seat motor having three armatures. *(Chrysler Corporation)*

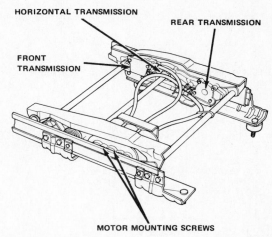

Fig. 16-18. Power seat mechanism. *(American Motors Corporation)*

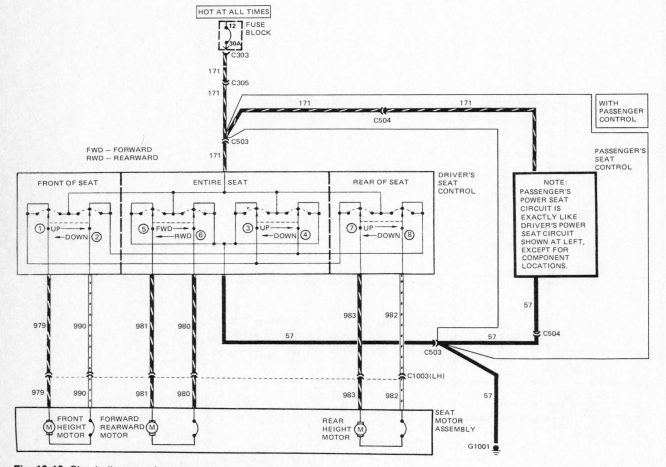

Fig. 16-19. Circuit diagram of a power seat. *(Ford Motor Company)*

A seat control switch assembly directs voltage to the three seat motors (Fig. 16-20). If the seat control switch is moved to the UP or DOWN position, both the front-height and rear-height motors operate at the same time. If the front-tilt or rear-tilt switches are operated, only one of the height motors operates. If the seat control switch is moved to the forward or rearward position, the forward-rearward motor operates.

Figures 16-21 and 16-22 show the current flow with the seat control in the FORWARD and REARWARD positions. Notice the difference in the direction of current flow in the two switch positions. Figures 16-23 and 16-24 show the current flow with the seat control in the FRONT-OF-SEAT-UP and FRONT-OF-SEAT-DOWN positions. The switch contacts that control the rear of the seat operate in the same manner as those that control the front of the seat. Figures 16-25 and 16-26 show the current flow with the seat control in the SEAT-UP and SEAT-DOWN positions.

Some power seat systems use a single motor with three solenoids. The seat control switch directs voltage to the solenoids. The solenoids then engage the drive cables to the motor armature to move the seat (Fig. 16-27).

On vehicles with separate front seats, the passenger seat has a similar arrangement of motors with a seat control switch. Some passenger seats provide four-way operation instead of the six-way operation common on driver's seats. The four motions are forward, rearward, front of seat up, and front of seat down.

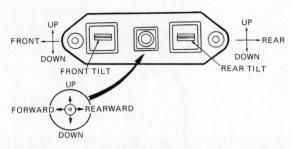

Fig. 16-20. Power seat control switch. *(Ford Motor Company)*

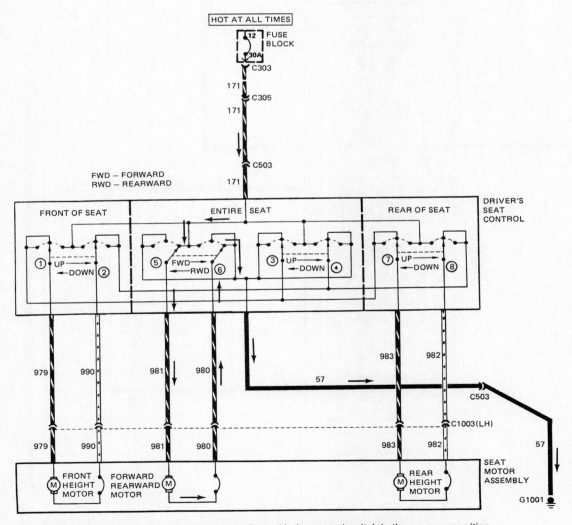

Fig. 16-21. Power seat system, showing current flow with the control switch in the FORWARD position. *(Ford Motor Company)*

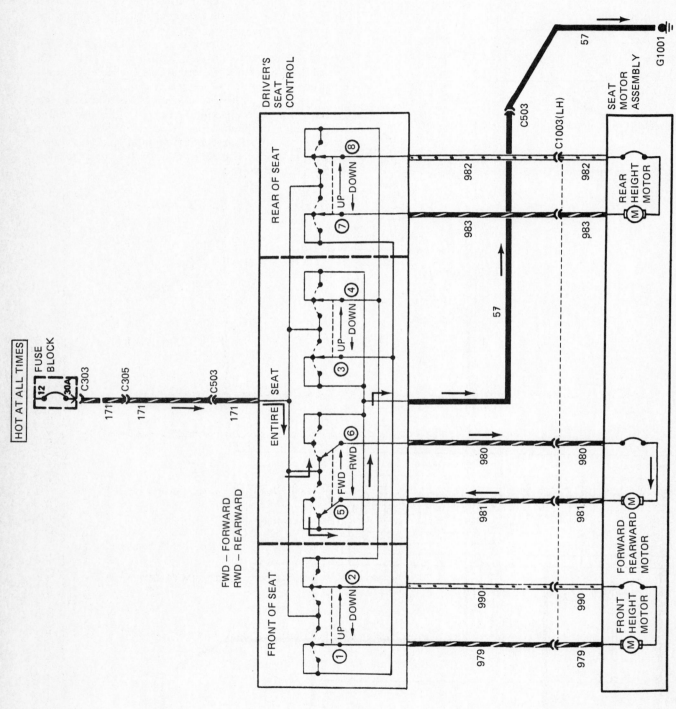

Fig. 16-22. Power seat system, showing current flow with the control switch in the REARWARD position. *(Ford Motor Company)*

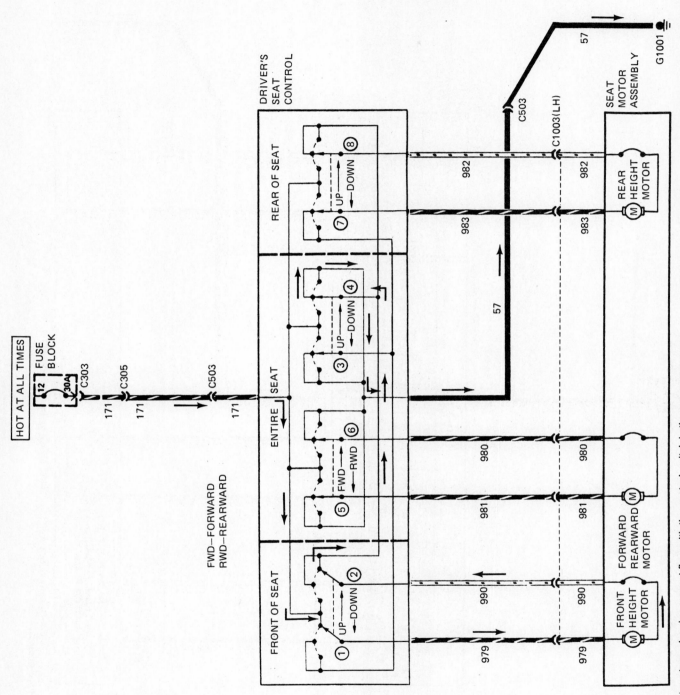

Fig. 16-23. Power seat system, showing current flow with the control switch in the FRONT-OF-SEAT-UP position. *(Ford Motor Company)*

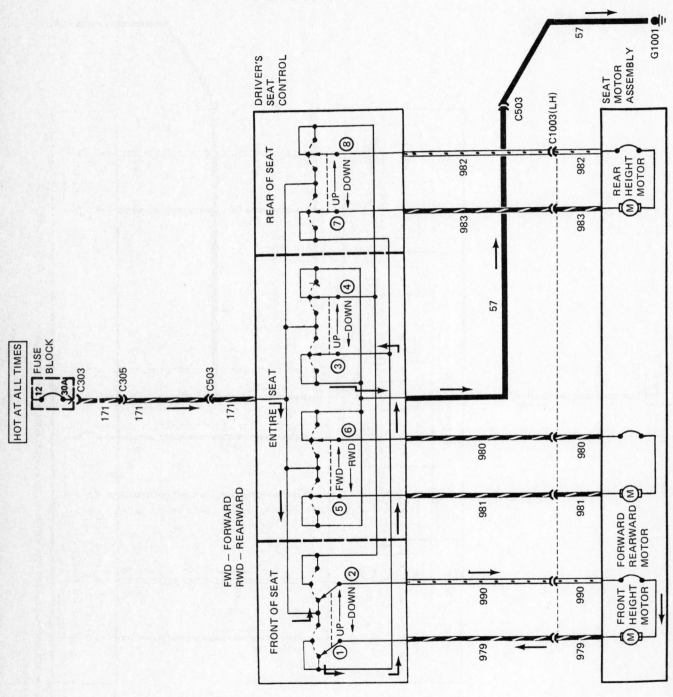

Fig. 16-24. Power seat system, showing current flow with the control switch in the FRONT-OF-SEAT-DOWN position. (*Ford Motor Company*)

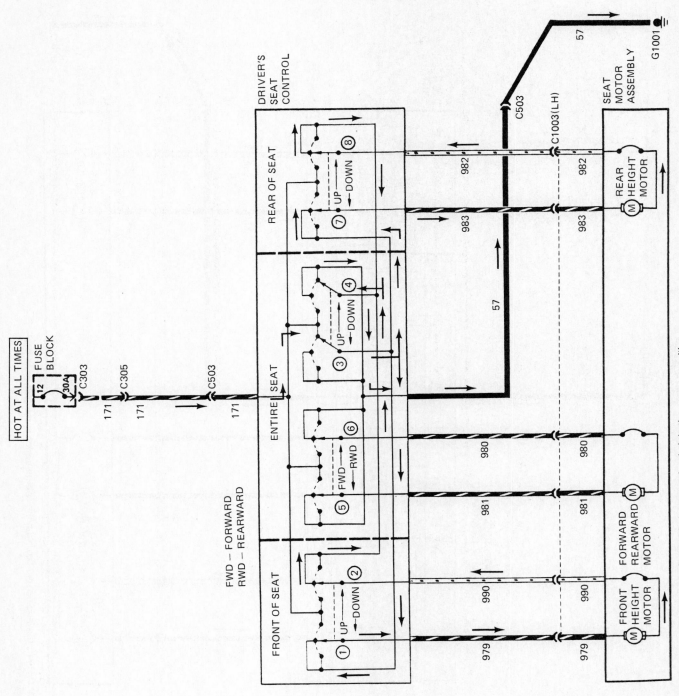

Fig. 16-25. Power seat system, showing current flow with the control switch in the SEAT-UP position. *(Ford Motor Company)*

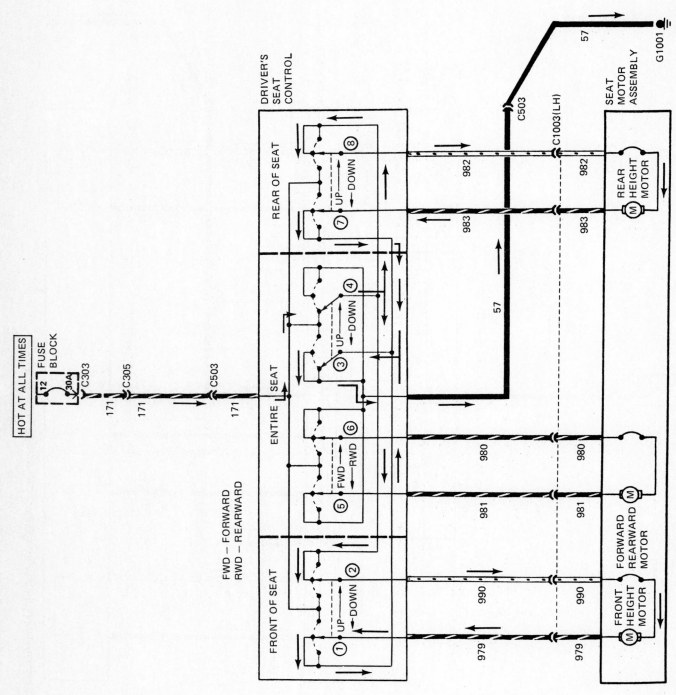

Fig. 16-26. Power seat system, showing current flow with the control switch in the seat-down position. *(Ford Motor Company)*

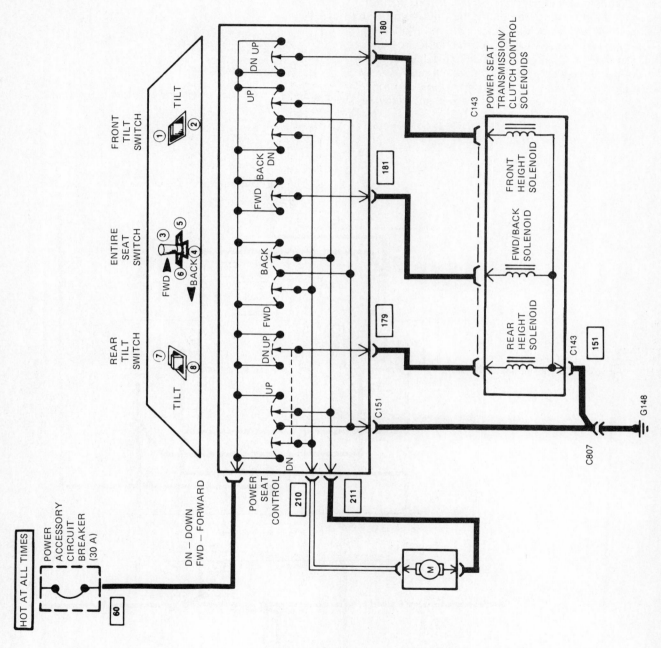

Fig. 16-27. Power seat system which uses a single motor with three solenoids. (*Chevrolet Division of General Motors Corporation*)

POWER DOOR LOCKS

Power door lock systems use motors to actuate the locking mechanism on the vehicle doors (Fig. 16-28). On some vehicles, the switch that controls the motors is operated by the door-locking rod, and on other vehicles, it is operated by separate switches. The switches are usually located on the driver's door and the front passenger's door. On systems which have the switch on the door-locking rod, pushing the locking button beyond the normal locked position will lock all doors. Pulling the button beyond the normal unlock position will unlock all doors. When the driver or the passenger operates the switch, all the doors are either locked or unlocked. Figure 16-29 is a circuit diagram of a power door lock system. The driver's switch and passenger's switch operate relays. The relays perform two functions. They direct voltage to the motors and provide

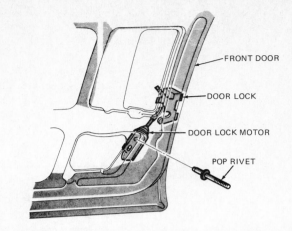

Fig. 16-28. Power door lock motor. *(Chrysler Corporation)*

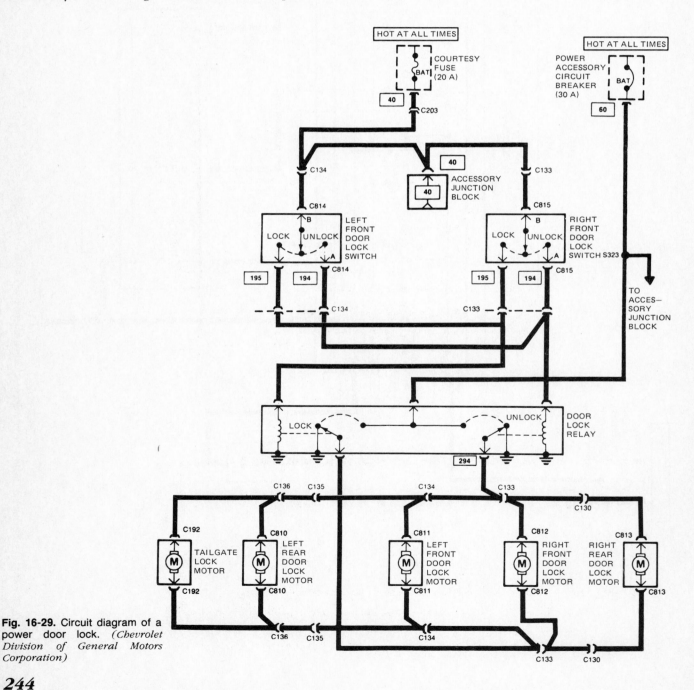

Fig. 16-29. Circuit diagram of a power door lock. *(Chevrolet Division of General Motors Corporation)*

244

ground for the motors. The door lock motors are reversible motors. The direction of motor rotation is changed by changing the direction of current flow through the armature of the motors.

Figure 16-30 shows the current flow with the driver's door switch in the LOCK position. The switch contacts supply voltage to the coil of the lock relay. This energizes the relay, so the relay contacts supply voltage to all the lock motors. The motors are grounded through the normally closed contacts of the unlock relay. When the switch is released, it returns to a neutral position and the lock relay

deenergizes. The passenger switch operates in a similar manner.

Figure 16-31 shows the current flow with the driver's door switch in the UNLOCK position. The switch contacts supply voltage to the coil of the unlock relay. This energizes the relay, so the relay contacts supply voltage to the lock motors. The motors are grounded through the normally closed contacts of the lock relay. The current flow is reversed through the motors, and the doors are unlocked. When the switch is released, it returns to a neutral position and the unlock relay deenergizes.

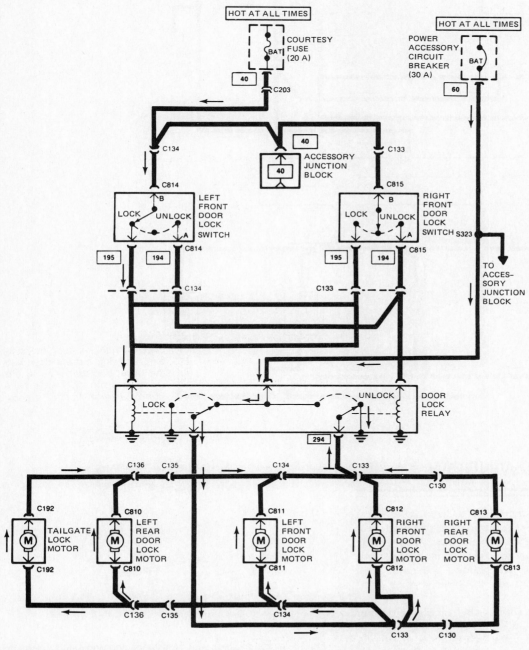

Fig. 16-30. Power door lock system, showing current flow with the driver's door switch in the LOCK position. *(Chevrolet Division of General Motors Corporation)*

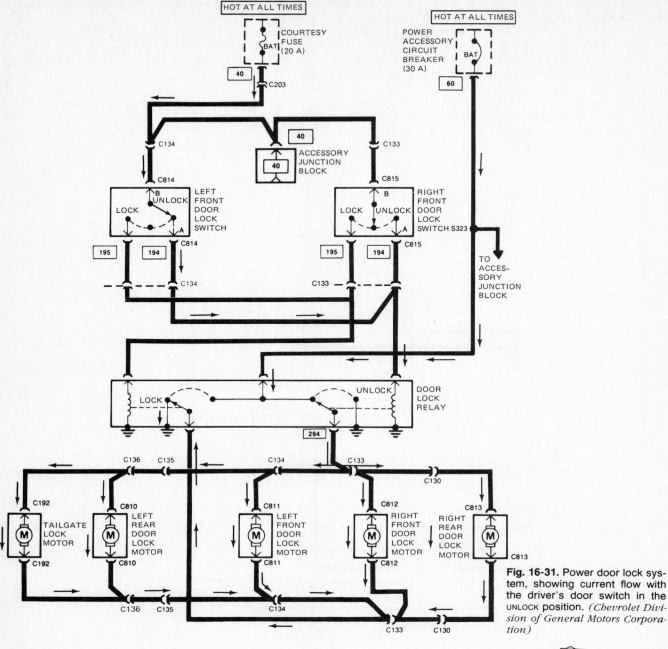

COURTESY
FUSE
(20 A)

BAT

40

C203

C134

C133

40

ACCESSORY
JUNCTION
BLOCK

40

HOT AT ALL TIMES

POWER
ACCESSORY
CIRCUIT
BREAKER
(30 A)

BAT

60

C814

C815

B
UNLOCK

LOCK

LEFT
FRONT
DOOR
LOCK
SWITCH

A

B
LOCK   UNLOCK

RIGHT
FRONT
DOOR
LOCK
SWITCH S323

A

195   194   C814

195   194   C815

TO
ACCES-
SORY
JUNCTION
BLOCK

C134

C133

LOCK

UNLOCK

DOOR
LOCK
RELAY

294

C136   C135

C134   C133

C130

C192

C810

C811

C812

C813

M
TAILGATE
LOCK
MOTOR

M
LEFT
REAR
DOOR
LOCK
MOTOR

M
LEFT
FRONT
DOOR
LOCK
MOTOR

M
RIGHT
FRONT
DOOR
LOCK
MOTOR

M
RIGHT
REAR
DOOR
LOCK
MOTOR

C192

C810

C811

C812

C813

C136   C135

C134

C133   C130

Fig. 16-31. Power door lock system, showing current flow with the driver's door switch in the UNLOCK position. *(Chevrolet Division of General Motors Corporation)*

HEATED-REAR-WINDOW SYSTEM

A heated-rear-window system uses a heating element bonded to the inside of the window to clear the window of fog or ice (Fig. 16-32). When current flows through the heating element, its temperature rises and melts the ice or evaporates the fog. Figure 16-33 shows a diagram of a Chrysler heated-rear-window circuit. Other systems operate in a similar manner.

The circuit includes a control switch, a relay and timer circuit, an indicator lamp, and the heating element. The control switch and timer relay are included in a single unit called the *control unit* (Fig. 16-34). When the control switch is turned on, the relay energizes and supplies cur-

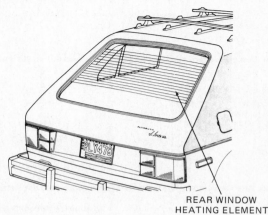

REAR WINDOW
HEATING ELEMENT

Fig. 16-32. Heated-rear-window system, showing heating element bonded to the inside surface of the rear window. *(Chrysler Corporation)*

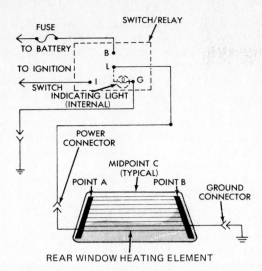

Fig. 16-33. Heated-rear-window circuit diagram. *(Chrysler Corporation)*

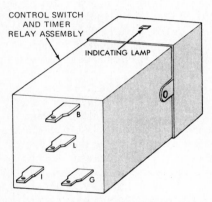

Fig. 16-34. Heated-rear-window control unit (control switch and timer relay). *(Chrysler Corporation)*

rent to the heating element. An indicator lamp is illuminated to show that the system is operating. After a certain time has elapsed (10 minutes for the system shown), the timer circuit turns off the relay and stops the current flow to the heating element. The circuit can be manually turned off at any time by turning the control switch to OFF.

Battery voltage is supplied to the system from two sources. The relay control circuit receives voltage from the ignition switch (in the RUN position) through a fuse in the fuse block. The heating element receives voltage from the battery through a fusible link when the relay contacts are closed.

The heating element consists of strips of silver ceramic material which are bonded to the glass (Fig. 16-35). A vertical strip at each side of the window has a terminal which connects to a wire. One wire supplies battery voltage to one vertical strip. The other wire connects the other vertical strip to ground. A series of thin horizontal strips connects the vertical strips together in a parallel circuit. When voltage is applied to the vertical strip, current flows through all the horizontal strips to the other vertical strip to ground. The strip material is electrically conductive, but it does have a certain amount of resistance. The current flow through the resistance causes the heat.

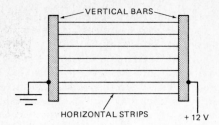

Fig. 16-35. Rear-window heating element.

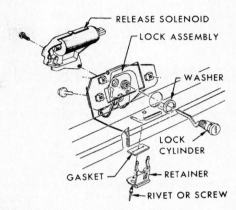

Fig. 16-36. Rear deck-lid release latch and solenoid. *(Chevrolet Division of General Motors Corporation)*

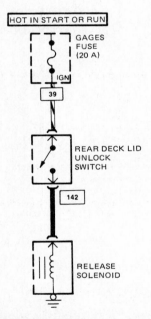

Fig. 16-37. Rear deck-lid release circuit. *(Chevrolet Division of General Motors Corporation)*

REAR DECK-LID RELEASE AND LOCKING CIRCUITS

A common deck-lid release circuit uses a solenoid to operate a latch on the deck-lid lock assembly (Fig. 16-36). The latch holds the deck lid closed. A diagram of the circuit is shown in Fig. 16-37. A single-pole single-throw switch controls the solenoid. In one design, the switch is located in the glove compartment (Fig. 16-38). When the switch contacts close, the solenoid energizes and releases the latch. This action opens the deck lid.

In another type of circuit, a solenoid is used to release the latch. A locking motor is used to close and latch the deck lid (Fig. 16-39). When the deck lid is pushed to the closed position, a hook on the lock contacts the striker. This starts the motor, and the motor operation causes the striker to move downward. The downward movement of the striker pulls down the deck lid. When the lid reaches the closed position, a portion of the lock frame operates a switch, which opens the circuit to stop the motor.

ENTERTAINMENT SYSTEMS ≡

Entertainment systems include AM and FM radios, tape players, and CB radios. These accessories are described in this section.

Radio

A radio converts a broadcast signal from a transmitting station into an *audio* signal. An audio signal is a sound that can be heard by the human ear. An audio signal can be either voice or music, or a combination of both.

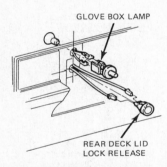

Fig. 16-38. Rear deck-lid lock-release switch. (*Chevrolet Division of General Motors Corporation*)

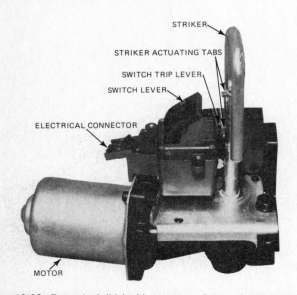

Fig. 16-39. Rear deck-lid locking motor. (*Chevrolet Division of General Motors Corporation*)

A radio broadcast signal consists of two parts: the *carrier* and the *modulation*. The carrier is the most basic signal a radio station can transmit. It is a high-frequency alternating-current (ac) signal (Fig. 16-40). The height of the vibrations of the carrier is called the *amplitude*. The *frequency* is the number of cycles (vibrations) of the ac signal which occur each second. One cycle per second has been given the name *hertz* (Hz). The name was chosen to honor Heinrich Hertz (1857–1894), who did the first experiments in transmitting and receiving electromagnetic energy (later known as *radio waves*). Because the frequencies of broadcast stations are in thousands or millions of hertz, two additional units of measurement are used. One kilohertz (kHz) is one thousand hertz, and one megahertz (mHz) is one million hertz.

The carrier alone produces no meaningful sound. Therefore, an audio signal must be combined with the carrier. The process of combining an audio signal with the carrier is called *modulating the carrier*. The audio portion of the signal is called the *modulation*.

There are two common ways of modulating a carrier. If the carrier is modulated in a way that causes its amplitude to vary with the audio signal, this is called *amplitude modulation* (AM) (Fig. 16-41). If the carrier is modulated in a way that causes its frequency to vary with the audio signal, this is called *frequency modulation* (FM) (Fig. 16-42).

Electrical disturbances in the atmosphere (lightning, for example) can cause brief changes in the amplitude of the radio signal. Because an AM radio reacts to changes in the amplitude of the signal, these disturbances are heard as static. Electrical disturbances do not affect the frequency of the radio signal. For this reason, FM reception is less affected by atmospheric disturbances. The AM broadcast stations transmit on frequencies that range from 535 to 1605 kHz (Fig. 16-43). The FM broadcast stations transmit on frequencies that range from 88.1 to 107.9 mHz. Figure 16-44 shows a combination AM and FM radio.

Because radio signals travel through the air, an antenna is needed to receive the signal. The most common automotive antenna is a vertical rod which is usually mounted in the right front fender of the vehicle. Coaxial

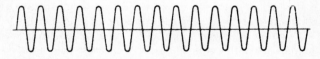

Fig. 16-40. High-frequency ac signal.

Fig. 16-41. Amplitude-modulated carrier signal.

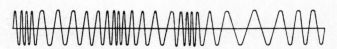

Fig. 16-42. Frequency-modulated carrier signal.

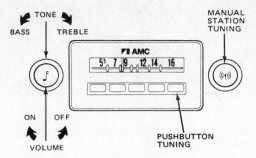

Fig. 16-43. AM radio. *(American Motors Corporation)*

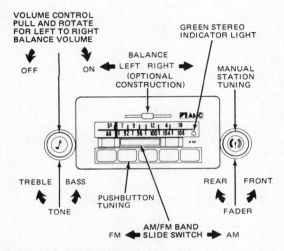

Fig. 16-44. AM-FM radio. *(American Motors Corporation)*

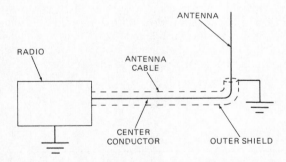

Fig. 16-45. Antenna connected to a radio with coaxial cable.

cable is used to connect the antenna to the radio (Fig. 16-45). Some antennas are motor-driven and are concealed when the radio is not in use. These antennas are called *power antennas*. When the radio is turned on, a motor raises the antenna to its normal position. Power antennas are covered later in this chapter. Another type of antenna consists of a wire built into the windshield. A connector at the lower edge of the windshield connects to a coaxial cable which leads to the radio.

The active components of a radio are transistors. The circuits are designed to operate on battery voltage. A single wire supplies battery voltage to the radio from a fuse in the fuse block. The metal case of the radio provides the ground connection. An additional wire provides voltage for the lamp or lamps which illuminate the radio dial.

Loudspeakers are placed in one or more locations in the vehicle to provide the sound from the radio (Fig. 16-46). A loudspeaker converts a varying-voltage signal into sound. The speaker consists of a paper cone mounted in a metal frame (Fig. 16-47). A small coil, called a *voice coil*, is attached to the small end of the cone. A permanent magnet is located near the voice coil. The output signal from the radio is applied to the voice coil. This is a signal that varies in voltage with the audio signal. When this voltage is applied to the voice coil, it becomes an electromagnet. The strength of the magnetism varies with the voltage of the audio signal. Because the voice coil is near the permanent magnet, the two magnetic fields interact. This causes the voice coil (and its paper cone) to move rapidly back and forth as the audio signal varies. The movement of the cone causes the air to vibrate. This is heard by the human ear as sound.

Loudspeakers can be either grounded or ungrounded (Fig. 16-48). With grounded speakers, one wire connects the output of the radio to the speaker. The other terminal of the speaker voice coil is grounded at the speaker. With ungrounded speakers, two wires connect the output of the radio to the speakers.

Loudspeakers are specified by the resistance of the voice coil. A commonly used speaker has a voice-coil resistance of 8 ohms (Ω).

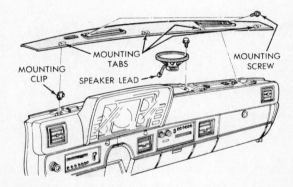

Fig. 16-46. Dash-mounted radio speaker. *(Chrysler Corporation)*

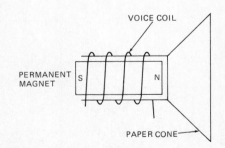

Fig. 16-47. Construction of a loudspeaker.

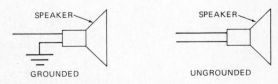

Fig. 16-48. Loudspeaker connections.

The speaker must be matched to the output circuit of the radio. If the output circuit of the radio is designed to operate with an 8-Ω speaker, an 8-Ω speaker should be used. If a speaker of a different resistance is used, the quality of the sound will be reduced. In addition, adding more speakers than a radio was designed to operate with will change the resistance connected to the output circuit of the radio. This will also reduce the quality of the sound.

Radios are commonly designed to operate with more than one speaker. Speakers are often located in the door panels (Fig. 16-49) and in the rear package shelf (Fig. 16-50). Controls, called *fader controls,* may be used to balance the sound levels between speakers.

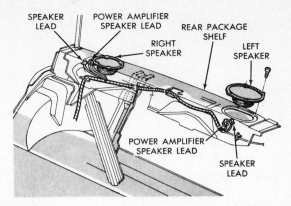

Fig. 16-50. Radio speakers mounted in the rear package shelf. *(Chrysler Corporation)*

Stereo

Some FM stations broadcast a *stereophonic* (or stereo) signal. This signal is a signal that has two separate audio channels which are electronically combined. The stereo receiver (radio) separates the two channels. Each channel is connected to a different speaker or set of speakers. Stereo provides a more accurate reproduction of the actual sound than a single channel can provide.

Premium-Sound Systems

Premium-sound systems use a separate amplifier and high-quality speakers to provide accurate sound reproduction. These systems operate at higher-than-normal sound levels and are commonly used only with stereo radios. Figure 16-51 shows the amplifier used with one premium-sound system. A switch controls the operation of the system (Fig. 16-52). When the switch is turned on, the output of the radio passes through the amplifier and then to the speakers. When the switch is off, the output of the radio bypasses the amplifier and connects directly to the speakers.

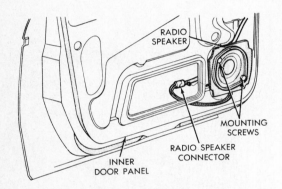

Fig. 16-49. Door-mounted radio speaker. *(Chrysler Corporation)*

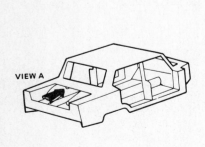

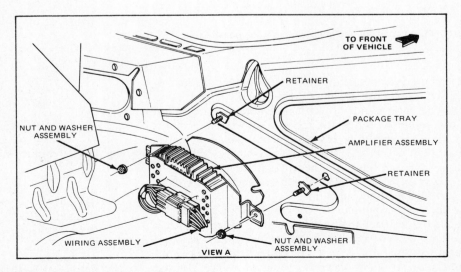

Fig. 16-51. Premium-sound amplifier installation. *(Ford Motor Company)*

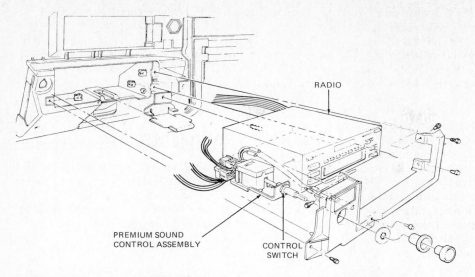

Fig. 16-52. Location of premium-sound control switch. *(Ford Motor Company)*

Radio-Noise Suppression

Radio interference can be caused by an electric spark. A spark releases energy in the form of radio waves (electromagnetic energy). This energy, when received by the radio, is heard as static or noise. Some spark interference, such as atmospheric disturbances or the ignition systems of other vehicles, reaches the radio through the antenna. Electric sparks within the vehicle can also cause radio noise. The ignition system, the alternator, and the windshield wiper motor are common sources of radio noise. The coaxial cable from the antenna to the radio minimizes noise pickup from within the vehicle through the antenna circuit. The shield of the coaxial cable is grounded at both ends. This prevents electromagnetic interference from reaching the center conductor.

Radio interference can also enter a radio on the 12-volt (V) power lead. For this reason, a series coil, also called a *filter choke* (Fig. 16-53), or a parallel capacitor is often used at the radio for noise suppression (Chap. 4). Noise can also be eliminated at the source. Figures 16-54 through 16-56 show noise-suppression capacitors located at the alternator, the ignition coil, and the instrument-panel instrument voltage regulator (IVR).

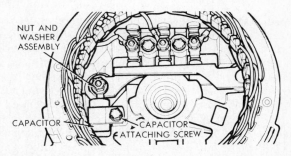

Fig. 16-54. Radio-noise-suppression capacitor in the alternator. *(Chrysler Corporation)*

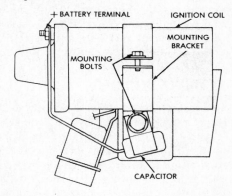

Fig. 16-55. Radio-noise-suppression capacitor on the ignition coil. *(Chrysler Corporation)*

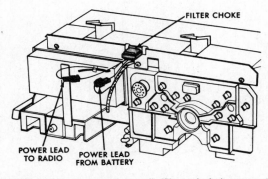

Fig. 16-53. Noise-suppression coil (filter choke) connected in series with the 12-V power lead to the radio. *(Chrysler Corporation)*

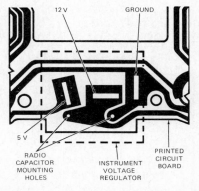

Fig. 16-56. Radio-noise-suppression capacitor on the IVR. *(Chrysler Corporation)*

Poorly grounded parts, such as the hood or the engine, can help to radiate interference caused by electrical components in the vehicle. For this reason, ground straps are used between the hood and the body and between the engine and the body. The manufacturer's service manual shows where all the radio-noise-suppression devices are located on the vehicle.

Sparks in the ignition system are the main cause of static in the radio. The higher the current jumping the gap at the spark plug (secondary current), the greater the amount of noise. Therefore, resistor spark plugs and resistance spark plug wires are used to limit the secondary current without affecting engine performance. Resistance spark plug wires are also called television-radio-suppression (TVRS) wires. The gap between the rotor and the distributor cap electrodes may also be a cause of static. Some vehicles have a resistor in the distributor rotor to limit the secondary current.

Magnetic Tape

Magnetic tape is usually made of a strip of polyester plastic film coated on one side with a powder or particles of ferric (iron) oxide. The oxide coating can be magnetized and will retain any magnetic fields that are applied to it. An audio signal can be recorded on the tape by passing it over a *record head.* The record head converts the varying audio signal into a varying magnetic field, which is retained by the tape. To play back a recorded tape, it is passed over a *playback head.* This device converts the varying magnetic field of the tape into the varying voltage of an audio signal.

A magnetic-tape system includes a playback head, a transport mechanism to move the tape past the head, and electronic circuitry. The electronic circuitry amplifies the weak signal produced by the playback head to a strong signal for driving the loudspeakers. Magnetic-tape players are often included as part of the automotive radio (Fig. 16-57).

Citizens Band Radio

The citizens band is a range of frequencies from 26.965 to 27.405 mHz which was provided by the Federal Communications Commission for commercial or personal communication. The band is separated into 40 channels. A CB radio is a transmitter-receiver combination called a *transceiver.* A switch located on the microphone switches the operation of the transceiver from receive to transmit. A single antenna is used for both operations. On some cars, the same antenna is used for AM, FM, and CB operation. These antennas usually have two cables; one is for AM and FM, the other for CB. Figure 16-58 shows a CB radio which is combined with an AM-FM radio.

POWER ANTENNAS

A power antenna is an antenna that is raised and lowered by an electric motor (Fig. 16-59). Some power antennas are operated by an antenna switch. Others operate when the radio is turned on. Figure 16-60 shows a power-antenna circuit diagram. The radio ON-OFF switch supplies voltage to

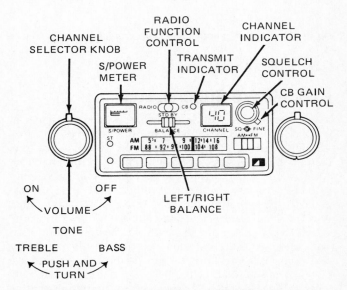

Fig. 16-58. CB radio combined with an AM-FM radio. (*American Motors Corporation*)

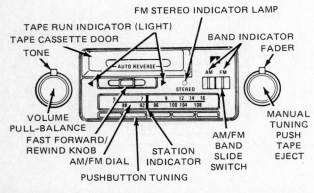

Fig. 16-57. Tape player and radio combination. (*American Motors Corporation*)

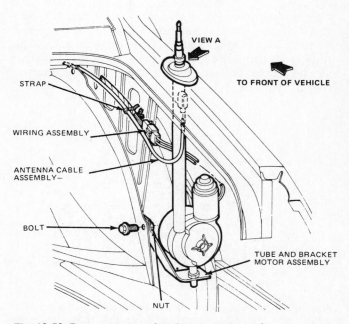

Fig. 16-59. Power antenna. (*Ford Motor Company*)

252

an antenna relay. The relay switches voltage from the battery to a reversible motor. The motor is connected to two switches. One switch is open when the antenna is in the fully up position. The other switch is open when the antenna is in the fully down position.

When the radio is turned on, the antenna relay is energized. Current flows through the motor as shown in Fig. 16-61. The motor rotates in the direction which raises the antenna. When the antenna reaches the fully up position, the motor contacts open and the motor stops.

When the radio is turned off, the relay deenergizes.

Current flows through the motor as shown in Fig. 16-62. The motor rotates in the direction which lowers the antenna. When the antenna reaches the fully down position, the motor contacts open and the motor stops.

Figure 16-63 shows a power antenna circuit which does not use a relay. An antenna switch supplies voltage to a motor which has two fields. When voltage is applied to one field, the motor rotates in the direction which raises the antenna (Fig. 16-63*a*). When voltage is supplied to the other field, the motor rotates in the other direction, which lowers the antenna (Fig. 16-63*b*).

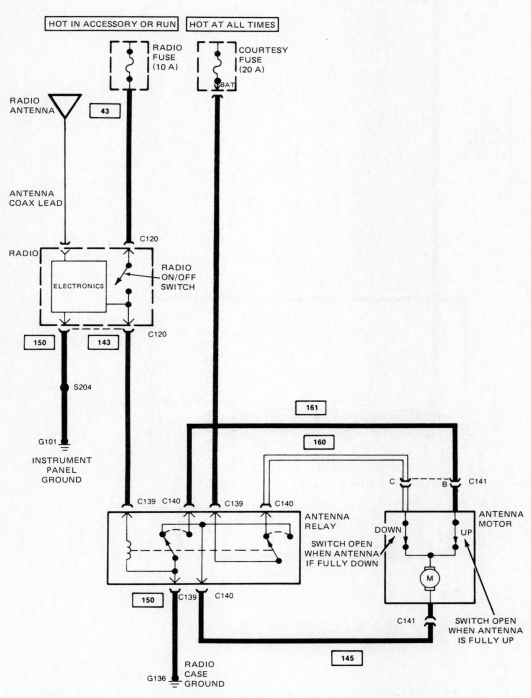

Fig. 16-60. Power antenna circuit diagram. *(Chevrolet Division of General Motors Corporation)*

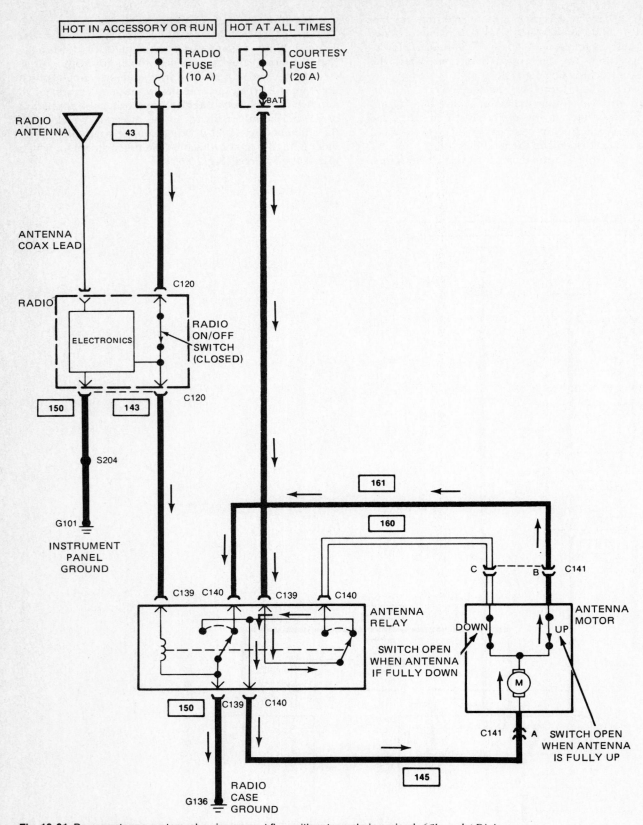

Fig. 16-61. Power antenna system, showing current flow with antenna being raised. *(Chevrolet Division of General Motors Corporation)*

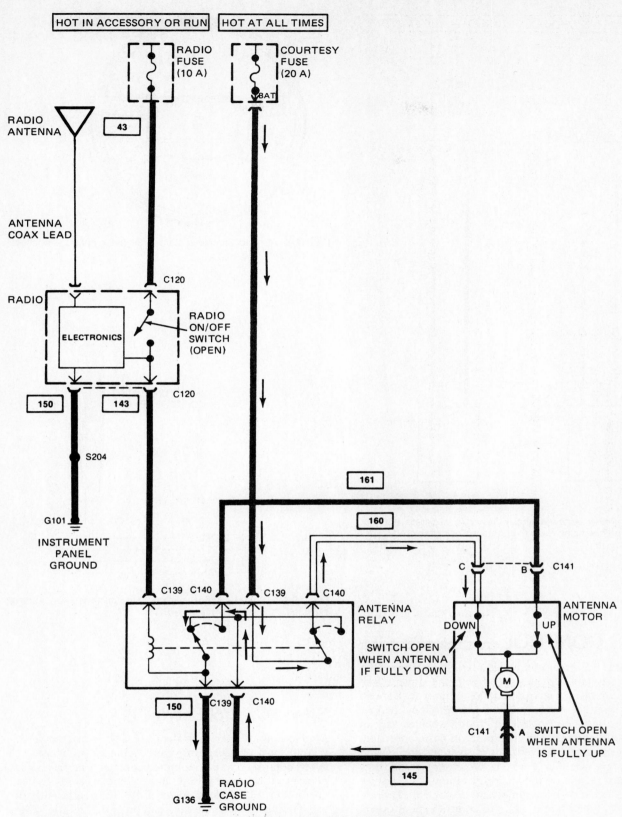

Fig. 16-62. Power antenna system, showing current flow with antenna being lowered. (*Chevrolet Division of General Motors Corporation*)

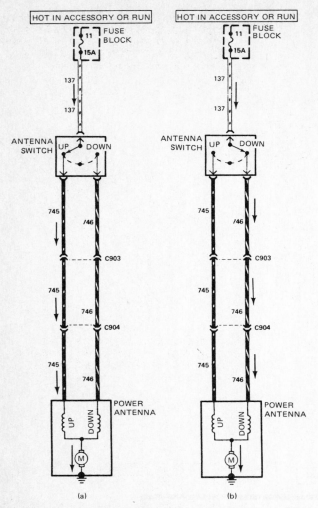

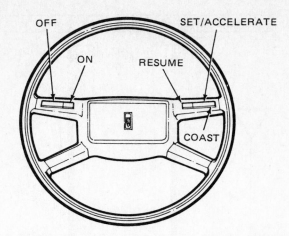

Fig. 16-64. Speed control system with driver control switches. *(Ford Motor Company)*

Fig. 16-63. Power antenna circuit having a separate antenna switch. (*a*) Antenna being raised. (*b*) Antenna being lowered. *(Ford Motor Company)*

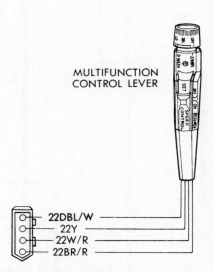

MULTIFUNCTION
CONTROL LEVER

22DBL/W
22Y
22W/R
22BR/R

Fig. 16-65. Speed control system with stalk-mounted control switches. *(Chrysler Corporation)*

SPEED CONTROL

Speed control (or *cruise control*) is a system that allows the vehicle to maintain a preset speed with the driver's foot removed from the accelerator pedal. The purpose of speed control is to reduce driver fatigue when frequent changes in speed are not needed. Speed control systems vary in construction, although they are similar in basic operation. On some systems, the driver control switches are located on the steering wheel (Fig. 16-64). On other systems, they are on a stalk (lever) on the steering column (Fig. 16-65). Some systems use an electromechanical controller, while others use an electronic module to control system operation. The components of a Ford speed control system are shown in Fig. 16-66. A circuit diagram of the system is shown in Fig. 16-67. The components are a speed control servo assembly, a speed sensor, an electronic module, a stoplamp switch, a vacuum dump valve, and a control switch assembly. The purpose of each component is described below.

Speed Control Servo

A servomotor, or *servo,* is a control device that converts a vacuum or a pressure into a mechanical movement. The speed control servo is a vacuum diaphragm unit that is connected to the engine throttle linkage with a cable or a bead chain (Fig. 16-68). Movement of the diaphragm pulls the cable or chain to change the position of the throttle valves. This action affects the vehicle speed. On a spark-ignition engine, intake manifold vacuum controls the position of the diaphragm. Two solenoid-operated valves control the vacuum applied to the diaphragm. The *charge valve* admits vacuum to the servo assembly. The *vent valve* releases vacuum from the servo assembly. The electronic module operates the solenoids.

voltage is applied to the switch assembly. Because each resistor has a different value, operating each switch will apply a different voltage to the electronic module. The module determines which switch has been operated by the voltage it receives.

Other Components

Some vehicles use a vacuum reservoir, which is a storage container for intake manifold vacuum. The vacuum reservoir provides a vacuum source which is free from rapid changes in vacuum. This prevents a brief change in engine vacuum from affecting system operation.

Vehicles with a manual transmission use a clutch switch. When the clutch pedal is depressed, the system is turned off and vacuum is vented from the servo assembly.

System Operation

When the driver presses the ON switch, and the vehicle speed is above 30 miles per hour (mph) [48 kilometers per hour (km/h)], the system is ready to operate. When the vehicle reaches the speed to be maintained, the driver presses and releases the SET/ACCEL switch. When the SET/ACCEL switch is depressed, the electronic module operates the charge valve in the servo assembly. This valve admits intake manifold vacuum to the servo assembly, and the diaphragm pulls the cable or chain to hold the throttle in position. If the vehicle climbs a hill and speed begins to drop, the electronic module increases the vacuum applied to the servo. Therefore, the servo maintains the set speed.

If the driver wishes to raise the set speed, this can be done in either of two ways:

- By depressing the accelerator pedal until the vehicle reaches the desired speed and then depressing and releasing the SET/ACCEL switch.

- By depressing and holding the SET/ACCEL switch. This causes the electronic module to increase vacuum to the servo, which increases vehicle speed. When the

desired speed is reached, releasing the switch will maintain that speed.

If the driver wishes to decrease speed, this can be done in either of two ways:

- By tapping the brake pedal to turn the system off and vent vacuum from the servo. Then, when the desired speed is reached, depressing and releasing the SET/ACCEL switch will maintain that speed.

- By depressing the COAST switch. This causes the electronic module to decrease vacuum to the servo, which decreases vehicle speed. When the desired speed is reached, releasing the switch will maintain that speed.

On a system which has the RESUME feature, if the brake pedal is momentarily depressed, pressing the RESUME switch will return the vehicle to the preset speed. Speed control operation can be stopped at any time by depressing the OFF switch.

ILLUMINATED-ENTRY SYSTEMS

On some vehicles, illuminated-entry systems light the door lock cylinders. This provides light for key insertion in the dark. In the Ford illuminated-entry system, the lock cylinders are illuminated by light-emitting diodes (LEDs). The courtesy lamps are also illuminated in the interior of the vehicle to assist entry.

This system includes an electronic actuator module (Fig. 16-71), door latch switches (Fig. 16-72), and illuminated door lock cylinders. The system is activated when either the left or right outside-door handle is raised. The system is deactivated when the ignition switch is placed in the ACCESSORY or RUN position. A timing circuit in the module deactivates the system after 25 seconds of operation. This prevents the system from continuously operating if a door handle becomes jammed in the raised position.

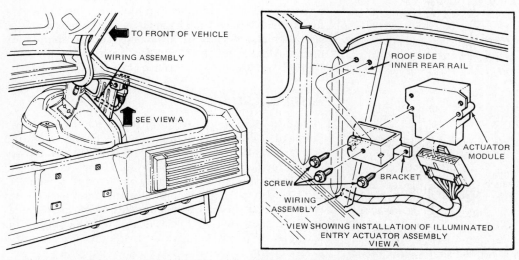

Fig. 16-71. Location of illuminated-entry actuator module. *(Ford Motor Company)*

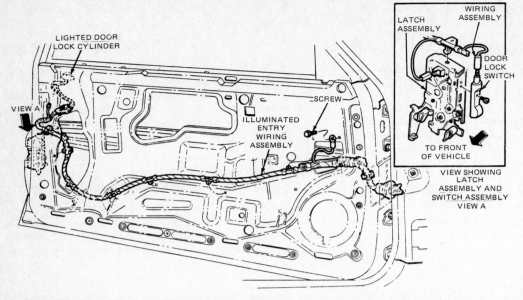

Fig. 16-72. Location of door latch switch, illuminated lock cylinder, and wiring harness. *(Ford Motor Company)*

A diagram of the Ford system is shown in Fig. 16-73. The electronic actuator module receives battery voltage on terminal 8 from a fuse in the fuse block. The door latch switches are connected to terminal 2 of the module. Raising a door handle closes the switch contacts and provides a ground at terminal 2. This triggers the module, which then switches battery voltage to terminal 4. The LEDs, which are connected to terminal 4, are illuminated. A resistor in series with each LED drops the battery voltage to the

operating voltage of the LED. If 12 V were applied directly to the LED, it would be destroyed. When the module is triggered, it also switches battery voltage to terminal 6 to operate the courtesy lamps.

ANTITHEFT ALARM SYSTEM ═

Some manufacturers provide an antitheft alarm system as an accessory item. The Ford system is shown in Fig. 16-74. The system includes an electronic module, a trigger relay, an alarm relay, a start-interrupt relay, doorjamb switches, and door lock cylinder switches.

For the system to operate, it must first be *armed*. Arming means placing the system in readiness to detect an illegal entry. To arm the system, the power door lock switch is placed in the LOCK position (with the door open and the ignition switch off). Then the door is closed. If a door is opened or the lock cylinder is pulled from the trunk after the system has been armed, the alarm will be activated. The alarm consists of the horn, headlamps, and taillamps being operated intermittently. In addition, a start-interrupt circuit prevents the engine from starting.

Arming Circuit

Figure 16-75 shows a portion of the alarm-system circuit. Terminal G of the electronic module is connected to the power door lock "locking" circuit. Terminal M is connected to the power door lock "unlocking" circuit. The door lock cylinder switches are connected to terminal H and are open when the doors are locked. An indicator lamp is connected between a fuse in the fuse block and terminal D of the electronic module (Fig. 16-76). The lamp is on whenever terminal D provides a ground. The indicator lamp is used to advise the driver of the operating condition of the system.

Fig. 16-73. Circuit diagram of an illuminated-entry system. *(Ford Motor Company)*

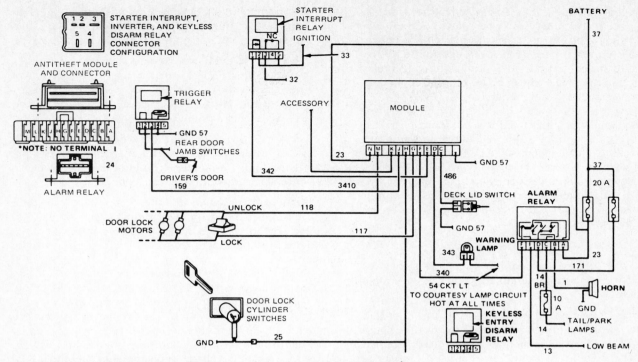

Fig. 16-74. Circuit diagram of an antitheft alarm system. *(Ford Motor Company)*

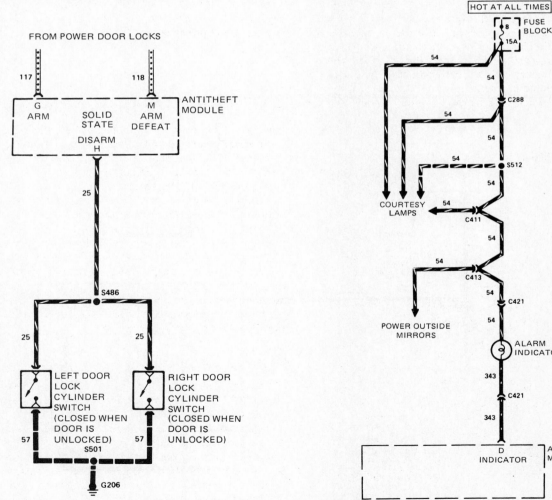

Fig. 16-75. Antitheft alarm system, showing the arm-disarm circuit. *(Ford Motor Company)*

Fig. 16-76. Antitheft alarm system, showing the indicator lamp circuit. *(Ford Motor Company)*

A trigger relay (Fig. 16-77) is operated by the doorjamb switches. The relay is energized when a door is open. Figure 16-78 shows the current flow with the left door open. Current flows from the fuse block through the left doorjamb switch, through a diode, to the coil of the trigger relay and to ground. When the trigger relay is energized, its contacts ground terminal J of the module.

Opening the right door will also energize the trigger relay. However, current through the right doorjamb switch does not flow through the diode. The diode prevents current from the right doorjamb switch from flowing to the lights-on warning system. The lights-on warning system is operated only from the left doorjamb switch.

The arming sequence for the system consists of four steps. These steps, and a description of the circuit operation, are described below.

- *Step 1* Turn off the ignition switch. This removes battery voltage from terminal K of the electronic module.

- *Step 2* Open the door. This closes the doorjamb switch, which supplies battery voltage to the trigger relay. The trigger relay energizes and grounds terminal J of the module. A ground at terminal J causes the module to provide an alternating ground at terminal

D. An alternating ground at terminal D causes the indicator lamp to blink on and off. When the lamp is blinking, it advises the driver that the system is not armed.

- *Step 3* Place the power door lock switch in the LOCK position. This applies battery voltage to terminal G of the module. The module now provides a steady ground at terminal D, which causes the indicator lamp to remain on continuously.

- *Step 4* Close the door. This opens the doorjamb switch, which deenergizes the trigger relay. Terminal J is no longer grounded. The indicator lamp remains lit for 2 seconds and then turns off.

To disarm the system after the door is closed, the door lock must be opened with a key. Unlocking the door closes the lock cylinder switch, which grounds terminal H of the module. A ground at terminal H of the module disarms the system.

If the driver wishes to disarm the system before closing the door, the power door lock switch is placed in the UNLOCK position. This applies battery voltage to terminal M of the module, which cancels the arming operation. The system can also be disarmed before the door is closed by turning the ignition switch to the ACCESSORY or RUN position. This causes battery voltage to be applied to terminal K of the module, which disarms the system.

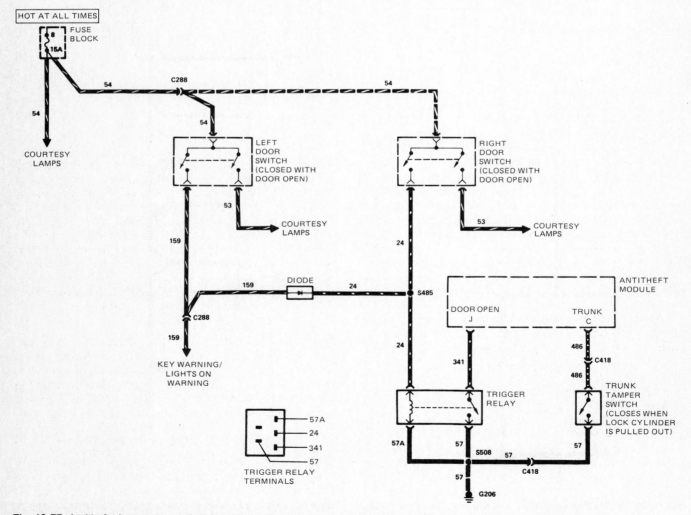

Fig. 16-77. Antitheft alarm system, showing the doorjamb switch and trigger relay connections. *(Ford Motor Company)*

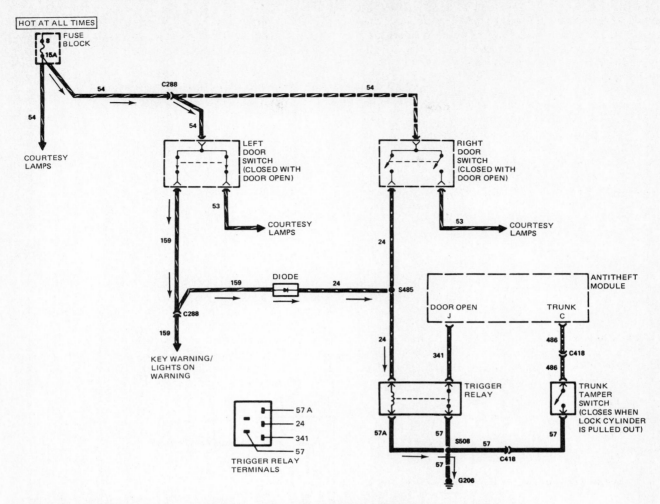

Fig. 16-78. Antitheft alarm system, showing current flow with the left door open. *(Ford Motor Company)*

Alarm Input Connections   Figure 16-77 shows the portion of the circuit that includes the alarm input connections to the module. If either terminal J or C is grounded while the system is armed, the alarm will be activated. Terminal J is grounded when the trigger relay contacts close. Terminal C is grounded when the trunk tamper switch contacts close.

The trigger relay is operated by the doorjamb switches. If either door is opened, the doorjamb switch closes. This energizes the trigger relay which grounds terminal J to activate the alarm.

The trunk tamper switch contacts close if the lock cylinder is pulled out of the trunk lid. When this occurs, terminal C is grounded to activate the alarm.

Alarm Activation   When an alarm is activated, terminal F of the module becomes an alternating ground (Fig. 16-79). A ground at terminal F grounds the coil of the alarm relay, which energizes the relay. When the relay is energized, its contacts close and supply battery voltage to the horn, the headlamps, and the taillamps. Because the ground at terminal F is alternating, the horn, headlamps, and taillamps continually turn on and off.

Start-Interrupt Circuit   When an alarm is activated, the start-interrupt circuit prevents the engine from

starting (Fig. 16-80). A start-interrupt relay receives battery voltage through the ignition switch (in the START position) and through the closed contacts of the neutral safety switch. Battery voltage to the starter relay and the ignition system is supplied through a set of normally closed contacts in the start-interrupt relay. An alarm causes the electronic module to provide a ground at terminal E, which energizes the start-interrupt relay. When the start-interrupt relay is energized, its contacts open to disconnect battery voltage from the ignition system and from the starter relay. This action prevents the engine from starting.

Deactivating the Alarm   Once the alarm has been activated, it may be turned off by unlocking a door with a key. The alarm will turn itself off after 2 to 4 minutes, but the system will remain armed. Even though the alarm has turned itself off, the start-interrupt circuit will prevent the engine from being started until a door is unlocked with a key.

System Variations   On vehicles with keyless entry (Chap. 15), the system may also be armed by pressing two buttons simultaneously on the keyless-entry module. This system is disarmed by entering a code into the keyless-entry module before a door is opened.

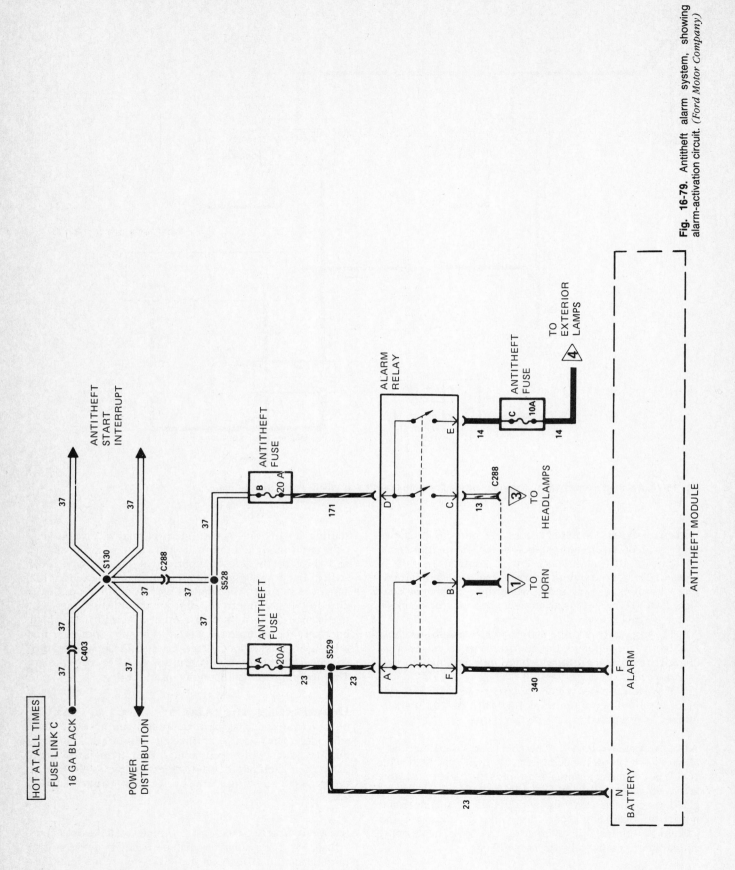

Fig. 16-79. Antitheft alarm system, showing alarm-activation circuit. *(Ford Motor Company)*

HOT AT ALL TIMES

FUSE LINK C

16 GA BLACK

ANTITHEFT START INTERRUPT

POWER DISTRIBUTION

C403

S130

C288

S528

ANTITHEFT FUSE

B 20 A

171

ANTITHEFT FUSE

A 20A

S529

23

ALARM RELAY

D

A

F

E

C

B

23

340

ANTITHEFT FUSE

C 10A

14

14

TO EXTERIOR LAMPS

C288

13

TO HEADLAMPS

TO HORN

ANTITHEFT MODULE

ALARM

BATTERY

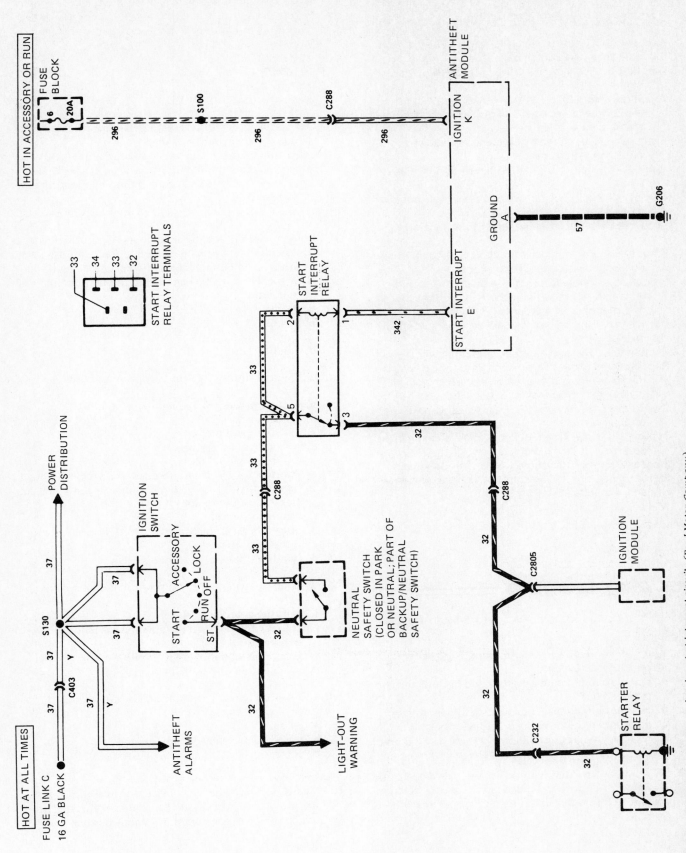

Fig. 16-80. Antitheft alarm system, showing start-interrupt circuit. *(Ford Motor Company)*

265

VOCABULARY REVIEW

Accessory A device which is not essential to the operation of an automobile.

Amplitude The height of the vibrations of an ac signal.

Amplitude modulation (AM) A method of combining audio with a carrier signal in a way that varies the amplitude of the carrier.

Arm To place an alarm system in readiness to detect an illegal entry.

Audio A signal which can be heard by the human ear.

Carrier A radio signal which does not contain modulation.

Filter choke A coil use in series to eliminate radio noise.

Frequency The number of cycles (vibrations) of an ac signal which occur each second.

Frequency modulation (FM) A method of combining audio with a carrier signal in a way that varies the frequency of the carrier.

Hertz (Hz) The unit of frequency (one cycle per second).

Modulation The audio portion of a radio signal.

Regulator, window The mechanism that converts the rotary motion of a window crank handle into the up-and-down motion of the window.

Sector gear A section of a gear which is part of a window regulator.

Servo A control device that converts a vacuum or a pressure into a mechanical movement.

Stereo A short form of the word "stereophonic."

Stereophonic signal A signal that has two separate audio channels.

REVIEW QUESTIONS

Select the *one* correct, best, or most probable answer to each question.

1. All of the following statements about a power window system are true *except*
   a. a nongrounded motor is grounded through the control switch
   b. a nongrounded motor has one field winding
   c. a grounded motor has two field windings
   d. with a nongrounded-motor system, the control switch only supplies battery voltage to the motor

2. Mechanic A says that two motors operate when a six-way power seat switch is placed in the SEAT-UP position. Mechanic B says that only one motor operates. Who is correct?
   a. A only
   b. B only
   c. both A and B
   d. neither A nor B

3. Mechanic A says that in the circuit of Fig. 16-29 current flows through both the lock relay and the unlock relay when the power doors are locked. Mechanic B says current flows through the lock relay only. Who is correct?
   a. A only
   b. B only
   c. both A and B
   d. neither A nor B

4. All of the following statements about a heated-rear-window system are true *except*
   a. silver ceramic material is bonded to the glass
   b. current flow through the resistance causes heat
   c. both vertical strips of the heating element receive battery voltage
   d. the timer turns the system off after 10 minutes

5. Which of the following statements is (are) correct?
   I. The basic operating principle of a loudspeaker involves the interaction of two magnetic fields.
   II. A speaker must be matched to the output circuit of the radio.
   a. I only
   b. II only
   c. both I and II
   d. neither I nor II

6. All of the following are noise-suppression devices *except*
   a. an instrument voltage regulator
   b. a filter choke
   c. resistor spark plugs
   d. an alternator capacitor

7. Which type of radio interference *cannot* be reduced by connecting a noise-suppression capacitor to the power lead of the radio?
   a. alternator noise
   b. atmospheric disturbances
   c. ignition noise
   d. windshield wiper motor noise

8. The motor switches in the power antenna system are used to
   a. start the antenna motor
   b. stop the motor when the antenna has reached a certain position
   c. ground the antenna relay
   d. protect the radio from an overload

9. In a speed control system, which component applies a force to the throttle linkage?
   a. solenoid
   b. speed control sensor
   c. servo
   d. control switch

10. Mechanic A says the vacuum dump valve turns off the speed control system. Mechanic B says the stoplamp switch performs this function. Who is correct?
    a. A only
    b. B only
    c. both A and B
    d. neither A nor B

11. All of the following statements about speed control systems are true *except*
    a. the charge valve releases vacuum from the servo
    b. the system will not operate below 30 mph [48 km/h]
    c. intake manifold vacuum is applied to the servo diaphragm
    d. the speed control servo is a small voltage generator

12. Mechanic A says the Ford illuminated-entry system is activated by a ground connection at the electronic module. Mechanic B says the module grounds the LED to illuminate it. Who is correct?
    a. A only
    b. B only
    c. both A and B
    d. neither A nor B

13. When the antitheft system described in this chapter is armed, the alarm will be activated by
    a. battery voltage applied to terminal G of the module
    b. a ground at terminal M of the module
    c. battery voltage applied to terminal D of the module
    d. a ground at either terminal J or C of the module

14. The indicator lamp of the antitheft alarm system is illuminated by a ground at terminal
    a. J of the module
    b. C of the module
    c. E of the module
    d. D of the module

15. In the antitheft alarm system, the start-interrupt relay is energized by a ground at terminal
    a. C
    b. E
    c. M
    d. J